DOUBLE CROSS

The True Story of the D–Day Spies

Ben Macintyre

BLOOMSBURY

LONDON · BERLIN · NEW YORK · SYDNEY

First published in Great Britain 2012

Copyright © 2012 by Ben Macintyre
Map by John Gilkes

The moral right of the author has been asserted

Bloomsbury Publishing Plc
50 Bedford Square
London
WC1B 3DP

www.bloomsbury.com

Bloomsbury Publishing, London, Berlin, New York and Sydney
A CIP catalogue record for this book is available from the British Library

ISBN 978 1 4088 1990 6 (hardback edition)
ISBN 978 1 4088 1991 3 (trade paperback edition)

10 9 8 7 6 5 4 3 2

Typeset by Hewer Text UK Ltd, Edinburgh
Printed in Great Britain by Clays Ltd, St Ives plc

For Callum, Pablo, Minnie and Wilf

'Tangle within tangle, plot and counter-plot, ruse and treachery, cross and double-cross, true agent, false agent, double agent, gold and steel, the bomb, the dagger and the firing party, were interwoven in many a texture so intricate as to be incredible and yet true.'

– Winston Churchill

'The enemy must not know where I intend to give battle. For if he does not know where I intend to give battle he must prepare in a great many places. And when he prepares in a great many places, those I have to fight in any one place will be few. And when he prepares everywhere he will be weak everywhere.'

– Sun Tzu

CONTENTS

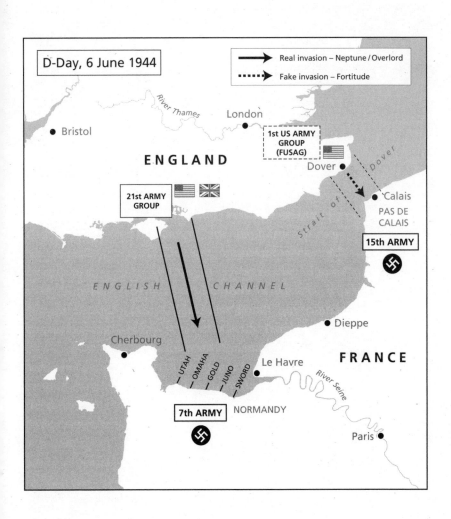

THE AGENTS AND THEIR HANDLERS

Dusan 'Dusko' Popov
MI5 codename: Tricycle, Skoot
MI5 case officer: Billy Luke, Ian Wilson
Abwehr codename: Ivan
Abwehr case officer: Ludovico von Karsthoff, Johnny Jebsen

Roman Czerniawski
MI5 codename: Brutus, Armand, Walenty
MI5 case officer: Christopher Harmer, Hugh Astor
Abwehr codename: Hubert
Abwehr case officer: Oscar Reile

Lily Sergeyev
MI5 codename: Treasure
MI5 case officer: Mary Sherer
Abwehr codename: Solange, Tramp
Abwehr case officer: Emile Kliemann

Juan Pujol García
MI5 codename: Garbo, Bovril
MI5 case officer: Tomás Harris
Abwehr codename: Arabel
Abwehr case officer: Karl-Erich Kühlenthal

Elvira de la Fuente Chaudoir
MI5 codename: Bronx, Cyril
MI5 case officer: Christopher Harmer, Hugh Astor
Abwehr codename: Dorette
Abwehr case officer: Helmut 'Bibi' Bleil, Berndt Schluetter

Preface

In the summer of 1943, a genteel and soft-spoken intelligence officer, wearing tartan trousers and smoking a pipe, put the finishing touches to a secret weapon he had been working on for more than three years. This weapon – unique in its power and unlimited in its range – was quite different from any built before or since. It was so shrouded in secrecy that its inventors were, for some time, unaware that they possessed it, and unsure how to use it. This weapon did not kill or maim. It did not rely on science, engineering or force. It did not destroy cities, sink U-boats or pierce the armour of Panzers. It did something far more subtle. Instead of killing the enemy, it could get inside his head. It could make the Nazis think what the British wanted them to think, and therefore do what the British wanted them to do.

Tar Robertson of MI5 had built a weapon that could lie to Hitler, and at the most critical juncture of the Second World War, he urged Winston Churchill to use it.

Allied military planners were already working on plans for the great assault on Nazi-occupied Europe. The D-Day invasion, so long awaited, would decide the outcome of the war, and both sides knew it. If the Allies could sweep across the English Channel and break through the massive German coastal defences known as the 'Atlantic Wall', then the Nazis might be rolled back out of Paris, Brussels, and then across the Rhine all the way to Berlin. Hitler, however, was convinced that if the invaders could be successfully resisted in the early stages of an assault, even for one day, then the attack would fail; Allied morale would slump, and it would take many months before another invasion could be attempted. In that time, Hitler could concentrate on destroying the Red Army on the Eastern Front. The first twenty-four hours would be, in Erwin Rommel's famous words, the 'longest day': how that day would end was far from certain.

D-Day stands today as a monumental victory and, with hindsight, historically inevitable. It did not look that way in prospect. Amphibious assaults are among the most difficult operations in warfare. The Germans had constructed a 'zone of death' along the French coast more than five miles deep, a lethal obstacle course of barbed wire, concrete and over 6 million mines, behind which lay heavy gun emplacements, machine-gun posts and bunkers. As Field Marshal Sir Alan Brooke, Chief of the Imperial General Staff, observed in a gloomy diary entry just before D-Day: 'It may well be the most ghastly disaster of the whole war.'

In war, no variable is more important, and less easy to control, than the element of surprise. If the Germans could be confused or, even better, actively misled as to where and when the landings would take place, then the odds on success improved dramatically. German forces in occupied France greatly outnumbered the invaders, but if they could be kept in the wrong place, at the right time, then the numerical equation appeared less daunting. By 1944, the war was claiming the lives of 10 million people a year. The stakes could not have been higher, or the margin for error smaller.

At the Tehran Conference in November of 1943, the first of the 'Big Three' meetings bringing together Churchill, Roosevelt and Stalin, the Allies laid plans for the invasion of Europe, codenamed 'Operation Overlord', that would take place in May 1944 (later delayed by a month), with

General Dwight Eisenhower as Supreme Allied Commander, and General Bernard Montgomery as Allied ground forces commander, for the assault across the Channel. During the conference, Winston Churchill turned to Josef Stalin and uttered a typically Churchillian remark that has since become a sort of myth: 'In wartime, the truth is so precious that she should always be attended by a bodyguard of lies.' Stalin, who had little time for literary metaphor, replied: 'This is what we call military cunning.' The D-Day invasion would be protected and supported by a comprehensive, worldwide deception campaign, a body of lies to shield the truth: in a tip of the hat to Churchill's remark, it was codenamed 'Bodyguard'.

The central aim of Operation Bodyguard was to fool the Germans into believing the invasion was coming at a point where it was not, and that it was not coming in the place where it was. More than that, to ensure that those troops preparing to fight off the bogus invasion were not redeployed to repel the real one, the deception must be maintained *after* D-Day. Goliath could be cut down to size only if he didn't know which direction David's sling-shot was coming from, and was kept guessing. The target range for a cross-Channel invasion, however, was extremely narrow. The Germans were sure to spot the build-up of troops in Britain, and since the assault had to take place within fighter range, there were only a handful of suitable spots for a massed landing. In the words of one planner, it was 'utterly impossible to disguise the fact that the major attack would come somewhere between the Cherbourg Peninsula and Dunkirk'.

The most obvious target was the Pas de Calais in the northeast, the region nearest the British coast. Deep-water ports at Calais and Boulogne could easily be resupplied and reinforced once they were in Allied hands, and a bridgehead in Calais would offer the most direct route for a march on Paris and the German industrial heartland in the Ruhr. The logic of attacking Calais was not lost on German tacticians. Hitler himself identified Calais as the likeliest target: 'It is here that the enemy must and will attack, and it is here – unless all the indications are misleading – that the decisive battle against the landing forces will be fought.' Hitler was fully alert to the possibility of being misled: he had been wrong-footed over the invasions of North Africa and Sicily. He would be far harder to dupe this time.

By July 1943, Allied military planners had concluded that, 'in spite of the obvious advantages of the Pas de Calais provided by its proximity to our coasts', the coast of Normandy north of Caen represented a better target. The Normandy beaches were long, wide and gently sloping, with suitable gaps in the dunes through which an invading force could spread quickly inland. The lack of a deep-water anchorage would be ingeniously solved by constructing vast artificial ports, codenamed 'Mulberry harbours'.

The successful deception surrounding the Sicilian landings in 1943 had persuaded the Germans that the most likely target was *not* the real target. Now, the aim was reversed: Hitler must be made to think that the most plausible target really *was* the target. Along the mighty Atlantic Wall the brickwork was thinnest in Normandy. That was where the wrecking ball would hit. But in order to strike with maximum effect, the truth would need to be protected by a bodyguard of liars, which is precisely what Tar Robertson had created.

Robertson and the small team of intelligence officers under his command specialised in turning German spies into double agents. This was the 'Double Cross System', coordinated by the intensely secret Twenty Committee, so named because the number twenty in Roman numerals, XX, forms a double cross. Hitherto these double agents – several dozen in number – had been used defensively: to catch more spies, obtain information about German military intelligence, and lull the enemy into believing he was running a large and efficient espionage network in Britain, when he was running nothing of the sort. In June 1943, Robertson reached the startling conclusion that every single German agent in Britain was actually under his control. Not some, not most, but *all* of them – which meant that

Robertson's team of double agents could now begin feeding the Germans not just snippets of falsehood, but a gigantic, war-changing lie.

The D-Day deception plot involved every branch of the secret war machine: scientists laid false trails, engineers built dummy tanks, radio operators put up a barrage of fake signals, and counterfeit generals led non-existent armies towards targets that were never in danger. While the overall, global deception campaign was codenamed Bodyguard, the plan specifically covering the cross-Channel invasion, the pivotal element in the deception, was named 'Fortitude', the quality most essential to its success. Operation Fortitude, the ruse to bottle up German troops in the Pas de Calais and keep them there, was an extraordinary collective effort, but at its core it depended on Robertson's spies, and a web of deception so intricate and strong that it would snare Hitler's armies, and help to carry thousands of soldiers across the Channel in safety.

The military saga of D-Day has been described many times, and the role of Operation Fortitude in that victory, though long shrouded in secrecy, has slowly emerged since the war. But the story of the five spies who formed the nucleus of the Double Cross system, Robertson's secret weapons, has never been fully told before. The spies themselves expected their story to remain hidden, as it would have done had the Security Service (better known as MI5) not chosen, in recent years, to declassify its wartime intelligence files. Indeed, if their stories had been told at the time, no one would have believed them.

For the D-Day spies were, without question, one of the oddest military units ever assembled. They included a bisexual Peruvian playgirl, a tiny Polish fighter pilot, a mercurial Frenchwoman, a Serbian seducer and a deeply eccentric Spaniard with a diploma in chicken farming. Together, under Robertson's guidance, they delivered all the little lies that together made up the big lie. Their success depended on the delicate, dubious relationship between spy and spymaster, both German and British.

This is a story of war, but it is also about the nuanced qualities of psychology, character and personality, the thin line between fidelity and treachery, truth and falsehood, and the strange impulsion of the spy. The Double Cross spies were, variously, courageous, treacherous, capricious, greedy and inspired. They were not obvious heroes, and their organisation was betrayed from within by a Soviet spy. One was so obsessed with her pet dog that she came close to derailing the entire invasion. All were, to some extent, fantasists, for that is the very essence of espionage. Two were of dubious moral character. One was a triple, and possibly a quadruple, agent. For another, the game ended in torture, imprisonment and death.

All weapons, including secret ones, are liable to backfire. Robertson and his spies knew only too keenly that if their deception was rumbled, then rather than diverting attention from Normandy and tying up German forces in the Pas de Calais, they would lead the Germans to the truth, with catastrophic consequences.

The D-Day spies were not traditional warriors. None carried weapons, yet the soldiers who did owed the spies a huge and unconscious debt as they stormed the beaches of Normandy in June 1944. These secret agents fought exclusively with words and make-believe. Their tales begin before the outbreak of war, but then overlap, interconnect, and finally interlock on D-Day, in the greatest deception operation ever attempted. Their real names are a mouthful, a sort of European mélange that might have sprung from a period novel: Elvira Concepcion Josefina de la Fuente Chaudoir, Roman Czerniawski, Lily Sergeyev, Dusko Popov and Juan Pujol García. Their codenames are blunter and, in each case, deliberately chosen: Bronx, Brutus, Treasure, Tricycle and Garbo.

This is their story.

1

Raw Recruits

Dusko and Johnny were friends. Their friendship was founded on a shared appreciation of money, cars, parties and women, in no particular order, and preferably all at the same time. Their relationship, based almost entirely on frivolity, would have a profound impact on world history.

Dusan 'Dusko' Popov and Johann 'Johnny' Jebsen met in 1936, at the University of Freiburg in southern Germany. Popov, the son of a wealthy industrialist from Dubrovnik, was twenty-five. Jebsen, the heir to a large shipping company, was two years older. Both were spoilt, charming and feckless. Popov drove a BMW; Jebsen, a supercharged Mercedes 540K convertible. This inseparable pair of international playboys roistered around Freiburg, behaving badly. Popov was a law student, while Jebsen was taking an economics degree, the better to manage the family firm. Neither did any studying at all. 'We both had some intellectual pretensions,' wrote Popov, but we were 'addicted to sports cars and sporting girls and had enough money to keep them both running'.

Popov had a round, open face, with hair brushed back from a high forehead. Opinion was divided on his looks: 'He smiles freely showing all his teeth and in repose his face is not unpleasant, though certainly not handsome,' wrote one male contemporary. 'A well-flattened, typically Slav nose, complexion sallow, broad shoulders, athletic carriage, but rather podgy, white and

Dusko Popov

well-kept hands,' which he waved in wild gesticulation. Women frequently found him irresistible, with his easy manners, 'loose, sensual mouth' and green eyes behind heavy lids. He had what were then known as 'bedroom eyes'; indeed, the bedroom was his main focus of interest. Popov was an unstoppable woman-iser. Jebsen cut a rather different figure. He was slight and thin, with dark blond hair, high cheekbones and a turned-up nose. Where Popov was noisily gregarious, Jebsen was watchful. 'His coldness, aloofness, could be forbidding, yet everyone was under his spell,' Popov wrote. 'He had much warmth too, and his intelligence was reflected in his face, in the alertness of his steel-blue eyes. He spoke abruptly, in short phrases, hardly ever used an adjective and was, above all, ironic.' Jebsen walked with a limp, and hinted that this was an injury sustained in some wild escapade: in truth it was caused by the pain of varicose veins, to which he was a secret martyr. He loved to spin a story, to 'deliberately stir up situations to see what would happen'. But he also liked to broker deals. When Popov was challenged to a sword duel over a girl, it was Jebsen, as his second, who quietly arranged a peaceful solution, to Popov's relief, 'not thinking my looks would be improved by a bright red cicatrix'.

Jebsen's parents, both dead by the time he arrived in Freiburg, had been born in Denmark, but adopted German citizenship when the shipping firm of Jebsen & Jebsen moved to Hamburg. Jebsen was born in that city in 1917, but liked to joke that he was really Danish, his German citizenship being a 'flag of convenience' for business purposes: 'Some of my love of my country has to do with so much of it actually belonging to me.' A rich, rootless orphan, Jebsen had visited Britain as a teenager, and returned a committed Anglophile: he affected English manners, spoke English in preference to German, and dressed, he thought, 'like a young Anthony Eden, con-servatively elegant'. Popov remarked: 'He would no more go without an umbrella than without his trousers.'

Johnny Jebsen

Preoccupied as they were with having fun, the two student friends could not entirely ignore the menacing political changes taking place around them in the Germany of the 1930s. They made a point of teasing the 'pro-Nazi student intelligentsia'. The mockery, however, had a metal strand to it. 'Under that mask of a snob and cynic and under his playboy manners', Jebsen was developing a deep distaste for Nazism. Popov found the posturing Nazi Brownshirts ridiculous, and repulsive.

After graduation, Popov returned to Yugoslavia, and set himself up in the import-export business, travelling widely. Jebsen headed to England, announcing that he intended to study at Oxford University and write books on philosophy. He did neither (though he would later claim to have done both). They would not meet again for three years, by which time the world was at war.

In early 1940, Popov was living in Dubrovnik, where he had opened his own law firm, and conducting affairs with at least four women, when he received a telegram from his old friend, summoning him to Belgrade: 'Need to meet you urgently'.

Their reunion was joyful, and spectacularly bibulous. They went on a bender through Belgrade's nightspots, having enlisted 'two girls from the chorus of one of the clubs'. At dawn, all four sat down to a breakfast of steak and champagne. Jebsen told Popov that in the intervening years, he had become acquainted with the great English writer, P. G. Wodehouse. With his monocle and silk cravat, Jebsen now looked like an oddly Germanic version of Bertie Wooster. Popov studied his old friend. Jebsen wore the same expression of 'sharp intelligence, cynicism and dark humour', but he also seemed tense, as if there was something weighing on his mind. He chain-smoked, and 'ordered his whiskies double, neat, and frequently. In style, his clothes still rivalled Eden's, but his blond hair was no longer so closely trimmed and he had a neglected moustache, reddened by tobacco.'

A few days later, the friends were alone, at the bar of a Belgrade hotel, when Jebsen lowered his voice, looked around in a ludicrously conspiratorial manner, and confided that he had joined the Abwehr, the German military intelligence service, 'because it saved him from soldiering, of which he was very much afraid as he is a heavy sufferer from varicose veins'. Jebsen's recruiter was a family friend, Colonel Hans Oster, deputy to Admiral Wilhelm Canaris, the chief of the Abwehr. He now had the formal but vague Abwehr title of *Forscher*, meaning researcher, or talent scout, with the technical rank of private, attached to a 400-strong special detachment of the Brandenburg Regiment. This unit was in reality 'a wangle by Canaris to keep a number of young men out of the clutches of compulsory service'. Jebsen was a freelance spy, on permanent leave from the army, with a personal assurance from Canaris that he would never wear uniform, never undergo military training, and never be sent to war. He was free to spend his 'time travelling throughout Europe on his private business and financial affairs, so long as he held himself available to help the Abwehr when called upon to do so'.

'Hitler is the undisputed master of Europe,' Jebsen declared. 'In a few months' time, he'll probably finish off England, and then America and Russia will be glad to come to terms with him.' This was pure Nazi propaganda, but Jebsen's expression, as usual, was glintingly ironic. 'Would you dine with a friend of mine,' Jebsen asked suddenly, 'a member of the German Embassy?' The friend turned out to be one Major Müntzinger, a corpulent Bavarian and the most senior Abwehr officer in the Balkans. Over brandy and cigars, Müntzinger made his pitch to Popov, as subtle as a sledgehammer. 'No country can resist the German army. In a couple of months, England will be invaded. To facilitate the German task and to make an eventual invasion less bloody, you could help.' Müntzinger shifted to flattery. Popov was well connected. His business was the ideal cover for travelling to Britain, where he must know many important and influential people. Why, did he not know the Duke of Kent himself? Popov nodded. (He did not admit that he had visited Britain only once in his life, and had met the Duke for a matter of minutes at Dubrovnik's Argosy Yacht Club.) Müntzinger continued: 'We have many agents in England, quite a number of them excellent. But your connections would open many doors. You could render us great service. And we could do the same for you. The Reich knows how to show its appreciation.' Jebsen drank his whisky and said nothing. Müntzinger was somewhat vague about the kind of information Popov might gather: 'General. Political.' And then, after a pause: 'Military. Johnny will introduce you to the proper people when and if you accept.' Popov asked for time to think the offer over, and in the morning, he accepted. Jebsen had recruited his first spy for German intelligence. He would never recruit another.

Popov, meanwhile, had begun to develop what he called 'a little idea of my own'.

In 1941, the Interallié was the most important spy network in Nazi-occupied France. Indeed, as one British intelligence officer remarked, it was virtually the only one, 'our sole source of information from France' in the early part of the war. The network consisted of scores of informers, agents and sub-agents, but ultimately the Interallié was the creation of one spy, a man to whom conspiracy and subterfuge were second nature, who regarded espionage as a vocation. His French collaborators knew him as Armand Borni; he also used the codename 'Walenty', or 'Valentine'. His real name was Roman Czerniawski, and in a very short time, through sheer energy, conviction and a soaring sense of his own worth, he had become the most valuable British spy in France.

Czerniawski was a Polish patriot, but that phrase cannot do justice to his essential Polishness, and the depths of his attachment to his motherland. He lived for Poland, and was perfectly prepared (at times, almost anxious) to die for it. 'His loyalty is entirely to his own country, and every problem he sees is bound up with the destiny of the Polish people,' wrote one of his fellow spies. He loathed the Germans and Russians with equal intensity for carving up his country, and dreamed only of restoring the Polish nation. Every other loyalty, every other consideration, was secondary. He stood just five foot six inches tall, with a thin face and intense, close-set eyes. He smiled readily, and spoke at machine-gun speed.

The son of a well-to-do Warsaw financier, Czerniawski had trained as a fighter pilot before the war, but a serious crash had left him partially sighted and deskbound. The German invasion of Poland in September 1939 found Captain Czerniawski at air force headquarters in Warsaw, a specialist in military intelligence and the author of a well-received treatise on counter-intelligence. Czerniawski was a professional, 'a man who lives and thinks spying', as one colleague put it. He regarded the spy trade as an honourable calling 'based on the highest ideals of human endeavour'. As the Polish army crumbled beneath the German onslaught, Czerniawski escaped to Romania, and then, using forged documents, made his way to France, where Polish forces were regrouping. When France fell in 1940, his division was disbanded, but rather than join his compatriots in

Britain to continue the fight from there, Czerniawski went underground. He persuaded a young French widow, Renée Borni, to lend him her late husband's identity. As German became their occupation, a peasant whose papers identified him as Armand Borni wobbled along beside them on a borrowed bicycle, taking mental notes, and already congratulating himself. 'Every signpost, every sign on a truck, every distinguishing mark of any sort, meant far more to me than to anybody else.' Here

Roman Czerniawski

were the seeds of what he would grandly refer to as his 'vision'. While the Polish government-in-exile in London fought one kind of war, he would mount another. He imagined 'small cells of resistance, multiplying with great speed, joining together and forming one screen of eyes'.

Czerniawski made his way to the unoccupied South of France, where he made contact with the Polish secret service and obtained formal approval for his plan to establish a network in the occupied zone. A few nights later, he was dining alone at La Frégate, a restaurant in Toulouse, when a young woman asked if she might occupy the empty seat at his table. 'She was small, in her thirties. Her pale, thin face, with thin lips, was animated by very vivid eyes.' Mathilde Carré simultaneously sized up her diminutive and accidental dining companion: 'Thin and muscular, with a long narrow face, rather large nose and green eyes which must originally have been clear and attractive but were now flecked with contusions as the result of a flying accident.' Czerniawski introduced himself 'in an appalling French accent'. They fell into conversation. After dinner he walked her home.

Mathilde Carré was highly intelligent, overwrought and, at the moment she met Czerniawski, teetering on the edge of a nervous breakdown. The child of bourgeois Parisian parents, she had studied at the Sorbonne, worked briefly in an insurance company, trained as a teacher, and then married a childhood friend, before swiftly discovering she could not stand him. The war was the excuse she needed to leave her husband. With the French army in retreat, she found work in a dressing station, treating the wounded. There she met a lieutenant in the French Foreign Legion, and made love to him 'under the eyes of an enormous crucifix' in the bishop's cell of a seminary at Cazères sur Garonne. He was gone in the morning, and she was pregnant. She decided to keep the baby, and then miscarried. One night, she stood on a high bridge, about to kill herself, but then changed her mind: 'Instead of throwing myself into the Garonne, I would fling myself into the war. If I really intended to commit suicide, it would be more intelligent to commit a useful suicide.' To celebrate this decision, she had taken herself out to dinner at La Frégate.

Czerniawski's abundant self-assurance made Mathilde feel instantly secure. 'Every time he spoke of the war his eyes flashed. He would not accept that Poland had been defeated. He radiated a kind of confidence and the enthusiasm of youth, an intelligence and willpower which would alternately give place to the airs of a spoilt, affectionate child.' They met again the next night, and the next. 'A great bond of friendship was swiftly forged.' Both would later deny they had ever been lovers with such vehemence that the denials were almost certainly untrue.

Three weeks after their first meeting, Czerniawski confessed that he was a spy, and asked Mathilde to help him realise his 'vision' of a multi-celled intelligence network. She said he could count on her; together they would 'do great things'. The theatricality of the moment was compounded by Czerniawski's announcement that he had already selected a codename for his new accomplice: she would be 'La Chatte', the She-Cat, because 'you walk so quietly, in your soft shoes, like a cat'. She raised the slim fingers of one hand in a claw: 'And I can scratch as well if I wish.' Perhaps it was a warning.

Roman Czerniawski and Mathilde Carré formed a most effective spy partnership. In Paris, they rented a room in Montmartre, and set about constructing an entire espionage network. 'It will be inter-Allied,' Czerniawski announced. 'The boss will be a Pole, the agents mostly French, and all working for the Allies.' The Interallié network was born.

Mathilde acted as chief recruiter (since some Frenchmen declined to work for a Pole), while Roman gathered, collated, typed and dispatched intelligence material to London. The first recruits were Monique Deschamps, codenamed 'Moustique' (Mosquito), a tiny, chain-smoking firebrand of a woman, and René Aubertin, a former French army tank commander. Gradually the network expanded to include railway workers, police, fishermen, criminals and housewives. They sent whatever intelligence they had gathered to one of numerous 'post boxes' across Paris: the lavatory attendant at La Palette, the Berlitz language school by the Opéra, and a concierge on Rue Lamarck 'who had received a bayonet thrust in the buttocks when the Germans entered Paris, so it was only natural that he should hate them'. Mathilde gathered up their intelligence. 'In her black fur coat, red hat and small, flat, red shoes she moved swiftly from one appointment to another,' wrote Czerniawski, 'bringing new contacts, new possibilities, leaving me free to concentrate on studying the news from our agents and condensing it into our reports.'

Czerniawski's aim was to build up a complete picture of German forces in occupied France, the Order of Battle: troop positions and movements, ammunition dumps, aerodromes, naval and radar installations. 'To defeat the enemy you have to know where he is; the more exactly you know where he is, the easier it can be,' he wrote. He typed up the condensed reports on tissue paper. Every few weeks, a courier codenamed 'Rapide', 'a tall, thin Pole of indeterminate age with a muddy complexion and a small black moustache', boarded the 11 a.m. Marseille train for Bordeaux at the Gare de Lyon. Ten minutes before departure, he locked himself in the first-class toilet. Over the toilet bowl was a metal sign reading: '*Remplacez le couvercle après l'usage*'. Inserting a handkerchief between screwdriver and screw to avoid tell-tale scratching, Rapide carefully loosened the sign-plate, inserted the tissue-paper report behind, and then screwed it back on. After the train had crossed the border into unoccupied France, an agent of Polish intelligence would perform the procedure in reverse, retrieving the report and inserting a reply to be picked up when the train arrived back in Paris. From unoccupied France, Polish intelligence relayed the message via courier through the neutral Iberian Peninsula to the Polish government in exile in London, which passed it on to the British Secret Services. Every one of Czerniawski's reports ended up with MI6, Britain's foreign intelligence organisation, more formally known as the Secret Intelligence Service, or SIS.

The network, or La Famille as they called it, expanded swiftly. A radio the size of a portable typewriter was smuggled across the border from Vichy France, installed in a top-floor flat near the Trocadero and used to send coded information. Renée Borni, the widow who had furnished Czerniawski's false identity, moved to Paris to work on coding and decoding the wireless messages. Czerniawski gave her the codename 'Violette'. She became his lover. By the middle of 1941, Czerniawski could boast that his 'Big Network composed of French patriots, directed by a Pole and working for England, was now the last stronghold of Allied resistance against Germany'. Three more underground wireless stations were established. Some reports were 400 pages long, including maps and diagrams. Impossible to send by radio, these were photographed, and the undeveloped film smuggled across the Spanish border, 'packed in such a way that, opened by an unauthorised person, it would be exposed to the light and so made useless'.

Interallié intelligence poured into London in a swelling torrent, ever more detailed and precise, and sometimes so fast that its recipients could not keep up. When a spy discovered the route intended for the personal train of Hermann Goering, the Luftwaffe chief, Czerniawski immediately radioed the information to London, and was dismayed when the train was not attacked. A message arrived the next day. 'RE: GOERING TRAIN SORRY WE GOT THE NEWS TOO LATE TO USE IT FOR THE RAF STOP.'

Inevitably, there were tensions within the group. Mathilde loathed Renée, considering her 'a typical little provincial woman, and badly dressed'. Czerniawski insisted there was 'no question of any jealousy', but he reflected that Mathilde was a 'strange woman, idealistic but ruthless, ambitious, very nervous and highly strung'.

In the autumn of 1941, Czerniawski was told to report to an airfield near Compiègne, where a plane would pick him up to bring him to London for a debriefing. On 1 October, an RAF Lysander glided out of the sky, piloted by a man with a moustache, Squadron Leader J. 'Whippy' Nesbitt-Dufort, whose only French, by way of greeting, was '*C'est la vie*'. On arrival in England, Czerniawski was met by Colonel Stanislaw Gano, the head of Polish intelligence. 'You've kept us all busy on this side,' said Gano, who looked, Czerniawski thought, like 'the head of some business firm'. For twenty-four hours he was quizzed on every aspect of his network. Gano seemed particularly interested in Mathilde Carré. 'We are perfect partners,' Czerniawski assured him. Finally, to his amazement, he was ushered into the presence of General Wladislaw Sikorski, the Polish Prime Minister. Sikorski gravely declared that Czerniawski had been awarded the *Virtuti Militari*, the highest Polish military decoration. 'I was petrified by the suddenness, unexpectedness and solemnity of the moment,' Czerniawski later wrote. He would soon be dropped by parachute back into France to continue his work. The little Polish spy was proud, but with gratification came a niggling doubt, a small premonitory stab of anxiety: 'Subconsciously I felt a disturbing uneasiness.'

Elvira de la Fuente Chaudoir spent night after night at the gaming tables in Hamilton's Club or Crockford's Casino in Mayfair, and though she sometimes won, she always lost in the end. It was most frustrating. But when Elvira wasn't gambling, she was bored to death; which was why she had agreed to have lunch with a man who, she had been told, might offer her a most interesting and well-paid job.

Boredom stalked Elvira Chaudoir like a curse. Her father, a Peruvian diplomat, had made a fortune from guano, the excrement of seabirds, bats and seals, collected off the coast of Peru and exported as fertiliser. Elvira grew up in Paris, where she was expensively educated, and tremendously spoilt. In 1934, at the age of twenty-three, to escape the tedium, she had fled into the arms of Jean Chaudoir, a Belgian stock exchange representative for a gold-mining firm. Jean turned out to be a crashing bore, and life in Brussels was 'exceedingly dull'. After four years of marriage, and a number of unsatisfactory love affairs with both men and women, she came to the conclusion that 'she had nothing in common with her husband' and ran away to Cannes with her best friend, Romy Gilbey, who was married to a scion of the Gilbey gin dynasty, and very rich. Elvira and Mrs Gilbey were happily losing money made from gin in a casino in Cannes when the Germans invaded France; they fled, in an open-top Renault, to St Malo, before taking a boat for England.

In London, Elvira moved into a flat on Sloane Street, but the tedium of life swiftly descended once more. She spent her evenings shuttling between the bar at the Ritz and the bridge tables, losing money she did not have. She would have borrowed from her parents,

but they were stuck
in France. She tried
to join the Free
French forces gath-
ering around the
exiled Charles de
Gaulle, but was told
she was unsuitable.
She did a little trans-
lating for the BBC,
and found it dreary.
She complained, to
anyone who would
listen, that she could
not get an interest-
ing job because she
was Peruvian. One

Elvira de la Fuente Chaudoir

of those who happened to be listening, one night at Hamilton's,
was an RAF officer, who told a friend in military intelligence,
who passed her name on to someone in MI6. And so it was that
Elvira Chaudoir now found herself, at the age of twenty-nine,
in the grill room of the Connaught Hotel, sitting across the table
from a middle-aged man in a rumpled suit with a bristling white
moustache and the eyes of a hyperactive ferret. He had introduced
himself as 'Mr Masefield'. His real name was Lieutenant Colonel
Claude Edward Marjoribanks Dansey, also known as 'Haywood',
'Uncle Claude' and 'Colonel Z'. He was assistant chief of MI6.

Claude Dansey was witty, spiteful and widely disliked by his
fellow spies. Hugh Trevor-Roper, the waspish historian who
worked in wartime intelligence, considered him to be 'an utter
shit, corrupt, incompetent, but with a certain low cunning'.
Dansey was a most unpleasant man, and a most experienced
spy. They made an odd couple: Elvira, tall and over-dressed,
with a sweet, rather innocent face, her auburn hair arranged
into a question mark over her forehead; Dansey, small, bald,

bespectacled and intense. Elvira rather liked this fizzing little man, and as the conversation unfolded it became clear that he knew a great deal about her. He knew about Mrs Gilbey and the unsuccessful evenings at the bridge table; he knew her father had been appointed Peruvian chargé d'affaires to the collaborationist Vichy government in France; he knew what was, or rather what was not, in her bank account. 'I realised he must have been tapping my telephone. There was no other way he could have learned so much about me and my friends,' she later reflected.

Dansey offered her a job. Her Peruvian passport, he explained, meant that she could travel with comparative ease in occupied Europe, and her father's diplomatic status would provide cover for an extended visit to Vichy France. She could report on political matters, but more importantly she might get herself recruited as an agent by the Germans. This is the intelligence technique known as 'coat-trailing', dangling a potential recruit before the opposition in the hope that, if recruited, they can then be put to work as a double agent. She would be well paid for her efforts. Elvira did not hesitate.

The MI6 assessment of their new recruit was blunt: 'Attractive in appearance. She speaks fluent French, English and Spanish. She is intelligent and has a quick brain but is probably rather lazy about using it. A member of the international smart gambling set, her friends are to be found in any of the smart bridge clubs in London.' Surveillance revealed that her 'tastes appear to be in the direction of the "high spots"'. Police reported 'hilarious parties' at the Sloane Street flat, with 'rowdy behaviour, singing and shouting late at night, and the arrival of drunken men and women in the small hours'. Deputy Chief Constable Joseph Goulder noted, with disapproval and some understatement, that Mrs Chaudoir 'favours the companionship of women who may not be careful of their virginity'. Though Elvira might have come across as some dizzy-headed socialite, in reality she was bright and resourceful, and with a cast-iron cover: a good-time girl with no interests beyond the next cocktail, the next bed partner and the next bet. She was also attractive to both sexes and hungry for cash, qualities which might come in useful. As Dansey knew from a lifetime of espionage, even the most intelligent and discreet of people will tend to indiscretion if they think they are talking to a foolish and beddable woman.

In a flat in Knightsbridge, Elvira was taught how to use secret ink using a match head impregnated with a chemical powder. Once in France, she would write 'apparently innocuous letters' to a cover address in Lisbon. 'Between the lines of those letters I was to insert my intelligence reports penned in an undetectable fluid that could be developed by Dansey's technicians.' Elvira was a swift learner. 'She is very intelligent and quick to grasp essentials,' her instructor reported.

Her budding spy career very nearly came to an early end when a certain Sub-Lieutenant Burnett of the Royal Naval Volunteer Reserve reported that, one night at Crockford's, he had overheard Elvira Chaudoir boasting 'she was being taught a secret service code in the neighbourhood of St James's and that shortly she was to be sent to Vichy'. Elvira was given a severe scolding, and told 'she must abstain from divulging information which may have come to her knowledge'. Chastened, she promised to be more discreet, but the incident had demonstrated one of her more aggravating (and endearing) traits: like many spies, she found it hard to keep a secret.

Elvira was given the oddly masculine codename 'Cyril', and told to stand ready to go to France. Her war was about to become very interesting indeed.

Juan Pujol García had been many things in his short life: cinema proprietor, businessman, cavalry officer (though he feared horses) and reluctant soldier. He had spent most of the Spanish Civil War in hiding from Francoist forces. A graduate of the Royal Poultry School at Arenys de Mar, Spain's most prestigious college for chicken farmers, he ran a poultry farm outside Barcelona, though he hated chickens. Pujol had no head for figures and the business went bust. Stocky and spry, with a high forehead and 'warm brown eyes with a slightly mischievous tint', he looked like a fighting bantam. When the Second World War broke out, Pujol decided he wanted to spy for the British. 'I must do something,' he told himself. 'Something practical; I must make my contribution towards the good of humanity.' Hitler was 'a psychopath', Pujol concluded, and so he must support the Allies. 'I wanted to work for them, to supply them with confidential information which would be of interest to the Allied cause, politically or militarily.'

Quite where and how he would obtain such information, he had yet to work out. 'My plans were fairly confused,' he later admitted. His memoirs, written many years later, suggest that his quixotic, deeply held determination to fight Hitler sprang from an aggressive form of pacifism, and an abiding distrust of political extremism in any form. He was a supremely gentle soul, proud never to have fired a gun; he planned to fight Nazism in a different way. 'I was fascinated by the origin of words,' he wrote many years later. 'The pen is mightier than the sword. I believe this sincerely and absolutely. I have devoted the greater part of my life to this ideal, using all my talents, all my convictions, all possible schemes, machinations and stratagems.' Pujol would fight a unique sort of war, with words as his only weapons.

In January 1941, the twenty-nine-year-old Catalan approached the British Embassy in Madrid, with an offer to spy against the Germans. He was politely but firmly told to go away. In a variant of Groucho Marx's dictum, the British did not want anyone in the club who wanted to be a member. Pujol next tried the Germans, pretending to be a keen fascist willing to spy against the British – in the hope that, once recruited, he could then betray them. The Germans told him they were 'extremely busy'. But the little Catalan with the oddly intense eyes continued to badger the Germans in Spain, schooling himself in National Socialism until he could 'rant away as befitted a staunch Nazi'. Finally (mostly to get him to shut up), the Germans said that if he could get to Britain, via Lisbon, he would be considered for intelligence work. This was enough for Pujol. From that point on, he began to worm his way into German confidences, and in particular those of Major Karl-Erich Kühlenthal of the Madrid Abwehr station.

Kühlenthal would be comprehensively duped in the course of Operation Mincemeat, the deception in which a dead body was floated ashore in Spain, carrying forged documents indicating an Allied landing in Greece rather than Sicily. The German officer was efficient, paranoid and stupendously gullible. From Pujol's point of view, he was the ideal case officer. Kühlenthal duly equipped Pujol with secret ink, cash, the codename 'Agent Arabel', and some advice: 'He should be careful not to underestimate the British, as they were a formidable enemy.' On his arrival in Lisbon, Pujol once more contacted the British, and once more was rejected. This left him in something of a quandary, since he needed to start feeding information to the Germans as soon as possible. On 19 July 1941, he sent a telegram to Kühlenthal announcing his safe arrival in Britain.

THE NATIONAL ARCHIVES

But he was not in Britain. Pujol was still in Portugal. Denied the opportunity to gather real intelligence, for either side, he decided to invent it, with the help of the Lisbon public library, second-hand books and whatever he could glean from newsreels. He dug out the names and addresses of real British

Juan Pujol

munitions companies, consulted a *Blue Guide to England* for relevant place names, and a Portuguese publication entitled *The British Fleet* as a primer on naval matters. Pujol had never been to Britain. He simply imagined it, sending back detailed, long-winded reports about things he thought he might have seen had he been there. Pujol's style was exhaustingly verbose, a thicket of clauses and sub-clauses, adjectival swamps and overwrought sentences that stretched to a distant grammatical horizon. He would later claim that this extraordinary writing style was a way of filling up the page without saying very much. Though he loved to play with words, his reports were full of glaring errors. He could never get to grips with British military nomenclature or culture. He imagined that Glaswegian drinking habits must be similar to those in Spain; he wrote: 'There are men here who would do anything for a litre of wine.' His German controllers not only failed to spot his mistakes, but heaped praise on Agent Arabel, particularly when he claimed to have recruited two sub-agents in Britain who were, of course, entirely fictional. For nine months, Pujol remained in Lisbon, doing what spies, when stuck for real information, have always done: he invented what he thought his spymasters wanted to hear. He would continue to make it up, magnificently, for the rest of the war.

Major Emile Kliemann of the German Abwehr was having a most agreeable war. Occupied Paris was an exceptionally pleasant place to be, if you happened to be one of the occupiers. He had an office on the Champs-Elysées, a comfortable apartment near the Bois de Boulogne, plenty of disposable cash and very little to do. Most importantly, he had a new mistress, named Yvonne Delidaise. A French woman with a German mother, Yvonne was demanding, expensive, and twenty years his junior. His dumpy Austrian wife was still in Vienna, and certain to remain there. This was also a source of satisfaction. Kliemann's job was recruiting informers and ferreting out French spies, but his indefatigable colleague Hugo Bleicher seemed happy to do the hard work, which was just fine with Kliemann. A Viennese businessman, posted to Paris in June 1940, Kliemann had little time for Nazism. Indeed, he 'did not particularly like Germans', and rather hoped that Germany would not win the war too quickly as he wanted nothing more than to continue his newfound Parisian life, making love to Yvonne and meeting the odd dodgy character in his favourite café, Chez Valerie. Portly and broad-shouldered, Kliemann wore a neatly clipped moustache, and a gold signet ring on the third finger of his left hand with the initials 'EK'. He dressed with what he considered understated elegance, dyed his sideburns, and wore his hair carefully parted and greased down. He played the violin and collected antique porcelain. At forty-three, Major Emile Kliemann was vain, romantic, clever, staggeringly lazy and consistently unpunctual. As befits a spy chief, he had assembled an impressive number of aliases – 'Killberg', 'von Carstaedt', 'Polo', 'Octave' and 'Monsieur Jean' – though not a single workable spy.

On 13 October 1941, Kliemann reluctantly arranged to meet a potential recruit, a twenty-nine-year-old Frenchwoman of Russian origin, recommended by one of his colleagues. Her name was Lily Sergeyev.

Kliemann was two hours late for their rendezvous at the Café du Rond-Point. The young woman waiting at the corner table was handsome, without being beautiful. She had curly brown hair, bright blue eyes and a square chin. In fluent German, Lily Sergeyev explained that she was a journalist and painter. Her father had been a Tsarist government official but after the Revolution, when Lily was five, the family had emigrated to Paris. Her grandfather, she announced with pride, had been the last Imperial Russian Ambassador to Serbia. Her uncle, General Yevgeni Miller, had commanded the Fifth Russian Army in the First World War and then vanished in 1937, and was executed in Moscow two years later. Her father now sold cars. Her mother was a dressmaker. She considered herself French. She wanted to spy for Germany.

Lily Sergeyev

Kliemann was intrigued. Lily seemed vivacious, intelligent and, most importantly, interested in Kliemann. He invited her to dinner at the Cascade restaurant, near the Bois de Boulogne, explaining that Yvonne, his 'secretary', would meet them there. The young woman insisted on bringing her dog, a small, white, male terrier-poodle cross named Babs, to which she was obviously devoted.

Once they were seated in the restaurant, Lily told her story. A restless spirit, she had made a number of epic journeys across Europe by bicycle and on foot, including one that had taken her through Hitler's Germany. There she had been impressed by the efficiency of the Nazi regime, and had written a series of admiring articles for the French press. She had even interviewed Goering, who had 'promised to obtain for her a personal interview with Hitler'. This had not materialised. In 1937, a German journalist named Felix Dassel, whom she had met on her travels, told her he was working for German intelligence, and asked Lily if she wanted a job. She had declined, but when the Germans marched into Paris, Dassel had reappeared. Over dinner at Maxim's, she told him that the British had 'let the French down badly and that she had no love for them'. Dassel asked her again if she was prepared to work for the Germans; this time, she accepted. It was Dassel who had recommended that Kliemann arrange this meeting.

Yvonne was yawning by this point in Lily's story, but Kliemann was curious. She seemed genuine enough, and enthusiastic, though nervous. 'It might be quite easy for me to get to Portugal, to

Australia, or to England,' she said. 'I have relatives in all those places and nobody would be surprised if I wanted to get out of France.'

Kliemann pondered. 'I am interested in your project,' he said finally. 'I think we will send you to Portugal. I very much doubt that you will be allowed to go to England.'

Then, suddenly, Kliemann caught Lily's wrist, and fixed her with what he plainly believed was a penetrating, spy-masterly stare: '*Why* do you want to work for us?'

There was a long and uncomfortable pause. Her reply, when it came, was an odd one.

'Major, you are an intelligent man: how much can my answer be worth to you? I can tell you that it is from conviction, a matter of principle, or because I love Germany, or else I hate the British. But if you were the enemy, if I were here to spy on you, to betray you, do you think that my answer would be any different? So will you allow me not to answer?'

He smiled and replied that 'of course, she was right'.

Kliemann dropped off Lily and her little dog at her parents' flat near the Trocadero. 'I will make contact again soon,' said the Major. Then, as usual, he did nothing at all.

In her diary, Lily wrote: 'Babs lifts up his shaggy, truffle-like nose and looks at me inquiringly.' (The diary is written entirely in the present tense, and much of it is devoted to her dog.) 'I take Babs on my knees, on the drawing-room sofa, and say in his pink ear: "It's a fine game, it's a grand game, but, you know, if we lose it, we'll lose our lives . . . or mine, at any rate."' Babs would be the first to perish in the game.

A Bit of an Enigma

Dusko Popov, the Serbian playboy, was not as feckless and apolitical as he seemed. The invitation from his old friend Johnny Jebsen to work for German intelligence was an attractive one. The year of 1940 was a time of deep anxiety as the German army rampaged across Europe. Poland had been under German occupation since September the previous year; Denmark had been invaded in April, followed by Norway; Belgium and the Netherlands surrendered in May; France had fallen in June. Yugoslavia might be next. A Serbian businessman with interests across Europe would need German friends and, as Popov told Jebsen, he was keen 'to get an easy living'.

But within days of accepting Major Müntzinger's offer, Popov began to work on his own plan. A small seed of courage had taken root in this hitherto callow and shallow soul. A few days after the dinner with Müntzinger, he contrived to bump into John Dew, First Secretary at the British Embassy in Belgrade, at a legation party. In a quiet moment on the terrace, he told Dew that an old university chum, now an Abwehr officer, had made moves to recruit him. 'Interesting,' said Dew (who privately suspected Popov was 'an awful crook'). 'Be a good thing for you to keep in touch with that chap.' Dew put Popov in contact with the MI6 station chief in the Yugoslav capital. 'Continue your conversation with the Germans,' Popov was advised. 'Be friendly but don't overdo it. Ask for time to prepare your trip.'

Johnny Jebsen laid out Popov's mission on behalf of German intelligence: he would travel to London, via neutral Portugal, under the guise of a businessman exporting raw materials from Yugoslavia to Britain. Once there, he should begin sending back information by writing letters in secret ink. This was the principal method of covert communication between spies, a way of passing information that was becoming something of an espionage art in 1940. Jebsen showed Popov how to make the ink using a tablet of Pyramidon, a common treatment for headache, dissolved in white gin. When Popov had something to report, he should write an 'insignificant letter in type' on one side of a piece of paper, and use the ink and a sharpened matchstick to write invisibly on the other. The letter should then be sent to 'Maria Elera', at an address in Lisbon, where it would be picked up by the Abwehr. When a developer chemical was applied to the paper, the secret writing would appear.

Maria Elera was described by Jebsen as 'a young girl, about twenty-two, a journalist, Mulatto, who would pass as his girlfriend'. She would soon become exactly that. Popov would report to the Abwehr station in Lisbon. 'Your spymaster will be Major Ludovico von Karsthoff,' Johnny explained. 'You may find yourself liking him.' Finally, Popov was handed a list of questions, covering subjects as diverse as Britain's coastal defences, deployment of troops, civilian morale and politics: 'Who were Churchill's enemies? Who was in favour of starting to negotiate peace with Germany?' Popov immediately handed the questionnaire over to MI6. By November, Popov, codenamed 'Ivan' by his German handlers, was ready to go.

Popov and Jebsen met for a farewell drink at the Serbian King Hotel in Belgrade. 'We are now both in the same service,' Jebsen remarked. There was something about his smile that gave Popov pause. Here was a German spy who was a devotee of P. G. Wodehouse; a mouthpiece for Nazi propaganda who said he was terrified of fighting, but who obviously relished the risky world of espionage, knew how to make secret ink and professed himself 'strongly pro-British'. Jebsen even employed a British secretary, Mabel Harbottle, a starchy English spinster who might have stepped from the pages of a Wodehouse novel. Miss Harbottle had formerly worked for Joachim von Ribbentrop, Hitler's Foreign Minister, and though a German citizen, Mabel remained 'British at heart'. She flatly refused to type his letters unless reassured that whatever Jebsen was doing for the Germans 'could not hurt British interests'. Jebsen gave her that assurance – an odd commitment from a man specifically employed by the German Reich to do as much damage as possible to British interests. As Popov put it, Johnny was 'a bit of an enigma'.

The same was true of Jebsen's new boss, Admiral Canaris, one of the most puzzling figures of the Second World War. Supple and sinuous, and a master of the espionage game, Canaris was held in some awe by the other leaders of the Third Reich, including Hitler. Himmler loathed and distrusted him. So did Ribbentrop. Canaris was determined to win the espionage battle for Germany, yet his loyalties were shifting, his personal convictions opaque. He was openly friendly to Jews, and would help save many from the gas chambers. He made little secret of his disdain for the hysterical violence of the Nazis. And he ran the Abwehr, the great sprawling German intelligence machine, as a personal fiefdom, with little reference to the High Command. But then, the Abwehr was itself an anomaly within the Nazi military structure. Its officers tended to be drawn from the German upper classes, old-fashioned military types with little sympathy for the boorish ideology of Nazism: some were professionals, but many were lazy and corrupt, and a number of senior officers were actively opposed to the Hitler regime.

'What is Canaris like?' Popov asked his old friend. 'A sensitive man, unobtrusive,' came the considered reply, 'with much curiosity, vast intelligence, and a great sense of humour. He gives the impression of preferring to listen rather than to speak.' Johnny Jebsen might have been describing himself.

Popov would later insist that Jebsen knew, from the outset, that he would make contact with the British, and wanted him to do so. Secretly anti-Nazi, a devoted Anglophile, Jebsen was already playing a subtle and dangerous double game. Popov was only pretending to work for the Germans and Jebsen, it seemed, was only pretending to believe that he was. Each was lying, both knew it, and neither admitted it. 'There was a curious ambiguity about friendship for people in our positions,' wrote Popov. 'You tried to convince yourself that a friend would be on the right side, yet you couldn't dare trust that friendship far enough to reveal yourself.'

Popov arrived in Lisbon a week later, where he was met by a chauffeur and driven in an Opel sedan to a large stucco villa in the Moorish style in the seaside resort of Estoril. At the door of Villa Toki-Ana he was greeted by a gentlemanly figure with a warm smile and a mass of 'blackish hair on his hands'. Popov was training himself to spot distinguishing features.

'I have been instructed to help you to the utmost,' said his host. 'You have inspired a lot of faith at the Tirpitzufer [Abwehr headquarters in Berlin], and they are making ambitious plans for you.' Johnny had been right: Popov felt immediately drawn to Ludovico von Karsthoff: 'He was tall and dark and his movements were those of a big cat.' Von Karsthoff gave Popov the name of another German agent in London, a Czechoslovak named Georges Graf, who could be contacted in case of emergencies. In the evening they drank champagne and dined sumptuously. Though Popov would never know it, von Karsthoff's real name was Kremer von Auenrode, an educated and worldly aristocrat from Trieste whose main objective was to get through the war with maximum pleasure and minimum danger.

At dawn on 20 December 1940, Dusko Popov, Yugoslavian businessman, alighted at Whitchurch airport near Bristol. There he was met by Jock Horsfall, a pre-war racing driver who was MI5's most trusted chauffeur. As they neared the capital,

Popov's registration card

Popov could see the menacing roseate glow over London: the Luftwaffe's bombers had departed, but the fires were still burning.

In the lobby of the Savoy Hotel, a tall officer in the striking tartan trousers of an officer in the Seaforth Highlanders strode forward, hand outstretched. 'Popov, hello. I'm Robertson.' He looked, thought Popov, 'like Hollywood's concept of a dashing British military type'. Popov felt an instinctive liking for another spymaster, this one on the other side. 'Let's get acquainted,' said the Englishman, ushering him towards the bar. 'We'll get down to business tomorrow.'

This urbane, upper-class Englishman with distinctive trousers might have been welcoming a new member into one of London's more exclusive clubs – which, in a way, he was.

Major Müntzinger's boast that Germany had 'many agents in England' was entirely correct. But so far from being 'excellent', most of them were hopeless, many were actively disloyal, and a number were already working against Germany as double agents.

The counter-espionage section of MI5, known as B Section, was presided over by Guy Liddell, a shy, cello-playing spy-hunter, whose voluminous diaries offer an extraordinary insight into the wartime work of this remarkable secret organisation. In combating German espionage, Liddell faced two overriding and interconnected problems: a huge host of spies that did not exist, and a second, much smaller body of secret agents that most certainly did.

With the outbreak of war, Britain was gripped by what Liddell called a 'Fifth Column Neurosis', the unshakable and all but universal belief that the country was riddled with enemy spies, preparing to rise up if Hitler launched an invasion. This fear was stoked by spy novels, an excitable press and a peculiarly British urge to play amateur sleuth. 'There is a well-defined class of people prone to spy-mania,' wrote Winston Churchill, who had the mania himself. These imagined spies came disguised as nuns, butcher's boys, churchwardens and travelling salesmen. They appeared perfectly respectable. The head of Home Forces insisted that 'the gentlemen who are the best behaved and the most sleek are the stinkers who are doing the work and we cannot be too sure of anybody'. A spy might look like your bank manager. Indeed, he might *be* your bank manager. Robert Baden-Powell, the original Scout master, insisted he could identify a German spy from the way he walked, but only from behind. Reports flooded in to MI5 detailing the nefarious activities of this hidden spy army: they were poisoning the ice cream, leaving marks on telegraph poles to guide the invading forces, drugging cigarettes and training the inmates of lunatic asylums as suicide squads. When six cows stampeded on the tiny island of Eilean Mor in the Scottish Hebrides, this was immediately adduced to secret enemy activity. That the spies were invisible was merely proof of how fiendishly clever they were at disguising themselves. Even pigeons were suspect, since it was widely believed that enemy agents had secret caches of homing pigeons around the country which they used to send messages back to Germany. Britain's fear of spy-pigeons would eventually come home to roost in a most unlikely fashion.

These spy sightings were, as Liddell put it, 'junk', but the suspicion that Germany had launched an espionage campaign against Britain was entirely accurate. In July 1940, the Abwehr held a conference in Kiel, attended by Germany's most senior intelligence officers, at which a plan was drawn up (codenamed 'Operation Lena', after the wife of a senior Abwehr officer) to recruit and train dozens of spies, and dispatch them to Britain to conduct sabotage operations, infiltrate British society, and collect information on troops, airfields, civilian morale and anything else that might aid a German invasion. German spies began slipping into the country: they came by boat, submarine and parachute; some, like Popov, came legally, or disguised as refugees. Of the two dozen spies or so deployed to Britain between September and November 1940, five were German, while the others were variously Dutch, Scandinavian, Cuban, Swiss, Belgian, Spanish and Czechoslovak. These were far removed from the super spies imagined by a nervous British public. Most were poorly trained and petrified; some spoke no English at all, and had only a sketchy notion of the country they were supposed to blend into. They did not look like your next-door neighbour – they looked like spies. Only a few were genuine Nazis. The rest were variously motivated by greed, adventure, fear, stupidity and blackmail. Their number included several criminals, degenerates and alcoholics. According to one MI5 report, 'a high proportion suffered from venereal disease'. Some had opportunistically volunteered to spy against Britain, with the intention of defecting. Some were anti-Nazi from the outset. This motley collection of invasion spies had only this in common: not a single one escaped detection.

The task of intercepting enemy spies was made immeasurably simpler after cryptanalysts at Bletchley Park, the British code-breaking centre in Buckinghamshire, cracked the Abwehr wireless code, and began reading Germany's most closely held secrets. The breaking of the 'Enigma', the German cipher machine, was the most important intelligence triumph of this, or any other war: here was an information gold mine, referred to variously as 'Ultra' or the 'Most Secret Sources' (or 'MSS'), and guarded more jealously than any other wartime secret. With access to the wireless traffic passing between Berlin and its Abwehr stations, from the end of 1940 the British could track German intelligence operations from start to finish, and plan accordingly. With advance warning from the Bletchley Park codebreakers, these incompetent and highly visible spies were 'easy prey'. Once in custody, they were taken to the secret wartime interrogation centre at Latchmere House in Richmond, Camp 020, under the command of Captain (later Colonel) Robin Stephens.

Known as 'Tin-eye', on account of the monocle permanently screwed into his right eye, Stephens was xenophobic, rude, manipulative, ruthless and brilliant. Spies were subjected to intense interrogation using every method to extract the truth short of physical violence. Those deemed unsuitable as double agents were either imprisoned, or tried and executed. The others, a small minority, were offered a choice: work for Britain against Germany, or face the hangman's noose. 'You have forfeited your life, but there is a way of saving your life,' was how Tin-eye framed the issue. Unsurprisingly, this argument proved persuasive. Of the twenty-five German spies sent to Britain between 3 September and 12 November 1940, all but one was caught (the lone evader shot himself); five were executed; fifteen were imprisoned; and four became double agents, the first recruits of what would grow into a substantial army of deceivers.

The officer in command of this fledgling force was Thomas Argyll Robertson, known as Tommy, but more usually Tar, on account of his initials. Spymasters are expected to be intense types, ferociously clever and faintly sinister. On the surface, Tar Robertson appeared to be none of these. The son of a Scottish banker, he was cheery, amiable, funny and self-mocking. If he ever opened a book, there is no record of it. As a young man he had, according to one relative, 'an almost suicidal appetite for dusk to dawn partying, pretty women, and fast cars', expensive tastes that put paid to his army career in the Seaforth Highlanders when he ran out of funds. After an undistinguished stint in the City, in 1933 he was recruited into MI5 through the old boy network. He retained a military air, and the tartan

Tar Robertson

army trousers which earned him the nickname 'Passion Pants'. In demeanour, he was 'a perfect officer type, who could have been played by Ronald Colman', the English actor, with 'friendly eyes and an assertive way about him'. His family considered him 'less than promising'. But once installed in MI5, Tar revealed a natural talent for hanging around in pubs and picking up gossip. He was 'immensely personable and monstrously good looking', according to one colleague, 'with a charm that could melt an iceberg' and an 'unmistakable twinkle' that encouraged the spilling of confidences. Beneath the affability and 'delightful chuckle' was a personality of granite determination, and a ruthless streak. Hugh Trevor-Roper considered his Secret Service colleagues 'by and large pretty stupid – some of them very stupid'. But Tar he regarded as a 'real genius', with an uncanny knack for reading character and knowing, instinctively, when he was being misled. Robertson knew better than anyone else in British intelligence how to spot a lie, and therefore how to tell one.

The British Secret Services traditionally took a fastidious approach to double agents, regarding the practice of 'turning' intercepted spies and using them to mislead the enemy as faintly disreputable. Such creatures were classed as '*agents doubles*' – in French, as if to underline that this was typically duplicitous Continental behaviour. But before the war, MI5 recruited only one truly important double agent, an experiment that had almost ended in disaster. Arthur Owens was a Welsh-born electrical engineer with a 'shifty look', who began his spying career by providing information to MI6 after his visit to German shipyards. Owens also made contact with the Abwehr, which gave him the task of recruiting radical Welsh nationalists for sabotage operations. (This was an early hint of the Abwehr's bizarre but firmly held belief that the Welsh valleys were filled with violent secessionists awaiting the opportunity, with Nazi encouragement, to rise up against their English oppressors.) He then turned double agent, and agreed to work against the Germans. Tar was made case officer to Owens (codenamed 'Snow', a partial anagram of his surname) and eventually concluded that this 'stupid little man given to doing silly things at odd times' was playing each side against the other, but inefficiently. The case was eventually wound up, largely because Owens was a fantasist, whose mind did not 'work on logical lines'. Yet the Snow case had helped Bletchley Park to break the Abwehr code, provided useful leads on tracking down other German spies, and 'saved us from absolute darkness on the subject of German espionage', according to Dick White, Liddell's deputy. It also gave Robertson an early taste of just how fickle, troublesome and yet valuable a double agent could be.

It was Tar who had pointed out that simply capturing, executing or interning enemy spies, however satisfying as an act of war, offered no long-term benefit. There was nothing tender-hearted in Tar's desire to preserve German spies from the gallows: this was hard-eyed calculation. The questions asked of spies by their German spymasters offered useful clues to what the Abwehr did not know; if the Germans believed they had a functioning network of spies in Britain, they might feel it unnecessary to send more; if the Abwehr thought its spies were alive, at liberty and functioning well, it would open up possibilities for dialogue and deception. A live spy was more useful than a dead one, though a lot more trouble. Section B1A was launched, a new subsection of Liddell's B Section, with Tar Robertson at the helm.

The first spies selected as double agents proved to be duds. Georges Graf (codenamed, punningly, 'Giraffe') was a Czechoslovak citizen who had served in the French army before being dispatched to Britain by the Abwehr. Popov had been given his name by von Karsthoff, so the Germans obviously trusted him, and Popov's willingness to pass his name on to the British, unaware that Graf had already been turned, was proof that he was playing straight. Kurt Goose (codenamed 'Gander', naturally), landed by parachute in October with only a transmitting wireless; unable to receive messages from his handlers, he was of limited use, and the Gander case was swiftly wound up, as was Giraffe. Of greater interest were two Scandinavians, who had trained together in the Hamburg Abwehr station: Gøsta Caroli, a Swedish journalist who had lost a fortune in an Uppsala silver fox farm, and Wulf Schmidt, a Danish fascist. Caroli parachuted into the Northamptonshire countryside on the night of 6 September 1940, landed badly, and staggered into a ditch to try to sleep off his concussion, where a farmhand spotted his feet sticking out of a hedge. He was carrying a radio transmitter, £200 and a loaded pistol. Schmidt landed two weeks later, sprained an ankle, limped into the Cambridgeshire village of Willingham in a natty blue suit but with an unmistakable foreign accent, and was promptly arrested.

Though a 'fanatical Nazi', in the view of Tin-eye Stephens, Caroli agreed to work as a double agent if Schmidt's life was spared. With cruel but effective psychological manipulation, Schmidt was told that his friend had betrayed him; enraged, he spilled the beans and agreed to change sides. Caroli was given the codename 'Summer', but the Swede seems to have had second thoughts. One evening, in his safe house in Hinxton, near Cambridge, Caroli crept up behind his minder while he was playing patience and tried to throttle him with a piece of rope. When this failed, he apologised, tied the man to a chair and ran off with a tin of pilchards, a pineapple and a large canvas canoe. He then stole a motorcycle and motored, very slowly, towards the coast, with the canoe balanced on his head. He intended to paddle to Holland. A roadman reported to police that a man with a canoe had fallen off his motorcycle on the Pampisford Road, and 'he had helped the man throw the canoe over a hedge'. Caroli was arrested outside Ely. Clearly unreliable, the Swede was declared unfit for double-agent work, and imprisoned for the rest of the war. After initial resistance, Schmidt proved much more cooperative, and was given the codename 'Tate' because Robertson thought he looked like the music-hall comedian Harry Tate. He would prove to be the longest-serving double agent of them all.

The handling of double agents, Tar concluded, was going to require considerable subtlety: 'The double agent is a tricky customer and needs the most careful supervision. His every mood has to be watched.' These erratic characters showed an alarming propensity to swap sides. If any of them managed to break away and make contact with the Germans, Robertson reflected, this could 'blow our whole show'. If the Germans invaded, and there was a danger the double agents might fall into enemy hands, 'they will be liquidated forcibly'. Robertson was becoming fond of his brood of double agents. But he would not hesitate to kill them if he had to.

This, then, was the newly formed club into which Dusko Popov was welcomed by a smiling Tar Robertson in the lobby of the Savoy Hotel. The new double agent had already been given the codename 'Skoot', a play on his name, carrying the hint that Popov might 'pop off', or scoot, at any moment. (Under wartime rules, a spy's codename, or *nom de guerre*, should contain no hint of his or her identity. Robertson joyously and consistently ignored this directive, and established his own rule: every spy name must contain a joke, a pun, a hint or a nudge.) Tar had already learned enough about his new recruit's mode of life to know that a cell at Camp 020 and a grilling from Tin-eye Stephens were neither necessary nor advisable. Instead, Popov was lodged in a comfortable room at the Savoy, where Robertson and his colleagues interrogated him on his story: his recruitment by Johnny Jebsen, the meeting with Müntzinger, his encounter with the suave, hairy-handed von Karsthoff in Lisbon; his questionnaire and his instructions for making secret ink.

Popov struck his interrogators as open and honest, and his story was corroborated by information from Most Secret Sources. He made no monetary demands, and seemed to want to work as a double agent for the British out of a combination of anti-Nazi conviction and a thirst for adventure. Tar was impressed. 'I have a strong feeling we are on to something good.' As a businessman from a neutral country, Popov could travel freely between London and Lisbon, and maintain direct, personal contact with his German handler. The Germans seemed 'absolutely obsessed with the idea that he has a wide circle of friends and business connections in England', even though he knew virtually nobody in the country. 'It will be necessary to supply him with the names of a number of supposed friends.'

After four days in his company, Tar was convinced that the young Serb with the carefree attitude was playing straight, and prepared to risk his life. 'Skoot left an exceedingly favourable first impression upon all of us. His manner was absolutely frank and we all considered without question that he was telling the truth.' A token of appreciation was in order, and Tar knew exactly what sort of reward Skoot would enjoy: on Christmas Eve 1940, MI5 laid on the most extravagant party that bomb-battered London could provide.

Courtnay Young, a junior officer in B Section, was appointed Popov's carousing partner. They began by consuming a substantial lunch with Robertson at Quaglino's restaurant. The remainder of the afternoon was spent playing billiards at the Lansdowne Club, with plenty of beer. In the early evening they drank sherry at the Universities' Club, before heading back to the Savoy for dinner. Young then suggested that they go dancing at the Suivi Club, where they met two attractive young women who danced with them all night. These, too, had been furnished by MI5. Skoot 'was obviously pleased by the interest shown by the two girls', reported Young, who had some difficulty keeping up with the pace of Popov's revelry. 'He enjoyed himself thoroughly [and] took part in the usual Christmas bonhomous rioting, well lubricated with champagne.' In the early hours, Popov and his minder staggered back to the Savoy, 'both viewing things through slightly rose-tinted spectacles'.

To retain German confidence, Agent Skoot would need to feed his handlers some true, but harmless information – known in spy jargon as 'chicken-feed', filling and substantial, but lacking in real nourishment. He would also need a convincing cover story. For this, Tar turned to Ewen Montagu, an officer in naval intelligence who would later devise Operation Mincemeat. Montagu was rich, well-connected, and a keen yachtsman – just the sort of person that the Germans would expect Dusko Popov to befriend. They met in the bar of the Savoy, where Montagu handed over a batch of true, low-level information on naval matters that could be passed to the Germans without danger, and some minor untruths, including the suggestion that British merchant convoys would be accompanied by at least one submarine in the future. In a small way, that might give the U-boat wolfpacks pause for thought. Before they parted, Montagu handed Popov a handwritten note, to show to the Germans as proof that he had indeed met this friendly and indiscreet naval officer. 'I much enjoyed meeting you,' wrote

Montagu. 'It is so nice at these troubled times to meet another who is as mad as I am about sailing.' In response to the question of which British figures were opposed to Churchill, he was told to cite Lords Brocket, Lymington and Londonderry as 'definitely members of the party that would be prepared to accept peace terms with Germany'. The three peers were widely suspected of pro-German sympathies, and there could be no harm in confirming what the Germans must already know.

Montagu was captivated by Popov: 'I found him a most charming person and would be most surprised if he is not playing straight with us,' he told Tar. 'I hope that his having met me and having laid the foundation for further information will satisfy his employers. I should have thought it ought to be enough to show for a first visit to this country.'

On 2 January 1941, the Twenty or XX Committee was formed to oversee the Double Cross system, the first and only government body named with a Roman numerical pun. The committee was formed to coordinate the work of double agents and supply these agents with a stream of chicken-feed to build up the credibility of the spies. John Masterman, an Oxford history don, part-time detective novelist and sportsman, was appointed Chairman of the Twenty Committee, which included directors of intelligence for the Army, Navy and RAF, and representatives of MI5, MI6, Home Forces and Home Defence. While Robertson and the case officers of B1A would be responsible for the day-to-day running of the double agents, the Twenty Committee would manage overall strategy and cook up a diet of harmless truths, half-truths and uncheckable untruths to feed to the enemy. The committee met, at MI5 headquarters in 58 St James's Street, every Thursday afternoon for the rest of the war. 'Giraffe's case died chiefly through lack of nourishment,' in Masterman's opinion. No double agent would ever go hungry again.

The Twenty Committee was referred to by its members as

'The Club', and Masterman organised it with a particular sort of club in mind: a cricket club. 'Running a team of double agents is very like running a club cricket side,' he wrote, and as a first-class cricketer himself, he approached the task exactly as if he was assembling 'a thoroughly well-trained and trustworthy team' of cricketers. Masterman was a cold fish, apparently without romantic feelings for either sex. But cricket was different. 'Cricket was my first and most enduring passion,' he wrote. He thought of espionage in terms of stumpings, no balls, innings and over rates, and of spies as 'players', some of whom 'required a good deal of net practice before they were really fit to play in a match'. The relationship between cricket (that most English of sports) and spying (at which the British have always excelled) is deep-rooted and unique. Something about the game attracts the sort of mind also drawn to the secret worlds of intelligence and counter-intelligence – a complex test of brain and brawn, a game of honour interwoven with trickery, played with ruthless good manners and dependent on minute gradations of physics and psychology, with tea breaks. Some of the most notable British spies have been cricketers, or cricket enthusiasts. Hitler played cricket, but only once. In 1930, it was claimed that, having seen British POWs playing in southern Germany during the First World War, the Nazi party leader asked to be 'initiated into the mysteries of our national game'. A match was played against Hitler's XI, after which he declared that the rules should be altered by the 'withdrawal of the use of pads' and using a 'bigger and harder ball'. Hitler could not understand the subtlety of a game like cricket; he thought only in terms of speed, spectacle, violence. Cricket was the ideal sport on which to model an organisation bent on stumping the Führer.

Tar Robertson was no mean cricketer himself – a left-arm spinner, whose speciality was a 'cunningly spun, deceptively slow ball'. As Tar assembled his team, Masterman was already imagining a time when they would be 'ready to take the field for what might be a decisive match' against German intelligence.

'The prime difficulty was that we never knew the date when this decisive match would take place.' It would be many months before the Double Cross players were ready to compete, but Masterman knew that in Dusko Popov, he had already found a singularly talented opening batsman.

On the day the Twenty Committee was born, Tar took his new protégé to lunch, and rehearsed, in detail, the story he was to tell the Germans. Twenty-four hours later, Skoot was on a plane back to Lisbon. 'We have in him a new agent of high quality,' Tar reported, confident that the sheer force of Popov's personality would protect him. If Tar was right, then Agent Skoot might help win the war; if not, then Dusko Popov was already as good as dead.

Roman and the Cat

Roman Czerniawski, the diminutive Polish spy, parachuted back into occupied France at dawn on 8 November 1941. He landed in a melon field, in the rain, not far from Tours. As he headed back to Paris on an overcrowded bus, wearing a beret and mackintosh, he reflected: 'I wonder if anybody here could imagine that I had my dinner in England.'

Safely back among his family of spies, Czerniawski announced that a celebration was in order. The 16th of November would mark the first anniversary of the Interallié network, and there was much to be proud of: some fifty agents, each with two or three sub-agents, had so far produced no less than ninety-seven reports, furnishing the British with 'a complete picture of the German Order of Battle'.

The leaders of the network assembled at the Montmartre flat – Roman, Mathilde Carré, Renée Borni and Maurice Wlodarczyk, a former Polish naval radio operator who worked the transmitter. They ate sandwiches and sipped the black-market champagne Czerniawski had managed to scrounge. At 8 p.m., they gathered around the wireless to listen to the BBC. Each section head of the Interallié had instructions to tune in. At 8.15, the BBC announcer played a snatch of patriotic French music, and then intoned: 'Many Happy Returns to our Family in France on the occasion of their anniversary.' They clinked glasses. Maurice sent a wireless message to London: 'AGAINST

THE GERMANS ALWAYS AND IN EVERY WAY. *VIVE LA LIBERTÉ!*'

The team drifted away. Czerniawski, a little tipsy, reflected that their underground work was taking its toll: Mathilde, in particular, was 'overworked and was obviously tired'. As co-founder of the network she seemed irked that Czerniawski had received a medal, the *Virtuti Militari*, while her work was barely acknowledged. The next night Roman and Renée Borni dined in their favourite restaurant. He asked the band to play 'Gloomy Sunday', also known as 'The Hungarian Suicide Song', a hit that year for Billie Holiday. 'Why did you ask for that?' asked Renée. 'It's so sad.' In the rainy street, as they were walking home, Roman noticed a man in a raincoat, his face obscured by an umbrella. He tried to recall the half-remembered face. 'I must be tired,' he thought.

Czerniawski was in deep sleep when a gunshot went off, and the Gestapo burst into his bedroom. Renée screamed. 'The light was switched on and in front of me I saw the man in the mackintosh and beret with a revolver in his hand.' Now he recognised him: Hugo Bleicher, the most feared German counter-intelligence officer in Paris. It was an 'intelligent face', Roman reflected, with eyes that were 'sharp, but not violent'. He was bundled into a waiting car, and driven directly to the Hôtel Edward VII, headquarters of the secret military police. 'If only someone could warn Mathilde,' Roman thought.

When Mathilde Carré got home from her early morning walk she saw, without immediately comprehending, that her door was splintered, hanging off its hinges. At the same moment, a burly Gestapo officer appeared at her elbow. She felt oddly calm as he led her away. 'It was a great gamble and today I have lost. But I'm a good gambler,' Mathilde reflected.

The Interallié network, so painstakingly assembled, had been torn apart in days, destroyed from within because of 'an ordinary denunciation dictated by personal spite'.

Hugo Keiffer, a former airman with a reputation as a 'wide boy', had been responsible for smuggling messages into France from Britain on the Normandy fishing boats. One of his own informants ratted on him, a certain Madame Denbié, because, it was said, he had refused to sleep with her. Under torture, Keiffer revealed the name of his contact in the network, a Pole named Krotki, who in turn directed the Gestapo to the flat in Montmartre. When Bleicher burst into Roman Czerniawski's bedroom, he did not even know the name of the man he was arresting.

Mathilde Carré was also brought to the Hôtel Edward VII, and cracked at once. 'I was like an animal caught in the headlights,' she recalled. Hugo Bleicher offered her a deal. Other senior members of the network had already confessed, he lied, and implicated her. 'You have committed enough crimes to be shot several times over.' He offered her the choice between collaboration and death, warning: 'If you double-cross me you will be shot immediately without trial.' He pushed a cup of ersatz coffee towards her across the desk. If she cooperated, he would pay her 6,000 francs a month. 'Great Britain makes other people work hard for her, and doesn't even pay them decently,' he added sourly. In the First World War, Bleicher had been sent on an espionage mission across the lines, dressed in British uniform, and was captured. A prisoner for two years, he claimed he had been treated 'inhumanely' by his British captors, 'not only with handcuffs on his wrists but manacles on his ankles'. Bleicher 'loathed Britain'.

It took Mathilde just ten minutes to accept Hugo Bleicher as her new master. She would look back on this decision as 'the greatest act of cowardice of my life'. Yet it had been a 'purely animal' reaction, prompted by survival instinct: 'winning Bleicher's confidence seemed the surest means of one day being able to escape'. That morning, Mathilde had a pre-arranged meeting with an agent at the Pam Pam restaurant. Bleicher told her to keep the rendezvous: 'You must behave normally.

Your life and liberty depend on it.' The agent was arrested as he
entered the café.

Afterwards Bleicher took Mathilde to lunch. 'You see how easy
it is,' he said. Unable to eat, she caught sight of herself in the mirror,
with 'a strangely haunted look in my eyes'. She began passing
names to Bleicher, and 'one by one' all her former comrades
were picked up and interrogated: Madame Gaby at la Palette,
Maurice the radio operator, 'Rapide' the courier. Some broke
down and implicated others. 'A few men proved their mettle, but
in comparison women showed better spirit,' Czerniawski later
wrote. A week after the first arrests, more than sixty Interallié
agents and sub-agents had been rounded up. Mathilde revealed
every aspect of the network she had helped to build, enough
evidence to ensure Roman Czerniawski's death many times over.

Bleicher was delighted. Another man might simply have
smashed the network and killed everyone in it, but Bleicher
was cleverer than that. Ostensibly for her own safety, Mathilde
was moved into Bleicher's home, a large mansion in the elegant
Paris suburb of Saint Germain en Laye. 'We have decided to
continue the messages from Interallié,' Bleicher told her. 'We're
going to play some fine tricks on the British. We shall inform
them that Armand [Roman Czerniawski] and Violette [Renée
Borni] have been arrested, but you are going to stress in a
message to London that you managed to save the third [wireless]
set and that you will continue with your principal agents. No
one in the network knows you are in our hands.' This was the
German version of Double Cross.

Mathilde claimed that Bleicher treated her with perfect
courtesy during these weeks. Refined and teetotal, in the
evenings he would play the piano for her. Soon, they became
lovers. Later, in overwrought prose, Mathilde struggled to
explain why: 'I had felt the icy breath of death and suddenly
found warmth once more in a pair of arms. I hated myself
for my weakness, and as a result of my abasement I hated the
Germans even more.'

At the Hôtel Edward VII, Roman Czerniawski was subjected to an exhausting interrogation, but no violence. He told Hugo Bleicher nothing. What annoyed him most was the small, fat Gestapo officer who had rubbed his hands with glee as Roman was marched in, and 'started to laugh contentedly'. The Pole had expected to be tortured, and then killed. Instead, he was transferred to Fresnes prison, south of Paris, and left in a dank cell.

Czerniawski had been in prison for six weeks, and was rather surprised to still be alive, when he learned of Mathilde Carré's treachery. He had been 'treated severely but without brutality', questioned repeatedly, denied exercise and fed scraps, yet no one had laid a finger on him. German and Vichy newspapers, predicting imminent Nazi victory, were left in his cell. Bleicher appeared from time to time, but instead of issuing threats he was full of flattery, remarking that he was most impressed by the Interallié organisation, and 'the completeness of the records which they found at his HQ'.

Roman did not know what to make of this red-faced man with the thick glasses, who, though 'intelligent and quick-witted', was 'always boasting'. He was nettled to see the German was wearing *his* pullover, stolen from his flat, but he conceded that there was something impressive about the Abwehr counter-espionage officer. 'He is a man of great ability and ingenuity and a specialist in running double agents,' he noted. 'Also a man of great personal ambition.'

One morning, Renée Borni appeared in Roman Czerniawski's cell, ushered in by a warder. The last Roman remembered of his lover was her 'terrified eyes' as she was frog-marched away from the Montmartre flat. Renée quickly explained what her jailers had told her: that Mathilde had 'given everything away'; the Interallié network was destroyed. Even so, 'the Germans felt an extraordinary admiration for our methods', she said, suggesting that Roman 'might exploit this favourable circumstance'.

Renée was certainly a plant, whether willing or otherwise – sent to weaken his resolve. Roman's first response was to try to make sense of Mathilde's betrayal. 'It is possible she acted under German blackmail,' he reasoned. 'When working in this terrain one cannot apply any rules concerning the trust one may place in individuals. The only value is a man's character and his resistance in moments of crisis and his loyalty to ideals.' Many years later, he was still pondering her behaviour, and his own.

Roman's morale improved after Renée's visit. He had been contemplating suicide, fearing interrogations 'by force', but now Czerniawski was once again plot-hatching, his favourite activity. As one of his spymasters observed, 'a firing squad did not fit in with his grandiose and dramatic ideas of his own destiny'. Renée's visit had suggested a way out of this predicament. Which was, of course, precisely what Bleicher had intended.

On 29 November, Roman Czerniawski handed his jailers a letter addressed to General Otto von Stülpnagel, Germany's military commander in France. For sheer gall, it was remarkable even by Czerniawski's standard: 'No collaboration which might be proposed to me could come about unless I was convinced that I was working for the good of the Polish nation,' he told Stülpnagel. 'If the German nation has amongst its plans the reconstruction of the rights of the Polish nation, in this case alone discussions about my collaboration could take place. Any such discussion must take place with an officer of the General Staff who knows these problems and is authorised to discuss them with me.'

No one had actually *asked* Czerniawski to collaborate. He was making an offer, but in such a way that it sounded as if he was accepting one.

The next day a man in the uniform of a colonel entered the cell, and saluted. Czerniawski bowed. The fellow was middle-aged and 'lantern-jawed', with 'thick grey hair and an intelligent look'. He introduced himself as Oscar Reile, chief of counter-intelligence for the Paris Abwehr office. Roman noted his 'manicured' fingernails. This man was a negotiator, a fixer, not a fighter.

Without preamble, Reile launched into a lecture on Nazi history. The National Socialists were the New Romans, he explained. The Führer did not wish to oppress Poland, and asked only for Polish support to counter the Bolshevik threat from the East: 'We do not deny the rights of the Polish nation, but we ask its cooperation.' In defying Germany, Poles like Czerniawski were opposing the tide of history. 'You have tied yourself on one hand with capitalist-Jewish England and, on the other, with Communist-Bolshevik Russia,' the Colonel continued. 'By joining us you will contribute to our programme to advance Europe by several centuries in one leap.' General Sikorski, he said, was backing the wrong horse: 'Whatever collaboration Poland might have with Great Britain would be merely to help the selfish aims of Great Britain. All things considered, the best solution would be to come under the cultural protection of Germany, since German culture is preferable to barbarian culture.'

It was an extraordinary performance, revealing an 'excellent knowledge of Polish history' and perfectly pitched to appeal to a patriotic anti-communist Pole, weakened by hunger but fattened up on a diet of Nazi propaganda, and fearful that his country might fall under Soviet rule. Above all, it played on Roman Czerniawski's abundant vanity, suggesting that he alone could 'raise the Polish nation on the side of Germany'.

Thus began what Czerniawski described as the 'war of nerves'. He would later claim that he had merely played a part, pretending to discuss collaboration, 'as though I had really swallowed their propaganda', when it is unlikely he ever had any such intention. He was determined, however, to keep fighting for Poland, and in order to do that, he needed to get out of prison. As the German officer rose to leave, Czerniawski dropped an unsubtle hint: 'In my opinion England is leading us Poles, up the garden path . . .'

When Oscar Reile returned a few days later, he was in civilian clothes. The propaganda lecture continued. 'The Germans were at the doors of Moscow . . . The war against England would certainly be won.' If Roman Czerniawski sided with Germany, and persuaded his compatriots to do likewise, he would 'be working for the good of the Polish nation'. The Pole responded hotly that 'he would never under any circumstances work against my countrymen'. Colonel Reile smiled broadly.

Czerniawski composed another letter. 'The future of Poland lies in German hands, the British will do nothing for us, and deliver us to the Russian barbarism,' he wrote. 'I am prepared to discuss placing myself at the disposal of Germany while at the same time being of use to my own country, Poland.' If the Germans could smuggle him into Britain, he said, he would spy for Germany. Once in place, he could gather information on British aircraft and tank production, troop deployments and above all 'preparations for, and the possibilities of, a second front'. In short, he would 'do for Germany what he had been doing in France against them'. He promised great things: 'I will group around me persons dissatisfied with the British alliance and thus create a powerful fifth column' ready to rise up 'the moment that Germany attacks England'. He made just two demands: 'That the agents of Interallié captured with him were not to be put to death and were to be set free at the conclusion of the war [and that] Germany would, after winning the war, assist his country and people in a manner commensurate with the valuable work he would no doubt have achieved.'

Much of this was posturing nonsense, but some was undoubtedly genuine. With his re-ignited self-confidence, Czerniawski truly believed that he could negotiate on behalf of Poland, and change the course of the war. It was, Reile admitted, 'an extremely odd situation: a captured spy was laying down conditions'.

The effect of the letter was instantaneous. Two new German officers appeared in his cell and 'in unusually polite and friendly terms, expressed their pleasure at the fact that, after all, I had come to realise the good brought by National Socialism to the "New Europe".' If Roman Czerniawski could deliver all he promised, then he would find Germany 'highly appreciative'. But how, they asked, could they be sure he would not betray them? The Pole's response was indignant: 'I told them I could carry out my mission successfully only on condition that I enjoyed their absolute trust.' But Reile knew better than to rely on the word of a man who had already amply demonstrated his talent for subterfuge. Czerniawski's mother was in occupied Poland, he pointed out; his brother was in a German POW camp; his lover sat in a nearby cell, and dozens of members of his network had been rounded up. 'Your companions are in prison,' Reile remarked pointedly. 'You know yourself what the sentence will be, if the courts have to impose a punishment for spying in wartime.'

Czerniawski responded hotly: 'If I work for you, it will be for ideological reasons. There will be no need for reprisals.' But the German did not need to spell out the threat: if he should double-cross them, his friends, colleagues and family would be killed.

The Pole had long considered himself as a prime candidate for martyrdom, but more than his own life was now at stake. 'Should I fail, the fury of the Germans would know no bounds,' he reflected. 'I knew that the fate of my former colleagues was practically a foregone conclusion, but now I was involving my mother and my brother. This time I had no right to commit any mistakes.'

On the afternoon of 14 July 1942, two Gestapo NCOs entered Czerniawski's cell and ordered him to put on his shoes. One was small and pudgy. The other looked tough and cunning, 'like an intelligent boxer'. Czerniawski wondered, for a moment, if he was about to be killed. He was led out of the prison gates, and driven to a flat on the Rue Dufrenoy where Colonel Oscar Reile was waiting. Reile handed over a set of civilian clothes, false papers taken from him at the time of his arrest, 10,000 francs in ration coupons and some money, to 'enable him to go to the barber and have a shave'. Reile laid out his instructions: Czerniawski should make his way to unoccupied France, re-establish contact with the Polish underground, and get himself smuggled to Britain. Bleicher would shadow him in the Vichy zone, in case of difficulties. Czerniawski should tell Polish intelligence that he had given the Germans the slip while being transferred between prisons. 'The prison would be notified that I had escaped en route to the car.' His new German codename would be 'Hubert'.

Canaris himself had approved the plan to woo Czerniawski, play on his patriotism, recruit him and then send him to Britain, but Reile was fully aware of the dangers. 'The English knew that Armand had fallen into our hands,' he later wrote. 'Our English opposite numbers would quite obviously assume that he had been released from prison by us, and sent over with secret orders. There was the risk that the enemy Intelligence Service would then attempt to transmit misleading information to us.' But Reile was confident that if Czerniawski began feeding him falsehoods, he would spot the deception and be able to pick up important clues as to the real intentions of the British by reading Roman's messages 'in reverse'. 'If the enemy attempted to mislead us we could, under certain circumstances, gather important information.' Czerniawski could hardly believe his 'fantastic' luck. He went to a barber on the Rue Pigalle to have his prison beard removed, and then ate in a Russian restaurant. Walking back to the flat, he stopped from time to time to check if he was being tailed. No one seemed to be following him. He was free, after a fashion.

Coat Trailing

Elvira de la Fuente Chaudoir, boredom-prone good-time girl
and aspiring spy, was perched at the roulette table in a Cannes
casino when she was approached by a Frenchman named Henri
Chauvel, a wealthy Nazi collaborator, who asked her out to
dinner. She had no hesitation in accepting.

Elvira had spent several weeks 'coat trailing' through the South
of France, spending time in casinos and expensive restaurants
while maintaining her 'cosmopolitan cover as a society girl
mixing in the very top circles', without so much as a sniff from
German intelligence. Cannes was an oasis of self-indulgence.
In her diary, Elvira described the 'small class of unscrupulous
millionaires', living it up in southern France while war raged.
'People who get all the food they want, who wear lovely clothes,
and who, though dancing is forbidden even to them, spend their
nights gambling in the casinos.' There was nothing she liked
better than dancing and gambling. But having spent the funds
provided by MI6, she was almost broke again. Her existence was
'altogether more agreeable than enduring the Blitz in London',
but Elvira was beginning to feel guilty. 'I felt I was doing little to
justify Dansey's investment in me.' She needed someone to pick
up her coat. Henri Chauvel seemed like a good start.

Of the millionaires enjoying life in the South of France in
the spring of 1941, few were more unscrupulous than Chauvel,
a property owner and entrepreneur who had discovered that

currying favour with the Germans was a most effective way of making money. He took Elvira to dinner at the Carlton Hotel, which he owned, and ordered champagne. Chauvel was 'obviously rolling in money'. At the bar, a group of men was getting noisily drunk. One stood out from the others, 'very tall, with pitch-black hair'. He spoke French, but even from a distance Elvira could hear his strong German accent. 'The German seemed very interested in me and looked at me all the time,' she wrote. 'He was young and good-looking.' She asked Chauvel if he knew him.

'I'll introduce you to him, but in the end he's just a pig like the others,' said the Frenchman, piqued at Elvira's interest in another man. She pressed him for a name. Chauvel shrugged: 'He is a secret agent of Goering's and changes his name every day.'

A few days later, Elvira was at the bar of the Miramar Hotel, drinking a whisky, when the German appeared at her shoulder, bowed, and introduced himself as 'Bibi'. His real name was Helmut Bleil. He had arrived in unoccupied France in 1940 as part of the commission enforcing the terms of the Franco-German armistice, but his role as an economic expert was a cover. Like Johnny Jebsen, he was a freelance spy. But unlike Jebsen, he had no formal role in the Abwehr, having 'been recruited personally by Goering'. Bibi bought Elvira another drink, and then invited her to dinner at 'one of the most expensive black-market restaurants'. He seemed an odd, but intriguing fellow. His hands shook and he drank heavily, but he had the most 'graceful walk' and was 'obviously a gentleman'. He appeared deeply anxious. Elvira wondered if he might have an 'inferiority complex'. Later he confessed that he feared he might be 'spotted as a German', and shot in the street by the Resistance.

At first, Bibi 'seemed to want to keep the conversation to ordinary things'. When she asked him what he did, 'he laughed and said he was supposed to be attached to the Madrid Embassy as an "economic specialist"'. He didn't elaborate. Elvira explained that she was separated from her husband, and visiting her parents in Vichy. Casually, she remarked that she had run out of money, and would soon be returning to England. After dinner, he said he would like to take her to the casino. Despite his peculiar combination of swagger and paranoia, Elvira found him a 'pleasant fellow'.

Elvira and Bibi met again the next evening, and the next. One moment he was full of laughter, and 'enjoyed everything like a child', the next he would be saturated in alcoholic gloom, telling her: 'The war was very silly and such a pity and the Russians were awful and it would have been much more sensible for England and Germany to unite against Russia.'

'Why are you going back to England?' he asked. 'You could have a much better time in Paris, and London is going to be bombed worse than ever.'

Finally, Bibi made his move, but tentatively. Apropos of nothing at all, he observed that 'his Portuguese banker had told him there were packets of money to be made in England at the moment'. There was a pause. 'We might do some little business together.' Elvira sensed that here, at last, was 'an opportunity to start justifying my SIS salary. I pricked up my ears.'

'How much does a woman like you need to live really well in London?' asked the German.

Elvira told him she would be quite happy with 'anything over a hundred a month'.

'That is very little,' said Bibi, looking relieved. 'And very easy to make.'

'How?' asked Elvira.

They sat talking on the deserted Cannes seafront until three in the morning. Bibi explained that he had 'friends' who would pay generously for political, financial and industrial information about Britain. 'After the war, everyone will be very poor so it is up to each one of us to try to make some money now. After all, that is the only thing that counts.' He was 'rather vague' about exactly how she should obtain this information. As Bleil stared out over the dark Mediterranean, he said soberly: 'You will have to be terribly careful and never tell a soul about it. Because, if you do, you will be the first to pay.' The words hovered somewhere between a warning and a threat.

Within forty-eight hours, Bibi reported that his 'friends' had agreed to pay her £100 a month 'to start with, and extra sums for good information'. The money would be paid through Swiss and Portuguese accounts, disguised as alimony payments from her ex-husband. Her codename would be 'Dorette'. She would communicate using secret ink, he said, a 'marvellous trick' by which she could write to them without ever being discovered. Letters should be sent either to Chauvel at the Hôtel de Paris, Monte Carlo, or to a cover address in Lisbon. 'We just want facts, not opinions or reactions . . .'

Elvira interrupted him.

'This is already quite different to the "little business" we were originally meant to do together.'

'This is infinitely more interesting, and if you are successful, it represents a life job.'

Ten days later, an excited Bleil, already quite drunk, met Elvira in a Cannes park shortly before noon. 'He looked around nervously and asked me if I was sure I wasn't being followed.' Then he reached into his pocket and handed her a small bottle of colourless liquid. 'The Germans are the greatest chemists in the world and this is their newest and best invention.' Elvira did not say that she already had a bottle of British secret ink in her handbag. They repaired to the empty lounge of the Hôtel Majestic, where Bleil ordered champagne.

'I always act on intuition,' Bleil said. 'And I feel I can just trust you. If I am wrong, it will ruin my whole career.'

Elvira felt a stab of remorse. Bibi might be a sozzled Nazi spy, but in character he was a child, and seemed hopelessly out of his depth. 'I felt rather sorry for him, and frankly almost wished I had kept out of all this, but bucked myself up by thinking that since you start doing a job you must do it fully and shut all softness away.'

Bleil's hands were trembling. He reached for his hip flask. 'You must never breathe a word of this to any living soul,' he said, and swigged.

Elvira merely remarked: 'I have no desire to spend the rest of the war in prison.'

Lily Sergeyev was being driven mad by the waiting. She had volunteered to spy for Germany, but Germany was in no hurry whatever to take up the offer. Even her terrier-poodle Babs seemed to be feeling the strain. For almost a year she had kicked her heels in Paris, while Major Emile Kliemann, nominally her Abwehr case officer, arranged meetings which he failed to turn up for on time. When he did appear, he enthusiastically discussed the missions Lily might perform for the Third Reich, and then did nothing at all. Plans to send her as a spy to Syria, Australia and Dakar all came to nothing. Kliemann was far more interested in exploring the pleasures of Paris and discussing his love life. He remained besotted with Yvonne Delidaise, 'a nice girl but without much principle' in Lily's opinion. Yvonne had long fair hair, blue eyes, a turned-up nose, and dressed in frills, which Kliemann liked to buy her. In her diary, Lily described Yvonne as 'pretty but rather fat in build and has very broad hips'. She was, however, twenty-six years old, and Kliemann, nearing fifty, was infatuated. He played her the violin until he wept. One night he told Lily that he had decided to divorce his wife and marry Yvonne, but had not yet got around to telling his wife, or Yvonne.

Kliemann paid Lily a retainer of 3,000 francs a month. She was taught Morse code by Richard Delidaise, Yvonne's brother, a barman at Le Bourget airport and a keen Nazi collaborator who had qualified as a wireless instructor before the war. Once she had mastered the rudiments of Morse, he revealed to her the mysteries of coding. Next, in an apartment near the Opéra, she was introduced to two bald men who 'looked a little like birds of prey'. They taught her how to make secret ink by melting a special, unidentified substance, dipping a toothpick in it, and then writing on 'ordinary writing paper that has been rubbed all over with dry cotton wool in order to raise the fibres very slightly'.

Lily, however, felt no closer to being sent on a spying mission than she had been when she first met Kliemann, and her patience was fraying fast. Unpredictable and ambitious, her motives were complicated. She would later claim to have been driven by the purest patriotism, and always intended to switch sides as soon as possible. But she was also motivated by adventure, and the belief that she was destined to play the leading lady in her own drama. She had become fond of genial, romantic, inefficient Kliemann, but found him infuriating. Lily was not a patient woman. To make matters worse, she was suffering from painful kidney stones. 'This has been dragging on so long, the war will be over before I have had time to do anything,' she complained to her diary.

Finally, after Kliemann failed to turn up for yet another meeting, Lily Sergeyev threw an almighty tantrum. Yvonne Delidaise found herself on the receiving end. 'I am sick of it,' Lily ranted. 'I don't like to be made a fool of. It is always the same: he is not there, or he's just left, or he's in a conference. Nothing has been done for over a year. So let's call it a day . . .' Then she slammed down the telephone.

When Kliemann turned up the next day and tried to pacify her, she tore a strip off him. 'You shall not continue to treat me as if I was an old boot. I am not going to listen to you. I'm fed up, and you can look for someone else.'

Perhaps it was this histrionic performance that jolted Kliemann into action. More likely the Major realised that unless he actually demonstrated some sort of activity to his bosses, his lotus life in Paris might be in jeopardy. But whatever the reason, the sluggish German espionage machine cranked into life.

Kliemann arranged for them to rendezvous and then, to Lily's astonishment, kept to it. 'It is the first time the Major has ever arrived on time for an appointment,' she wrote. He was suddenly a paragon of crisp efficiency. He had orders from Berlin: Lily was to make her way to Britain, via Madrid, posing as a refugee keen to 'serve the Allied cause by any means in your power'. She would use the codename 'Solange', while Kliemann would sign his messages 'Octave'. She would be met in Madrid by one of the local Abwehr agents: 'He could recognise you by your little dog, as you insist on taking Babs with you.' Kliemann would join her in Madrid in a few weeks' time and bring her a wireless transmitter hidden inside a gramophone player. He ended with a pompous exhortation: 'I have confidence in your success. You must not doubt. You MUST succeed.'

As the train pulled out from Gare d'Austerlitz, Lily – Agent Solange – wrote in her diary: 'I wave a handkerchief at Mummy standing on the platform. Babs sniffs with satisfaction. I pull up the window, make a place for Babs. I'm leaving France, to try to help those who want to set her free.'

The Club

In the MI5 offices on St James's Street, John Masterman was thinking, as usual, about spies and cricket. The Double Cross team was shaping up into a decent squad, he reflected, with new contenders for the First XI appearing all the time. Some of the new arrivals were naturals, eager to play, and signed up almost immediately; others were untalented or uncooperative, and dealt with accordingly.

Josef Jakobs, a forty-three-year-old German dentist, was found in a Cambridgeshire field in early February with a broken ankle. Unable to move, he had fired his revolver to attract attention. After interrogation at Camp 020, Tin-eye Stephens briskly concluded that Jakobs was a 'scrofulous Nazi' and 'manifestly unemployable as a double agent', since he showed no inclination to collaborate. He was tried and sentenced to death by firing squad. 'He died at the Tower of London,' wrote Tin-eye, 'a brave man. His last words directed the firing squad to shoot straight.'

Much more promising were two young Norwegians, John Moe and Tör Glad, who had been dropped off the Scottish coast by German seaplane, and then rowed ashore to the rocky shoreline of Banffshire in a rubber dinghy loaded down with sabotage equipment, a wireless and two bicycles. They immediately turned themselves in to the astonished Scottish police. Their story was corroborated by Bletchley's Most Secret

Sources, and they were duly enrolled into the Double Cross system with the codenames 'Mutt' and 'Jeff', after the popular American comic strip about two mismatched and somewhat dim-witted gamblers. The names were unfair, as Mutt and Jeff would develop into unflashy but solid middle-order all-rounders.

Danish fascist Wulf Schmidt, alias Agent Tate, was also proving a useful player, though he was not allowed to operate his own transmitter, owing to lingering doubts that his 'newfound loyalty to this country would survive any real strain'. But the chicken-feed Tate sent to Germany appeared to be going down well, and in time he would become, in Masterman's words, 'a pearl among agents', setting the record for the longest continuous radio contact with Germany.

By far the most talented of the early recruits was Dusko Popov – Agent Skoot – the libidinous Serb playboy, who was not only proving good at the game, but slightly too good to be true. First one side, and then the other, trusted him, and then began to wonder whether they should. The first to raise serious doubts was William (Billy) Luke, the MI5 case officer assigned to handle him. An industrialist from Glasgow who owned a linen thread company, Luke was not unlike Popov in character, with a roving eye and a taste for the high life – which was exactly why Tar Robertson had chosen him for the job. He could match Popov drink for drink, and almost girl for girl. But Billy

Billy Luke

Luke was worried: 'I cannot help regarding him with a good deal of suspicion. I just have the general feeling that he may be a most accomplished liar.' Had Popov lied to MI5? Might he be a plant?

After a month in Lisbon, Popov flew back to London, where he was subjected to a second interrogation even more penetrating than the first. Popov told Robertson and Luke that he had been warmly welcomed at Lisbon's Portela airport by von Karsthoff himself. Back at the Villa Toki-Ana, he had recited his rehearsed story in detail, describing the meeting with Ewen Montagu and the snippets of information he had supposedly gleaned. Von Karsthoff had then flown to Paris to report to his Abwehr superiors, and returned with the verdict that although they were 'not very impressed and thought the answers too general', they felt Popov would make an excellent agent. There was no hint of suspicion. Indeed, they seemed to have 'blind confidence' in 'Agent Ivan', and wanted him dispatched back to England to gather more intelligence as soon as possible. Von Karsthoff had issued Popov with fresh secret ink, and a lengthy new questionnaire, covering a vast array of subjects, including morale, military matters and politics. 'You'll soon want to know what Churchill had for dinner,' Popov remarked.

The Abwehr 'expected much from his second visit', von Karsthoff observed. Great rewards would be his if Popov worked hard and improved the quality of his information. He hinted at a possible mission to the United States. Popov had happily spent the remaining weeks in Lisbon, wining and dining at von Karsthoff's expense, establishing business contacts, and conducting an affair with a divorced French marquise. Popov was certain: the trip to Lisbon had been a resounding success.

The amusements laid on for Popov the previous Christmas had given him a taste of London's wartime highlife, and he was a little disappointed to find he was now expected to make his own entertainment. 'London is rather a dull place,' he wrote to Johnny Jebsen, in secret ink. 'Most of the nice girls have gone to the country and whisky is 16 shillings a bottle. That would make you very unhappy.' Popov did not demand to be paid – the Germans were already rewarding him handsomely – but as MI5 would soon discover, he did expect to be provided with what he considered the necessities of life: namely, wine, women and song. Especially women. Tar Robertson was a man of the world, but even he was mildly taken aback when Popov 'hinted that a little high-class feminine society would be most acceptable'. Robertson had never been asked to act as a procurer before, but he knew where to find an expert. Sergeant Lewis of the Metropolitan Police Vice Squad was asked for 'suggestions as to possible female acquaintances who might be used as agents'. MI5 was not looking for a prostitute, Tar insisted, but 'a woman purely and simply to entertain Skoot and keep him out of mischief, at the same time to keep us informed of the various curious associations which he is making in this country'. Lewis said he had a candidate in mind.

Popov's MI5 file contains a number of amorous notes sent to Popov from 'Gwennie', who was married to 'Charles' and worked, during daylight hours, for the Red Cross. (A typical example reads: 'I won't be able to see you tomorrow after all as Charles is unexpectedly coming to London!! He won't be here for long so I'll ring you as soon as I can. I'm so sorry as I was ready for you! Love Gwennie.') She was almost certainly an MI5 plant; Popov almost certainly knew it, and he certainly did not mind. Gwennie's full name has been carefully expunged from the record. She remains one more unsung heroine, performing sterling, though unconventional, wartime service for her country.

Von Karsthoff's new questionnaire indicated significant German interest in Scotland's coastal defences, and so it was decided that Billy Luke would take Popov on a tour of his homeland: that way Popov could accurately describe to von Karsthoff what he had seen, while being steered away from things he should not see. It would also be an opportunity for

Luke to test Popov's honesty, and show him a good time. Just how a good a time Popov was having could be measured by the colour of his face. 'Complexion depends on previous night's activity,' Tar Robertson noted dryly. 'If the night has been a good one, from his point of view, the complexion is rather white and blotchy.'

Their tour of the north turned into an extended pub crawl, the days spent among 'typical Scottish scenery' and the nights 'filled with jovial entertainment in congenial company'. They visited Loch Lomond and Gareloch, stopping for regular refreshments, and then headed to Edinburgh. Popov later recalled: 'There was a law that existed at that time that you couldn't have a drink unless you had travelled five miles and so my case officer, being a true Scotsman, interpreted this as meaning that you *had* to stop and have a drink every five miles.' In Edinburgh they stayed at the Central Hotel, drank at the American Bar and the Piccadilly Club, and dined at the Malmaison and the Mirabel. Popov was plainly not spying for Germany, Luke reported, since 'he made no effort to obtain information of any kind, nor did he ask any questions which could be connected with espionage'. But in the course of their evening pleasures, Popov did drop one particularly interesting hint, about his friend Johnny Jebsen: 'He did not think it would be difficult to persuade Jebsen that he is fighting on the wrong side. Jebsen is at heart pro-British.' Popov even suggested he might be able to recruit for MI5 the man who had recruited him to German intelligence, 'especially if he could meet him in Madrid, provide him with vivacious and beautiful feminine society and lose money to him at poker'. Here was a tempting prize: a member of the Abwehr who might be lured into the Double Cross pack. 'It may be desirable to enlarge on this theme,' wrote Luke.

After three days of carousing and sightseeing, Luke returned to London, white and blotchy, impressed by Popov's stamina, and fully reassured that he was not, after all, playing a triple game. 'He is quite definitely working for us and not the

Germans,' wrote Luke. 'Clever, versatile and firm of purpose, he has personality and charm and would feel at home in society circles in any European or American capital, being much the usual type of international playboy. He misses no opportunity of disparaging the Germans and the Nazi leaders and has a great hatred of Goebbels, a whole-hearted admiration and respect for the English and is convinced that Great Britain will win the war.' His prodigious womanising might eventually be a problem, Luke predicted: 'He is fond of the society of attractive women, who are apparently plentiful in Dubrovnik, where it seems that virtue is at a discount. His amorous exploits would provide material for Maurice de Kobra' – the French erotic novelist. But Luke was now certain that Popov was dependable, and ready to risk his life again by returning to Lisbon: 'Skoot is an ingenious, cheerful and amusing companion of whose sincerity and loyalty I, personally, am satisfied.' Unknown to Popov, his older brother Ivo, a doctor in Belgrade, had also approached MI6 with an offer to spy against the Germans: the Popov family was firmly on side.

Reassured, Tar set about 'building up' Popov with some first-class chicken-feed, verifiable but harmless answers to his questionnaire that would convince his Abwehr handler that he was, indeed, the efficient and energetic spy he seemed to be. Von Karsthoff had suggested that Popov should recruit some sub-agents, should he find anyone suitable. MI5 obliged: the first was Dickie Metcalfe, a former army intelligence officer. To von Karsthoff, Metcalfe would be portrayed as a disgruntled, broken-down gambler working for an arms dealer, who had been cashiered for passing fake cheques and was prepared to spy on his former colleagues because 'he hates them all'. The real Metcalfe was portly (he was given the codename 'Balloon'). A second sub-agent was lined up in the more svelte form of Friedl Gaertner, a thirty-four-year-old Austrian cabaret singer, well connected in London society, who had already done work for MI5. Her father had been a member of the Nazi party so it was hoped that, when the Germans came to check up on her, she would be considered reliable. Gaertner was a 'link with people of a high state of society in this country' and therefore 'in a position to get good information from indiscretions of well-placed friends in government and diplomatic circles'. She was given the codename 'Gelatine' because the B1A men thought she was a 'jolly-little-thing'. Popov also saw her that way. Inevitably, they became lovers.

Now that he was no longer considered likely to 'scoot', Popov was also awarded a new codename, more fitting to his status as the most promising of double agents. He was rechristened 'Tricycle'. This may have been, in part, a reference to Popov's insatiable appetites and his reputed but probably apocryphal taste for three-in-a-bed sex. It also recognised that the Tricycle network now consisted of one big wheel – Popov – supported by two smaller ones, Agents Balloon and Gelatine.

While Robertson was playing word games with his agent's *nom de guerre*, Popov had some fun with Tar's nickname. He had asked MI5 for help in setting up his own import-export business, which would provide good cover as well as a genuine income. 'They propose to buy and sell anything in any market,' wrote Tar, who arranged for Popov to occupy a lair of offices in Imperial House, 80 Regent Street. MI5 even produced an attractive part-time secretary to handle Popov's correspondence and mind the business. In a tip of the hat to his spymaster, Popov named the new company 'Tarlair Ltd'.

As he prepared to head back to Portugal once again, Popov was a little anxious that 'the answers we had given him to his questionnaire were lacking in detail and would jeopardise his supposed position as a good spy'. He was also suffering 'slight moral scruples about the part he was playing', simultaneously befriending and betraying von Karsthoff. Masterman offered a typically donnish and convoluted reassurance: 'The strictest moral censor, having regard to his motives, would not cavil his conduct.' Popov, whose English was not quite Oxbridge standard, surely had not a clue what he was saying. Luke spoke a simpler language, telling him 'that the work he had undertaken was extremely valuable to this country'. That conversation seemed to reassure Popov, for he penned a farewell letter to his case officer that revealed an unexpected depth of purpose in this apparently pleasure-seeking young man. 'It would be difficult for me to define the feeling I experience on leaving your brave country. I am leaving with a heart filled with hope. You, my dear Luke, are the classical example of English calm, [a] manifestation of the most powerful English weapon, "to remain human". It is this that will demolish Hitler's machine.'

On the day of Popov's departure, Luke took him to lunch at the Savoy and found him cheery, but 'somewhat tired', pale and blotchy. He had spent what he called 'an expensive evening' the night before, after an exhausting week featuring Friedl, Gwennie, the 400 Club, Coconut Grove and dinners at the Hungaria. Popov requested 'a small automatic revolver in case of need', and seemed entirely unfazed when Luke explained that this might be tricky, and possibly unwise. Popov was stepping back into extreme danger, and they both knew it: 'We could do nothing to help him if things went wrong.' Agent Tricycle sauntered off with 'a slightly rolling gait, the very reverse of military', to catch the Lisbon plane, leaving MI5 to pay his stupendous hotel bill.

Luke and Popov were birds of a feather, and Tar observed the bond growing between them with satisfaction. In the shifting, shadowy world of Double Cross, the relationship between agent and handler was fundamental: 'A case officer should be personally responsible for each agent, with his hands, as it were, on the pulse of the patient from morning until night, and with an eye on every twist and turn of the patient's mind.' David Petrie, the chief of MI5, had ordered that B Section should 'command the best talent and experience that the service possesses', but it was not easy to find people equipped to act as friend, psychologist and patient nursemaid to a group of

individuals who were, almost by definition, erratic, frequently
infuriating and quite possibly disloyal.

Section B1A was expanding, and what had started as an
experiment was fast becoming a major enterprise. 'The running
and control of double agents', wrote Masterman, 'is a very long,
laborious and infinitely complicated task. A truly formidable
work of coordination, preparation and crucial analysis.' Each
double agent required 'the whole-time service of a case officer
to control and organise him, a wireless officer to monitor and
perhaps submit his messages, at least two guards, possibly an
officer with a car to collect his information and probably a
housekeeper to look after and feed the whole party.' The MI5
offices in St James's Street were becoming distinctly crowded.
Tar Robertson sat in the first office, while the adjoining room
was shared by Masterman and John Marriott, Tar's chief assistant
and deputy. A solicitor in civilian life, Marriott was 'the collector
of facts', a stickler for rules and economies; the dry, nit-picking
counterpoint to Tar's extravagance and ebullience, who peered
at the world suspiciously through bottle-top spectacles. The case
officers, already five in number, sat together in the largest office,
along with two filing clerks and another officer responsible for
disseminating intelligence arising from the cases.

   The officers, each handpicked by Robertson, were a
distinctly unorthodox crew: in addition to Billy Luke, their
number included Cyril Mills, a part-time circus impresario,
Hugh Astor, the son of *The Times* owner Lord Astor, and two
very different lawyers, Ian Wilson, methodical and withdrawn,
and Christopher Harmer, witty, intuitive and glintingly clever.
As shown by the effort that went into choosing codenames, the
agent-runners delighted in word play, and the atmosphere at
Number 58 was relaxed, and frequently hilarious. They were
an extraordinarily youthful team: Tar was just thirty when war
began, and Hugh Astor was just twenty-three when he joined
the team. Harmer, a year younger than Tar, described B1A as

a group of 'overgrown schoolboys playing games of derring-do absorbed from reading schoolboy books and adventure stories'. There was also one 'schoolgirl', although it would have taken a brave man to describe her as such.

Gisela Ashley, who went by the spy name of Susan Barton, was at this time the only woman in the section, and a most formidable intelligence operative. German-born and vigorously anti-Nazi, Gisela had left Germany in the 1920s, appalled by the rise of German fascism. She married a British man and then divorced him when he turned out to be homosexual, retained her British citizenship, joined MI5, and established a lifelong partnership with another intelligence officer, Gilbert Lennox, with whom she wrote a number of successful stage plays. 'Mrs Barton' had been a 'casual agent' for some years before the war, reporting on the German community in Britain. Her play *Third Party Risk* opened at St Martin's Theatre in 1939, shortly after she moved to The Hague under diplomatic cover to spy on the Germans. There the secretary of the German naval attaché took a shine to her, and Gisela appeared to be on the point of penetrating the German legation when disaster struck. In November 1939, two MI6 agents were lured to a rendezvous at Venlo on the Dutch border, in the belief that they were meeting an anti-Nazi officer, and were kidnapped. One of them, astonishingly, was carrying a list of British agents' names in his pocket, including, it was feared, that of Gisela Ashley. She was hurriedly recalled, and assigned to Robertson's section. Gisela's brother was by now a U-boat captain, but Mrs Barton's loyalty was never in doubt. With her 'real understanding of German and Nazi mentality', she played a vital role in B1A, and as the lone woman in a unit composed of men, she offered an important corrective to some of the more extreme chauvinism around her. Masterman barely noticed women; Marriott found the opposite sex tiresome and unpredictable; Wilson refused to allow women solicitors in his law firm. But they could not ignore Gisela Ashley. The vivacious Mrs Barton, the secretary who opened his mail and ran the Tarlair office, was Gisela Ashley, special agent, carefully placed at Popov's elbow to keep an eye on him.

Christopher Harmer would later remark: 'Thank God for Tar, I say, he gave us all our heads and encouraged us and, if we were doing something stupid, he pulled us up by tact and persuasion rather than by direction.' Tar Robertson was a 'born leader', according to Masterman, 'gifted with independent judgement', but he was also a firm believer in mixing business with pleasure. Indeed, he saw no distinction between the two, and was a devotee of the three-hour lunch. Rank counted for little: Robertson was a major, and would end the war as a lieutenant colonel, but most of the staff of B1A had no military rank at all. But beneath the public-school banter, the puns and badinage, ran deep veins of anxiety, in a community cauterised by secrecy and suffused with uncertainty. Every case officer was acutely aware that a single slip could bring the entire project crashing down, with catastrophic consequences. Most Secret Sources showed that the Germans were constantly assessing and reassessing their agents, trusting them and doubting them, and those judgements, in turn, had to be evaluated and re-evaluated by Section B1A, prompting Tar to remark: 'In this game one never knew quite how things would appear to the opposition, although one did one's best to guess.'

The Germans, he reasoned, must assume that some of their agents had been intercepted, and would surely suspect that at least some of these were working as double agents. Perhaps that suspicion could be used to advantage: if a double agent was run 'in an obviously bogus fashion', the Germans might assume general incompetence on the part of the British and therefore overlook the real double agents. Alphonse Timmerman, a Belgian ship's steward, was arrested as a spy in early 1941, but declined to cooperate. While Timmerman (codenamed 'Scruffy') languished in prison, B1A began sending secret ink letters in his name to his German handler. These contained a number of glaring errors, to indicate that Timmerman was being controlled. It was a brilliant plan, typical of the lateral thinking beloved of the Double Cross team, and it failed utterly. The Germans never spotted the deliberate mistakes, and 'seemed unable to realise that Scruffy was obviously controlled'. This unshakeable faith in their spy was confirmed by Most Secret Sources. The Scruffy case was terminated. This was a disappointment for B1A, but far more so for Alphonse Timmerman, who was executed. The Abwehr even failed to spot his death notice in *The Times*. Slowly, it began to dawn on Tar Robertson that the Abwehr really might be as gullible as they seemed. Yet Tar remained convinced that other spies must be at large in Britain, perhaps even working within MI5. And he was right.

In February 1941, Guy Liddell, the head of B Section, took on a new personal assistant. He was tall, thin, good looking and homosexual; a brilliant art historian and a linguist with all the right social connections. His name was Anthony Blunt, and he was a Soviet spy. Four years earlier, Blunt, a secret and dedicated communist, had been recruited into the NKVD (later the KGB) by Dr Arnold Deutsch, alias Otto, the cultured espionage talent spotter responsible for forging the so-called Cambridge spy ring. At the urging of his Soviet handlers, Blunt had applied to join the intelligence services, and by 1941 he was at the very heart of Britain's secret war machinery. Liddell had little need of an assistant 'since he always does all the work again himself', and Blunt soon moved on to other work within the section. He had a finger in many of the most secret pies, working on German counter-espionage, running B Section's surveillance section, and intercepting the diplomatic bags of neutral countries. Languid, erudite and whimsical, he cut a distinctive figure in the corridors of the St James's building: he quoted *Winnie-the-Pooh*, while sipping on a bottle of cod-liver oil and malt and remarking 'that's what Tiggers like for breakfast', and liked to play leapfrog in the canteen.

Despite his charm, Blunt was not universally liked, although much of the animus was coloured by hindsight. 'He was a very nice and civilised man,' recalled Dick White, Liddell's deputy;

'and he betrayed us all.' Tar Robertson disliked Blunt intensely, but his attitude sprang not from any doubts about his loyalty but from a homophobia common to the time. 'I couldn't stick the man. One knew that he was queer and before the war one would not have countenanced letting him anywhere near the office.' Tar's distaste for Blunt's homosexuality did not stop him from discussing the most secret aspects of his work with him. In the public school parlance of the time, a gay man was said to be 'batting for the other side'; but Blunt was batting for the other side in a way that no one inside MI5 could possibly have imagined, and making a remarkable score.

Blunt first began passing secret information to his Soviet handler, Anatoli Gorsky, in January 1941, when the USSR and Germany were linked under the Molotov-Ribbentrop pact: passing military information to a power in alliance with Britain's enemy was an act of treason. Blunt would continue to feed secrets to Moscow, in vast volume, for the rest of the war. The Soviets gave him the codename 'Tony', the only example of a wartime codename that was actually an agent's real name – either a clever double bluff, or amazingly stupid. Blunt met his handler once a week to hand over documents, both originals and copies. He memorised vast amounts of material, consulted the MI5 archive to answer Moscow's special requests, and spent his lunch hour rummaging through the desks of colleagues. He passed on personal files, operational information, intelligence summaries, Bletchley Park intercepts, diplomatic wireless traffic, and details of MI5 tradecraft including surveillance and interrogation techniques. Seldom has an intelligence organisation been so comprehensively penetrated. 'Tony is a thorough, conscientious, efficient agent,' his Russian handler reported to Moscow. 'He tries to fulfil all of our tasks in time and as conscientiously as possible.' Britain and the Soviet Union would become allies against Hitler, but Blunt's torrential leakage of information to Moscow still represented the single gravest threat to the Double Cross operation. If Soviet intelligence was penetrated by the Germans, then the information he was passing to Moscow would end up in Berlin. Over the next four years, Blunt would hand the Soviets a staggering total of 1,771 documents.

But not for an instant did the Double Cross team suspect the double agent in their midst.

6

Garbo Takes the Stage

In the winter of 1941, the Bletchley Park team decoding Abwehr wireless traffic between Madrid and Berlin made a most alarming discovery. Tar Robertson's fears, it seemed, were justified: the Germans did indeed have an agent active in Britain, writing secret missives to a controller in Madrid. His codename was Agent Arabel. He seemed to be well-informed, energetic and resourceful, and had recruited at least two sub-agents. Most Secret Sources revealed that Berlin was delighted with his work.

The implications were potentially catastrophic. This mysterious Arabel was in a position to contradict information supplied by the Double Cross agents, in which case 'the duplicity of all MI5's double agents might be revealed'. An uncontrolled agent, particularly one as good as this, could not only unravel the network in Britain, but expose the agents, most notably Popov, to mortal danger. 'Who was this Arabel and how had he got into the country? Where had he sprung from? Where was he getting all this information from?'

The task of analysing intercepted traffic for counter-espionage purposes fell to B1B section of MI5, known as 'Special Research', headed by Herbert Lionel Adolphus Hart, a young Jewish lawyer who would go on to become Professor of Jurisprudence at Oxford. The more H. L. A. Hart and his team pored over the Arabel traffic, the stranger it appeared. His fabulously drawn-out messages appeared to be written by someone suffering from chronic verbal incontinence. But more than that, the information supplied by Arabel was frequently, and sometimes hilariously, wrong.

Arabel reported, for example, that the people of Liverpool indulged in 'drunken orgies and slack morals at amusement centres'. He appeared to believe that the summer heat was so intense in London that the diplomatic corps decamped *en masse* to Brighton for the summer months. He reported major naval manoeuvres on Lake Windermere (which is landlocked), involving an American-made amphibious tank (which had not been invented). He provided details of unreal army regiments, and even provoked the enemy into attempting to intercept a convoy, sailing from Malta, that did not exist. Arabel was submitting meticulous monthly expenses to Berlin, but in a most curious form. He claimed, for example, to have visited Glasgow by train, at a cost of '87 shillings and 10 pence' (this should have been rendered as £4 7s 10d). Britain's pre-decimal currency was confusing, but not so baffling that someone living in the country would not have grasped it after nine months. Such errors escaped the notice of the Abwehr, but the 'very wild messages' being relayed through Madrid presented MI5 with a peculiar riddle: this rogue spy was eccentric and innumerate, or a fraud, or mad.

In Lisbon, former chicken farmer Juan Pujol, invulnerable to rejection, had continued to pester the British to recruit him. Despite producing evidence to show he was now in the employ of the Germans, he was repeatedly turned down. His wife, Aracelli, his accomplice from the start, took up the cause and approached the American naval attaché in Lisbon, who contacted his opposite number in the British Embassy, who duly (but very slowly) sent a report to London. Finally, MI6 twigged that the German agent sending the bogus messages must be Juan Pujol García, the Spaniard who had repeatedly approached them in Lisbon. In the ancient British tradition of pointless inter-departmental rivalry, MI6 (responsible for intelligence overseas) still did not inform MI5 (responsible for counter-espionage in the UK) of Pujol's existence. Only a chance conversation between Tar Robertson and an MI6 officer from Lisbon alerted B1A to what was going on. Even then, MI6 was unwilling to allow Pujol to join the Double Cross team. 'I do not see why I should get agents and have them pinched by you,' was, according to Guy Liddell, the attitude taken by MI6's head of counter-intelligence. 'The whole thing is so narrow and petty that it really makes me quite furious,' wrote Liddell.

A 'walk-in', in spy jargon, is an informant or agent who, without prompting, contacts an intelligence organisation with an offer of information. Pujol had walked in to the British time after time, and then, when told he was not wanted, walked out again. Forced to rely on secondary sources and a first-rate imagination, he was in constant danger of exposure. His guide book, for example, compared Brighton to the Spanish town of San Sebastián. Since diplomats escaped the summer heat of Madrid by moving to San Sebastián, Pujol logically, and wrongly, assumed that the same must be true of Brighton. It was, MI5 observed, 'a miracle that he had survived so long'.

The squabble over control of Pujol was finally won by Tar Robertson, who was delighted by this inventive new addition to his team. The Catalan was smuggled out of Lisbon on a steamer to Gibraltar, and then flown by military aircraft to Plymouth, arriving on 24 April 1942. After two weeks of interrogation, MI5 declared that, despite his 'inexhaustibly fertile imagination', he was telling the truth. The Twenty Committee initially wondered whether he might be a plant, but evidence from Most Secret Sources (which MI6 now, reluctantly, agreed to share in full with the Double Cross team) proved the truth of his story beyond doubt. Pujol's wife and young son were brought out of Lisbon, and the family was reunited in a safe house at 35 Crespigny Road, Hendon, in the north London suburbs. Pujol was provided with a housekeeper, and a cover job translating for the BBC. Most importantly, he acquired a case officer.

Once again, Tar's choice was inspired. Tomás 'Tommy' Harris was a thirty-four-year-old half-Spanish artist, whose imagination was as vivid as Pujol's, but tempered by solid common sense. The son of a rich Mayfair art dealer, Harris moved in bohemian circles, and was friendly with the trio of Soviet moles, Kim Philby, Anthony Blunt and Guy Burgess, an association that would later lead to the (baseless) claim that he too had been a double agent. Of all those recruited to run double agents, Masterman considered Harris to be 'in some ways, the most remarkable'. One colleague described him thus: 'With fierce black eyes and a hawk-like nose, thick well-oiled hair slicked back from a low forehead, he looked like a casting director's ideal choice for a desert sheikh or a slinky tango lizard.' Harris and Pujol made an extraordinary double act. They spoke the same language, literally and metaphorically, and in time the combination of Harris's artistry and Pujol's flamboyant ingenuity would spin a web of deception that is as close to a thing of beauty as espionage can offer. Pujol's lexophilia had led him into spying: over the next three years, he and Harris would bombard the Germans with hundreds of thousands of words, 315 letters in secret ink, and more than 1,200 wireless messages. Pujol would clock up an innings like no other double agent. 'He played his game with masterly skill,' wrote Masterman, who dubbed him the 'Bradman' of the Double Cross team, after the Australian cricketer Donald Bradman, the greatest batsman of all time.

MI6 had given Pujol the codename 'Bovril', after the thick, salty meat extract which, like Marmite, appeals only to British palates, and only to some of those. It was possibly intended as a compliment, since Bovril was seen as a 'war food' that had sustained soldiers in the trenches during the previous war. MI5 changed his codename, partly to make a point to MI6, and partly because, after his dramatic work of subterfuge in Lisbon, he deserved something grander, more fitting to 'the best actor in the world' of spying. Juan Pujol García became Agent Garbo.

★

Where Garbo had been secretly smuggled to London from
Lisbon, Tricycle openly shuttled back and forth between the
two capitals, ostensibly as director of Tarlair Ltd, but in reality
building up his credentials with both his German and British
spymasters. The British authorities furnished the necessary
paperwork for his 'mysterious business deals', while noting: 'We
are going in very deep with Popov'. Seats on civilian flights
between Lisbon and London were in hot demand, but space
was always made for Popov, creating another source of concern.
'In time of war only diplomats, journalists and spies can travel
about freely, and everyone knows Tricycle does not come into
the first two categories.' Popov was confident von Karsthoff
suspected nothing, but Luke was not so sure. 'The Germans
may know he is doubling, but may consider that they get more
information by letting him continue doing so than they would
if he disappeared. I am not suggesting that Tricycle is aware that
they know he is doubling.' Dusko Popov might be an unwitting
pawn in a clever German bluff.

From Lisbon, Popov kept MI5 fully updated on his love life,
which now incorporated Maria Elera, the twenty-two-year-old
Brazilian journalist whose home in Lisbon had been supplied
by von Karsthoff as the cover address for sending secret letters.
Popov sent back photographs of Maria posing in sultry fashion
on the steps of an aeroplane. In his file, these are labelled: 'His
latest girlfriend'. But he did not neglect Gwennie: 'Missing
you terribly darling, I adore you, hope to be back soon.' Was
it possible, MI5 wondered, that someone so pathologically
faithless in his romantic life could be loyal to one cause?

By the summer of 1941, Popov had passed over to the
Germans vast swathes of information, some of it true, none of
it harmful, and much merely confusing. He described various
new military inventions: a new anti-gas battledress which the
troops hated because of the smell; a silent aircraft engine; a
high-velocity ammunition for machine guns; and an incendiary
bomb made from a derivative of tar. His reports were garnished

with snippets of political gossip, such as the news that Oswald Mosley, the interned British fascist, was 'degenerating in prison and has lost his personality'. Popov's sub-agent Dickie Metcalfe also began passing information, distinctly flavoured with the personality of a former soldier. The British infantry, Balloon reported, had been issued with a new seven-inch bayonet, 'which makes for much easier withdrawal from Huns'. MI6 was appalled by this joke: 'I wonder whether Balloon realises he is working for the Germans.'

The Double Cross 'traffic' sent to Germany was growing more sophisticated, as the Twenty Committee served up an increasingly potent cocktail of information and deception, mixing falsehood, half-truth and real, verifiable information approved by the relevant military authority. Gisela Ashley analysed incoming messages, and Tar began 'submitting to her all the traffic in its original German as a matter of routine'. It was she who first argued that the double agents should be used, not just to deceive individual spymasters, but to influence German thinking. 'We are the Double Cross section in that we send over to the Germans information which is either misleading or which we want them to have. It seems to me there is a much wider scope for such a section. Would it not be possible to push across propaganda or to give the Germans ideas that we want them to have?' The men of Double Cross tended to think exclusively in military terms, but Gisela suggested that they paint a misleading picture of Britain itself, by exaggerating anti-Jewish feeling, domestic fascism and industrial unrest: 'After all, any decent spy would naturally try to get over warnings and pointers with regard to domestic news in the country in which he is spying.'

Popov was supposed to be gathering his information from senior figures in the British establishment, so to fortify his cover story, he was introduced to some. Victor Cavendish-Bentinck, chairman of the Joint Intelligence Committee, met the young spy and wrote up his impressions. 'He is by temperament an adventurer who is very partial to the fleshpots of this world and he realises that a person of his type can enjoy the fleshpots better under democratic than totalitarian conditions.' There was some truth in this cynical assessment, but Popov was more than a mere sybarite. In lieu of payment, he hinted that he would like to be made British Consul in Dubrovnik after the war, and receive 'some sort of decoration' for his services. For all his insouciance, he was playing a deadly game, particularly after the German occupation of Yugoslavia from April 1941 left his family under direct Nazi threat. The Germans had reassured him that his relatives would be protected. 'I do not like this "protection" much,' he told Tar. 'My own life is much less important to me than that of my family.' Brave, self-indulgent, committed, venal and unfaithful, Popov was a man of the strangest honour: 'I am still satisfied that he is playing straight with us,' Luke reported to the Twenty Committee.

When in Lisbon, Popov stayed at the Palacio Hotel, gambled in the Estoril casinos, and squired one woman or another around town, often in the company of his spymaster and friend, whom he was comprehensively betraying. Ludovico von Karsthoff took his duties lightly and his pleasure seriously, and professed himself 'extremely pleased with the information provided'. Von Karsthoff rarely rose before midday, and spent much of his time in the gardens of Villa Toki-Ana, playing with his pet monkey, Simon, and his twin dachshunds, Ivan and Ivan. He had found in Popov, he believed, a man as self-indulgent as himself, who could improve his standing in the Abwehr, and perhaps make him some money on the side. One evening, over cognac, he announced that Berlin wanted Popov to go to America. German espionage operations in the US were a mess; the FBI was picking up German spies 'like whores on the Reeperbahn'. Popov should go to New York and build a spy network from scratch, just as he had done in London. That way, when the Americans finally entered the war, Germany would be ready. Popov would be paid a great deal of money.

When Popov returned to London and reported this approach, Tar Robertson was initially resistant, arguing that he was too valuable to be spared. Tricycle was running smoothly, highly respected in Berlin, and a means of direct personal contact with the enemy. But if he refused this mission, it might raise German suspicions. Popov himself was eager to go. He had never visited the United States, and New York sounded like his kind of town. If the FBI played its cards well, here was an opportunity to create an American version of Double Cross. Von Karsthoff seemed most accommodating and unsuspicious. And Johnny Jebsen, his best friend and patron, could be relied on to watch his back.

Whenever Popov returned to Lisbon, Johnny would come to meet him. Their friendship was as solid as ever, though neither could afford to be fully candid. To Popov's surprise, Jebsen revealed he had recently got married, to Eleonore Bothilde Petersen (known as Lore), an actress and the leading lady at the Frankfurt Theatre, though he still maintained a mistress in Paris, and another in Dublin. Jebsen seemed able to travel freely, but his activities, as both a businessman and a freelance spy, were deeply mysterious: he told Popov he had recently visited Finland, Sweden, Greece, Persia, and the coast of Italy to draw up a report on Italian defences for Japanese intelligence – Japan was not yet in the war, but Tokyo's secret interest in coastal defences would take on an ominous significance after Pearl Harbor.

Jebsen was supposed to be recruiting spies, but he happily admitted that the enrolment of Popov was his only success to date 'in this business'. He was clearly a figure of some importance within German intelligence. When the conversation shifted to one Professor Miller, a teacher and Nazi at Freiburg they had both disliked, Johnny remarked, half-casually: 'I am not cruel enough, but now I am in a position to get rid of anyone I hate. If I want to get rid of that man all I have to do is say that Professor Miller said this and that, and they will kill him at once, without question.' Then he added: 'If there is anyone you particularly want to have set free I might be able to arrange it.'

The situation in Germany was deteriorating, Jebsen reported. Aircraft production was down; food was becoming scarce and even clothing was in short supply. The dapper Jebsen, still styling himself as Anthony Eden, was having trouble maintaining his wardrobe: 'I would be willing to pay £600 for a suit of English clothes, but you cannot get them,' he complained. Even more intriguing was Jebsen's description of the in-fighting between factions within German intelligence, some of which were secretly opposed to Hitler. The turf war between the Abwehr and the SD (Sicherheitsdienst, the intelligence agency of the SS and the Nazi party) was particularly venomous, and getting worse. 'They are like cat and dog with each other,' Johnny observed.

This sort of information was intelligence gold dust, which made Jebsen's remarks either extraordinarily indiscreet, or entirely calculating. He made no secret of his disdain for Hitler, and dropped hints that he had fallen foul of some powerful people who disapproved of his louche lifestyle. 'Whenever I go to Germany, I can never be sure whether I will get out alive,' he said. Jebsen seemed thinner and more ravaged than before. His limp was worse, and his teeth stained brown from the cigarettes he smoked in a never-ending stream. Jebsen had good cause to fear returning to Germany, though he did not yet divulge the real reason to Popov. The Gestapo were after him. More than a year earlier he had been approached by one Heinz Jost, a high-ranking official in the SD, who said he had some forged British bank notes which he wished to exchange for dollars. Jebsen cautiously observed that the Reichsbank had 'advised it was contrary to international law to forge currency'. There the matter rested for a while. When Jost reappeared with bundles of £5 and £10 notes, Jebsen was told (or chose to believe) that this was genuine British currency, seized in Paris. Through a contact named Avramedes at the Bank of Greece in Switzerland, he began exchanging the notes for dollars, passing the bulk to Jost and keeping a substantial commission for himself. Some senior Gestapo officers also began passing him British cash to exchange. For nine months the arrangement had proved most satisfactory, as larger and larger amounts passed through Jebsen's hands.

Jebsen spent his profits on his wife, his mistresses, himself, and his favourite novelist – for some of the ill-gotten gains ended up in the hands of P. G. Wodehouse. The British writer had remained in France at the outbreak of war, and was duly interned, as an enemy alien, in Upper Silesia ('If this is Upper Silesia, one wonders what must Lower Silesia be like . . .?' he wrote). Released in June 1941, just before the age of sixty under the terms of the Geneva Convention (he was playing a game of cricket in camp when he heard he was to be freed), Wodehouse and his wife Ethel eventually took up residence in occupied Paris, but since the royalties from his books were blocked, they were extremely short of funds. Jebsen gave money to his old friend. After his release, Wodehouse had made a series of whimsical and deeply foolish radio broadcasts through the German propaganda service, in the naive belief that he would be admired for keeping a 'stiff upper lip' during his internment. Instead, he became a hate-figure in Britain, accused of collaborating with the Germans. It can only be imagined what Wodehouse's critics would have said had they known that this comic genius was being bankrolled by a German spy through an illegal currency scam involving the Gestapo, the Nazi security service and a fortune in forged British banknotes.

The forgery fiddle worked well for nine months, and then dramatically unravelled. A Swiss bank spotted the fakes, and Jebsen's Greek middleman refused to deal in them any more. Jebsen would later claim that he had honestly believed the notes were legal tender, and when he found out about the counterfeiting 'he did all he could to stop it', by reporting the matter to his superiors. More likely, he had known all along that he was dealing in duds, and cut his losses when he discovered the fiddle had been found out. In the ensuing row, Heinz Jost was dismissed from his comfortable post in the SD's foreign intelligence department and sent to the Eastern Front where he was placed in command of Einsatzgruppe A, the death squad responsible for killing thousands of Jews. Jost was now Jebsen's sworn enemy, whose friends in the Nazi hierarchy were determined 'to take revenge on his behalf'. Jebsen also had allies, most notably Canaris, the Abwehr chief. He confided to Popov that he had set up a crude form of insurance policy: 'I know too much about the dirty things that happen. I have got papers in a bank abroad, and if the bank does not receive a cable from me on this or that day, they will send the papers to a publisher.'

Jebsen's anti-Nazi remarks, and his willingness to discuss the most secret aspects of German intelligence, could only mean one thing: Jebsen knew Popov was working for British intelligence, and that the secret information he was supplying so casually would be passed straight back to London, as indeed it was. Popov was convinced his old friend knew what he was up to, a conviction that was strengthened when Jebsen observed: 'If you are caught by the British, you can tell them that I will come over to the British side and work in whatever way I can.' Jebsen was no more a loyal Abwehr officer than Popov was a genuine German agent. Each was lying to the other, and both knew they were being lied to. Theirs was a curious dance of deception, in which neither could afford to admit the truth.

Popov again urged MI5 to approach Johnny Jebsen in a neutral country, and recruit him. 'He is very pro-British and I think if he was sure he would be safe he would come over here. At heart he is anti-Nazi and he is always in difficulties with his superiors owing to his extravagant habits.' If Jebsen was smuggled to Britain, Popov urged, he would reveal everything he knew, and could then be 'placed in honourable retirement at some resort'.

Billy Luke was doubtful. 'I am not at all sure we could gain very much by having him here as he seems very much of the playboy type.' MI6 was also unconvinced by Popov's character reference for his friend, and 'not as confident as he is that Jebsen is anti-Nazi'. It would be better to keep an eye on Jebsen, and wait to see what else he might reveal.

Like all start-ups experiencing rapid expansion, a flood of new employees and increasing overheads, the Double Cross operation faced cash-flow problems. No double agent was cheap to run; those with extravagant tastes, like Dusko Popov, were fantastically expensive. But the Abwehr's money problems were even more acute. MI5 had to ensure that the Abwehr found a way to pay its spies, otherwise it would soon stop believing in them: if a spy continues to work without getting paid, then someone else must be paying him. The spies sent to Britain were always short of cash. The Abwehr attempted to get money to their agents in a variety of ways, including air drops, but with little success.

Knowing this, B1A had the double agents make ever more pressing demands for cash. Wulf Schmidt (Agent Tate) kept up a steady litany of complaint in what Masterman called his 'virile telegraphese': 'I am beginning to think you are full of shit,' he told his Hamburg controller, when the latter failed to supply funds. 'I shit on Germany and its whole fucking secret service.' Tate was finally told to wait in Victoria station, follow a Japanese man carrying a copy of *The Times* onto a double-decker bus, and then pick up the newspaper when he left it on the seat. The entire episode was covertly photographed by MI5. It yielded £200 in £1 notes, and the identity of a Japanese diplomat, assistant naval attaché Mitinori Yosii, who was working for German intelligence in violation of his country's neutrality. But leaving packets of cash on buses was no way to finance an entire spy ring. The Abwehr needed a better way to get money to its agents, and MI5 needed to find a way to help it.

Only a mind as supple as that of Dusko Popov could have come up with 'Plan Midas', a way to manufacture gold. His sub-agents, Gaertner and Metcalfe, needed payment but, as Popov explained to von Karsthoff, if he entered Britain carrying large quantities of cash this would certainly raise suspicions. Why not find a middleman in London who could plausibly pretend to be passing money to German agents, in return for reimbursement by the Germans in another country? The Germans would be reassured that their agents were being properly paid at last, and MI5 could simply pocket the cash. The enemy, believing it was financing its own agents, would end up paying for the double agents.

The chosen middleman was Eric Glass, a successful and wealthy Jewish theatrical agent. Glass would pretend to be fearful of German invasion, determined to save his skin and his fortune, and prepared to transfer funds to the US by unscrupulous means. The Germans would be told that Glass was willing to hand over money to Wulf Schmidt, who could then finance other agents in Britain by leaving cash in pre-arranged places. The Germans would then reimburse Glass by transferring money to his New York bank account, which MI5 could then appropriate.

Eric Glass was a flamboyant figure, half-Austrian and half-British: 'his delight in approaching a deal, and his inventive sagacity in clinching it, were a byword in theatre and film circles'. The part offered by MI5 appealed to him, and a deal was struck. Plan Midas was put into action. Glass, however, had developed doubts. The more he thought about what he was involved in, the more terrified he became. What if the Germans rumbled the plot? Would they try to kill him? In the best theatrical tradition, Glass grandly declared he could no longer play his part, and wanted to leave the stage.

In fact, he was no longer needed, as MI5 had direct access to the New York account set up in his name. The show could go on without him. But Glass knew enough about Plan Midas to jeopardise the project. Superintendent George Leanore of Special Branch, the police unit working with MI5, was deployed to put the frighteners on the theatrical agent, a job he seems to have carried out with ugly anti-semitic relish. 'He was in a complete flat spin and scared nearly out of his life,' Leanore reported, having told Glass 'to keep his mouth shut' or face the consequence. 'I said enough to let him feel that his life depended on that. He can be trusted not to tell anyone. This trust is based on the only thing that in this case really counts – sheer fright. Sorry to appear somewhat ruthless, but we are at war and I see no reason why the fears of a little Jew should in any way deflect us from our path.'

Midas would prove to be one of the most profitable and least-known operations of the war. On the German side, the plan was approved by the Abwehr's senior financial officer, who authorised an initial transfer of £20,000. Money which the Abwehr believed was being used to finance espionage operations in the UK poured into a New York bank account in the name of Eric Glass, and from there directly into MI5's coffers. Popov took a 10 per cent cut. Von Karsthoff also took a commission. The Germans were overjoyed. 'Heartiest congratulations,' read the message sent to Wulf Schmidt when he reported the first cash handover by Glass. 'On no account spend all the money at once on drink, for that you can wait until we come. We consider ourselves invited.' The Double Cross system was now not only self-financing but profitable, to Masterman's delight: 'The actual cash supplied by the Germans to maintain their and our system between 1940 and 1945 was something in the region of £85,000' – the equivalent of more than £4.5 million today.

Popov Goes Shopping

On a hot afternoon in August 1941, Dusko Popov boarded a plane at Portela field in Lisbon, bound for the United States. He was carrying $70,000 in cash and a telegram, on which were eleven microdots, barely visible to the naked eye, the latest in German espionage technology. Enlarged under a powerful microscope, these tiny specks would reveal themselves to be photographs of a new set of questionnaires drawn up by von Karsthoff. Recruited to spy on the British, Popov had spied on the Germans and now, in yet another twist, he was being sent by the Germans to spy on the Americans, with British approval.

Popov's mission for MI5 was to create an American counterpart to Double Cross by building up a network of fake double agents. MI5 had already sent the FBI a glowing character reference: 'Popov is a clever, attractive and courageous young man of whose sincerity and loyalty we are satisfied. He has an excellent brain, but dislikes work. He is fond of women, and yachting is his principal pastime. He has personality and charm and would be at home in society anywhere. He has refused payment from us of any kind, as he has received adequate payment from the German secret service and we are hoping that this happy state of affairs will continue.' Tar Robertson had been reluctant to see Popov go west. 'For the moment we can spare you,' he said, but 'we shall probably ask you to come back in the not-too-distant future.' Tar knew the opportunity to replicate the Double Cross system stateside was too good to pass up. Popov's American mission should have been a triumph. It was an unmitigated disaster.

The problem was partly cultural. The FBI, under the dictatorial and dynamic leadership of J. Edgar Hoover, took a very different approach to counter-espionage. The foreign spy, in Hoover's mind, was just another species of criminal, to be caught, tried and then executed with maximum publicity. The bureau had achieved a breakthrough success in 1941 with the capture of no fewer than thirty-three German spies, using one of their number as bait, in what Hoover proclaimed to be the 'greatest spy round-up in US history'. With time, the FBI would come to appreciate the value of double agents, but the immediate effect of that success was to convince Hoover that the only use for a captured spy was to capture more spies. As usual, MI5 reached for a cricket analogy: 'His first innings was too easy and he imagined apparently that the Huns would not learn the lesson.' The FBI was not equipped, psychologically or practically, to run double agents. 'It is a great pity,' wrote Masterman. Dusko Popov was exactly the sort of person Hoover loathed: dissolute, extravagant, sexually voracious and foreign. As Ewen Montagu observed: 'Hoover obviously only regarded Tricycle as potential fly-paper,' useful to trap more pests, but rather disgusting to handle. Relations between Popov and his new FBI handlers started badly, and grew steadily worse.

The questionnaires in the microdots Popov had brought to the US furnished an important insight into German thinking: Popov was instructed to set up a network to gather information on atomic research, military preparations, convoys, industrial production, politics and morale. With hindsight, the most crucial part of Popov's questionnaire asked for intelligence on Pearl Harbor, the Hawaiian naval base: its anchorages, submarine port, floating docks and mine defences. Popov later claimed that he (and, for that matter, Johnny Jebsen) had realised from the start that this questionnaire pointed to a looming Japanese attack on Pearl Harbor. This is unlikely. There is nothing in Popov's file to indicate that he understood, let alone warned anyone about, the significance of the questions. Four months after Popov's arrival, the Japanese attacked, catapulting America into war. Had the Allies missed a vital tip-off that might have changed history?

Certainly some in MI5 believed so, and blamed the FBI for failing to spot the clues. 'The mistake we made was not to take the Pearl Harbor information and send it separately to Roosevelt,' Tar Robertson said many years later. 'No one ever dreamed Hoover would be such a bloody fool.' Masterman was similarly critical: 'The questionnaire indicated very clearly that in the event of the United States being at war, Pearl Harbor would be the first point to be attacked, and that plans for this attack had reached an advanced stage by August 1941.' Actually, the questionnaire showed no such thing: it did not indicate that an air assault was planned, and still less that a Japanese attack was imminent. It merely demonstrated that the Germans were acutely interested in Pearl Harbor which, given that the US Pacific Fleet was based there, was hardly surprising. The simple truth is that no one – neither Popov, Jebsen, MI5 or the FBI – saw the questionnaire as the harbinger of the attack on Pearl Harbor, until after it happened.

Popov expected to be welcomed by the FBI, just as MI5 had embraced him, but in place of Tar's clubby congeniality he found only deep suspicion. From the moment he checked into the Waldorf Astoria, Popov was put under surveillance, which the FBI's 'G-men' made little effort to disguise. Under FBI control, he began sending secret letters back to von Karsthoff in Lisbon, but the US military authorities declined to provide any genuine information to put in these. He was told he could not visit Hawaii to investigate the defences there. Popov had been instructed to establish a radio link with Lisbon and Rio de Janeiro (home to an active Abwehr spy cell), but when the FBI did finally establish a radio transmitter, based on the North

Shore of Long Island, Popov was not permitted to know what information was being sent in his name. The FBI did not go in for jocular codenames: Popov was 'Confidential Informant ND 63', an austere title that aptly reflects the bureau's chilly attitude.

Held at arm's length by the FBI, and prevented from conducting any active espionage, Popov went on a spending binge of epic proportions. Hoover was already worried that the spy's playboy habits could 'embarrass the bureau', and the scale of his expenses seemed calculated to do just that. Within a short time he had acquired an apartment on Park Avenue, a summer house in fashionable Locust Valley on Long Island, a red Buick convertible and another girlfriend, the French film star Simone Simon, whom he had met before the war. When challenged over his wild expenditure, Popov blandly insisted that he needed to maintain his cover as a wealthy roué. Among the accoutrements he considered necessary for this purpose were a butler called Brooks, a half-deaf Chinese manservant called Chen-Yen, and a team of gardeners; he had his apartment refurbished by an interior designer, and spent $12,000 on furniture, antiques and several hundred gramophone records; he drank and danced at the Stork Club, skied in Sun Valley, Idaho, and motored south for a sunny vacation in Florida. He also began an affair with an expensive Englishwoman, soon to be divorced, named Terry Richardson, and set off a fresh spasm of disapproval within the FBI when he took her on holiday, since transporting a woman across state lines for 'immoral purposes' was illegal under the ludicrous Mann Act. The FBI suspected Mrs Richardson might be a German spy, but finally concluded she was merely a 'gold-digger'.

Popov's gold supplies, however, were dwindling. He kept half the money brought from Lisbon, and swiftly spent it. The Abwehr handed over another $10,000, and he spent that too. When the Germans failed to send more money, he demanded a loan from the FBI, in order to pay his tailor, shirt-maker, florist and staff. Popov treated the FBI as his private bank and although the bureau, with extreme reluctance, began to subsidise his high-living, relations deteriorated still further. Popov's Midas Plan was bringing in a steady stream of cash, but even MI5 expressed astonishment at Popov's spending. 'His financial behaviour in the US cannot be justified,' wrote John Marriott, noting that Popov was burning through more than $5,000 a month. 'I cannot distinguish his handling of this money from embezzlement.' The man with the tricky job of reining in Popov's profligacy was Colonel Walter 'Freckles' Wren of MI6. 'Tricycle should have a good talking-to,' he was told, 'so that he should adjust his expenditure to a more reasonable basis.' It was a vain hope.

Popov was living a Gatsbyesque life, but he was far from happy. Ewen Montagu, on a visit to the US to solidify intelligence relations between the Allies, 'found him depressed and worried, with all the gaiety which exudes from him completely gone'. Popov's family was in Yugoslavia, under Nazi rule, and by handling him so ineptly and undermining his credibility with the Germans, the FBI was placing them in extreme danger. 'Hoover's management of Tricycle could not have been more calculated to blow him if Hoover had sat down to devise and plan a method of doing so,' said Montagu, who tried to lift Popov's spirits by telling him 'that there were people who still believed in him, that we were ready to go to real trouble to keep him "alive" as a double agent [and] continue the work against the Nazis for which he had risked his life'.

Popov's fear that the Germans would lose faith in him was fully justified. In March 1942, Bletchley Park deciphered an Abwehr message revealing just how far Popov had fallen in German estimation. 'Berlin suspected Tricycle to be working for both sides and recommended extreme caution when dealing with him.' Popov was not told of the Germans' suspicions. Intriguingly, the intercepts also showed that 'a larger sum in dollars ought to have been paid to him' in the US, but his handlers in Lisbon had not passed it on: von Karsthoff and

Johnny Jebsen, it seemed, were skimming off funds intended for Popov. His spymaster and friends were using him to rip off their own bosses.

By the summer of 1942, Popov and the FBI had had enough of each other. 'I cannot continue under this strain,' Popov wrote. The bureau had even begun interfering in his love life – the ultimate offence – by intercepting his telegrams to Simone Simon. 'Tricycle suspects the evil hand of the FBI in everything,' MI5 noted. He wanted out, and the FBI wanted him out. By July he had racked up a debt to the FBI of $17,500, and the bureau declared it was no longer prepared 'to maintain him in his present state of living'. The Germans also failed to send any more money, despite Popov's urgent appeals – yet another indication of their waning confidence. An internal FBI report stated: 'Popov has been totally unproductive so far as developing any German espionage or other subversive activities in the United States is concerned, and has been a continuous source of annoyance in connection with his lavish expenditures . . . It is therefore recommended that he be turned back to the British for use by them in London.'

Tar Robertson was only too happy to bring Tricycle back into the fold, but reintegrating him into the Double Cross system would be tricky. The Germans were mistrustful, and Popov would face an uphill task in regaining their trust. If he failed to do so, then his sub-agents, and all the other connected double agents being paid through Plan Midas, would fall under suspicion: 'I need not repeat the importance to us of preserving the Germans' faith in Tricycle because of his linkup with other B1A agents,' wrote Tar. A choice was put to Popov: 'He could end his double-agent work with our gratitude, or he could come back via Lisbon and try to explain away his failure in America and rehabilitate himself with his Abwehr masters.' He chose to go back to Lisbon.

There was still the matter of Popov's debts. MI5 calculated he had managed to spend $86,000 in just nine months, including

$26,000 on 'entertaining, social life, etc.'. Ian David Wilson, the thirty-eight-year-old London solicitor who had taken over from Billy Luke as Popov's case officer, was sent out to New York to try to extricate him from the mess, and prepare Popov for what was likely to be his toughest test so far. Wilson was an intriguing figure: with prominent ears, an awkward manner and a 'razor-keen mind', he was fiercely conventional and set in his ways: he worked in the same law firm all his life, never moved house, and avoided all forms of small talk. 'Quiet and introverted, he contributed very little to conversations.' Yet he had a truly remarkable capacity for concentration and absorbing detail. He completed *The Times* crossword, every morning, in a few minutes, never missing a clue. Happiest immersed in minutiae, he memorised every aspect of the case: he lived through Popov.

Wilson needed to find out what information Popov was supposed to have sent to the Germans, and explain where he got it; he would also need an explanation for his lack of productivity in the US, and some juicy new intelligence to convince von Karsthoff that he was still to be trusted. All of this required American cooperation, but the FBI, in Wilson's words, 'failed to produce any worthwhile information for Tricycle to take with him'. So Wilson and Popov simply invented a slew of American informants to explain 'how he had come into possession of certain information in the USA'. These fake informants were real people, including a Russian journalist named Igor Cassini, and Sol Bloom, 'a very pro-British Congressman and chairman of the House Foreign Affairs Committee', who had never exchanged a word with Popov. Hoover was outraged, and denounced the subterfuge as 'extremely objectionable'.

Wilson compiled a caustic report on the American handling of the case: 'The FBI have lost all interest in Tricycle. The FBI were either through incompetence, lack of power, lack of interest or lack of goodwill, of no assistance, and let us down badly.' Popov's debts to the bureau should be paid off, he recommended, 'to prevent any further deterioration in relations . . . in spite of the fact that the FBI have handled the case in such a way that they do not deserve to be repaid'. Tar Robertson read Ian Wilson's tirade with relish: 'It is a very outspoken document, but I do not see any object in mincing matters with such an organisation as the FBI.'

Now that he was back in the Double Cross team, Popov's old ebullience returned: after weeks of coaching by Wilson and Wren, he felt sure he could tell von Karsthoff a convincing tale. But Wilson was anxious. To repurchase German confidence, Popov would have to describe information he had never obtained from people he had never met. 'Tricycle himself showed great confidence in his ability to survive his meetings in Lisbon. His story is thin and cannot expect to survive searching interrogation, but he is satisfied that his personal relations with Johnny Jebsen and von Karsthoff will pull him through.'

Thrusting Popov back into suspicious German hands after the American debacle was Robertson's biggest gamble so far, and he knew it: 'His chances were nothing like even money. The odds must be at least two to one that he was blown. And, if he was, it was pretty certain that he would be tortured to squeeze him dry of information about our system, and there was an equally probable death sentence awaiting him at the end.'

Dusko Popov flew from New York on 12 October 1942, leaving behind 'an enormous number of gramophone records', a number of broken hearts and a stack of bills that would follow him, unpaid, for the rest of the war. Montagu thought Tricycle's decision to return to Lisbon was 'the greatest instance of cold-blooded courage that I have ever been in contact with'.

Before leaving New York, Popov had sent a telegram alerting von Karsthoff that he would be arriving in Lisbon on 14 October 1942. 'Will telephone office on arrival. Hope Johnny will be waiting for me.'

Instead he was welcomed back to Portugal by a smiling von
Karsthoff, along with a clean-shaven, dark-haired man Popov
had never met before, who gave his name as Kammler. Popov
described this new officer, a lieutenant, as about twenty-eight
years old, 'stiff in manner', and speaking English 'as if he learned
it from a book'. His real name was Otto Kurrer: an officer in
the Abwehr espionage division, he was there to take part in the
debriefing of the prodigal agent. Their manner was friendly, but
businesslike, and Popov could sense he was being regarded with
'some suspicion'.

Settled in the large salon of a comfortable apartment on the
Avenida de Berna, von Karsthoff came straight to the point,
and presented Popov with what sounded oddly like a school
report. His work in England, before leaving for the US, had
been 'very good'; in America it had initially been 'excellent';
then 'medium'; and then, for the last three months, 'terribly
bad'. Von Karsthoff eyed him keenly: 'Now you know what
Berlin thinks of you.'

Popov responded by telling von Karsthoff what he thought
of Berlin. He delivered a furious broadside against the Abwehr
for sending him to the US, under-supported and under-funded.
He was now deeply in debt, he said, and it was all the fault of his
German handlers. 'You send me there with no help whatsoever,
no contacts, a few miserable dollars, and you expect me to
produce results in no time . . .' It was a bravura performance,
and put von Karsthoff on the defensive: 'We did all we could.
It was Berlin's fault.' The Abwehr man seemed uninterested in
the meagre haul of intelligence Popov had brought back from
the US; he did not try to pick holes in his story; he did not
even discuss the little intelligence he *had* sent. Von Karsthoff,
it seemed, was not only willing to believe Popov's story, but
unwilling to ask him anything that might make it harder for
him to do so. The reasons for his eagerness were personal,
professional and financial. Popov had long assumed that his
German handlers were skimming off money that should have

been passed to him. Kammler observed darkly that Popov had not received adequate funds in the US because Jebsen had 'embezzled' at least $10,000. They were all making money, illicitly, from Popov's spy salary: von Karsthoff, Jebsen, and even, it seemed, this man Kammler.

'Berlin are stupid fellows,' Kammler remarked. 'They are sitting at desks and don't realise the difficulties of being without money. Please work hard in the future or we shall all have trouble here. And you'll see we will be able to give you big bonuses.' Popov had become more than a spy in the eyes of his German handlers. He was a valuable business, and thus in a powerful bargaining position since von Karsthoff and Kammler were clearly terrified that he 'might make a scene with Berlin'. He now demanded full payment of all the money he claimed to be owed. The financial wrangling continued for days, but Popov had the upper hand. 'Kammler begged him not to make difficulties over money arrangements because such difficulties might cause Kammler to be removed from Lisbon and sent to the Russian front.' If Popov continued as before, they would all make money, and Berlin would be pleased. If he did not, then they were all in deep trouble. They could not afford for him to fail.

He had absolute faith in his own powers of persuasion and seduction, and rightly so, for three days later, London intercepted a message sent by von Karsthoff to Berlin, in which he reported that Popov had been subjected to 'severe' interrogation and no evidence had been found that he was engaging in 'double work': Popov was in the clear. 'Lisbon seem to have satisfied themselves that Tricycle was not double-crossing them,' Tar reported.

Popov spent a week in Lisbon arguing over money, until a deal was finally struck: the Germans would pay him $25,000, plus 6,000 Portuguese escudos, and a salary of $2,500 a month, depending on his performance. From Popov's standpoint, this was a remarkable bargain: a lump sum to repay debts he had not incurred, for services to the Third Reich he had not rendered, and a future stipend to continue betraying the Germans and supplying information that was either useless or false. The origin of the money, and Jebsen's role in the deal, were unclear, but Popov's old friend was somewhere in the background, pulling strings and lining his pockets.

Following the script laid out by Wilson, Popov declared that he intended to return to London and continue spying as before. 'Berlin wants information of direct use for military purposes,' von Karsthoff told Popov. Reports on public morale, industrial output and political gossip were all very well, but 'we are not so interested in people's feelings, not in production, but interested in purely military facts'. Specifically, Berlin wanted advance warning of Allied military plans. Now that America had entered the war, there would surely be a counter-attack to try to roll back the German occupation, in North Africa, France, Norway, or somewhere else. 'What about invasion?' von Karsthoff demanded. 'Where will it be? See what kind of training and instruction the army has. Are they learning any languages? What kind of beaches are they training on?' Popov should furnish as much information on military preparations as possible, and they would make their own deductions.

Popov landed back in Britain with this new mission, $25,000 in cash in his pocket, and five matches impregnated with a new type of secret ink sewn into the shoulder pads of his overcoat. A room was waiting for him in Claridge's Hotel, but Tar Robertson asked Jock Horsfall, the MI5 chauffeur, to drive Popov directly from the airport to his own house in west London, 'so that I can satisfy my curiosity and at the same time welcome him home'.

Popov seemed 'voluble and rather confused', expressing 'a great deal of vague feelings of grievance with regard to his American visit'. But there was no doubt whose side he was on. 'He is entirely friendly towards us and I have no doubt about his loyalty.' At a debriefing session the next morning, attended by Robertson, Masterman and Wilson, Popov searched through his pockets for the cash given to him by von Karsthoff, finally located the wads in his trenchcoat pocket, and dumped it all on the table. Masterman was stunned at his 'extraordinary casualness about money', and observed: 'It is quite probable that he would have lost or been robbed of this large sum of money without worrying very much about it.' Popov explained, without rancour, that his German handlers were on the fiddle, 'both by making profit on exchange and taking a considerable rake-off from money from Berlin'. He seemed to regard this as normal business practice. 'I was cheated by Johnny, I was cheated by von Karsthoff,' he said. 'I think Kammler earned a lot of money from the exchange.' Once again he urged MI5 to recruit Jebsen, whom he described as 'very anti-Nazi'. If properly handled, 'Johnny would give him a great deal of information'.

He was adamant that any German doubts about his loyalty had been dispelled: 'Any suspicion against me was cleared up on the first day.' Popov's best defence was the sheer force of his personality, Tar reflected, his uncanny 'ability to impose himself and his views on the Germans when personal contact could be made'. Von Karsthoff was 'not in any way suspicious', and had promised to send a letter to the Savoy Hotel with three microdots containing questionnaires for his new mission. The MI5 team was deeply relieved: 'Von Karsthoff has defended Tricycle as his agent and made a good deal out of the business.' Here were fine opportunities for blackmail and manipulation. But it was the German hunger for information about Allied invasion plans that set Tar thinking. Von Karsthoff wanted raw military intelligence, as much as possible, and urgently. 'We may be able to draw our own conclusions,' he had told Popov.

It was a revealing observation, for it suggested that with careful planning, the Germans might be guided into drawing, not their own conclusions, but the conclusions the Double Cross team wanted them to draw.

8

The Great Game

Roman Czerniawski met Hugo Bleicher, his German handler, in the lavatory of the Brasserie Georges in Lyon, on 15 August 1942. In the intervening weeks, the Polish spy had learned how to construct a wireless transmitter, memorised his code, and consumed food 'in enormous quantities' at a Chinese restaurant next door to the safe house on Rue Dufrenoy, rebuilding his strength after months in prison. Concealed in the heels of his shoes were two transmitting crystals. Czerniawski had slipped across the border into Vichy France, and made contact, as instructed by Colonel Oscar Reile, with Polish intelligence, explaining that he had escaped and now needed to get to Britain, quickly. He revealed nothing about his deal with the Colonel. The Polish secret service contacted MI6, and plans to evacuate the leader of the defunct Interallié network, who had miraculously evaded the clutches of the Germans, were set in motion: he would be smuggled into neutral Spain, using the underground route for escaping POWs, and then put on the next flight to Britain.

Bleicher had been shadowing him and thoroughly enjoying his 'free holiday' in southern France. He even brought along one of his French mistresses. The meeting in the Brasserie Georges was the first time they had met since Roman Czerniawski's 'escape'. Their conversation in the restaurant lavatory was brief, and quite odd.

With some embarrassment, Bleicher said that although he 'realised that any manifestation of mistrust on their part would jeopardise the affair', German bureaucratic rules required a 'written guarantee' of Czerniawski's loyalty. This was 'a mere formality'. Bleicher then handed over a piece of paper which stated, in German, that Czerniawski was 'starting to work for the National Socialist State in a military capacity, and undertaking his mission voluntarily, and if he failed in his duty the Germans would be entitled to take reprisals'. Here was a bold threat disguised as form-filling, a guarantee that if he reneged on his promises, then the people he loved would be killed. Only a state as murderous and bureaucratic as the Third Reich would require a man to sign his own family's death warrant, and consider it binding. Czerniawski signed.

The next day, Bleicher picked up a letter at the Hôtel d'Orléans. It read: 'Long Live Hitler, the Great Builder of a new Europe!' Czerniawski was on his way to Britain.

In London, Roman Czerniawski was greeted by the Polish community as a returning hero: a patriotic 'super-spy' who had defied the Germans in occupied Paris and then, astonishingly, managed to slip out of their grasp. During October 1942, he was interviewed by both British and Polish intelligence officers, and subjected to the 'most exhaustive and painstaking' interrogation. No one smelled a rat. The Polish pilot was praised for his 'great daring and initiative' in forging the Interallié network. 'He is a natural leader of men and has great organising ability,' MI5 noted. Colonel Stanislaw Gano of Polish intelligence, who had met Czerniawski in London the year before, welcomed him back with open arms. The story of his flight from German custody was 'amazing' and 'everyone was prepared to accept it as genuine'. Or almost everyone. Some found Czerniawski's account a little too heroic to be credible. A rumour began to circulate that 'there was something funny about his escape'.

Czerniawski was not the only member of the French network to reappear in Britain. Monique Deschamps ('Mosquito'), the 'tiny, vivacious and attractive' head of the Interallié's southern sector, had also escaped the Gestapo and made her way across the Channel. So, too, had Mathilde Carré. Like Czerniawski, she had agreed to work for the Germans as a double agent in Britain. Under Bleicher's instruction, she had used the captured Interallié wireless to maintain the fiction that she had escaped the round-up and was continuing her work as an Allied agent. In the spring of 1942, Bleicher had her send a message to London, asking to be evacuated as she feared she was about to be arrested. The British agreed to send a boat to collect her from the French coast. 'The plan was that in London I should get as many names as I could of agents working in France for the Allies . . . after that, the great roundup would take place. They promised me an enormous sum of money, a trip to Germany and the publication of my memoirs in the largest Nazi newspaper.' Mathilde was in thrall to her German lover. She promised to bring back for Bleicher 'a couple of pairs of shoes' from a London bootmaker. Bleicher may have hated the British, but he was partial to handmade English shoes.

Mathilde Carré was picked up by a fast British motor gun boat at Bihit point near Lannion, on the Brittany coast (Bleicher having ensured that no German patrol would be on hand to interrupt the rendezvous). In London she was interrogated by a uniformed British officer with impeccable manners and a steely look. 'Anglo-Saxon hypocrisy is so often preferable to Gallic excitability,' she later reflected. Once again, she broke almost immediately, confessing that she had been recruited as an Abwehr agent but insisting that she had always intended to betray the Germans as soon as she was on British soil. She did not, however, explain her relationship with Hugo Bleicher, or her role in the break-up of the Interallié network. The British did not quite know what to make of Mathilde Carré. She was lodged in a safe house, and kept under close surveillance.

Czerniawski's arrival in London sealed her fate. Mathilde had betrayed them all, he explained: 'Her guilt is the greater since, although she must have fully realised the extent of the catastrophe, she helped the Germans in their work.' Bleicher had doubtless put her under intense pressure, 'but there is no excuse whatever for treason and betrayal to the enemy of her colleagues, knowing that they will face the firing squad'. Czerniawski did not of course mention that he, too, had been recruited by German intelligence.

Mathilde was arrested and lodged in Aylesbury prison: she would spend the rest of the war behind bars.

Czerniawski, the decorated war hero, was given a desk job by the Polish government in exile. He moved into a flat in Brompton with Monique Deschamps, who became his lover. For the first time since the war began, Roman's life appeared to achieve a sort of calm. Then he dropped what MI5 called 'the bombshell'.

Six weeks after arriving in Britain, Czerniawski presented Colonel Stanislaw Gano of Polish intelligence with a sixty-four-page, typewritten document, written in English and entitled 'The Great Game'. It began: 'The Germans are entering the final stage of losing the game. It has become my ambition to conclude this affair in grand style . . .' Czerniawski then proceeded to describe, in detail, his recruitment by the German secret service: the conversations in his jail cell at Fresnes, the deal struck with Bleicher and Reile, the terms of his mission, and his faked escape from German custody. As proof he produced 'the wireless crystals which he had kept hidden in the heels of his shoes'. He had merely been playing a part, he said, 'carrying out a carefully worked out plan to fool the Germans'. He insisted: 'During the whole period of my "collaboration" with the Germans they did not receive from me the slightest hint which might have helped them in combating our or Allied organisations on the Continent.'

The double agent now offered to turn triple agent, pointing out that he was in a unique position to tell the German High

Command, via wireless, anything that Allied intelligence wanted
to tell them. Czerniawski laid down the rules of his game: 'I shall
discuss personally all data with the British, or rather with one
Englishman, an officer who alone would hold the entirety of
the affair in his hands and would be in charge of it . . . I would
act as the expert.' No one else in Polish intelligence should
know the truth about how he had really got out of France: 'The
story of my escape, for the good of the cause, must continue to
be regarded as true.'

This extraordinary document ended with a characteristically
grandiose flourish: 'I am convinced that if an exact plan is laid
down now and carried out logically and adhered to strictly,
then the Great Game has all the chances of success and may
yield great results. If I have acted wrong in organising the Great
Game the news that I have perished in an air accident will save
my family and my colleagues.'

When Colonel Gano had finished reading, he looked up,
staggered, but before he could speak, in a final dramatic gesture,
Czerniawski 'demanded a revolver to shoot himself, if his request
were refused and he was found to have failed in his military duty'.

Gano's first reaction was shock, but his second was blind
fury. Czerniawski had lied to his superior officers. He had
deliberately concealed the true circumstances of his escape. He
had struck a deal with the enemy, and had continued to hide
the truth for weeks after arriving in Britain. He had made Gano
look a fool. Czerniawski responded that he had not revealed
the truth until now because he was not 'certain of the degree to
which the Germans had penetrated Polish HQ in London'. The
suggestion that the Polish government in exile might harbour
enemy spies made Gano even angrier. He ordered Czerniawski
to return to his flat and await further orders, and declared his
belief (from which he never wavered) that Czerniawski was a
'sinister individual' who deserved to be shot.

Czerniawski's treatise (he called it 'his book') was passed to
Tar Robertson at B1A. If Czerniawski was telling the truth,

then he might be useful to the Double Cross team. If he was lying then, like Mathilde Carré, he should be locked up and, if necessary, tried and executed. The decision must be made quickly, since if Czerniawski was to demonstrate his worth to the Germans, he would need to make radio contact as soon as possible. Christopher Harmer was once again tasked with teasing out the motives of a potential double agent, and deciding his ultimate fate.

Harmer spent days interrogating Czerniawski. The resulting report is a masterpiece of psychology, a remarkable insight into the mind of a spy. Czerniawski was telling the truth, Harmer concluded, but not the whole truth, and only those parts of the truth that suited his purposes. He claimed the Abwehr had recruited him, whereas he had plainly volunteered to spy for them; he insisted he had been acting a part, but the Germans had successfully plied him with propaganda and stroked his vanity; he had come to Britain planning to see which way the winds of war were blowing, and only after assessing the situation had he decided to come clean.

'There are considerable doubts about his integrity,' wrote Harmer. 'It seems possible that he might be embarking on some form of triple cross.' But Czerniawski was reliable in one, important respect:

His loyalty is entirely to his own country, and . . . every problem he sees is bound up with the destiny of the Polish people. He is of an intensely dramatic and egotistical nature. This may be due in some part to his size. It is necessary to avoid taking him at his own valuation. His character, sense of drama, and the feeling of self-importance which his intelligence work has given him – which makes him regard himself in some way as a sort of Joan of Arc of Poland – causes him to dramatise and overrate the part he has played.

Harmer tried to imagine what it must have been like for Czerniawski in Fresnes prison, 'a loyal and fervent Pole in a weak state, physically and mentally', and he reproduced the scene:

> As his condition gets lower, so his credibility of propaganda and ideas of grandeur become greater. Their confidence in him grows, and when he suggests that he might also act as a spy for them, they take this suggestion seriously. He himself really thinks that there may be a possibility of fixing up an arrangement between Poland and Germany.

But on reaching Britain, Harmer surmised, Czerniawski realised that his German jailers had misrepresented the political situation.

> He finds that so far from wanting collaboration, the Polish official circles here are determined to continue the fight against Germany. His health and strength and sense of judgment return, he realises that as a loyal and patriotic Pole, it is impossible for him to carry out his mission. With a dramatic gesture, therefore, he presents his book to his chief.

Czerniawski's loyalties depended entirely on what he perceived to be Poland's best interests. 'I do not think he is a spy using this story as his cover,' wrote Harmer. 'There is no evidence, nor any probability, that he has worked here to the detriment of Britain and for the benefit of her enemies.' He had already 'rendered very great service to this country', and properly handled, he could do so again:

> The Germans would have confidence in him given their hold on him. There is no reason why we should not open up his transmitter. With imagination, and with his very original mind, we might possibly confuse and deceive the Germans to a remarkable extent [but] a successful

exploitation of the opportunities is dependent on his willing cooperation.

Yet again, some senior members of B1A were unconvinced. Marriott, the stickler for rules, pointed out that it had been agreed 'we are never going to tolerate any person who has worked for our service agreeing in any circumstances to work for the Germans'. Masterman argued that 'the Germans have really lost nothing by letting him go: for they have cleaned up the whole of his organisation, and the only thing left would have been the doubtful satisfaction of executing him'. It seemed possible that the Germans had sent Czerniawski to Britain as a plant, 'knowing pretty well certainly that he would throw in his hand with us'. If so, they would know his messages were false from the outset. Were Bleicher and Oscar Reile simply using the Pole to try to find out what the British wanted the Germans to believe? 'We are not yet at all convinced as to his *bona fides*,' Guy Liddell wrote in his diary.

The dispute over Czerniawski provoked a blazing row between Masterman, representing the cautious old guard, and Christopher Harmer, the young enthusiast keen to run the Polish spy. Masterman seemed 'hell-bent on chopping him', thought Harmer, and even 'intrigued behind my back' to do so. The day before his wedding to his secretary Peggy, Harmer wrote Masterman 'one of the rudest letters I have ever sent'. They later made up. 'I loved the old boy,' wrote Harmer. 'I suppose he was only doing his job – of exercising a wise and mature restraint on the irresponsibilities of the hot-headed youngsters.' But the hothead stood his ground, insisting they should not 'throw the case away'. Tar Robertson agreed. The Abwehr radio station in Paris had been trying for weeks to make wireless contact. It was decided that Czerniawski should begin sending radio messages back to his German controllers, but only on a temporary basis 'under close supervision'. The Polish authorities, suspicious and resentful, convened a military court of inquiry, which issued a severe reprimand to Czerniawski and relegated him to a 'non-job'.

Czerniawski was delighted with the way matters had turned out. 'The NEW GAME is beginning,' he wrote to Harmer. 'The Germans lost the old one. They must lose the new one as well. In my opinion it is a difficult game, but it might yield enormous advantages, especially during the decisive moments which are drawing nigh.' More puffed up than ever, he now set out on the third lap of his extraordinary espionage career, with a new mission and a new name. As a spy in occupied France he had adopted the codename 'Walenty' (Valentine); as a spy for the Germans he had become 'Hubert'; and now, as a double agent for the Double Cross team, he was renamed once again. Henceforth he would be Agent Brutus.

The classically educated Harmer came up with this *nom de guerre*. 'Roman Czerniawski had been turned by the Germans, and then re-turned by us, so I thought "Et tu, Brute?" Of course he had carried out a very brave mission in Paris during the first year of occupation, so I thought of Brutus's final speech from *Julius Caesar* which begins "He was the noblest Roman of them all".' The words 'Et tu, Brute?' are also, of course, the most famous denunciation of treachery in literature; the words of a man who has been stabbed in the back by a friend he trusted. Harmer was convinced that Roman Czerniawski, unlike Shakespeare's famous Roman, would not betray him, but his playful choice of codename carried the unmistakable hint of anxiety.

9

The Flock

Agent Cyril, a potential new recruit to the Double Cross team, was not quite what MI5 had been expecting. Elvira de la Fuente Chaudoir was, Harmer later recalled, 'one of the most elegant women I had ever met'. She wore a cloche hat, and as she sat down she peeled off a pair of silk gloves, revealing 'beautifully varnished nails'. For a moment, Christopher Harmer was lost for words. 'She was really very striking.'

On her return from France, Elvira had been debriefed by MI6, which concluded her mission had been 'carried out to the best of her ability' and then handed her on to Tar Robertson with the recommendation that she be deployed as a double agent.

Harmer's task was to assess her usefulness. He introduced himself as 'Mr Palmer', while John Masterman, who sat in on the interview, called himself 'Masterson'. (Case officers used – and still use – pseudonyms as close as possible to their own names. That way, if someone happened to use their real name, the person who was not supposed to know it might assume he had misheard.) Over the next hour, Elvira told the story of her recruitment in Cannes by a German agent named 'Bibi', and the deal to furnish political and military information for £100 a month. She 'made a good impression', thought Harmer.

Tar Robertson was cautious. 'It is by no means clear that she has told us everything she knows.' Further investigation into her private life raised the possibility that she might be blackmailed over her 'Lesbian tendencies'. (For some reason, the word 'lesbian' is frequently capitalised in MI5 files: perhaps this was the result of a classical education, since the word is associated with the island of Lesbos, or perhaps the officers thought such an exotic species deserved special grammatical treatment.) She had been reprimanded before for indiscretion, and although 'she would appear to have learned wisdom, that point will have to be taken into account in considering her employment as a double agent'. Her German recruiter was also an unknown quantity. Britain's MI5 and M16 had, by now, amassed a great deal of information about German intelligence personnel. This data was entered onto punchcards and fed into a 'Hollerith Machine', an electrical tabulating apparatus originally invented to process data for the US census. Elvira's detailed description of Helmut Bleil was run through the device but 'disclosed no possible trace'. This anxious, amateur and alcoholic spy seemed to be operating semi-independently. 'We have not come across this man before.'

The most vigorous sceptic was Masterman, who did not want a woman on the team and pointed out that an indiscreet, cash-strapped 'Lesbian' with a gambling habit represented a serious security risk. 'We ought *not* to plunge into this case,' he wrote. 'I cannot help feeling that the Germans would not have given Cyril so much secret ink etc. unless they had fairly good evidence of her attachment to them. So I am driven back to the fear that she may in fact have deceived SIS.' Elvira had made no secret of her interest in money. 'She is a rather expensive woman,' noted Masterman. 'Has she cost SIS a packet?'

Harmer won the day. 'I think this woman is telling the truth,' he insisted. 'Bleil regards her as a bona fide agent and has so represented her to his masters.' Her social contacts, as a 'typical member of the cosmopolitan smart set', would enable her to report all sorts of misleading political and social gossip from the gaming tables and salons of London. Elvira was asked to explain why she wanted to become a double agent; her answer was revealing: 'She replied that she had no such desire at all, although she would do it if it was any use.' Whatever Masterman's suspicions, she was not motivated solely by money. On 28 October 1942, Elvira was officially brought into the Double Cross team. Harmer, now her case officer, 'impressed on her the absolute need for secrecy'. She, like Garbo, would be provided with a cover job at the BBC, and paid a monthly salary equal to the money she was receiving from the Germans. Under MI5 control, she should begin writing secret letters to Bleil at once. In case of difficulty she could contact 'Mr Palmer' on Grosvenor 3171. As a precaution, her letters would be intercepted, and her telephone bugged.

All she now needed was a suitable new codename; something sophisticated, racy and intoxicating, as befitted this beautifully manicured spy. 'I chose the name of a rum-based cocktail,' Harmer later recalled. (The Bronx Martini is usually made with gin, but the barman at the Hyde Park Hotel made a wartime version from rum, orange juice and sweet and dry Vermouth.) 'It was one of the very few cocktails you could buy during the war when gin was in short supply,' said Harmer. 'It was a very appropriate, short name for an exceptional woman.'

Elvira de la Fuente Chaudoir became 'Agent Bronx'.

The little Spanish gentleman who had moved into Number 35, Crespigny Road, Hendon, was a refugee from Franco's Spain, it was said, who did translation work at the BBC. Every morning Señor Pujol caught the Underground train into central London, and every evening he came back home to his family. He spoke little English, and seemed polite, shy and rather dull. Indeed, the only interesting thing about the new arrivals, from the neighbours' point of view, was the state of their marriage: their nightly rows in loud and incomprehensible Spanish were a source of considerable entertainment in Crespigny Road. The neighbours would have been surprised to discover that the Pujols were arguing over the finer points of espionage. They would have been even more astonished to learn that, instead of working at the BBC, the little Spanish man spent his days in a small office in Jermyn Street, making up an army of fake spies.

Juan Pujol possessed what his case officer, Tomás Harris, called a 'remarkable talent for duplicity'. Harris was no slouch in that department, but Agent Garbo was in a league of his own, a master of invention whose 'entire existence remained wrapped up in the successful continuation of the work'. Unlike other double agents, Pujol's 'absolute loyalty' was never questioned. He was, in the best way, an extremist and a fanatic. The pair spent all day at the Jermyn Street office, located conveniently close to the Double Cross headquarters, inventing a world of spies, devising stratagems, cooking up new chicken-feed and composing messages. They would break for lunch at Garibaldi's Italian restaurant, and then resume in the afternoon. Their make-believe sessions sometimes extended far into the evening.

By the end of 1942, the Garbo network included an airline employee, the courier who supposedly smuggled Garbo's letters to Lisbon, a wealthy Venezuelan student named Carlos living in Glasgow, his brother in Aberdeen, a Gibraltarian waiter in Chislehurst whose anti-British feelings were said to be exacerbated because 'he found the climate in Kent very disagreeable', a senior official in the Spanish section of the Ministry of Information, an anti-Soviet South African, and a Welsh ex-seaman living in Swansea described by Pujol as a 'thoroughly undesirable character'. The personality, activities and messages of each spy were carefully imagined, refined, and entered in a log book. Some of these sub-agents were supposedly conscious collaborators, while others were unwitting sources of secret information; some were given names, others remained anonymous. The information they theoretically supplied was written up in secret ink and dispatched inside innocuous letters that the Germans believed were either brought by courier or sent by air mail to various cover addresses in neutral Spain and

Tommy Argyll 'Tar' Robertson, the mastermind of Double Cross.

Camp 020: Latchmere House, the top secret interrogation centre in southwest London, where captured spies were imprisoned, grilled and 'turned'.

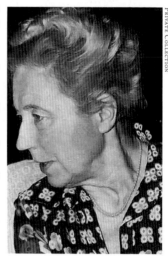

Gisela Ashley, alias 'Susan Barton', German-born expert on Nazism and the most senior woman in B1A.

J. C. Masterman, Oxford history don, cricketer, and the 'elder statesman' of the Double Cross system.

French film star Simone Simon, one of Popov's many lovers.

Dusko Popov, 'Agent Tricycle', Serbian playboy, international businessman and double agent.

Maria Elera, Brazilian model: photograph from the MI5 files labelled wearily, 'Popov's latest girlfriend'.

Popov with his first wife, Janine.

Roman Czerniawski, 'Agent Brutus': Polish patriot, trained intelligence officer and the most professional of the Double Cross spies.

Captain Czerniawski (*fourth from right*) with his Polish regiment shortly before the fall of France in 1940.

Colonel Oskar Reile, Czerniawski's German case officer.

Hugo Bleicher, the Abwehr's ruthless counter-espionage officer in Paris.

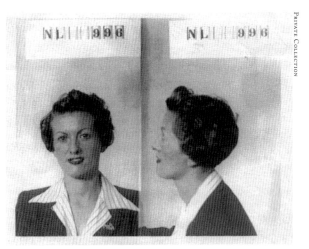

Monique Deschamps, 'Agent Moustique' (Mosquito), the French Resistance agent who would later marry Roman Czerniawski.

Mathilde Carré outside the Montmartre restaurant where she betrayed the Interallié intelligence network.

Mathilde Carré, 'The Cat', the Resistance agent who helped to build, and then destroy, Czerniawski's network.

Elvira Josefina Concepcion de la Fuente Chaudoir, 'Agent Bronx', seen here at the Hurlingham Club with MI5 case officer Billy Luke.

Major Christopher Harmer, a lawyer in peacetime, case officer for Brutus, Bronx, Mutt and Jeff.

Hugh Astor, case officer for Brutus and Bronx.

Helmut Bleil, the alcoholic German intelligence agent who recruited Elvira Chaudoir in the south of France.

Juan Pujol Garcia, 'Agent Garbo', and his wife Aracelli, in Spain *c.* 1940, during a rare moment of domestic harmony.

Garbo in disguise, a man of 'great ingenuity, and a passionate and quixotic zeal for his task'.

Karl-Erich Kühlenthal of the Madrid Abwehr, Garbo's gullible German case officer.

Tomás Harris, the half-Spanish art dealer who helped Garbo to create a fictional network of twenty-seven sub-agents across Britain.

Johann JEBSEN

Johnny Jebsen, 'Agent Artist'.

Johnny Jebsen in Turkey in 1942.

Johnny Jebsen on the day of his marriage to actress Lore Petersen, to whom he was serially unfaithful, but deeply loyal.

Admiral Wilhelm Canaris, the chief
of the Abwehr, German military
intelligence.

Hans Oster, Canaris's deputy and secret
anti-Nazi plotter who recruited Jebsen to the
Abwehr.

Paul Fidrmuc, 'Agent Ostro', prized
Abwehr agent-runner and fraud.

Anthony Blunt, MI5 officer, art expert and Soviet mole. 'He was a very nice and civilised man, and he betrayed us all.'

Guy Liddell, the shy, cello-playing head of MI5's counter-intelligence B Branch.

Code-breakers at work at Bletchley Park, the secret code-breaking centre in the Buckinghamshire countryside codenamed Camp X. Deciphered German wireless messages were circulated as 'Most Secret Sources', or 'MSS'.

With information from the code-breakers, MI5 intercepted scores of enemy spies, such as John Moe and Tör Glad, double agents 'Mutt' and 'Jeff', pictured before their departure from Norway in 1941.

Lily Sergeyev's French identity card issued in November 1941, soon after her recruitment by German intelligence. In Paris, she was trained in the use of wireless, secret inks and coding.

Lily Sergeyev, 'Agent Treasure', who brought 'a rich dowry: the confidence of the Germans'.

Babs, Lily's beloved dog, a critical, if unlikely, player in the D-Day story.

Mary Sherer, the only woman officer in the Double Cross team.

Pigeons were used to pass messages, gather intelligence from behind the lines and plant false information on the enemy.

D-Day troops at Weymouth heading into battle: 'It may well be the most ghastly disaster of the whole war.'

Portugal. In fact, they were transported in the diplomatic bag. Pujol's sub-agents were able to correspond with the Germans independently after he was authorised to supply them with secret ink; those agents then began recruiting their own sub-sub-agents. The network began to self-replicate and metastasise, until the work of Pujol and Harris came to resemble a limitless, multi-character, ever-expanding novel.

The early objective of the Garbo network, in the words of Harris, was 'to swamp the Germans with information, misinformation and problems'. The information, true and false, was vetted by the Twenty Committee; the problems were the fruit of pure creativity; all of it was written up in Pujol's bombastic style. 'I do not wish to end this letter without sending a *Viva Victorioso* for our brave troops who fight in Russia, annihilating the Bolshevik beast.' If the Germans could be inundated by this deluge of intelligence, 'in as much confusing bulk as possible', from myriad fake spies, it would at the very least dissuade them from trying to send over any more genuine ones. 'The greater the work we caused them to put into the Garbo case, the more they would become conscious of his importance to them.' By continually emphasising 'the fanatical loyalty, the quixotic temperament and the untiring energy' of Pujol himself, the Germans could be made increasingly dependent on this 'temperamental genius', who needed to be placated and flattered at all times. They sent money, encouragement and ever more extravagant 'expressions of high satisfaction'.

In response, Juan Pujol threw periodic hissy fits. His tone was that of a testy and demanding lover: 'Why have I been made to suffer?' His complaints were exhaustingly long-winded: 'I want you to know that if it were not for the esteem which I feel personally for you, which I feel you reciprocate, as well as the interest which I have in helping our cause for which I have fought for three years during our war, and continue to fight for, though in a more responsible position in order to terminate this plague of Reds, I must tell you that in all sincerity, and as a friend, that I would have returned to Spain some time ago.' The relationship between Pujol and his handler Karl-Erich Kühlenthal began to resemble an abusive marriage, in which one partner holds the other in abject submission. Pujol battered Kühlenthal with verbiage. 'The more we dictated our terms, the more they cooperated; the more arrogant and temperamental Garbo became, the more considerate they were in return.'

The information provided by the Garbo network was voluminous, but of strictly limited worth: low-grade military information, political gossip, reflections on public opinion, the occasional item of real deception, and physical evidence when this was requested, such as gas mask crystals sent to Spain inside a tin of Andrew's Liver Salts. When Garbo did send important, real information, this was carefully timed to arrive too late to be of use. It never occurred to Kühlenthal to wonder why items of little importance, such as gas mask crystals, arrived promptly, whereas the most significant nuggets were invariably delayed in the postal system. It certainly occurred to John Marriott, Robertson's silky deputy, who wondered how the Germans could fail to see their agents as people 'who seldom or never say anything untrue, but who equally never say anything which is new'. The infatuated, dominated partner in any relationship tends to overlook, sometimes wilfully, the small clues to infidelity. In German eyes, Garbo's failure to supply high-grade information in a timely way was not his fault, but theirs; and the more often he tried and failed, the more they loved him.

One by one, as the flock of double agents fluttered into MI5's coop, Tar Robertson began to imagine new ways of combating German espionage, and using enemy spies to Allied advantage. His thoughts, increasingly, turned to pigeons.

For some time, Robertson had been receiving long and detailed reports on 'the possible uses, and actual uses, that Pigeons can be put to from the point of view of espionage'. (Pigeons, like Lesbians, frequently merited a capital letter.) The author

of these reports was one Flight Lieutenant Richard Melville
Walker, who headed one of the most secret and peculiar units
of MI5: 'The Pigeon Service Special Section, B3C,' charged
with disrupting the enemy's use of pigeons, and deploying
Allied pigeons for passing on secret intelligence.

To describe Flight Lieutenant Walker as a 'pigeon fancier'
does not quite do justice to the depth of his passion. He adored
pigeons. He lived for pigeons. His reports were long, cooing
poems of love. 'Years of breeding have made the Carrier Pigeon
into a thoroughbred,' he told Tar, with a 'magical' ability to find
its way home over a range of up to 700 miles. Walker wrote
about his homing pigeons in the same way that Robertson
described his most valued agents: 'Out of a hundred birds of the
same stock perhaps one will be that bird all breeders hope for – a
bird of highly individual character, courageous and resourceful.
Much depends on the individual bird and especially its character
and intelligence.'

Britain had abandoned its military pigeon service after the
First World War. But even before the outbreak of the Second
World War, Walker realised that Britain was falling behind
Germany in the pigeon race since these birds remained an
important way of passing information across enemy lines:
fast, reliable and virtually impossible to intercept. The Nazis
incorporated pigeons into the very heart of the Reich: each of
Germany's 57,000 pigeon fanciers had to have a certificate of
political reliability from the Gestapo; Jews were banned from
keeping pigeons, and the German Pigeon Federation was placed
under the control of the SS. 'Himmler, who has been a pigeon
fancier and enthusiast all his life, has brought his enthusiasm for
pigeons into the Gestapo,' Walker reported. Eugenics theories
were applied to pigeons, and 'any lofts where the pigeons did
not come up to standard were wiped out'. In 1937, a pigeon
race had been staged in which some 1,400 German pigeons
were brought to Britain by plane and then released to fly home.
Walker believed the race had been a cover 'to accustom as many

German pigeons as possible to the sea crossing from England to Germany'.

Walker was convinced that Nazi pigeons were now pouring into Britain, by parachute, high-speed motor launch and by U-boat, providing enemy spies in Britain with an undetectable method of sending information to occupied Europe. Walker was not alone in his pigeon paranoia: Basil Thomson, the veteran Scotland Yard spy-catcher, observed: 'It was positively dangerous to be seen in conversation with a pigeon.' Some experts claimed to be able to identify a pigeon with a German 'accent'.

With MI5's wholehearted backing, Flight Lieutenant Walker drew up maps of known pigeon lofts in occupied Europe, and logged suspicious pigeon sightings (homing pigeons tend to fly in a tell-tale straight line, particularly across water). He argued that agents should be sent into occupied territory with a knapsack of pigeons rather than a wireless, since 'they are easier to work and, once liberated, the agent has nothing incriminating to carry about'. Walker began to develop ever more elaborate ways for pigeons to carry secret messages: small holes burnt with a fine nail in the feathers; a tiny roll of rice paper inserted into the hollow part of the main wing feather; messages in Morse code written on the quills in waterproof ink. Evidence of enemy pigeon activity mounted: an exhausted bird dropped onto the Scilly Isles, off the Cornish coast, with an intelligence message in French; two German pigeons were blown across the Channel in bad weather, carrying routine training messages. 'Both birds are now prisoners of war, working hard breeding English pigeons,' Walker reported.

Flight Lieutenant Walker loved all pigeons, even enemy pigeons, but this was war. It was time to go on the attack. Walker brought in the falcons. In 1942, the falconry unit, comprising three peregrine falcons and a falconer, was established on the Isles of Scilly, with the task of intercepting enemy pigeons: it would eventually bring down a total of twenty-three pigeons, every one of which turned out to be British. These incidents of what might now be called 'friendly fire' did nothing to dampen Walker's enthusiasm: 'The falconry unit proved it could intercept pigeons,' he wrote triumphantly. Finally, the birds of prey went AWOL. But by this time Walker had come up with another ingenious plan. Homing pigeons are sociable creatures, and if a pigeon spots other pigeons flying about, it may join them and, particularly if tired, return with them to their home lofts. This gave Walker an idea: 'If all the fanciers living within ten miles of the coast from Cornwall to Norfolk could be organised to form a screen' by releasing their birds at staggered intervals, then 'any enemy pigeon on a homing flight would stand a good chance of coming across these pigeons exercising and would be tempted to join them.' Astonishingly, Walker was given permission to carry out the largest military deployment of pigeons ever attempted, a sort of aerial Home Guard. Walker boasted that the resulting screen 'covered an area roughly ten miles deep all along the coast from Land's End to Cromer'. It had no effect whatever, for the simple reason that the Germans had never attempted to use pigeons to send messages *from* Britain. Walker did not mind: 'Had they done so, it is fairly certain that the loft screen would have bagged a fair proportion of them.'

Walker's pigeon reports received an enthusiastic and supportive reception from Tar Robertson. The idea of using pigeons for deception lodged somewhere in his fertile mind, and would soon take flight.

True Agent, False Agent, Double Agent

As Brutus and Bronx joined the team, and Garbo and Tricycle spun their webs tighter, it dawned on Tar Robertson that he had built a form of weaponry that could inflict some major damage. Garbo (Pujol) had bewitched the Abwehr in Madrid. Brutus (Czerniawski) (assuming he was not playing some fiendish triple game) had established a brand new channel of communication to the Germans in occupied France. Bronx (Elvira Chaudoir) was up and running, writing letters to a mysterious branch of German intelligence, and Tricycle's (Popov) hold over the Lisbon branch of the Abwehr seemed even stronger, thanks to the corruption of his case officers. In each case, the German spy-handlers were being handled, unknowingly, by the spies: Garbo was running Kühlenthal; Brutus was in control of both Bleicher and Reile; Bronx had Bleil twisted around her elegantly manicured little finger; and Tricycle knew that the greed, ambition and paranoia of von Karsthoff and Kammler had turned his relationship with the Germans through 180 degrees. The double agents were now controlling their controllers.

The B1A team would later wonder why it had taken them so long to appreciate the full potential of the Double Cross system. Masterman put it down to an obsession with 'the idea there might be a large body of spies over and above those whom we controlled'. By the summer of 1942, Robertson felt 'reasonably certain' that no such body existed. Most Secret Sources gave no hint that the Abwehr was running any spies other than those already in the Double Cross team. By 1942, almost all the traffic of German intelligence services was being read, with over 200 messages decrypted every day. From this trove of information, MI5 constructed a detailed picture of the German intelligence, its personnel, methods, strengths and frailties; they knew who their enemies were, and what they were doing and thinking. Indeed, they probably knew more about the Abwehr than the Abwehr did.

In July 1942, emboldened and increasingly ambitious for his flock, Tar Robertson made an astonishing claim: he, and not Wilhelm Canaris, controlled the German espionage network in Britain and as a consequence, he could make Hitler and his generals think what he wanted them to think. The capabilities of this 'powerful weapon' were laid out in a formal memo to the Twenty Committee: 'The only network of agents possessed by the Germans in this country is that which is now under the control of the Security Service,' he wrote. 'The Combined General Staff in this country have, in MI5 double agents, a powerful means of exercising influence over the OKW' – the Oberkommando der Wehrmacht, the Supreme Command of the German Armed Forces.

The implications of Robertson's claim were extraordinary. Hitherto, the Double Cross organisation had been used to catch more spies, extract information on German intentions, seduce the enemy into believing he already had a functioning spy network, spread propaganda, and influence enemy thinking, but only at the margins. After months of passing over chicken-feed, true but harmless, there was now an opportunity to distribute information that was methodically misleading and potentially highly destructive. What had begun with the ad hoc interception and turning of enemy agents was developing into a genuine system in which the misleading information from one double agent could be bolstered by all the others, an intricate, self-reinforcing structure that could 'fill the German files with what we want'. From the summer of 1942, the Twenty Committee began trying to influence overall German strategy, to burrow into Hitler's thoughts in a way that could cause the Germans massive, and perhaps critical, damage.

'It was always in the back of our minds,' wrote Masterman. 'That at some time in the distant future a great day would come when our agents would be used for a grand and final deception of the enemy.' For the moment, caution ruled. Canaris was known to boast about his network of agents in Britain, but the Abwehr was becoming wary: 'The enemy is becoming increasingly ruthless and penetration of agent circles is not to be ruled out,' warned the Abwehr bosses in Berlin. The interconnected nature of the Double Cross system was a source of vulnerability as well as strength. As one German intelligence officer observed: 'if one pearl is false, the whole string is false'. It would take just one mistake or betrayal to reveal to the Germans that not one, not a few, not even most, but *all* their agents were false. In that case, so far from enabling Britain's High Command to shape German thinking, Hitler would know exactly what falsehoods the British were trying to feed him, and change his plans accordingly. For all his boldness, Robertson was haunted by the knowledge that if one of his double agents was really a triple agent, then so far from unveiling a war-changing new weapon, he could be leading the Allies towards disaster: 'It is always impossible to be certain in such cases whether the Germans are fooling us or we are fooling them,' he reflected. Gisela Ashley, B1A's expert on the German mentality, sought to reassure him, insisting that while 'the Nazis are very good double-crossers', they lacked the patience and guile to set up a 'carefully and cleverly worked out system of deception'.

'The very few really important agents', it was agreed, 'should be held in readiness for a large-scale deception which could at a crucial moment be of paramount operational importance.' This 'glittering possibility', as Masterman put it, was some way off, but it could be glimpsed in the distance, and it was brought an enormous step closer by the appointment, as Britain's chief deceiver, of a man with 'the most highly polished shoes in the British army'.

Colonel J. H. Bevan, the newest member of the Twenty Committee, was a strait-laced, cricket-playing, workaholic stockbroker of rare intelligence and impeccable attire. Johnny Bevan tended to judge others by appearances, taking particular exception to slovenly uniform, but there was probably no one in the British military establishment more acutely aware that appearances can be deceptive. From May 1942, he headed the London Controlling Section, known as LCS, with orders from Winston Churchill to 'prepare deception plans on a worldwide basis' and put in train 'any matter calculated to mystify or mislead the enemy'. As Controlling Officer, Bevan would become the mastermind of wartime deception, overseeing a worldwide web of deceit and mystification from the underground warren beneath Whitehall known as the Cabinet War Rooms.

In September 1942, Bevan was inducted into the arcane world of Double Cross. For the rest of the war, the double agents, no longer an exotic sideshow, would be fully integrated into military operations. 'We had an instrument which had been tried and tested and which we could offer to the Controlling Officer for his deception plans,' wrote Masterman. Bevan played this instrument like a virtuoso.

The initial test of Tar's claim came with Operation Torch, the invasion of North Africa in November 1942, the first great Allied amphibious offensive of the war. Bevan drew up a deception plan aimed at misleading the Germans into thinking the Allies intended to attack northern France and Norway, while simultaneously attempting to relieve Malta. Among the double agents used to put across the deception were the two Norwegians, Mutt and Jeff, Tricycle's sub-agents Balloon and

Gelatine, and Tate. But the main burden fell on Garbo and his fictional network. He and his agents reported troops massing in Scotland apparently poised to attack Norway, preparations for a fictional cross-Channel assault, and numerous other titbits which, when assembled, would encourage the Germans to tie down troops far from the real point of attack. At the very least it would sow confusion. Some of Garbo's fake agents, it transpired, were simply too well placed for their own good. 'William Gerbers' was a German-Swiss businessman living in Liverpool, who had been conjured into being by Garbo before he even arrived in Britain. Ships and troops were massing in the Mersey for the invasion of North Africa where Gerbers, had he existed, would surely have seen them. How to explain that this active agent had failed to report such an obvious prelude to invasion? The solution was simple and brutal: Gerbers was first rendered extremely ill with a 'lingering malady', and then put to death. MI5 even inserted a death notice in the *Liverpool Echo*, which Pujol clipped out and sent to his handlers. The Germans sent a letter of condolence.

To maintain his growing reputation, however, Garbo needed to demonstrate access to high-grade material. He therefore sent two letters, both containing correct information: the first accurately reported a convoy leaving the Clyde on 29 October ('I fulfil my duty by advising you of this danger'); the second relayed information, obtained through the Ministry of Information, indicating an imminent invasion of French North Africa. The B1A team contrived to ensure that these arrived in Spain on the eve of the invasion, too late to be of any use.

The Germans were wholly unprepared when Allied forces landed at Casablanca, Algiers and Oran in early November. Pujol's handlers were pleased, nonetheless, by the evidence of his loyalty and efficiency, even if the postal system had stymied his efforts. 'Your last reports are all magnificent but we are sorry they arrived late, especially those relating to the Anglo-Yankee embarkation in North Africa.' Bevan was promptly promoted. But Masterman was too hard-eyed a realist to claim credit for the Double Cross team: 'The success was not primarily a triumph for deception, and still less for the double-agent system.' The Germans seemed, in fact, to have fooled themselves into thinking that the Allies lacked sufficient shipping for such an invasion. The system might not yet be powerful enough to make the enemy believe a false plan, but it had helped disguise the real plan. Here was an exhilarating foretaste of what the spies might be able to achieve in the future.

With the eye of a successful coach, Masterman looked back on the season with satisfaction. By the end of 1942 'the team was distinctly stronger', he wrote. Some impressive new players were stepping up to the crease, in the shape of Bronx and Brutus. Garbo was piling on the runs. Tricycle was back in the squad. But cricket and espionage are games of patience as well as skill. 'If the agents were ever to have their big day in the future, they had to be built up and maintained so that at the right moment we could be sure that we had a team of trusted agents who would be ready when called upon.' The players, Masterman knew, are only the most visible parts of a successful team: winning also depends on the trainers, the specialist advisers, the backroom staff.

The double agents were a mixed, even a motley crew, but the men and women who ran the Double Cross system were, in some ways, even odder. Tar Robertson deliberately gathered around him people who were out of the ordinary. Their very strangeness set them apart from the herd, reinforcing secrecy but also a sense of exclusive camaraderie that a more conventional unit would never have achieved. There was John Masterman, dry and deliberate, 'an older, wiser statesman to stop the inexperienced young hotheads from doing something totally irresponsible'. Masterman could be 'guaranteed to argue each side of an issue with total logic and lucidity' and then 'come down with a dull thud on the side of the status quo'; John Marriott, the sharp-tongued Cambridge-educated solicitor, who did little to disguise his opinion that double agents were only one step removed from crooks, and that a short one; Tommy Harris, the extrovert art dealer; Billy Luke, the pleasure-loving industrialist; Cyril Mills from the world of the circus; and Hugh Astor, the scion of a newspaper dynasty. Each had been diverted from a more orthodox military path: Christopher Harmer was almost blind in one eye and therefore precluded from advancement in the service; childhood polio had left Astor with a permanent limp; Ian Wilson could handle humanity brilliantly on paper but found personal conversation almost impossible. Gisela Ashley would have made a fine military officer, had she not had the misfortune to be a woman. Ewen Montagu was too old for frontline action, and Masterman was troubled by guilt because he had been interned in Germany during the First World War, and had missed the action, and sacrifice, that claimed so many of his contemporaries. Unable to do battle physically, they compensated by devoting their talents to a form of intellectual warfare.

From behind their desks, these men and women fought a specialist conflict 'without any training whatsoever', using language, ideas and information as others fought with guns and bombs. It was the indefatigable Gisela Ashley who urged the team to come up with ever more extravagant forms of deception, and never to underestimate the literalness of the German mind. 'What may appeal to an Englishman, even an Englishman engaged in double-crossing, as absurd, unlikely or naïve, may be the very thing that a typical Nazi would swallow and do.'

Just as the double agents lived double lives, so each officer had to try to inhabit the life of his agent. 'The case officer had to identify himself with his case,' wrote Masterman. 'He had to see with the eyes and hear with the ears of his agent; he had to suffer himself the nervous prostrations which might follow an unusually dangerous piece of espionage; he had to rejoice with his whole heart at the praise bestowed by the Germans for a successful stroke.' More than that, the case officers had to imagine themselves into the lives of their German opposite numbers, after the 'most careful psychological study'. Through Elvira Chaudoir's letters, Hugh Astor sought to understand what made Helmut Bleil, her German handler, tick; Ian Wilson found himself trying to fathom the corrupt and charming Ludovico von Karsthoff; Tommy Harris began to feel something like kinship with Karl-Erich Kühlenthal, whose eager gullibility was the key to Garbo's fictional world. These were intimate enemies.

Handling such fissile human materiel, for such high stakes, was an emotionally demanding and highly stressful business. 'We were playing with dynamite,' said Masterman. Some, like Wilson, drank too much pink gin to alleviate the strain. Everyone smoked, all the time. Yet there was also a unique brand of merriment in the cramped and smoky rooms of St James's Street, a sense that their shared mission was not only important but was occasionally fun, and frequently absurd. Gisela Ashley found herself stumped, in a message to Popov, by a reference to the 'Gonorrhoea expert without hairs'. Who could the Germans be alluding to? Popov himself was miraculously free of VD. 'This might be a heavily jocular reference to Johnny Jebsen,' Wilson suggested, with convoluted delicacy. 'What we know of his habits makes the suggested description not entirely inapt. The hair on his head is described as thick, but the reference may not be to his head.' This was, truly, a strange war.

Much of the work was done on paper, with the careful gathering and sifting of material, the drafting and redrafting of messages. The Double Cross system was, in part, a triumph of filing. Masterman insisted that 'only a well-kept record can save the agent from blunders which may "blow" him or inconsistencies which may create suspicion'. The B1A files grew to 'a truly formidable size', each one indexed and cross-referenced, since 'the messages of any one agent had to be consistent with the messages sent by him at an earlier date and not inconsistent with the messages of other agents'. The evidence on enemy intelligence officers and agents grew to more than twenty volumes, a veritable *Who's Who* of German spying. The Garbo case alone would swell to twenty-one files, more than a million pieces of paper. The Germans continued to send over spies, though in dwindling number since the existing ones were doing such a good job: Josef Terradellas, a Catalan separatist who was turned to become 'Agent Lipstick'; Waldemar Janowsky, a German landed by U-boat in Canada, was run jointly with Royal Canadian Mounted Police and MI5. The most remarkable new arrival was Eddie Chapman, the British safecracker parachuted into East Anglia in December 1942 who would become 'Agent Zigzag'. Each fresh arrival, each intercepted spy, each potential new double agent, added to the strength of the system, and the mountain of paper.

With some trepidation, it was decided to introduce Winston Churchill to the Double Cross story. The hesitation did not spring from any sense that the Prime Minister was uninterested in spies. Quite the reverse; he was fascinated by deception, and would look back on wartime espionage with glee: 'Tangle within tangle, plot and counter-plot, ruse and treachery, cross and double-cross, true agent, false agent, double agent, gold and steel, the bomb, the dagger and the firing party, were interwoven in many a texture so intricate as to be incredible and yet true.' In fact, Churchill was far *too* interested in the delicate business of espionage, and there was a danger he might interfere. The Twenty Committee was unofficially approved by Churchill, but not subject to ministerial responsibility. That way, the committee 'could not claim to have been "authorised" to do' what they were doing, much of which was, strictly speaking, illegal. Today this would be called 'plausible deniability'. The arrangement gave the Double Cross team unusual freedom, and it kept Churchill at arm's length. When it was first proposed that the Prime Minister should be informed of what was actually going on, Guy Liddell, the head of B Section, feared that he might, 'on seeing some particular item, go off the deep end and want to take action, which will be disastrous to the work in hand'. But by the beginning of 1943, the system was running so well, its potential so great, and its substance so certain to appeal to Churchill's vivid imagination, that it was agreed to introduce him to the cast and the drama, a little at a time.

The first monthly report to Winston Churchill, in March 1943, offered an espionage inventory. 'In all, 126 spies have fallen into our hands. Of these, twenty-four have been found amenable and are now being used as Double Cross agents. In addition twelve real, and seven imaginary persons have been foisted upon the enemy as Double Cross spies. Thirteen spies have been executed.' The report described Garbo, Zigzag and Mutt and Jeff, who had just received a wireless, £200 in notes and sabotage equipment via parachute in a remote Scottish glen. Churchill was riveted. Across the report he scrawled: 'Deeply interesting'.

In time, he would be introduced to Tricycle, Brutus and Bronx. The reports were drafted by Anthony Blunt, who drew up a long version which was then boiled down for the Prime Minister; Agent Tony also passed the information to his Soviet handlers. Stalin was fully versed in the Double Cross system: indeed, as Christopher Andrew, the authorised historian of MI5, writes, the Soviet leader may well have 'seen more detailed reports than Churchill'.

The Prime Minister's marginalia showed why it had been wise not to get him too involved, too early. When informed that a clerk at the Portuguese Embassy was spying for both the Germans and Italians, he wrote: 'Why don't you shoot him?' But Churchill did not go off the deep end; instead he was gradually immersed in the story, the strange tale of cross and double cross, true agent, false agent, double agent.

Elvira Chaudoir was shaping up to be a 'very competent letter-writing agent', reported Masterman. The tap on her telephone had produced 'no evidence of any pro-German sentiments' and was maintained 'merely to keep an eye on her financial position'. This was, as usual, dire. Unpaid bills from various nightclubs showed that Elvira was enjoying her return to London's 'high spots'. 'She plays bridge or poker every night, principally at the Hamilton Club or Crockford's, obviously for high stakes,' her MI5 minder reported. 'She is not engaged in any sinister activity', although he added: 'It is not known whether she is continuing in her Lesbian tendencies.' (She was.)

Under the watchful eye of Hugh Astor, she began sending letters in secret ink to Helmut Bleil, care of the Banco Santo Espirito in Lisbon and the Hôtel de Paris in Monte Carlo. The cover letters consisted of 'completely meaningless feminine chat', according to Astor. 'This text is so much in her own style (which is very far removed from anything I could produce) that in my opinion any attempt to interfere with it would be liable to show that the text was written under control.' Between the lines, writing in capital letters with a matchstick dipped in secret ink, she began to record items that might be of interest to Bleil. Initially, her observations were banal: 'Last week I saw a man unloading a lorry full of foodstuffs into an old empty house next to the church at Roehampton.' But as she grew more confident, she and Astor began to insert half-truths, rumours, elements of propaganda and harmless military details. 'Her friends are to be found in any of the smart bridge clubs in London,' wrote Astor, and 'as a friend of several English "socialites" she has been in a position to pick up much indiscreet gossip from Government circles.' Among her acquaintance were aristocrats such as Lord Carnarvon, the Duke of Marlborough, Duff Cooper, Head of the Security Executive, and a number of senior military officers.

In addition to reporting items of interest she had really heard, with Astor's guidance Elvira made up additional snippets and attributed them to individuals she might plausibly claim to have met, including Churchill's son-in-law and the Chairman of a War Cabinet Committee, Duncan Sandys, and the press barons Lords Beaverbrook and Kelmsley. As ever, MI5 had no scruples about putting words in the mouths of real people. 'We took great care to make every detail as authentic as possible,' Astor later recalled. 'I'm afraid we took the names of a good many people in vain. We certainly suggested that the [former] War Minister, Oliver Stanley, and peers such as Lord Lovat and Lord Mountbatten were among her circle of friends. Of course, they had no idea Bronx was attributing some splendid indiscretions to them. If they'd known, they'd have been furious.' To supplement her income, Elvira wrote vigorously anti-Nazi articles for the British popular press, for which she apologised to Bleil in her secret letters: 'I hope you won't mind reading my article in *Sunday Graphic* as it was essential that I should get the reputation for hating Germany.'

The sum of £100 soon landed in her Swiss bank account, the first monthly payment from the Germans. It was a drop in the ocean of her debts. Harmer advised the MI5 accountants to be generous: 'As she is a woman with expensive tastes, we would come off better if we allowed her to keep what the Germans sent her.' The deposits to her account arrived with 'satisfactory regularity', but they were always 'minus several hundred pounds' suggesting that 'somebody on their side is taking a rake-off'. This fresh evidence of corruption planted the seed of an idea. Bronx sent a letter suggesting that Bleil or his associates should send her a large sum of money that she could invest, on their behalf, on the British stock exchange. 'It was hoped that an unscrupulous member of the Abwehr might see in this an opportunity of getting capital out of Germany' and creating 'a nest egg for after the war'. The money, of course, would be appropriated, enabling the case to become self-financing and solving her money problems. Elvira, needless to say, was enthusiastic about the plan, and extremely cross when her German handlers 'ignored this suggestion'. The Germans might be gullible, but they were not so foolish as to employ a woman with a gambling habit as a secret stockbroker.

Initially Elvira's reports consisted of economic morsels: as time went on, her range widened to include reports on political and military affairs. Her letters were a strange, almost surreal, mixture of the mundane, the personal and the important. 'Tank production retarded by lack of tracks,' she reported. 'Heavily in debt. Canadian invasion practices in Scotland. Increased number of American troops in London. Shortage of kitchen utensils.' She insisted on swift and regular payments: 'Money must be sent at beginning of month. Serious risk and no claims for expenses.' When the Germans asked for information on gas warfare defences, she gave 'a glowing account of the excellence of British preparations' and pointed out that 'the British had developed large stockpiles of chemical weapons to retaliate if the Germans resorted to a gas attack'. Masterman believed her report had helped to dissuade the Germans from mounting a gas attack, possibly saving many lives and proving that 'we can in some instances influence and perhaps change the operational intentions of the enemy'.

The only fly in the ointment sat in the secret intelligence service next door. Claude Dansey, deputy chief of MI6, took every opportunity to poison his protégée's mind against MI5, telling her that she was being grossly underpaid. 'He has apparently said that he did not think we were working along the right lines,' Astor reported through gritted teeth. 'It is interesting to note that the case is being supervised by Dansey in this indirect manner.' Interesting, and extremely annoying. A formal complaint was lodged, which only encouraged Dansey to redouble his interference.

MI5 began to wonder whether it was Bleil, or someone pretending to be him, who replied with letters in secret ink, praising her work. 'We have no knowledge of which section is running Bronx or who are the officers in control of her case,' wrote Astor. Even so, references to a female agent, 'a member of the international smart gambling set', began to appear in Most Secret Sources, indicating satisfaction at a high level with this new spy at the heart of the British social scene. 'Bronx is believed to be a reliable agent,' Astor recorded. 'It may be of course that Bleil or the officers running her know, or assume, that she is under control, but there is every reason to believe that the HQ at Berlin are led to believe that she is a reliable agent.' Six months after her return to Britain, Elvira was given a formal seal of approval: 'The evidence suggests that the Germans believe in Bronx.'

The clouds of doubt surrounding Agent Brutus took longer to disperse. The radio technicians of B1A constructed a wireless using the crystals he had brought from France, and under close supervision, Roman Czerniawski made his first radio contact with Paris shortly before Christmas 1942. The enthusiastic response from Oscar Reile, his German handler, suggested he had complete confidence in his agent. The same could not be said of the British, who still wondered whether the Germans had sent him to the UK knowing he would switch sides. 'They had studied him from the psychological standpoint,' Masterman observed. 'If they convinced themselves that he had thrown them over, his traffic from this country could be a source of great danger to us' since they would read his messages 'in reverse'. If, for example, he passed on evidence of an attack on Denmark, then the Germans, knowing he was controlled, would conclude that Denmark was safe. The Twenty Committee ruled that Brutus should be run 'sparingly' and not used for operational deception. He would be 'allowed to lead a free and normal life', but under close scrutiny, his telephone bugged and his mail opened. The Polish intelligence service also put him under surveillance. One false move, and he would be joining Mathilde Carré in prison.

Czerniawski was eagerly cooperative, and happily resumed a life of full-time espionage. Unlike so many of the spies sent

to Britain, Brutus was a professional military observer. His
first reports gave details of the Polish armed forces in Britain
(which the Germans already knew) and political attitudes
within the Polish community. After a month, he visited
Scotland, and sent a description of military deployments in
the north, which the Germans hailed as 'exceedingly good'.
This was followed by a 'lengthy report on the south coast'.
These field trips followed a pattern: Czerniawski, accompanied
by his case officer (initially Harmer, and later Astor), would
tour a given area, and then draw up his genuine observations
and discoveries, complete with maps, insignia, and even the
identities of individual commanding officers. Much of this
information was far too important to be passed on to the
Germans: the Twenty Committee would whittle it down, and
add new touches, which Czerniawski would translate into his
own distinctive 'telegraph French'. Sometimes he operated the
wireless himself, at others he was mimicked by one of B1A's
radio operators: 'Brutus is very easy to imitate because he
is a very bad operator and commits very distinctive faults.'
His messages to Colonel Reile were larded with self-praise:
'Several of my old agents who work in this country are very
discontented on account of their treatment at the hands of the
British. They are still bound to me by intense personal loyalty
and will work for me without question.'

Czerniawski continued to behave as if the destiny of
Poland lay in his hands, insisting he would continue to spy
for Germany only 'if I have your government's undertaking,
after the defeat of the Allies, to offer through me to the Polish
government liberal peace terms'. There were moments of high
anxiety. Whoever was operating the transmitter at the German
end sometimes tried to trip him up, to test if Czerniawski was
really the recipient: 'Every now and then they'd send us a trick
question. "What is the name of your mother-in-law? When
was she born?"' Astor noticed that when Czerniawski was
operating the transmitter himself, he spelled London in the

French way, 'Londres', but left off the s. Could this be his control signal, the distinctive 'mistake' to alert his German masters that he was operating under British control? Astor casually asked him to address a handful of envelopes to London addresses: it soon became apparent that Czerniawski simply couldn't spell. Gradually, the fear that Czerniawski was working with the Germans ebbed: 'Almost certainly Brutus did not have a triple-cross mission,' wrote Harmer. 'His position as a German agent is clear. Namely, he is working for us.'

The secondary anxiety, that the Germans might suspect he was working for the British, lingered longer. Three months after the first radio transmission, Robertson was still feeling 'a little anxious about Brutus', keen to use him in active deception, but worried that in so doing they 'might warn the Germans instead of deceiving them'. He wanted 'evidence that he is fully trusted by the Germans, in which case he would be eligible for use in deception'. Most Secret Sources duly obliged, revealing that Abwehr reports on Agent Hubert contained 'no qualification to suggest that the source was not a genuine one'. Berlin described him as a 'very valuable wireless agent'. Brutus was becoming a trusted source of military intelligence. 'As confidence grew both in him, and in the Germans' belief in him, he was used more and more.'

While Czerniawski's stock rose with both his British and German spymasters, it plunged to new lows within the Polish government-in-exile. He 'threw his weight about and gave himself airs' and was 'at loggerheads with all the other officers'. Harmer had grown fond of this bull-headed Pole, but had to concede 'he is a vain and conceited man who spent a considerable period of the war in exciting activities and now found himself doing a largely academic job'. Colonel Gano, the head of Polish intelligence, wanted this 'infernal nuisance' sent on a mission to Persia to get him out of the way: 'He spends his whole time making very damaging criticisms of other people's work [and] is inordinately ambitious, prying into everything.'

Within weeks of arriving in Britain, he was 'embroiled in Polish politics' which, as in many small and unhappy expatriate communities, were deeply rancorous. Czerniawski espoused 'extreme anti-Bolshevism', lecturing anyone and everyone on the iniquities of the Soviet regime. He was a pathological plotter, reflected Harmer, and dreamed of setting up a new network, this time to mislead the Germans. He suggested that he recruit his lover Monique as a sub-agent. Harmer firmly told him to do nothing of the sort, and 'sensed that he was hurt'. Restless, troublesome and self-important, Czerniawski needed another outlet for his boundless capacity for intrigue. He soon found one, with calamitous results.

To mark the twenty-fifth anniversary of the founding of the Red Army, General Stanislas Ujejski, Inspector General of the Polish Air Force, attended a reception at the Soviet Embassy in London. Anti-Soviet feeling was running high among Polish expatriates after the Katyn massacre, in which thousands of Polish officers had been murdered on Stalin's orders. Czerniawski was outraged by what he saw as Ujejski's cosying up to a murderous regime. In early June, he wrote a blistering attack on the General entitled 'In Defence of our Colleagues', ran off hundreds of copies, and distributed them throughout London. His denunciation was written in pungent style, littered with exclamation marks, and calculated to cause maximum offence, which it did. 'The Soviets committed terrible crimes against the Poles. These Red soldiers ill-treated Polish women and bestially murdered thousands of our defenceless colleagues. It is unworthy for the head of the Polish Air Force to go to a tea party where they danced on the newly made graves of many Polish soldiers.' Ujejski was attacked as an overpaid, immoral, flattering coward, who should be sacked. 'The Polish Air Force deserves a better leader.' This was a resounding political polemic. It was also an act of mutiny.

Within hours of distributing his 'pamphlet', Czerniawski was arrested by the Metropolitan Police Special Branch at the request of the Polish government and charged with 'the gravest military indiscipline'. His flat was searched, and Czerniawski was imprisoned in Scotland to await court martial. His enemies in Polish intelligence rejoiced that the 'little tin-pot hero' was getting his comeuppance. Christopher Harmer and Tar Robertson were appalled. Just as Brutus was developing into a first-class double agent, he had brought matters to a screeching halt and now 'threatened the extinction of the case'.

Harmer rushed to his prison cell and found Czerniawski quite unrepentant, declaring pompously that 'any patriotic Pole would have done likewise'. When Harmer ticked him off for 'meddling in affairs which were not within his province', Czerniawski insisted 'it was the duty of someone to expose this, and he was the only person in a position to do so'. He seemed to be relishing the attention, and positively proud of stirring up a hornet's nest. From his cell he wrote letters to Monique 'which demonstrate a desire to dramatise himself and his life and a capacity for exhibitionism which almost shows the first signs of delusions of grandeur'.

If Czerniawski's radio suddenly fell silent, the Germans would assume he had been caught. A message, mimicking Brutus's wireless style, was immediately sent to Paris, reporting that he and other anti-Bolshevik Poles were suspected of distributing anti-Soviet propaganda. 'I foresee my arrest as very probable. I am hoping for the best but the situation is very dangerous.' Two weeks later, he sent another message: '20th June arrested in the clandestine anti-Russian affair. Detained in Scotland. Await trial. Foresee light punishment. Fear I am being watched at present. Until the end of the trial too dangerous to transmit. I regret difficulties. Morale good. Am hopeful.' This would explain his absence from the airwaves, and was sufficiently near the truth to be plausible if the Germans got wind of his arrest. Whether they would actually believe him was another matter entirely. Harmer was gloomy, and doubted 'whether the Germans will ever accept Brutus as one hundred per cent reliable'. Awaiting trial on charges of 'indiscipline and offensiveness to superior officers', Czerniawski suffered a (brief) moment of contrition, and apologised 'for the harm he had done to the great game'.

His career as a double agent was over, at least for now. Brutus had managed to stab himself in the back.

Cockade

Garbo's (Pujol) network grew more and more elaborate, as new fictitious spies were added to his roster. The widow of Wilhelm Gerbers, the spy killed off in Liverpool, stepped in to take his place; 'Agent Dagobert', the 'undesirable' Swansea seaman, began recruiting his own sub-agents, eventually assembling a team of seven. Most importantly, Garbo enrolled a radio operator. Letters in secret ink were slow and cumbersome; a wireless link would speed up communication with Madrid. Garbo told his German handlers that the Gibraltarian waiter, 'Fred', had found a friend, a Spanish Republican, with a wireless set he was prepared to operate on Pujol's behalf. In reality, the set was operated by Charles Haines, a former Lloyds Bank clerk and amateur radio ham now in the Intelligence Corps Field Security Section.

The Germans provided Pujol with a code, which Liddell described as 'perhaps the highest-grade cipher ever used by the Abwehr'. The volume and speed of the Garbo traffic increased exponentially. 'The one-man band of Lisbon developed an orchestra which played a more and more ambitious programme,' wrote Masterman. A report to Churchill sang the Spaniard's praises: 'Garbo himself works on average from six to eight hours a day – drafting secret letters, enciphering, composing cover texts, writing them and planning for the future. Fortunately, he has a facile and lurid style, great ingenuity and a passionate and quixotic zeal for his task.' Everyone, it seemed, was pleased with

Juan Pujol, except Mrs Pujol. For while his secret life flourished, his domestic life was floundering.

Aracelli Pujol was lonely, homesick and fractious. She was banned from contact with London's Spanish community lest she let something slip. She spoke no English, had no friends and seldom left the house in Crespigny Road. Tommy Harris disliked 'Mrs G', describing Aracelli as a 'hysterical, spoilt and selfish woman'. But her complaints were not unreasonable: her husband was up at dawn and worked late; when he finally came home to Hendon, he was exhausted and irritable; she was expected to cook, clean and look after their son. She threatened to leave him, but had nowhere to go. Number 35 Crespigny Road echoed to the sound of raised Spanish voices and breaking crockery. The Pujols' relationship was under the sort of strain familiar to many marriages, the only difference being that their domestic disharmony represented a direct threat to the Double Cross project. Juan Pujol was not the only man to use 'winning the war' as an excuse for neglecting his wife. But in his case, it happened to be true.

Aracelli first asked, then pleaded, and finally demanded to be allowed to return to Spain, if only 'for a week'. Harris was coldly unsympathetic, suggesting she was 'unbalanced'. Aracelli snapped. On 21 June 1942, she telephoned Harris and threatened to destroy the entire Garbo network by revealing his activities to the Spanish diplomatic authorities: 'I am telling you for the last time that if at this time tomorrow you haven't got me my papers ready for me to leave the country immediately – because I don't want to live another five minutes longer with my husband – I will go to the Spanish Embassy. I shall have the satisfaction that I have spoiled everything. Do you understand? I don't want to live another day in England.' Harris certainly did understand. Aracelli had to be stopped. He arranged for the Spanish Embassy to be put under surveillance, so she could be arrested if she appeared there. He also considered warning the Spanish Embassy that 'a woman of Mrs G's description is anxious to assassinate the Ambassador [which] would ensure her being flung out if she attempted to go to the Embassy'. Liddell thought it might be best to lock her up. Robertson wondered whether to go to Crespigny Road himself and 'read her the Riot Act'. Even Churchill was informed of the 'outburst of jealousy' from Mrs Garbo and her threat to 'ruin the whole undertaking'. But it was Pujol himself who came up with a drastic plan to subdue his wife by subterfuge.

The next day, a Special Branch officer arrived at Number 35 and told Aracelli that her husband was under arrest, and that he needed to collect his toothbrush and pyjamas. Juan Pujol had tried to quit as a double agent, the officer explained, because she had threatened to 'give the whole show away'. The belief that she had caused her husband's arrest produced a 'hysterical outburst' from Aracelli. She telephoned Harris in floods of tears and insisted that 'her husband had always been loyal to this country and would willingly sacrifice his life for our cause'. Later that day, she was found by Charles Haines in the kitchen filled with fumes from the gas oven, an apparent suicide bid which Harris coldly dismissed as 'ninety per cent play-acting'. Weeping and distraught, poor Aracelli's capitulation was complete. 'She pleaded that it was she who had been at fault and that if her husband could be pardoned she promised she would never again interfere with his work, or behave badly, or ask to return to Spain.' Pujol's plan had been brutal, effective and revealing: beneath his gentle manner, he was absolutely dedicated and quite ruthless, prepared to go to extreme lengths to preserve the network he had created, even if that meant double-crossing his own wife.

Dusko Popov, as ever, was living in 'considerable comfort'. He moved into Clock House, a charming cottage in Knightsbridge, which he rented for twelve guineas a week, and recommenced his affair with, among others, Gwennie, whose passionate missives were intercepted and copied by MI5: 'Please try to be ¼ way decent till I can pick up where I broke off. You are a sweetie and I love you (a little) Gwennie.' He was simultaneously conducting an affair with 'Mairi', who lived on Park Lane, and a young Yugoslavian woman from a wealthy family, Ljiljana Bailoni. (Popov would 'undoubtedly be an easier agent to run if he became a little more settled in his domestic habits', sighed Wilson.) He was heartily congratulated by von Karsthoff for the legibility and content of his secret letters: 'Your writing is wonderful . . . we can read every word.' His business, Tarlair, was booming, although even Gisela Ashley, monitoring Popov's activities, found it hard to keep track of exactly how the company worked. 'He gets particularly obscure when discussing matters of international finance,' John Marriott noted. Popov's debts, large and small, trailed after him: more than $10,000 still owing to the FBI, several thousand more to MI6 in New York, several hundred dollars to the Long Island Telephone Company and $215 to 'Trivett's Tested Seeds'. He paid none of them. He simply forwarded the bills to MI5, along with his tailor's invoice for eighteen silk shirts and a dozen monogrammed handkerchiefs.

The tide of war was turning. Popov could feel it in the 'humour and spirit of Londoners'. The great counter-attack against occupied Europe was in sight: 'Everyone, the Germans included, knew the invasion was coming.' Again, he lobbied his spymasters to recruit Johnny Jebsen, pointing out that once his friend 'realised that Germany was going to lose the war he would be only too willing to re-insure himself with the victors by telling them all he could'. Popov offered to make the approach himself, on his next visit to Lisbon: 'Johnny has never been pro-Nazi,' he insisted, and had access to high-grade information including 'full details of the personnel of the Abwehr and its agents in many countries'. Wilson had qualms about Jebsen's suspect financial activities – 'Johnny is always carrying out various more or less irregular deals as well as acting as an agent of the Abwehr' – but he was tempted by the prospect of recruiting an 'amoral,

opportunist and not particularly Nazi' informant within the
Abwehr at this critical juncture. Wilson toyed with getting Popov
to offer a promise 'to arrange for Johnny to receive favourable
treatment, providing that Johnny has something worthwhile to
sell to the British'. Jebsen had recruited Popov; now Popov might
recruit Jebsen. 'The Germans regard their personal friendship as
an essential part of the set-up,' Wilson observed, and if Jebsen
really was as anti-Nazi as Popov said, then he might make a
useful double agent himself: 'We must seek to take advantage of
Jebsen's outlook.'

As the winter of 1942 closed in, Popov described himself
as 'the shabbiest and coldest man in London', a statement that
was demonstrably untrue. He amused himself by demanding
additional luxuries, and wrote to Colonel 'Freckles' Wren of
MI6 in New York:

> My heart is in very bad condition. My doctor who is my
> biggest friend says it is too much alcohol, tobacco and sin.
> The only remedy which I found efficient until now was
> milk and chocolates. Please send $100 worth of any kind
> of chocolate you can think of. I don't mind what they are.
> I am taking them as medicine. Please send me at the same
> time $100 of Nylons in 9, 9½ and 10 (Don't think I'm
> promiscuous.)

Wren did not swallow Popov's claim of a medical chocolate
emergency. 'The chocolates are intended to delight the interiors
of those same exteriors which he wishes to decorate with
stockings.' But it was a measure of Popov's status that he could
instruct the British secret services to buy nylons for him, and
they grudgingly obliged.

> We have done our best to carry out Tricycle's wishes with
> regard to comforts for his lovelies, but I have a strong feeling
> that this kind of business should now stop. It is legitimate for

an agent working abroad to supply douceurs if it is necessary to do so in the interests of the state at war: I cannot see how that principle can apply to Tricycle. Do you think it would be possible to bring home to Tricycle the fact that his country and we have a right to his unselfish duty?

Tar Robertson was indulgent, arguing that 'Tricycle has the Balkan outlook that all positions of influence can be turned to personal advantage'. To make matters worse, Popov's American creditors discovered that he worked for the British government in some capacity, and the Keystone Debt Collection Agency had begun demanding payment of his unpaid bills through diplomatic channels. 'The one thing that does strike me as urgent is that we should stop the debt collection agency trying to dun Tricycle further through the British Ministry of Information,' wrote Tar. Trivett's Tested Seeds finally got what it was owed, unaware that it had successfully extracted money from British intelligence.

At a meeting with Wilson in February, Popov announced 'his desire to do something more active in the way of outwitting the Germans', and was told there was 'certainly no intention of letting his case vegetate'. Popov asked to be parachuted into Yugoslavia to join the Chetnik partisans, insisting 'he was ready to take almost any risks to achieve anything that would be really useful'. The request was turned down. Popov was too valuable to be risked, but his demands and complaints, his restlessness and sexual shenanigans, his 'white silk shirts with soft collars and fancy ties' were starting to try even Wilson's vast reserves of tolerance: 'Tricycle is continuing to make an infernal nuisance of himself.' So it was agreed to send him back to Portugal.

'Every Double Cross agent is inclined to be vain, moody and introspective,' wrote Masterman, but these volatile personalities were proving ever harder to handle. One of the most important members of the team had got himself arrested, another was in the throes of a spectacular marital bust-up, and a third was demanding women, chocolates and silk shirts while living the life of a pampered prince. Even Elvira Chaudoir was asking for more money, and flirting with MI6. The constant need to monitor, cajole, flatter and sustain these difficult people was taking a toll. However, the effort, expense and frustration would all be worthwhile if the Double Cross spies managed to deceive the Germans into making some large and disastrous mistake.

At the Casablanca Conference in January 1943, the Allies agreed that a cross-Channel invasion could not be undertaken before the spring of 1944. The main thrust for 1943 would be into Italy, via Sicily, while Stalin's Red Army continued the epic battle in the East. The Germans knew that an invasion of France was only a matter of time, and were already laying plans to reinforce the Atlantic Wall with millions of tonnes of cement and steel, using slave labour. They could not know that the Allies had decided to focus elsewhere in 1943, and therein lay an opportunity.

A deception plan, codenamed 'Cockade', was drawn up by the London Controlling Section to mount bogus threats to Norway and northern France, in the hope of drawing off German troops from the Mediterranean and the Eastern Front, or at least pinning down those in northern Europe. In early September, a mock invasion fleet would set sail from Kent and Hampshire apparently heading for Calais, to draw the Luftwaffe into battle over the Channel; another fake invasion force, this time American, would threaten Brittany, while a third fake force would threaten Norway. The central plank of the deception was to be nailed down by planting false information through the double agents. Cockade was not quite the grand roll of the dice envisaged by Masterman, but it was the most ambitious gamble so far.

The B1A team sprang into action. Von Karsthoff's messages to Popov indicated that 'invasion questions are no doubt what the enemy is chiefly interested in'. Therefore 'he ought to be supplied with a lot of items from which it is possible to draw all sorts of inferences about our future intentions'. Popov was again 'in his best mood', and looking forward to seeing Jebsen again. 'He should be back here in time to put over some really effective misinformation when invasion of the Continent becomes imminent,' wrote Wilson. In July, Popov flew to Lisbon once more (leaving MI5 to pay his overdue rent), carrying a briefcase full of hints indicating that an invasion of France was at hand: his tailor told him senior officers were ordering new battledress, hospitals were preparing beds, and electrically propelled canoes were being manufactured in large numbers. He told von Karsthoff he had 'taken his girlfriends to different south coast towns on various weekends', and in Southampton he spotted that shelters were being prepared for a retaliatory air attack, indicating the port would be 'active as a supply base for the invading army'.

Popov's sub-agents, Gelatine and Balloon, added corroborative details, while Mutt and Jeff, the two Norwegians, reported that Norway was under threat of attack from Scotland. Bronx relayed invasion gossip picked up from politicians, journalists and others, including a conversation with an invented Harley Street surgeon called Nielson, who told her of 'hospital arrangements for an invasion in autumn'. On 11 July, she wrote: 'France to be attacked in September. Increased production of invasion barges. Good harvest and increase in pig farming.' The reply congratulated her: 'Pleased with work. Exact details on invasion, will pay expenses of travel for this.'

The Garbo network reported concentrations of troops in Wales and Scotland, while Pujol himself claimed to have seen seven divisions near Brighton (though he was careful to point out this might be just an exercise); his sub-agents spotted assault craft gathering in the Channel ports, military camps near Southampton and torpedo boats massing in Dover.

On Robertson's orders, even Flight Lieutenant Walker's pigeons were enrolled into the deception. For some time, British intelligence had been dropping homing pigeons into occupied France carrying questionnaires about German defences, 'in the hope that at least some of them will fall into the hands of people who are supporters of the Allied cause', who were urged to fill out the forms and release the birds to fly back across the Channel. The pigeons were dropped by parachute, in cardboard containers, each with a small bag of corn. 'I gather some satisfactory results have been obtained from the answers to these questionnaires,' wrote Robertson. 'But some fall into the hands of the enemy.' Any method of seeking the truth can also be used to plant a lie. 'It occurs to me that this is a possible means of putting deception over to the enemy by the careful framing of the questionnaires, as presumably the Germans must, if they capture some of these birds, take notice of the kind of question being asked.'

Robertson gave orders that 'the questionnaire carried by pigeons dropped in the Pas de Calais and west coast areas should convey the impression that we are very keen on getting detailed intelligence about these areas in beach and coast defences, airfields, focal points on road and rail communications, detailed locations of formation headquarters and units, bridges, ports and installations for demolition etc.'. The Germans would read this, and assume an imminent invasion. Walker prepared his flock, and in August more than a thousand homing pigeons, each carrying a list of questions deliberately framed to suggest a looming attack, were dropped in a flapping deluge on Calais and Brittany. 'The mere fact of increasing the number of pigeons used has a certain deceptive value,' Robertson gleefully reported.

Finally, the day of the dummy invasion arrived. On 8 September, Agent Garbo reported that troops had been confined to barracks and assault craft were gathering. A mock invasion flotilla of some thirty ships headed for France, preceded by mine-sweepers. With information coming in from all sides, the Germans surely could not fail to think that a huge invasion was taking place.

But that is exactly what happened.

In response to the great charade the Germans did . . . nothing at all. The shore batteries did not open up, the Luftwaffe did not take to the air, and the High Command did not redeploy troops from places where they were needed. As one British officer wryly remarked: 'It was an inspiring sight to see everybody doing his stuff to perfection . . . except, unfortunately, the Germans.' The only indication that they even noticed the elaborate performance put on for their benefit came when 'a German coast-artillery subaltern on the far shore [was] overheard calling his captain on the radio to ask if anybody knew what all this fuss was about'. About ten miles off Boulogne, the bogus invasion force stopped, waited for the Germans to do something and, when they didn't, trailed home.

From the Allied point of view the attempted deception was 'disappointing in the extreme', not to say downright humiliating. It would later emerge that instead of reinforcing their defences in light of a perceived threat, the Germans had actually reduced their troop numbers in the run-up to the mock invasion, apparently convinced that there were still insufficient troops in Britain for a full-scale invasion. Garbo scrambled to cover his back with a message to his German handler: 'It appears the operation has been suspended. Troops surprised and disappointed.'

Cockade was a cock-up, but the Double Cross team could extract some crumbs of comfort. Popov seemed even more firmly in favour with his German bosses, and Garbo's credibility was actually reinforced by the farce. 'Your activity and that of your informants gave us a perfect idea of what is taking place over there,' enthused Kühlenthal, who was becoming infected by Garbo's rococo prose style. 'These reports, as you can imagine, have an incalculable value and for this reason I beg of you to proceed with the greatest care so as not to endanger in these momentous times either yourself or your organisation.' Messages marked 'urgent' were being relayed from the Garbo network to Berlin in under an hour. 'There can be no doubt of the high standing which Garbo enjoys with his masters,' Johnny Bevan told Tar Robertson. 'Garbo will have a very important role to play in the future.'

Some useful lessons were learned from the failed plan: any future deception would have to involve every branch of the military, to the fullest extent, on a far wider scale; no fake invasion would be believed unless a real one was taking place at the same time. The Double Cross players would have to up their game. Despite the disappointment, Masterman eagerly 'looked forward to the day when we should take part in the great final deception'. The episode also instilled fresh confidence in Tar Robertson, along with a profound, but not entirely helpful belief in 'the actual uses that Pigeons can be put to from the point of view of espionage'.

Discovered Treasure

Kenneth Benton was, formally speaking, His Majesty's Passport Control Officer in Madrid, in charge of visas, immigration and customs formalities. In reality he worked for MI6, recruiting agents and potential double agents and, with his wife Peggie, also an MI6 officer, organising a rich range of skulduggery to confound German espionage in the Iberian Peninsula. His opposite number in Madrid, Karl-Erich Kühlenthal, considered him a 'sly fox', a description that Benton had read in Most Secret Sources, and found rather flattering.

At 10.30 on the morning of 17 July 1943, Benton's secretary, Mollie Gillard, rang through to say that there was someone in the Embassy reception demanding an urgent interview to sort out a visa. Moments later, a 'rather attractive woman of about thirty' was ushered into his office, carrying a small white dog. The visitor perched on a chair with a creaking wicker back, the dog on her knee.

'My name is Benton,' said Benton. 'If what I understood is correct you wish to go to England to rejoin your family.'

'Not exactly,' said the young woman. 'I'm going there to spy.'

In good English, Lily Sergeyev described her recruitment in Paris by Major Emile Kliemann as 'Agent Solange', her training in the use of a wireless and secret ink, and her spying mission to Britain: she now wished to swap sides.

They sized one another up. Lily saw a 'classic example of "the Englishman": young, tall, and slim, with a long narrow head and a straight brow with thinning red hair'. Benton saw a typical Frenchwoman, 'made up and dressed to kill', with a self-dramatising manner, but clearly intelligent. He wondered whether she might be 'first and foremost a self-server'. During pauses in the conversation, she whispered remarks, in Russian, to her dog.

Lily explained that, as instructed by Kliemann, she had made contact with an Abwehr agent in Madrid, a man she knew only as 'Hans'. Kliemann himself had promised to bring a wireless to Madrid. He was late.

Benton told Lily to report back to Hans, and tell him that the British authorities had agreed to issue a visa, but the process might take several weeks. She should then wait for Kliemann to arrive. That afternoon, Benton sent a coded telegram to London, describing his meeting with Lily Sergeyev, and asking whether MI5 might have any use for her. He himself was 'doubtful'.

Benton's doubts were shared by John Masterman. 'I should be very cautious about agreeing that she should become a double agent working for us,' he wrote. 'She ought to be thoroughly interrogated and a full account obtained of her activities before we decide we can use her.' MI5 began a background check, interviewing people in Britain who knew Lily. 'She has respectable friends and relatives,' noted Tar, but these offered a contradictory picture of her loyalties. Virginia Hall, an American SOE agent who had known the Sergeyevs in Paris before the war, said she suspected that Lily was 'pro-German'. Anthony Blunt, who also knew her slightly, described Lily as 'a White Russian with slightly left views' (which was rich, coming from him). Her cousin, Dr Elizabeth Hill, who lived in Cambridge, was 'perfectly sure that Lily was pro-Allied in her sympathies', and thought her 'something of an adventuress, but an exceedingly clever girl'.

The person assigned to investigate Lily Sergeyev was Mary Sherer, the latest addition to Tar's team and the only woman case officer in B1A (though she was denied full officer status). Mary Corrie Sherer was twenty-nine, robust, ambitious, and with a sharp sense of humour 'often at other people's expense'. She joined MI5 as a secretary in 1938, and spent the first part of the war in the counter-sabotage section and working for British Security Coordination in New York, the clandestine arm of MI6, MI5 and SOE that sought to bring America into the war by means of propaganda, blackmail and espionage. A child of the Indian Raj and the daughter of a brigadier, Mary was military in bearing, and often wore a red jacket with epaulettes which she thought made her look like a general. She walked with a long, martial stride, swinging her arms, and humming little songs to herself when she thought no one could hear. In a male world, she assumed a carapace of toughness, smoking filterless Kent cigarettes and holding her gin as well as the next man. 'Mary was someone you did not want to cross, and was not quick to forgive any misdoings.' But there was also a gentleness to her, and a resolute sense of purpose.

After conducting the background check on Lily Sergeyev, Sherer concluded: 'She appears to be a character well-suited to becoming a double agent.' Mary Sherer 'had a great deal of character', according to Benton, and not for the last time she stood up to her sceptical male bosses, insisting that a woman double agent, equipped with her own wireless and a gullible German handler, would be highly valuable in the run-up to the Allied invasion of northwest Europe. Mary gave her the codename 'Treasure'.

After nearly two months in Madrid, Lily was becoming oppressed by a city 'full of menace and intrigue; a place where everyone is plotting, betraying, bribing or selling themselves'. She urged Hans, her Abwehr contact, to tell Kliemann to come quickly. Still he did not appear. 'I have got very good at lying,' she wrote in her diary. 'I am beginning to feel the nervous strain [of] this double game, this constant change of personality without any let-up when I can be myself again.' The only creature she could trust was her dog. Lily wrote to her sister: 'The heat in Madrid is torrid. Babs sleeps blissfully on his back with four feet in the air and his tongue hanging out. I have just been talking to him about you. He opened one eye and raised an ear; that means he remembers.'

She arranged another meeting with Benton, who told her she had done extremely well. 'We know a certain amount about Major Kliemann,' he explained. 'He's an important man in German intelligence – quite a formidable figure, in fact. I have the impression that you underestimate him. He has his weaknesses certainly – you think him a little absurd because he is always late for appointments. If he finds out that you've double-crossed him, he won't be late for the next rendezvous, I can promise you.'

Finally, word came from Hans that Kliemann was on his way, and would meet her at the Café Bakanik. When he eventually arrived, the dog jumped up to greet him. 'Babs licks his face while he continues to waggle his tail and whole body.' Lily felt moved by the sight of her dog and her German spymaster, so pleased to see one another: 'I look at them and think: at last, something genuine.' Kliemann was excited by the way Lily's mission was progressing. He preened himself, and ordered a steady stream of drinks. 'It will be quite something for me: to have set up an agent and actually get that same agent into England. It's incredible. It looks as if it's going to work.'

Kliemann, usually so lethargic, was all business. He planned to provide her with a radio set hidden inside a gramophone, with operating instructions written on a microdot concealed in the case. In order to read it, she would need to buy a small microscope. She should pretend to be interested in microbes. Indeed she should carry a book with her as cover: he recommended *The Microbe Hunters* by Paul de Kruif. Lily declined to say that she thought this was a ridiculously overcomplicated plan. By now quite drunk, Kliemann was enjoying his role, though Lily could sense he had something else on his mind. He suddenly grew pensive and gazed 'thoughtfully at the space in front of him, sighing deeply'.

'Anything wrong?' Lily asked, knowing that the conversation was about to turn to his favourite subject: Yvonne Delidaise, his mistress.

Kliemann buried his face in his hands. 'You must think me ridiculous. Maybe I am. She is young and pretty, gay and witty. And I? Look at me. A married man of forty-six.' The German spymaster ordered another bottle of wine, and poured his heart out. Yvonne had spent May in Madrid, at the Ritz, he said. After she returned to Paris, she was no longer the same towards him; something must have happened while she was here. And he wanted Lily's help to find out what.

With a fierce twinge of irritation, Lily understood that Kliemann had come to Spain with an ulterior motive that had nothing to do with her, and everything to do with his love life. Like most jealous lovers, he had already fixed on the rival he believed Yvonne to have been seeing in Madrid: Edgar Espirito Santo. 'He's Portuguese. A very wealthy banker. He used to see a lot of Yvonne. He's a lady-killer. Yvonne amused him. She is jolly and witty, but Yvonne doesn't mean a thing to him. I think she met him here. He always stops at the Ritz – and I want to know if he was there at the same time as Yvonne. I must know if she has been carrying on with that damned Espirito Santo. And if she has made a fool of me . . .'

'Then what?'

'Then I shall ask for a transfer to the Russian Front.'

'But what do you want me to do?'

She could make enquiries, suggested Kliemann, and see if the banker had been staying at the Ritz when Yvonne was in Madrid. Lily had come to Spain as a German spy, not as a freelance private detective for a middle-aged married man besotted with a younger woman. She was outraged.

'Major Kliemann, I don't care a hang about your ridiculous affairs,' Lily railed. 'In a few days, I shall be in England and you will be in Paris. I shall probably never see you again. Why should I care whether Yvonne is deceiving you or not?'

Kliemann was pleading, and plastered. She left him in the café.

The next day, she related this bizarre conversation to Benton, who reported back to MI5: Kliemann 'appears to be extremely pleased with her progress' and 'pathologically jealous' of his mistress, he wrote, two discoveries which, in combination, rendered him uniquely vulnerable. Lily was Kliemann's only spy. If she now became a prop for his frail sexual ego, then he would be even more in her debt, and even easier to manipulate. Benton advised her to report back to the Major that 'the object of Kliemann's jealousy was not at the Ritz, or even in Madrid, in May'. The MI6 officer then made his own enquiries, which suggested that Yvonne probably *had* been carrying on with the Portuguese banker. There was no sense in telling Kliemann that. 'Whatever the truth may be, the report must prove that Yvonne is faithful to him. Now that we know all about Major Kliemann we want him to stay in the job. We must make quite sure he doesn't get sent to the Russian Front.'

Kliemann was delighted with Lily's 'purely fictitious but reassuring report' affirming Yvonne's fidelity. Predictably, he had failed to find her a wireless set, but insisted he would be able to get one passed to her in Britain, by a Spaniard 'who was under great obligation to Kliemann's friends'. (MI5 would later conclude that this must have been a reference to Angel Alcazar de Velasco, the press attaché at the Spanish Embassy and a known German agent.) He then handed over two pellets of ink for secret writing, and a long questionnaire, clearly aimed at discovering the Allies' invasion plans, which he told her to memorise, and then destroy. 'What view is taken in authoritative English circles of landing preparations? Where are the barracks placed in coastal towns?' Kliemann wanted information on uniforms and troop movements, stoppage of leave, armaments production, and much more. Lily, and British intelligence, seemed to have Kliemann exactly where they wanted him: she was 'the personification of his hopes, the evidence of his subtlety, his courage and his flair'.

Only once did the conversation take a more sinister turn when Kliemann, with studied nonchalance, observed that after her abrupt departure from Paris, the Gestapo had put her parents' flat under surveillance. Lily did not like the sense of threat in that remark, and told him that 'if any harm came to her parents while she was away he would find her working for the other side against him'. It was half a joke, but Kliemann's response was immediate, sharp and entirely without humour: 'Naturally, should she double-cross him, she must consider that the lives of her parents were at stake.'

Kliemann now reached into a pocket with an air of great munificence, and handed Agent Solange a small package wrapped in tissue: inside was a diamond solitaire ring and a two-inch brooch in the shape of a branch with five small diamonds representing blossoms. The ring had cost 95,000 francs in Paris, he said, and the brooch 39,000 Portuguese escudos. In England, she could sell the jewellery, and say it had belonged to her grandmother. To this he added a pile of 7,000 Spanish pesetas, with an additional 2,000 pesetas as a bonus for setting his mind at rest about Yvonne's visit to Spain, a token of thanks for her 'help and sympathy'. Dinner over, Kliemann climbed into a taxi in the Plaza del Callao, and drove off with 'a cheery wave'. He was a happy man: his mistress was faithful, his bosses were pleased, and his star agent was now about to help win the war for Germany. That night, Lily wrote in her diary: 'He has gone. He hasn't found out anything. And now: England.'

Kenneth Benton of MI6 had grown to like Lily. He liked her still more when she reappeared in his office, with Babs in tow, and handed over Kliemann's questionnaire, proof of mounting German anxiety over the coming invasion. She was dressed up to the nines, having spent all the Spanish cash from Kliemann on clothes. 'I was getting to know her and felt she had a good feeling for the job. Everything was in order for her onward travel to Lisbon. Then she exploded her landmine.'

'Mr Benton,' said Lily. 'I have one more request. I have worked for you; I will continue to work for you; I don't ask for any payment. But I have one favour to ask: I want to keep Babs with me.'

Benton was taken aback. It wasn't possible. It wouldn't be allowed. There were quarantine laws.

'That's exactly it. I want to skip quarantine,' Lily explained. 'Babs has been vaccinated. I've got his anti-rabies certificate, and there is no danger. It's the only thing I ask for, but I do insist on it.'

British laws preventing dogs from entering the country until declared disease-free were some of the oldest, and silliest, in the statute book, maintained long after science and technology had effectively removed the rabies threat. This strange animal-based xenophobia probably had something to do with Britain being an island. Benton was happy to break every law in the book to help win the war, but he was not about to break the sacrosanct quarantine laws. He prevaricated. 'I'll see what I can do . . .'

But Lily would not be fobbed off. She would not leave without Babs. 'If my work is important it is worth this exemption; if it isn't worth that, then it isn't worth my going to England . . . To you, it's just a dog; but to me, it's Babs, and worth more than a million pounds. Just tell your people in London that.' She was working herself up into one of her rages. 'Why can't I go by Gibraltar?'

'Even if you did you would have to leave the dog in quarantine for six months. In fact, I'm not even sure they would allow that.'

'You can persuade them. After all, I'm going to be an important double agent.'

'I cannot persuade them. This is wartime, Lily.'

'Then I will refuse to go. I will stay here in Spain. I won't leave my poor little Babs.'

Desperate for the interview to end, Benton offered to find a kind owner for Babs. It was wartime; she had to make sacrifices.

Lily whispered angrily in Russian to her dog, before turning back to Benton. 'You shall not have him . . . He knows nothing about your war; all he wants is to be with me.'

Benton (who rather liked dogs) told her he would do his best, though he knew 'it was going to be impossible to get that wretched dog into Britain without passing through quarantine'. He had resorted to a very English sort of temporising, a commitment to do what he could, when he planned to do very little and believed that nothing could be done. But Lily had heard something very different: she had heard an Englishman promise to get her dog into Britain. That misunderstanding would have the most profound ramifications.

Benton asked London what to do about Lily's dog. 'Get her to Gibraltar, then leave it to Gibraltar colleagues to sort out,' came the reply. Benton reported back to Lily: 'My Gibraltar colleagues might be able to find a way of smuggling Babs to Britain, perhaps by sea.' In reality, this had already been ruled out by the MI6 officer on the island.

On 7 October 1943, Lily Sergeyev, travelling under an alias, arrived in Gibraltar under escort, with her dog. Benton did not fail to notice the 'suspicious looks' she gave him as they said goodbye. Sure enough, when she reached Gibraltar, the customs officer insisted she surrender the dog. 'I picked up Babs and handed him over,' Lily wrote in her diary. 'The difficult moment had arrived.' But their separation, she assured herself, would be temporary. She had Benton's 'promise'.

The next day an MI6 officer in plain clothes, who introduced himself as O'Shagar, came to see Agent Treasure at the hotel.

'From now on, you have nothing to worry about. We will take charge of everything,' he told her.

Lily pressed him about Babs and 'Mr Benton's promise to arrange for his transport and to make sure that he wouldn't have to go into quarantine'. O'Shagar replied that they'd 'see to that too'.

That night, at the hotel bar, she met a friendly American pilot, Lieutenant Kenneth Larson, who liked dogs. 'Why don't you send him to London with one of our pilots? They don't have to go through customs or any controls at all,' he said. 'Would you like me to fix it up for you?' The next morning she reported the conversation to O'Shagar, pointing out that this arrangement would 'save an awful lot of bother and red tape'. But she wanted a promise that if the American failed to deliver Babs to Britain, then MI6 would find a way to do so.

'You have my word,' said O'Shagar. (That, at least, was how Lily remembered the conversation.)

By some immutable law of travel, luggage always lets you down when you are in the greatest haste. Lily was about to board the flight for England, when the clasp on her suitcase gave way, spilling its contents everywhere. O'Shagar gathered up her scattered belongings, stuffed them in the broken suitcase, and promised to get it repaired and sent over on the next flight. Lily ran for the plane.

A few hours later, 'Dorothy Tremayne' landed at Bristol airport. The policewoman detailed to collect her had been told to look out for a woman with a small white dog and a large record player. She had no gramophone and no dog; she also had no suitcase. But she was in no doubt that the Frenchwoman complaining loudly in the arrivals hall must be Lily Sergeyev. 'Treasure' had finally been smuggled into Britain, bringing with her, in Masterman's words, 'a rich dowry: the confidence of the Germans'.

Back in Madrid, Kenneth Benton of MI6 suffered a 'feeling of guilt' when he learned that Lily had flown to England, leaving her beloved dog behind in Gibraltar. But then he reflected: 'After all, it was wartime, and sacrifices, as I had told her, had to be made by people and consciences alike.' Besides, Benton had other things on his mind: he was about to reel in an even bigger fish, an officer within the Abwehr itself.

The Walk-in

On 14 September 1943, Dusko Popov flew back to Britain, and was immediately taken to Clock House, the cottage rented by MI5, for a debriefing by Tar Robertson and Ian Wilson. Both were in a state of high excitement to see what Tricycle had brought back from Lisbon. Solemnly, Popov opened the 'diplomatic bag' provided by von Karsthoff. 'First of all a very large number of silk stockings fell out,' wrote Wilson. These were followed by a radio transmitter, a Leica camera and six rolls of film, ingredients for making secret ink, $2,000 and £2,500 in cash and yet more questionnaires. This complete spy kit was proof enough of German faith in Popov, but additional reassurance came from Most Secret Sources which, as Wilson reported, 'make it clear that Tricycle's reports to us are accurate, that for the most part the Germans still believe him, and that those members of the Abwehr who have reason to doubt him are so corrupt or so afraid of losing their jobs by disclosing awkward facts that they are doing all they can to support him'.

Popov explained that he had met up once again with Johnny Jebsen, and was now 'absolutely sure' that his friend knew he was a double agent: 'The way he talks to me and his whole behaviour shows this very clearly.' Jebsen had been even more candid than before, talking of 'that idiot Hitler' and speaking with a 'funny smile in his eyes' that left Popov in no doubt that he knew every word he said would be relayed straight back to the Allies. Jebsen's enemies in Berlin were machinating against him, he said, and the Gestapo was circling. But the part of Popov's report that really made his listeners sit up was Jebsen's account of 'some new invention' causing great excitement in Berlin, a multiple rocket device 'with the same effect as a 2,000 kilo bomb'.

Robertson immediately sent a memo to the Twenty Committee, informing the board of this most alarming information from Jebsen who seemed to be, 'for the first time, acting as a conscious informant'. Popov did not say explicitly that he had advised his friend to go to the British and offer himself as a double agent, but he almost certainly had. A full report was sent to Churchill:

> Tricycle has just returned from a visit to Lisbon where he has been in contact with members of the German secret service. He gained the impression that they no longer hope to win the war and expect it to be over shortly. He learnt from his spymaster who is also a close personal friend that the latter believes in the existence of a rocket gun for shelling London. The spymaster added that the raids on Germany had delayed the production of the gun by about two months, but that it should be in action by December and Tricycle would be well advised to leave London before then. The Germans further told Tricycle that they are well informed about the British Order of Battle. The Germans said that they had practically no agents in the USA, but that they had ten or twelve in the UK (this corresponds to those under our control). They also told him the story of a Major in the German secret service in Berlin who had suggested that the agents in England were under British control but was sacked for this suggestion within 24 hours.

The 'rocket gun' was the V1, the flying bomb being developed in Germany in order to bombard Britain into submission.

Jebsen's information corroborated what was already known about the new weapon, while his description of the Germans' faith in their British spy network underlined Tar's claim to control the whole thing: any German intelligence officer who dared suggest the spies were false was regarded as a heretic, and liable to be fired.

The final element in Popov's Lisbon haul was a plan that had been stewing for some time – a way to smuggle additional double agents into Britain, with German help. With MI5's approval, Popov had spun von Karsthoff an ingenious tale: since numerous Yugoslavs were anxious to get to Britain, why not introduce some secret Nazi spies among the genuine refugees? Popov's older brother Ivo, living in Belgrade, could select potential candidates. Ivo was held in high regard by the Germans, who saw him as a keen and dedicated collaborator, so highly trusted that he had been issued with travel papers, a Wehrmacht uniform and the rank of *Sonderführer* (Specialist Leader). Ivo Popov would select recruits, who with German assistance would be smuggled into Britain, via Spain, as refugees. Once they arrived in Britain, the younger Popov brother would take them in hand and add them to his spy network. Von Karsthoff leaped at the idea, and on 23 July sent a message to Berlin describing Popov's wheeze for infiltrating spies into Britain: 'I consider this plan a good one,' he wrote. 'I still consider Ivan as reliable, if kept under supervision.'

What von Karsthoff did not know was that Ivo Popov, like his brother, was working for the other side and had already been recruited by British intelligence as Agent 'Dreadnought'. Instead of choosing Nazi sympathisers for the so-called 'slipping out' operation, he would select his own anti-Nazi collaborators, who had been briefed to play the part. At the other end, Popov, Robertson and the Double Cross Committee would be waiting to welcome them. Every link of the chain was false. Instead of introducing keen new spies into Britain, the Germans would be helping to recruit, train, finance and transport a stream of ready-made double agents, pre-cooked and ready to serve.

The first agent to be 'slipped out' in this way was the Marquis Frano de Bona, an aristocratic Yugoslavian naval officer, and a friend and former carousing partner of Dusko Popov. At Ivo's instigation, de Bona was recruited by the Abwehr and trained as a wireless operator, and slipped into Spain. While waiting for his transfer to London as a refugee, the Marquis took up residence in a Madrid brothel, where he spent four days and nights, finally emerging exhausted and happy, but with a nasty dose of venereal crabs. On arrival in Britain he moved into Clock House with Popov, and became a double agent, the wireless operator for the Tricycle network. No longer would Popov and his sub-agents have to rely on secret writing to communicate with Germany. Whether because of his long hair, licentiousness or lice, the Marquis de Bona was awarded a most unflattering codename: he became Agent Freak.

Intriguingly, Freak's briefing in Germany offered indications that elements within the Abwehr were ready to sue for peace. Churchill read of de Bona's arrival:

His main mission, it appears, was to contact Englishmen in high places and to impress upon them very strongly the view that Germany is open to approaches from this country with a view to stemming the flow of Communism across the Continent of Europe, and for this purpose they required the assistance of the British. The core of his instructions was that Germany was not to be forced to capitulate, but should be granted terms by this country to enable her to maintain a barrier in Eastern Europe against the Communist peril. It was emphasised that Germany was willing in order to obtain these terms, to get rid of Hitler, to introduce a democratic form of government acceptable to the English and Americans, [and] withdraw from all occupied territory.

This was the essence of the anti-Nazi resistance: to oust Hitler, ally with the West, defeat the Bolsheviks and salvage some

German pride. Anthony Blunt certainly passed this report to the Soviets, doubtless compounding Stalin's suspicions that the British and Americans might make peace with Germany and then turn on the Soviet Union. Churchill believed that the war could only end with Germany's unconditional surrender, but de Bona brought hard evidence that Abwehr officers were now actively manoeuvring to oust the Führer. Riven with conspiracy, double-crossed from within, under attack from its rivals, German military intelligence was starting to implode.

Kenneth Benton made his way upstairs in the British Embassy in Madrid to a small attic room usually 'used as a bedroom for escaped POWs'. There he found a young man 'who was chain-smoking and looking rather sweaty and apprehensive'. The man rose, shook hands, and spoke in perfect, accentless English: 'I am an officer in the Abwehr and I wish you to protect me from the Gestapo.'

Benton offered his guest a whisky. The Abwehr man 'smiled rather charmingly' revealing nicotine-stained teeth: 'Where I come from we love whisky, and I could certainly do with a drink right now.'

Sipping whisky and soda, in his well-cut suit and monocle, he might have been an Englishman. He wore a 'very small blond moustache', and fiddled restlessly, lighting one cigarette from another. 'My name is Johnny Jebsen,' he said. 'I suppose you are Mr Benton.' The MI6 man was taken aback. His real name was supposed to be a closely guarded secret, even within the Embassy. Jebsen smiled again.

'You're in trouble?' asked Benton.

'The Gestapo are on my tail because I made a report on their dealings in forged banknotes.'

'Have they followed you here?'

'No, I shook them off.'

Jebsen had every reason to be agitated. Not only was the Gestapo closing in, but he had learned that Kammler, the Abwehr official in Lisbon skimming Popov's pay, had denounced him to the bosses in Berlin. Jebsen feared that his hotel room in Lisbon might have been bugged and his 'indiscreet' conversations with Popov overheard. His supporters within the Abwehr had advised him to stay away from Germany. He might need an escape route.

They talked for two hours, and as Jebsen relaxed, he became ever more informative and opinionated, revealing the identities of senior Abwehr officers in Spain and 'their special fields of interest', his role as a freelance agent-recruiter, and sinking German morale: 'There is hardly a soul any more in Germany who believes in victory. Probably the only man who really does is Hitler.' He drank more whisky, and cracked dark jokes: 'During an air raid Hitler, Goering, Goebbels and Himmler took refuge in the same air raid shelter. The shelter received a direct hit. Who was saved? Germany.' He described again the 'secret weapon' being built in Germany, 'which would spread terror throughout the whole of the south of England'. Jebsen said he 'did not know any details about the mystery weapon', but could find out more.

'I'm giving you a lot of information, aren't I?' he remarked, with a grin. 'Well, it'll be up to you to help me in return.' Jebsen was ready to cut a deal. If the Gestapo came after him, he wanted the British to get him out, quickly. In return, he would reveal everything he knew. Benton knew that smuggling Jebsen back to Britain from Spain would be simple enough, but the consequences of such a move were unpredictable: when the Abwehr discovered Jebsen's defection, they would assume he had revealed all, and anyone associated with him would immediately become suspect. Jebsen had thought of a solution. He would leave a fake 'suicide note' to cover his sudden disappearance, in which he would write: 'I shall take poison and swim far out into the sea. It may be days before my corpse is washed up and it will then be no longer recognisable.' It is hard to imagine even the most idiotic Abwehr officer falling for such an obvious ruse. MI5 would later dismiss Jebsen's suicide plot as a 'piece of extreme foolishness brought on by excessive nervous strain'.

Benton felt drawn to Jebsen. The spy spoke warmly of his love for England, his wish to study at Oxford after the war, his friendship with P. G. Wodehouse, and his bossy English secretary, Mabel Harbottle, who refused to type letters that might undermine the Allied war effort. 'He was an interesting and well-educated man and very good company,' thought Benton, but also worldly, cynical and dissolute. 'He had a great liking for pornographic films and admitted that one of the reasons why he came so frequently to Madrid was the existence of two clandestine Madrid cinemas which specialised in this kind of film.' He made no secret of his fears, and no claims to courage. With a 'visible shudder' he described the Ablege Kommando, a 'trained hijack team, skilled in seizing a wanted man and smuggling him back across the frontiers without arousing suspicion'. Even in neutral Spain, he might be kidnapped at any time and taken back to Germany, a prospect that terrified him.

Benton advised Jebsen to spend that night at the Embassy. 'It is in your interest. By tomorrow I'll have a safe house.' Over a last nightcap, Benton asked his new recruit if there were other Abwehr officers who might be willing to defect. Jebsen replied: 'I'm sure some of them have been turned and I know one Abwehr agent, a man I recruited myself, who has either been turned already or would go over to your side at the drop of a hat.'

'Who is that?'

'Dusan Popov,' Jebsen answered. 'He's a prolific agent, run from both Berlin and Lisbon.'

Jebsen had recruited Popov into the Abwehr. Popov, once turned, had urged the British to recruit Jebsen. Now Jebsen, in the process of being turned, urged the British to recruit Popov. He was being deliberately disingenuous. Jebsen knew by now, and probably had known from the beginning, that Popov was working for the British. Henceforth, they would be working together.

Benton sat up late, drafting a long report to London about Jebsen, whom he codenamed 'Artist'. The reply read: 'Artist is telling you the truth. He is a *Forscher*, and well known to us. This contact has great potential value. Use utmost caution.'

Jebsen told him he would remain in Spain for the time being, see what developed, and keep in touch. 'I was very sorry to part with Artist,' Benton later wrote. Jebsen was plainly being honest about his espionage activities, if not his financial dealings: 'Artist told me that he suspected the Gestapo of lining their pockets with forged British banknotes, but I was never quite sure it was not the other way around.' With Jebsen, it was always tricky to work out which way round the truth lay.

Lily Sergeyev's first moments on British soil could not have been more inauspicious. She had been told not to answer questions until she was interrogated. 'You won't have to open your mouth from here to London,' O'Shagar had told her as she left Gibraltar. Mary Sherer had sent instructions that she 'should be dealt with at the airport in an absolutely normal manner', since Lily was 'particularly anxious that as few people as possible should know about her case, as she has a family still in Paris'.

The very first official she encountered was an immigration officer named Gold, 'fat, with big ears', and a stickler for the rules. Gold asked her name. She refused to answer. He asked where she was born. Lily said nothing. Finally, in what was later admitted to be a 'rather ill-advised attempt to make her feel at ease', Gold remarked: 'It's all right, you needn't worry. We know all about you, the Germans have sent you here.'

Lily exploded. She had been in Britain less than an hour, and already some lumpen official with outsize ears was telling her that everybody knew her secret. Lily was still shouting when a severe-looking policewoman appeared, saying she had been sent to escort 'Miss Tremayne' to London.

She was driven to a house in Balham, through the pouring rain, and put to bed by a motherly woman calling herself 'Mrs Maud'. The next morning, after a deep and exhausted night's sleep and breakfast of porridge, she was ushered into a second-floor room to find a woman in a red suit, sitting 'on the edge of a chair, her arms folded, chin resting on her hands'. Mary Sherer appraised Agent Treasure coolly 'through slightly slanted greenish eyes'. For a few moments, neither spoke. Lily then perched on the sofa, and reeled off her story. Mary took notes, saying little. After an hour, she stood up: 'You can be extremely useful to us, and the opening you provide may be of vital importance. We will be delighted to work with you, but you must realise the gravity of the situation. By helping the British you will be working for France, for her liberation.' She escorted Lily to a waiting car.

Lily was driven to Flat 19, Rugby Mansions, in Kensington, and introduced to a Yugoslavian woman named Maritza, who would be her housekeeper, Mary explained. She did not explain that the flat was an MI5 safe house under surveillance: the phone was bugged, the post monitored, and Maritza Mihailovic was herself a double agent, codenamed 'The Snark' (after the Lewis Carroll nonsense poem *The Hunting of the Snark*. Since Carroll himself could not explain what a Snark was, this may be one codename with no relevance whatever to its subject). A domestic servant, she had been recruited by the Abwehr in Yugoslavia and arrived in England as a refugee in 1941. B1A had run her as a double agent for a time, but for unknown reasons the Germans had lost interest in her, and since 1943 she had worked for MI5 as a cleaner, and as a spy. The Snark would be keeping a close eye on Treasure.

Tar Robertson soon arrived, exuding bonhomie: 'So you are here at last. Let me congratulate you on your work: it's a great success. Now you must relax, forget your fears and uncertainty; nothing more can happen to you. You are among friends.'

Lily made no reply. She was fairly impervious to English charm. Robertson ploughed on.

'We look on you as a trump card. There is no doubt the German intelligence people have complete confidence in you, so we are in a unique position to feed them false information. We can pull off what is known in the trade as an "intoxication".'

With Mary Sherer's help, Tar explained, Lily would write her own letters. 'I want you, yourself, to draft all the messages,' said Tar. 'If you think that any of the stuff we want to send will seem unlikely to the Germans, you mustn't hesitate to say so. The possibilities open to us are so precious that we must not take even the smallest risk.' For the next four hours, she went through her story yet again. She drew a map of Madrid showing where she had met her German contacts, and even sketched portraits of Emile Kliemann and Yvonne Delidaise.

Lily's sketches of Emile Kliemann and Yvonne Delidaise

'That only leaves the financial question,' said Tar, beaming. 'We'll take over the money and jewellery and give you £50 a month and 10 per cent of anything else they send. Is that all right?' Lily nodded, but reflected that the Germans had offered her £250 a month. 'I am not doing this for the money,' she told her diary, 'but I am a little surprised.' The brooch and diamond ring were locked in the B1A safe, but not before MI5 had valued them and found the jewellery was worth just £100, 'rather a far cry from the £400 that Kliemann thought she would get'. The arrival of this promising new double agent was relayed to Churchill:

A French citizen of Russian origin, she has lived most of her life in Paris, where she occupied herself with journalism, and at one time gained a considerable reputation as an artist. Through a fellow journalist, a German whom she had known before the war, Treasure gained her first introduction to the German secret service. It was a long time before Treasure was able to persuade her German masters to send her to this country. She has had extensive training in wireless transmission and in secret ink writing. She did not bring a wireless set with her, but was assured that arrangements had been made for one to be sent.

Anthony Blunt had made a special request 'to be informed when Treasure arrives'; news of Lily's arrival was certainly relayed to the Kremlin.

Mary Sherer was far too English to show it, but she was pleased with Lily, and already had the 'very strong conviction that this, her first double agent, was going to be a success, come what might'. Kim Philby, her colleague in MI6, remarked darkly: 'Poor girl. She's in for a disappointment. Never trust a Tsarist émigré.'

Lily glumly appraised her new home, the flat with its large, ill-furnished rooms, 'clean and impersonal, like the rooms of a hotel'. She went for a walk, Maritza hovering in attendance. The street was 'bleak and gloomy', and Rugby Mansions a 'plain-fronted house with neither imagination nor ornament, as sour as an old spinster suffering from jaundice'. She had imagined a London ferociously at war. This place was grey, damp and foggy. Lily thought of herself as a bird of colour, an artist, a child of bright adventure. This was not her world. 'What strikes me is the shabby appearance of everyone in the street: worn-out overcoats, shiny sleeves, dowdy clothes. In the shop windows the dresses are straight, without facing, lapels, or belt – everything remotely frivolous has been pitilessly sacrificed.' Her new handlers seemed detached and distant. Mary Sherer was a puzzle: 'I still cannot quite place her: is she my jailer, or nursery governess, or what?' she wrote. 'I don't even know what she feels about me, though I suppose this really doesn't matter very much.' Lowering her spirits still further was the nagging, and growing, pain in her kidneys, a recurrence of her old malady.

Lily missed Paris, stylish even under Nazi occupation. She missed the excitement of playing one side off against the other. She even missed Kliemann. But most of all, she missed Babs.

A Time for Fortitude

The D-Day deception plan went through many versions and many names in the months leading up to June 1944: Operation Jael (named after the Old Testament heroine who nailed her sleeping enemy's head to the floor with a tent peg) aimed to persuade the Germans there would be no invasion in 1944; then came 'Torrent' or 'Appendix Y', intended to convince them that Calais was the sole target. The plan for Operation Bodyguard, combining elements of the earlier plans, was finally completed by Johnny Bevan, 'haggard with sleeplessness', just before Christmas, 1943.

Bodyguard was worldwide in scope, and vaulting in ambition. Its aims were multiple: to tie down German troops in the Mediterranean with the bogus threat of assaults on the Dalmatian and Greek coasts; to dissipate German strength by suggesting that additional attacks might be made in northwest Italy, Bulgaria, Denmark and, most importantly, Norway; to implant the idea that the bombing of Germany would take precedence over land-based assaults, and make the Germans believe, for as long as possible, that no cross-Channel attack could take place until late summer. Bodyguard's aim was to baffle and bemuse, to keep German troops away from where they would most be needed, hold them down where they could do least harm, and lure them away from France and the Eastern Front, and towards Italy, the Balkans, Greece and Scandinavia.

Bodyguard would be implemented in various theatres of war, but its most important element by far was the plan to mislead Hitler over the planned Normandy landings.

The choice of codename for this particular operation – the crux of Bodyguard – was much debated. Churchill had given instructions that no codename should be selected that might seem flippant in retrospect, or give a hint of the individual or action involved. But he also disliked codenames that meant nothing at all, which is why the original choice, 'Mespot', was rejected. Also vetoed were 'Bulldog', 'Swordhilt', 'Axehead', 'Tempest', and, obscurely, 'Lignite'. Finally a name was selected that seemed to evoke the resolution required to pull it off: Operation Fortitude.

A vast, secret army set to work on Operation Fortitude, fabricating physical deception, including dummy landing craft and rubber tanks at key points, and technical deception in the form of great waves of radio traffic, a blizzard of electric noise mimicking great armies training and assembling where none existed. British diplomats dropped misleading hints at cocktail parties to be overheard by eavesdroppers and channelled back to Germany. Conspicuously large orders were made for Michelin Map 51, a map of the Pas de Calais area. The French resistance, SOE agents, Jedburgh saboteur and guerrilla teams, MI6, the code-breakers at Bletchley, secret scientists and camouflage engineers would each play a part in this great, sprawling, multi-faceted deception campaign. But at its core was Tar Robertson's tiny team of double agents, telling lies to their spymasters, in secret writing, by radio, and to their faces, forging a shield of deceit that would guard the soldiers, if it worked, onto the beaches of Normandy.

Many played a part in planning Operation Fortitude, but three principal architects of the deception plan stand out. Colonel Johnny Bevan, the head of the London Controlling Section; Major Roger Fleetwood-Hesketh, the leading intelligence officer within the Supreme Headquarters Allied Expeditionary

Force (SHAEF), whose task it was to merge military planning and deception, and Colonel David Strangeways, the head of General Montgomery's deception section. Christopher Harmer of B1A would act as liaison between the headquarters of the Expeditionary Force and the Double Cross team. These were very different men. Fleetwood-Hesketh – a barrister with 'one of the best claret cellars in England' – was 'charming and witty', with a fine sense of the absurd. Harmer described him as a 'most tidy and meticulous worker' but 'essentially a scorer rather than a player'. Strangeways, a hard-driving infantryman, was 'impossible and insufferable' according to Harmer, but frequently right, and occasionally inspired. Bevan, overworked and under stress, was liable to volcanic eruptions of temper, always followed by heartfelt apology. Their roles were often ill-defined and overlapping. Tempers frayed and snapped. The rows were spectacular, but the extent of their collaboration was even more remarkable. Between them, these individuals would fashion and then implement the most ambitious deception campaign ever attempted.

Operation Fortitude was revised over time. At one point, the acerbic Strangeways, in his own words, 'rewrote the thing entirely', igniting another furious argument (though his changes were finally accepted). In its final form, the plan had several, interlinked aims: to convince the Germans that the attack on Normandy (eventually scheduled for June) was merely diversionary, a ploy to draw off German forces before the main thrust of the invasion in the Pas de Calais around the middle of July; at the same time it sought to lure the Germans into preparing for an attack on Norway, along with another landing in the area of Bordeaux. Crucially, the threat to the Pas de Calais would be maintained for as long as possible after the Normandy landings, to ensure that the Germans did not send a large body of troops south to repel the real invasion.

The deception plan was divided in two: Fortitude North was the fake threat to Norway; Fortitude South would pose, and maintain, the threat to the Pas de Calais. In order for the plan to work, the Germans must be made to expect three separate invasions – a feint in Normandy and two major landings in Norway and the Pas de Calais – and therein lay a major hurdle. There were simply not enough soldiers in Britain to do what the planners wanted the Germans to believe they were about to do, so they invented them. It was Strangeways who came up with the idea of creating an entire fictional army in southeast England, poised to invade the northeast coast of France. This ghost army, supposedly stationed directly across the Channel from the Pas de Calais, was dubbed the First United States Army Group, or FUSAG. Another fake force, the British Fourth Army, would be created in Scotland, to keep German minds focused on a threat to Norway. These counterfeit armies would threaten bogus targets, while living soldiers prepared to attack the real target, in Normandy.

Masterman was itching for the game to start. 'We had always expected', he wrote, 'that at some one moment all the agents would be recklessly and gladly "blown" sky-high in carrying out the grand deception, and that this one great coup would bring our work to an end.' There were voices of caution, and some of scepticism, including the British Army representative on the Twenty Committee who insisted that 'the German General Staff will not move a single German division on an agent's report alone'. Unless, of course, they discovered the agent was a double agent, and the division was then moved in precisely the wrong direction. 'An agent who turned out not to be believed by the enemy might wreck the whole enterprise, or, even worse, his messages might be read "in reverse" and the true target of the attack be exposed instead of revealed.' There was every possibility the plan could backfire disastrously.

Churchill and Roosevelt were kept fully apprised of the roles planned for the double agents in the deception, as was Stalin, both officially and secretly. The NKVD mole Anthony Blunt, now promoted to major, was still burrowing deep into British intelligence, digging up every scrap of secret information he could find, and shipping it all to Moscow. 'I have managed to get myself in touch with Robertson who runs the double agents,' he told his Soviet handlers. 'In this way I can usually get an idea of what is actually planned and what is being put across as cover.' If there was an equivalent German mole within Soviet intelligence, then the entire deception would be blown. Or it might have been, had it not been for the paranoia ingrained into Soviet officialdom. Moscow did not believe what Blunt was telling them, because it was too good to be true. Having discovered that Britain was practising an intricate double-cross operation on the Germans, the Soviets convinced themselves that they, too, must be victims of such a deception. According to the warped logic of the NKVD, the Cambridge Five (Blunt, Kim Philby, Guy Burgess, Donald Maclean and John Cairncross) were sending such high-grade information that they must be double agents, sending deliberate disinformation; and since the information from the five tallied perfectly, this was further proof that they were in league.

The chief exponent of this gymnastic exercise in double-think was Colonel Elena Modrzhinskaya, a blonde, rotund, zealously conspiratorial NKVD officer responsible for assessing British intelligence. Her suspicion of Blunt and his fellow spies was based on the assumption, firmly held and quite wrong, that the British could not be so foolish as to allow former communists to occupy senior positions in the intelligence services. Therefore Blunt and the others must have been working for the British from the beginning. A splendidly incompetent NKVD surveillance team was sent to gather evidence of the Cambridge spies making contact with their British handlers. Since Blunt worked *inside* MI5, this 'evidence' of contact with British intelligence was not hard to find. As the D-Day deception was being crafted, Moscow sent a letter to its London spy chief warning of a vast, organised deception by these British double agents. 'Our task is to understand what disinformation our rivals are planting on us,' since 'all the data' from Blunt and the others indicated a double-cross operation. (The irony that Moscow was only aware of the existence of the British Double Cross system because Blunt had revealed it to them, was entirely lost on Colonel Modrzhinskaya.)

But in the mirroring world of espionage, Blunt and Modrzhinskaya might actually end up *supporting* the deception. If Agent Tony was a double agent, then his false information should be read in reverse; if he indicated that Normandy was the real target and the Pas de Calais a decoy, then the Pas de Calais must be the real target, and Normandy a feint. And if a German mole had penetrated Soviet intelligence, then that is the information he would be passing back to Berlin. In a nutshell: if the Germans believed that the Soviets thought the British were trying to make them believe something that was untrue, then the deception would still be on track. At the very least, Soviet suspicions would muddy the waters to an opacity beyond human penetration.

By the end of 1943, wrote Masterman, the Double Cross team was 'far more powerful and better equipped than it had ever been before'. The double agents were reaching peak fitness. Tricycle (Popov) was beloved and admired by his German handlers, with Jebsen, the latest addition to the team, on hand to protect him; Garbo sat in Crespigny Road, Hendon, arguing with his wife and spinning ever more elaborate fantasies; Treasure was now in place, lonely and lovesick without her dog, but ready to start feeding misinformation back to Kliemann. Bronx, the socialite spy, was in regular contact with Germany. Even the excitable Brutus might soon be back in play, if the Pole could be extracted from prison.

The Double Cross idea had always been based on lateral thinking without boundaries, a willingness to contemplate plans that others would dismiss as unworkable or, frankly, barmy. Flights of fantasy were integral to the system, which perhaps explains why, just as the D-Day deception plans were falling into place, the Double Cross system suddenly took wing, and soared into the surreal.

Of all the strands in Operation Fortitude, none was quite so bizarre, so wholly unlikely, as the great pigeon double cross, the first and only avian deception scheme ever attempted. Animal-based espionage and sabotage was all the rage among Allied plotters: SOE agents stuffed dead rats with explosives, and military zoologists explored the use of trained marine mammals for naval sabotage. In December 1943, Guy Liddell reported an American scheme for attacking Japan using thousands of exploding Mexican bats: 'These bats should be put into crates shipped to Seattle. Attached to the feet and wings of the bats were to be small incendiaries. The bats were to be released from an aeroplane near Tokio [sic], the idea being that they would fly down chimneys and that Tokio would go up in flames.' The idea never took off, but was taken seriously. 'It sounds like a perfectly wild idea but is worth looking into,' said Roosevelt.

People like Robertson and Walker flourished in that grey area between ingenuity and insanity; early in 1944 'our pigeon expert', as Robertson called Walker, approached B1A with an audacious new plan. With D-Day approaching, and having failed to make much impact on enemy pigeons in Britain (because there weren't any), the unstoppable Flight Lieutenant Walker 'began to wonder if there were not some more offensive way of attacking the German pigeon service'. He came up with the 'double-cross pigeon racket', a plan that might wipe out the enemy pigeon population at a stroke.

Every German intelligence station in occupied France had a pigeon section. Moreover, collaborationist French pigeon fanciers were being recruited as stay-behind agents, to harbour German homing pigeons and then release them with intelligence from behind the lines in the event of a successful Allied invasion. Walker began to wonder whether Himmler's interest in pigeons, and his taste for final solutions, could be manipulated to Allied advantage. If the Germans could be fooled into believing that British spy-pigeons had infiltrated their lofts, then it would throw suspicion on the entire German pigeon service: if they could no longer trust their own pigeons, they might kill the lot. In the winter of 1943, he presented MI5 with a top secret memo laying out his 'Pigeon Contamination Plan'.

A stray or lost pigeon will almost always find its way into some loft. If a number of British pigeons could be disguised as German pigeons by putting German rings on them and then released on the Continent (deliberately choosing second-rate birds which would be unlikely to attempt the long flight back), they would find their way eventually into German-controlled lofts. Sooner or later, the Germans would discover they were being fooled. They would find two birds with the same ring number, or a grey pigeon wearing a ring which their records clearly showed as belonging to a red pigeon. They would begin, then, to wonder how many of their pigeons were 'phoney', and the only thing they could do would be to call all their birds in and check them. Until they had checked all their birds in all their lofts they would be unable to use any pigeon services and by the time they had gone through them all, I would have delivered more 'phonies'.

MI5 was enthusiastic. With the Germans braced for an invasion, the discovery that their lofts had been penetrated by double-agent pigeons would 'throw them off balance at a critical psychological moment', in the words of Guy Liddell. The pigeon deception scheme was approved by MI5. After consulting expert technicians, Walker discovered a new aluminium welding process that could attach a forged leg-ring to a pigeon with a 'perfectly invisible joint'; he created a rubber stamp to counterfeit German wing markings; he constructed an automatic pigeon release system out of a weighted Hessian bag,

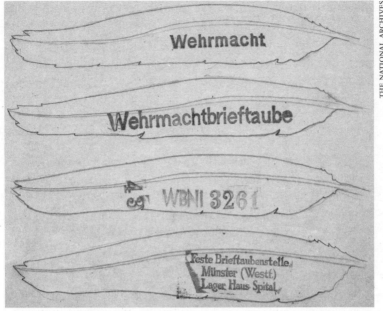

Flight Lieutenant Walker's diagrams for counterfeit wing markings

large enough to carry eight birds, that could be thrown from a plane with a strap attached that would pull off an elastic band and release the birds beyond the slip stream; he consulted the Air Ministry to find out 'when aircraft were going on special dropping missions'. And he began recruiting sluggish British carrier pigeons to be sent on this secret mission to infiltrate the German pigeon service, and destroy it from within. Soon there was a force of 350 double agent pigeons at his disposal, disguised as German pigeons, ready to do their bit.

The Allies now had a series of double-cross operations running simultaneously: a human one in Britain, another composed of pigeons, and a third, fledgling team of double agents, in America.

The Popov debacle in America had revealed the very different American and British attitudes towards double agents, but as the Allied intelligence services grew closer in the course of war, the FBI first became interested in the Double Cross system, and then extremely good at it. The chief impetus for this change of heart was a man not unlike Popov in character: a rich, profligate wastrel with an eye for the ladies and the main chance. Jorge José Mosquera, an Argentinian by birth, was the owner of a leather export company based in Hamburg. In 1941, he decided to relocate to South America. At this point the Abwehr had moved in, insisting that his funds would only be released if he agreed to spy for them in the New World. Mosquera agreed, headed to Uruguay, and promptly handed himself in at the American consulate in Montevideo. Described as 'a tall, pleasant-looking businessman with some glamour effect', he was given a new identity as Max Rudloff by the FBI.

Mosquera's German instructions were to make his way to New York, build a wireless transmitter, and begin sending military information as soon as possible. The FBI duly established a transmitter in a farmhouse on a secluded section of the Long Island coast, manned by three agents disguised as local workers and protected by a pack of guard dogs. Soon he was sending several transmissions a week, and recruiting fake sub-agents, in the manner of Garbo: an engineer who worked in an aircraft factory, an official in the War Department, and a civilian in the Navy Department. Mosquera had not been long in New York when he conceived a grand passion for a much younger woman of Italian extraction who wanted to be an opera singer. Mosquera demanded that the FBI hand over $15,000 to enable her to pursue her operatic career. The bureau arranged for Mosquera's inamorata to 'audition at the Metropolitan Opera', the first and only time that institution has taken an active role in international espionage.

Mosquera was only the first of the FBI's double agents. Next came a Dutchman named Alfred Meiler, a former diamond dealer sent to the US to gather information on atomic research, who turned himself in and was set to work reporting titbits of misinformation from naval dockyards. Helmut Goldschmidt, a Dutch-born Orthodox Jew who had renounced Judaism, deserted from the Dutch army, and then signed up with the Abwehr, was described by the FBI as 'an extremely selfish individual, arrogant, extremely difficult to control, and of a very low-grade moral character'. Goldschmidt handed himself in and became agent 'Peasant'. The most glamorous of the American–based double agents was Dieudonner Costes, a French former flying ace. Recruited by the Abwehr and sent on an espionage mission to the US, he turned himself in and was duly installed in New York's Park Lane Hotel, where he began sending letters in secret ink. 'Although he might not deliberately try to assist the Germans,' the FBI reported of the flamboyant, arrogant and dubious Costes, 'he does not hesitate to resort to falsehoods in any situations.'

The FBI took a cautious approach, seldom permitting double agents to fashion their own messages, 'chicken-feed' with misinformation thrown in. They reported on military production, insignia and the units departing for the European theatre. Folded into Operation Bodyguard, American double agents were set to work promoting the idea that the invasion would be postponed owing to lack of landing craft, industrial unrest and the slow build-up of American troops. The US agents were not in a position to report on the immediate preparations for the D-Day assault, yet the slow but steady trickle of corroborative material provided a distinct minor melody in the major symphony now under way.

As Masterman's small orchestra of double agents tuned up, a small, discordant note became audible, growing louder as the day of the grand performance approached. There was, it seemed, another band of spies in Britain, playing their own song. Early in 1942, Most Secret Sources revealed the existence of a highly regarded German agent codenamed 'Ostro'. A Czech businessman named Paul Fidrmuc, Ostro was based in Lisbon but boasted a wide espionage network, including five spies on British soil, as well as other parts of the British Empire, the Middle East and America. Ostro was highly paid for his reports, which were passed directly from the Abwehr in Lisbon to Berlin. Indeed, he was sometimes sent the reports from other agents for evaluation, and 'regarded in Berlin as a sort of prima donna who must not be ruffled'.

Ostro was reticent about his sources of information, for good reason: he was making it all up. Like Garbo before him, Fidrmuc had worked out that German hunger for information was so acute that the Abwehr would pay handsomely for invented information, and the more secretively that information was passed on, the more likely they were to believe it. Wartime intelligence often throws up such 'freelancers', canny individuals who realise that in a situation where the buyer cannot check the quality of the goods, dealing in false commodities is both easier and safer than genuine trade. The Germans had no idea that Ostro was feeding them nonsense, but the British did.

The Bletchley decrypts clearly showed that Fidrmuc's reports were an amalgam of imagination, half-baked deduction and quarter-baked gossip, bearing little relation to reality. Yet Ostro was anything but harmless. His reports would inevitably contradict, at times, what was being reported by the controlled double agents, and dilute their effect. More worryingly, his guesswork might accidentally reveal the truth. Ostro was spinning his own deception, and there was not room enough in the game for two. MI5, MI6 and the London Controlling Section discussed the options. Like Garbo, Ostro could be approached and brought under British control; alternatively, he could be discredited in Abwehr eyes if he was exposed as a fraud. A more radical alternative would be to kill him, an option backed by the shark-eyed John Marriott: 'If liquidation means the literal abolition of Ostro by doing away with him altogether . . . then I naturally consider that the best solution to the whole affair.' Garbo was a fabulist, who had been welcomed into the MI5 embrace; Ostro was also making it up, and might have to be murdered. 'We should try to buy him up or bump him off,' thought Liddell. For reasons more practical

than humanitarian, it was finally agreed that MI5 would 'try to
discredit Ostro rather than eliminate him'. Any move against
Fidrmuc risked revealing how he had been rumbled, and Most
Secret Sources must be protected at all costs. Ostro's life was
spared, a decision MI5 would come to regret.

Enriching the Chicken-feed

As 1944 dawned, Juan Pujol was in the highest spirits: he was beloved of both the British and German intelligence services, and he had a new girlfriend. Somewhat ungallantly he described her to his German handlers as 'less than beautiful and rather dowdy in her dress [and] unaccustomed to attentions of the opposite sex', but 'delightfully indiscreet' – which was ideal since she worked as a secretary in the War Office and had access to useful information on the forthcoming invasion. She was also imaginary. Garbo's acquisition of a fantasy lover was part of his job, but it was also surely a reflection on the state of Pujol's marriage.

Tommy Harris led Garbo into ever more extreme and colourful realms of make-believe. 'I would never have had the nerve to allow any of my agents to be as audacious as he was,' Christopher Harmer later said. In addition to his plain new lover, Garbo's fictitious web now included an American sergeant ('jocular and fairly talkative'), a Greek deserter, a commercial traveller and, strangest of all, a group of fiercely anti-semitic Welshmen dedicated to bringing National Socialism to the valleys and toppling the British government by a campaign of assassination. 'The Brothers in the Aryan World Order' had just twelve members, led by an Indian poet named Rags. Three of the 'Brothers' were brought into the network, and a 'Sister', Theresa Jardine, a Wren (in the Women's Royal Naval Service) and the Hindi-speaking girlfriend of Rags. None of these people existed.

It would be reasonable, at this point, to wonder if Garbo and Harris had gone wildly over the top. Rags and his posse of Welsh fascists seem like caricatures, the villains of cheap melodrama. Could the Germans really be expected to believe that a gang of murderous racists planned to destroy the government and seize power, killing Jews, communists and other 'undesirables'? They could; because, of course, that is exactly what had happened in Germany. Importantly, the new recruits offered an opportunity to establish the network in sensitive coastal areas, ahead of the travel ban that would precede Operation Overlord, the invasion of Europe.

The Garbo network now consisted of a staggering twenty-four agents, of whom only one, Pujol himself, was real. With a secure telephone link to both MI5 and the Expeditionary Force headquarters, Pujol and Harris fed directly into military planning and the overarching deception. Over the next six months, Garbo's network would send an average of four wireless messages a day. Pujol himself was privy to Operation Fortitude, the cover plan and the real plan; he knew which divisions were genuine, and which false, where the attack would take place, and where it would not. He was more trusted than ever, by both sides. The Germans began submitting wish lists of secrets: the dates and targets of the invasion, the troops involved, types of landing craft, warships and embarkation points. He was specifically asked to inspect the coast between Weymouth and Southampton, where troops were already massing for the Normandy invasion. 'There is no concentration at special points,' he reported. The Brothers in the Aryan World Order were deployed to Brighton, Exeter, Harwich and Southampton, where they would be ideally situated to relay misinformation about the forthcoming invasion.

The poultry farmer from Barcelona was getting all his ducks in a row.

★

Elvira Chaudoir, Agent Bronx, was also wheedling her way deeper into German affections, by rather different methods. Her early letters contained snippets of political and economic gossip supposedly gleaned from the military officers, politicians, society ladies, industrialists and journalists she encountered around the gaming tables of fashionable London. From late 1943, Hugh Astor began to make her letters 'more military in character to enable her to play a part in current deception policy'. The response from Germany was swift and gratifying. She was bombarded with questions about military installations, troop movements and even the possible use of radar to divert 'radio controlled rockets'. Bronx reported rumours that 'big magnetic deflecting fields' were to be deployed. The exchange, Tar observed, 'showed German faith in Bronx on a crucial matter'. She passed on harmless information about egg rationing, and small items she imagined might be true ('Great invasion problem is seasickness. Canadians studying new cure'), but also deceptive material to suggest that the vast, slowly assembling US Army was plagued by logistical problems that would delay any attack. In Liverpool docks, she reported seeing 'hundreds of American tanks, many Jeeps, cases, cranes etc.', but added that the newspaper baron Lord Kelmsley had told her there would be 'no invasion for months' owing to a 'shortage of barges'.

The Germans were pleased: 'Good work. Good reward. Information wanted. Movement of troops in Scotland and S. England. Details of preparations for European landing.' A gambling party girl picked up in a French casino was being transformed, in German eyes, into an important agent with access to top-grade military information: 'The principal thing is the invasion of Europe, above all in France,' Helmut Bleil told her.

For all Elvira's apparent capriciousness, Bronx was no Brutus, playing one side against the other: 'Of the cases I have had to deal with, Bronx is the only one who has told the entire truth about her recruitment and mission,' reported Harmer. The tap on her telephone had produced only 'a lot of perhaps interesting, but irrelevant details about her private life', including a close relationship with Monica Sheriffe, a racehorse owner. 'Bronx assures me that Miss Sheriffe knows nothing about her work with this Department and I think that this is true,' wrote Hugh Astor, who took over the case when Harmer was transferred to the Expeditionary Force HQ. Her loyalty was beyond question. 'She was a British agent before she was ever recruited by the Germans, and is probably one of our most reliable agents.'

The regular German payments into her Swiss and Portuguese bank accounts now included a substantial bonus, yet Elvira was flat broke, with ballooning debts. Dunning letters from her bookmakers, dressmaker and various casinos mounted up on the doormat of her Mayfair flat. She did not open them. MI5 already had. She owed the Hamilton Club alone more than £1,000. Elvira begged her mother for more money. 'It is absolutely impossible to pay for lodging, food, clothes, dentists, medicine, amusements etc., with the amount I receive.' She did not mention that her amusements included a gambling habit worthy of a shipping tycoon, and a whopping drinks bill. As ever, her most sympathetic listener was Claude Dansey of MI6, who clucked with disbelief when told what MI5 was paying her. He gave her £15, and seemed determined, Harmer reported, 'to twist our tails by telling Bronx to get as much out of us as she could'. MI5 was livid that an officer in the sister service was interfering in this way: 'She has no right to discuss the matter with Dansey at all.'

Bronx could communicate only by secret letters (of which she had now sent more than fifty), but the postal service was so slow that anything she sent in the immediate build-up to invasion would arrive too late to be of any use. This thought seems to have occurred to her German handlers, for in February 1944 a letter arrived at Elvira's flat, written in secret ink, suggesting that if she uncovered invasion information she should send a message to the bank in Lisbon to indicate where and when the attack would take place. The warning should be in a 'plain language code', a message that looks perfectly innocuous to the uninitiated. Here was a perfect opportunity to plug Bronx into the heart of the D-Day deception.

The code suggested by Bleil was very simple. If and when she discovered the target, she should send a telegram, in French, to Antonio Manuel de Almeida, Director and General Manager of the Banco Espirito Santo in Lisbon, asking him to make a money transfer. The sum requested would indicate the target area. If she asked for £80, that meant the attack was aimed at the Atlantic coast of France; £70 would indicate northern France and Belgium; £60, northern France; £50 for the Bay of Biscay; £40, the Mediterranean; £30, Denmark; £20, Norway and £10 for the Balkans. Elvira was told to send the message only when 'absolutely certain of what will happen and a week before the landings are to take place'. The Portuguese bank was known to have links to Deutsche Bank, and had been under British surveillance for some time. Its owner, Richard Espirito Santo, was a personal friend of the Portuguese dictator, Salazar, and had played host to the Duke and Duchess of Windsor in 1940. (He was also the brother of Edgar Espirito Santo, the sometime lover of Yvonne Delidaise, Emile Kliemann's French mistress.) The plan set out by Bleil proved that, although Portugal was neutral, 'the general manager of the bank had certainly lent his name and good offices to the Germans in an attempt to obtain from this country most vital information about forthcoming military operations'. There was enough evidence here to warrant a formal complaint to the Portuguese government, but this would instantly scupper Elvira's career as an agent, and 'in view of the part which Bronx should be able to play in current deception plans, it is clearly against our interests to blow Bronx'.

Harmer pointed out that the geographical areas indicated by the plain language code were broad, and did not fit precisely with the Bodyguard plan. 'If it is desired to send a telegram indicating that the landing will be in the Pas de Calais area, the difficulty is that the codeword covers the whole of northern France and Belgium.' But improving the code by subdividing the target areas 'would appear too professional for someone of the character of Bronx'. Elvira nonetheless sent back a letter suggesting some refinements: if she wrote that she needed the money '*pour mon dentiste*', that would mean the information was 'certain'; if she wrote '*pour mon docteur*' it was 'almost certain'; but if the words used were '*pour mon médécin*', it was only 'probable'. She also added a timescale: '*tout de suite*' meant the landing would be in one week's time; '*urgent*' indicated an attack in a fortnight; '*vite*' would indicate a month; and if she asked for the cash '*si possible*', then the date was still uncertain. Here was a simple, swift and effective way of sending the Germans barking up the wrong tree, neatly disguised as a medical bill.

In August 1943 a Polish court martial had found Roman Czerniawski guilty of gross insubordination. 'Anxious to hush the whole matter up', the Polish authorities sentenced him to just two months' imprisonment. Since he had already been inside for six weeks, the remainder of his sentence was postponed until after the war. He never served it.

Czerniawski was vigorously unrepentant. Indeed, his rebellion and punishment raised him yet higher in his own estimation. His handler Christopher Harmer reported wearily that Brutus 'declined to give any promise that he will not interfere in Polish internal affairs'. Monique Deschamps, once Czerniawski's sub-agent, now his lover, was waiting for him when he got back to the Brompton flat and he immediately asked her to marry him. She was somewhat taken aback by this 'most unorthodox proposal of marriage', but told MI5, with an irony that suggests she knew exactly what she was dealing with, 'Ah, but you must remember that he is a super-man, and super-men are always eccentric.' She accepted his proposal. An internal MI5 memo wondered how much she knew about Czerniawski's espionage, but concluded that if he had let her in on the secret 'her personal loyalty to him was sufficient to make her keep her mouth shut'.

Czerniawski saw no reason why he should not immediately resume his role in the Double Cross team. MI5 was less sanguine. The Germans were likely to be suspicious at the 'peculiar circumstances of his arrest and release'. Czerniawski was fickle, irritating and meddlesome. 'We can never guarantee that he will not intrigue,' wrote Harmer. 'He can be a great nuisance to us if he gets into trouble again.' Yet he had also shown how useful he could be. Until Czerniawski's arrest, the Germans had shown complete faith in him and as a professional intelligence officer, his information was taken seriously in Berlin: 'Of all the agents, Brutus appears to be the one who works most directly to the military authorities.' Harmer insisted that despite his vexatious personality, Czerniawski was 'dynamic and industrious' and 'an excellent agent who is very easy to run – of all the people I have run he is the only one who has never complained'.

It was agreed that Brutus would resume contact with the enemy, but cautiously, and under close supervision. He would be steered away from active deception since, if he was suspected, this could backfire. Left idle, Czerniawski would certainly start plotting again, but perhaps, wrote Harmer, the run-up to D-Day would 'become sufficiently exciting to occupy his thoughts'. Most Secret Sources would be combed for evidence of German mistrust, and he would no longer operate his own wireless. Instead, he would tell the Germans he had recruited a wireless operator, a disgruntled and cash-strapped Polish former air force officer living in Reading, whose family had been killed by the Soviets and who was therefore willing to aid the Germans against the Bolsheviks for ideological reasons. In intelligence jargon, radio operators were known as 'pianists'; this fictional sub-agent was therefore given the codename 'Chopin', in honour of Poland's great pianist and composer. Chopin's compositions would be performed by MI5, from a transmitter in Richmond.

In late summer 1943, Czerniawski resumed radio contact with Paris. Colonel Oscar Reile's response was welcoming, but reserved. Sure enough, Bletchley Park intercepts indicated that 'Agent Hubert' was no longer fully trusted. Reile had begun to wonder whether the radio was really being operated by Czerniawski, or 'an enemy radio-operator who transmitted only what the Intelligence Service allowed'. In his memoirs, written many years later, Reile claimed that he had made up his mind, with 'a probability bordering on certainty', that Czerniawski was a British double agent. 'Not the least of my reasons for arriving at this conclusion was that none of the radio messages which came from England contained any enquiry about the sixty-six members of the *Réseau Interallié* who were still in the hands of the Germans.' Czerniawski had agreed to spy for Germany on condition they were not ill-treated, yet he never inquired about the wellbeing of these hostages. This was a serious mistake on the part of Czerniawski and his handlers, but it seems unlikely that Reile really spotted it at the time. If Reile was genuinely suspicious, he kept his doubts to himself.

As the weeks passed, German concerns about Brutus seemed to evaporate. Czerniawski kept up a stream of chatty, informal banter with Reile. Indeed, their relations appeared so cordial that Harmer 'suggested, half-jokingly', that Brutus should 'send a personal message to the Colonel saying that in his view Germany had lost the war but might still save Europe from Bolshevism if the High Command were prepared to let the English and Americans land unopposed'. Czerniawski leapt at the idea of interceding personally with Hitler to ensure the success of D-Day, and pronounced it 'an excellent idea'. More surprisingly, Tar agreed: 'I like the suggestion,' he wrote. Czerniawski set to work drafting a message to Reile, in which he assumed the role of spokesman for the Polish nation.

Colonel! I conceive it my duty to speak frankly to you. I am now convinced that Germany has lost the war . . . I must ask you to state precisely the terms on which Germany is prepared to collaborate with my country. What will be our status in Europe and how far is Germany prepared to grant concessions before the end of the war? You know that I have risked everything for the ideals we have in common. The greatest service Germany could now offer to European civilisation would be for your High Command to indicate to the Anglo-American armies that when they land they can do so unopposed. Your armies could then unite with those of un-Bolshevised countries to save Europe from Communism.

It is not clear whether this message was ever sent. If it was, it had no effect.

By December 1943, Most Secret Sources had proved that the Brutus case was firmly back on track: 'The Germans appear to have regained confidence in him. They regard him once more as being genuine [and] once they have accepted him and regard him as an important agent, they are unlikely to go back on their judgment.' A few days before Christmas, the decoders sent through an intercepted message in which 'the Germans expressed their great appreciation of Brutus's work'. Harmer began lobbying for Czerniawski to be used for active deception in Operation Fortitude. 'The Brutus case could be developed as an effective means of deceiving the enemy,' he wrote. If not, it should be shut down, since continuing to stuff Reile with chicken-feed was 'a complete waste of time'. If the case was closed, Harmer suggested that MI5 send Reile a personal message saying: 'We have caught your man. It was clever of you to recruit him, but we know everything now. We think he is a little mad, and so we are not going to shoot him. We will, however, communicate with you from time to time to discuss matters of mutual interest.'

If, on the other hand, it was decided to keep the case running, then Czerniawski should send over high-grade military misinformation. Reile was asking specific questions about the forthcoming invasion, and so 'the opportunities for using this case for deception are very great'. Indeed, with Chopin tapping out regular messages to Paris, he might eventually rival the star of the team. 'Brutus is getting questions on the same level as Garbo' and the Brutus channel was an 'even better wireless link than Garbo'. In a note on the Brutus file, John Marriott observed: 'The objectives to be gained by running double agents are numerous, but there is one overriding objective: to delude the enemy to his undoing.' Czerniawski was reintegrated into the great deception.

Brutus marked his return to the team with a message to Reile laying down his conditions: the secret of the D-Day landings in exchange for Poland's liberty.

> The risks involved in helping the Axis to resist the coming offensive are justified only if I have your government's undertaking, after the defeat of the Allies, to offer through me to the Polish government liberal peace terms. In setting up an organisation to give you full and up-to-date information about military preparations for an invasion, I am acting solely from ideological motives and with the object of securing for Poland an honourable place in the new Europe. This is the only reward I ask.

The London winter wrapped around Lily Sergeyev like a soggy cloak. Her kidneys ached. She spent long hours alone in the Rugby Mansions flat, although Maritza Mihailovic, double agent Snark, was seldom far away. Every few days, Mary Sherer would march in with her attaché case, a model of brisk efficiency. Together, they would draft and redraft letters for Kliemann, cover letters to the address in Lisbon containing idle chat with messages beneath, in secret ink. 'The information doesn't seem to make much sense,' Lily wrote in her diary. 'Bits of conversations mentioning ranks and badges; trains supposedly seen in stations; information obtained by chance by overhearing conversations in the train.' She visited her relatives near Bristol, with Mary in attendance. Forces for the Normandy landings were already assembling in the area, but in her letters Lily described 'lonely countryside and empty main roads which were in fact bustling from dawn to dusk and through the night, with troop movements'.

Tar Robertson explained the plan in broad terms: 'For the last few months the Germans have been desperately trying to find out where we plan to land our forces. With your help, we can make them think that we have made our preparations to invade an area which in fact we have no intention of going anywhere near. If we succeed, the Germans will concentrate their troops in the worst possible places to cope with the landing when it is finally launched.' Lily was not told that the real target was Normandy, nor that Calais was the cover target: 'I don't try to guess what all these scraps might add up to. Obviously the Germans will make certain deductions from them,' she wrote in her diary.

Lily had expected to find excitement as a double agent. Instead, she was miserable. Mary Sherer and Gisela Ashley (whom she knew as 'Louisa') took her to lunch at Chez Kampinski restaurant, and tried to cheer her up. Lily liked Louisa – they called each other 'Ducky' – but could not warm to Mary, so proper, so reserved and so entirely unsympathetic to Lily's moods. Theirs was a head-on collision of culture and personality: the emotional, temperamental Frenchwoman and the buttoned-down, aloof Englishwoman. 'I want to love and hate; to be alive,' wrote Lily. 'I find the English cold, uncommunicative, undemonstrative, impenetrable. I would like to see Mary laugh, or cry, or scream; I would like to see her face express something. To me she seems almost an automaton.' Lily sensed, rightly, that beneath the no-nonsense manner was a far more vulnerable and interesting person. 'There is something about Mary, in the way she twists her legs in a spiral, in the way her stockings come down like a corkscrew, in the way she walks with a long stride, swinging her arms and perhaps humming a little song, which doesn't fit in with the tough face she wants to show the world.'

Lily repeatedly demanded to be reunited with Babs, but the response was always non-committal and evasive. She fired off increasingly irate telegrams to O'Shagar, the MI6 officer in Gibraltar, asking for news of the dog. In a note to Tar, Mary warned that Treasure was becoming 'very unreasonable' and that a major explosion was brewing. 'Treasure is very upset about the absence of her dog, and has seriously threatened that if the dog does not arrive soon she will not work anymore. I think this can be dealt with but it will mean a scene.' Mary was not as unsympathetic as she seemed; she was a dog lover herself, and felt for Lily; but in Mary's world, rules were sacred. 'I do not quite know what we can do to help, because if we have the dog sent over here officially it will have to go into quarantine, which from Treasure's point of view would be as bad as having it in Gibraltar. I am afraid that Treasure's American boyfriend has let her down and has no intention of smuggling the dog over here for her, I am wondering whether we could get the Royal Navy to help via Commander Montagu.' Britain was preparing for battle on an epic scale, and MI5 was seriously considering whether to deploy a Navy submarine to fetch a small dog, illegally, in order to placate a volatile double agent.

Lily had long complained of what she called 'her *internal* troubles'. In December she was 'seized with a fit of shivering and trembling'. Mary told her to snap out of it. 'You cannot be ill. You haven't any right to!' It was a joke, but not the sort that Lily appreciated. Ailing, lonely and filled with self-pity, Lily was spoiling for a fight. The ensuing exchange is detailed in her diary:

'Mary, it's obvious now that my pilot isn't going to bring Babs over. Could you do something about it?'

'No: I have already told you so.'

'Do you mean to say that you refuse to keep the promise made to me by Benton?'

'We can't help it if you were promised something contrary to the regulations.'

'In that case I don't have to keep the promise I made to work with you. From now on you can get on alone.'

Mary Sherer was furious. Her ingrained sense of duty simply did not accept that, in the middle of a war, someone could down tools and withdraw cooperation: 'You refuse to work?'

'Certainly.'

'But it's stupid. You know we need you.'

'Nevertheless, my work is not worth a small dog.'

'You act like a spoilt child! You want something and you mean to have it. Well, you can't. You're ill. You'll change your mind when you have thought things over.'

Mary stormed out of the room, slamming the door behind her. The next day, Christmas Eve 1943, Lily made a rambling entry in her diary. 'My brain is empty of thoughts. I'm lighter than the air, I'm gliding across the ceiling. I'm going to die.' Maritza, the housekeeper-spy, alerted Mary, who sent an urgent message to MI5 headquarters: 'Treasure is behaving in an eccentric manner, despite her fever, wandering around in her pyjamas, and sitting on the floor in the drawing room. Snark found her dancing.'

Delirious, Lily was rushed to St Mary's Hospital. Dr Hanfield Jones examined her, and diagnosed chronic kidney stones. When she came round, Mary Sherer was at her bedside. Lily was unwell, but not nearly as ill as she believed. The combination of a high fever and a highly developed sense of drama had convinced her that she was on her deathbed.

'It seems I won't live,' she told her case officer, with a gust of Gallic melodrama.

'Nonsense,' said Mary Sherer.

('I love the way Mary says nonsense,' Lily later wrote. 'She says it with so much conviction.')

Tar Robertson arrived the next day, carrying a bunch of jonquils and daffodils. Lily was feeling better, but still convinced she was dying, with maximum melodrama: 'I don't want to die here. If I died now, my soul would get lost in the fog.'

Robertson, usually so affable and cheery, struck Lily as oddly ill at ease. But she was feeling too weak for another row. She drifted off to sleep.

Over the next three weeks, Lily regained her appetite and some of her spirit. In early January, Lily sent a message in secret ink to Kliemann explaining that her long silence had been down to illness. She had obtained a Hallicrafter 'Sky Rider' radio that could receive but not transmit messages, she told him, and would be listening in for his messages on the agreed frequency. B1A's technicians duly set up the radio. Treasure could now receive orders and questions directly from Kliemann. His first message was encouraging: 'Information very interesting – Letters arrive well – Continue', and signed off with flirty courtesy: 'You are very charming.'

A shadow fell across Lily's brightening mood with the arrival of a telegram from Gibraltar, sent by Kenneth Larson, the American pilot who had agreed to bring over her dog, explaining that he had been forced to leave Babs in Algiers. The tone of the message struck her as odd. She showed it to her cousin: 'Why should he have left Babs in Algiers? I wonder if it's the truth. Maybe he has become attached to Babs and just wants to keep him.'

When she raised the matter of her dog with Tar Robertson, he changed the subject. Mary Sherer also declined to discuss it. Lily's sister Bimbo was living in Algiers: she would write and ask her to find out what had happened to Babs.

Mary Sherer had ambitions for Treasure. It was all very well receiving messages from Kliemann, but in order to play a full part in Operation Bodyguard she needed her own wireless set. Then, like Garbo, Brutus and Tricycle, she would be able to relay important misinformation instantly. 'Treasure could be used by us for deception,' Mary told Tar. 'She could cover various districts and could quote several reliable sources, notional and actual. The first message from the Germans indicated their confidence in Treasure. But she cannot be used for Overlord or other deception unless she gets her W/T [wireless transmitter].'

They tried to prod the sluggish Kliemann into providing a radio by reporting increased military activity: 'There is something in preparation,' Lily told him. 'I must have the promised radio transmitter.' Kliemann did nothing at all. Mary grumbled: 'If we let him "arrange" matters, either he won't know how to do it, or else it will take him so long that we will miss our opportunities.' They would have to set the ball rolling.

Mary Sherer drew up a bold plan: Lily should go to Lisbon, meet up with Kliemann, and get him to hand over a radio. It was a gamble, given Lily's volatility, but Sherer told Tar she was sure it would pay off: 'I believe, and I think you will agree, that Treasure is very capable of carrying out such a mission very successfully.' Tar gave his approval. A cover story was drawn up to explain how Lily had managed to travel to Portugal. She would tell Kliemann that through her cousin Elizabeth Hill, a Cambridge academic, she had obtained a job in the Film Division of the Ministry of Information working on the scripts of propaganda films to be shown in countries liberated from the Nazis. She would explain that she had been sent to Portugal to interview refugees and gather 'first-hand information about conditions in those countries'. It was a rather thin story, but Mary was bullish: 'You've made Kliemann swallow bigger pills than that.'

One evening, after a long day spent rehearsing her cover story with Mary, Lily returned to the flat to find a letter waiting from her sister, postmarked Algiers. She read the first sentence over and over, in stunned disbelief. 'My poor Darling, I hate the pain I will give you, but it's better you should know, so as not to make plans for the future: you will not see your Babs again: he has been run over.' Her dog, probably the only thing she had ever truly loved, the only creature to have shown her unconditional love, was dead.

Lily was distraught. 'Everything is indifferent to me now. The circle of loneliness has closed around me; I am alone, absolutely alone.' The account of Babs's death made no sense to her. Why had the dog been taken to Algiers? If he was in the care of the authorities, how had he been run over? Why had her handlers seemed so shifty when the subject was raised? Why had they failed to honour the promise to bring Babs to Britain?

When Mary Sherer arrived later that day, she said nothing about Babs, though Lily was convinced she knew what had happened to her beloved dog, and had known for some time. After the grief came boiling anger; Lily was in no doubt: the British had killed her dog. And she may have been right.

Lily believed, fervently and furiously, that Babs had been sacrificed by MI5, his death arranged as a convenient solution to a tiresome problem. Perhaps Babs was 'bumped off', sacrificed to the demands of war, or perhaps his death really was accidental. The fate of Babs the dog is a mystery. MI5's archives have been routinely 'weeded' since the war, but when a file is declassified it is usually accompanied by a file index which lists, in chronological order, all the items in the original file. In other words, one can see what has been removed. Between 25 November and 29 December 1943, no less than nine separate items were entered in the Treasure file relating to Babs. The index entry headings are specific: 'Report from Mary Sherer on Treasure and the dog'; 'Notes of enquiry re: quarantine regulations with regard to Treasure's dog'; 'To SIS request for enquiries to Gibraltar re: Treasure's Dog'; 'Note re: Treasure's dog', and so on. Every single one has been taken from the file and destroyed.

Mary Sherer was surprised how well, after her initial distress, Lily took the news of Babs's death. She seemed 'in good spirits and much more enthusiastic about her case', and eager to get to Lisbon and see Kliemann. Had she read Lily's diaries, Mary would have formed a rather different impression. Lily was a born actress, a slave to her feelings, but also quite adept at hiding them when she wanted to. 'I can change my skin quite easily now,' she wrote. Agent Treasure was in deep mourning for Babs, and quietly plotting revenge.

Artist Paints a Picture

Johnny Jebsen was getting cold feet. His disgust with the Nazi regime was undimmed, but something in his mottled conscience rebelled against the idea of betraying his German colleagues. Moreover, the danger from the Gestapo seemed to have receded. Kammler, the corrupt Lisbon Abwehr officer, had sent in a report claiming that Dusko Popov must be a double agent since his reports had deteriorated 'both in quantity and quality', and pointing the finger of suspicion at Jebsen. On hearing this, Jebsen launched a personal appeal to Admiral Canaris, the Abwehr chief, protesting 'violently against machinations by Kammler to discredit him' and declaring his 'intention of throwing up his work and returning to Berlin to enlist in the army' unless he was allowed to go to Lisbon to handle the Popov case in person. The bluff worked. Canaris ruled that Kammler's denunciation had been 'malicious', and packed him off to the Eastern Front.

Spiteful or not, Kammler's suspicions were spot on, and Canaris's motives for dismissing them were, like everything the Admiral did, opaque. Canaris was almost certainly plotting against Hitler. Jebsen was sent to Lisbon with vague orders to improve 'the cover under which correspondence with agents is carried out'. Reassured that he was no longer in immediate peril, Jebsen hinted to Kenneth Benton of MI6 that perhaps it would be better if, after all, he remained independent. He was firmly told that it was too late to back out, but reassured that 'if, as he says, he wishes to do everything possible to damage the Nazi regime, then he need have no scruples in dealing with us'. Jebsen's wobble was over: 'He was convinced that he had taken an irrevocable step and that it was only consistent with his anti-Nazi principles that he should henceforth participate actively and not merely passively in the fight against the present regime in Germany.' Agent Artist was in the team, for better or worse, and for ever.

The British now had, for the first time, a spy deep within the Abwehr, working 'unconditionally' for the Allied cause. 'The fact that Johann Jebson [sic] is prepared to give us information through Tricycle offers enormous possibilities,' observed Guy Liddell. But Jebsen was also a potential liability. A report to Churchill laid out the danger.

A difficult situation has arisen since [Tricycle's] spymaster has recently been in touch with British authorities in Madrid and has told them he is under serious suspicion from the Germans and might have to ask for asylum in the UK. He said he saw no hope of German victory and that if he could get a British passport which would enable him to live in peace after the war, he might be prepared to consider any reasonable offer. While this spymaster has in his possession an enormous amount of knowledge which would be very valuable, his defection at the present time would compromise agents who are working under him, and in whom hitherto the Germans have had confidence, such as Tricycle himself.

Popov's Tricycle network was not the only asset at risk. Jebsen simply knew too much. He knew which spies the Germans were running (or believed they were running) in Britain. If he passed on this information to British intelligence, and those agents continued to function, then he would know they were under British control. For the first time, a major disagreement erupted within B1A, a fierce turf war between competing case officers anxious to protect their own agents. Hugh Astor, now running Bronx, fired the opening salvo.

If Artist is energetic in providing information, he should in due course provide us with sufficient information to effect the arrest of at least Garbo and Treasure, and it seems to me that however delicately the matter is handled, it will ultimately become obvious to Artist that all of these agents are operating under control. Thus the fortunes of some of our most valued agents will be entirely dependent on the whims of a German whom we know to be brilliantly clever, but unscrupulous and dishonest, and who may turn over his knowledge to the Germans, either by his own volition or through force of circumstances. Artist has never acted out of loyalty to the Nazi party. It has always been his sole desire to serve his own interests. In the past it has always been to his advantage to safeguard the Tricycle organisation – this has freed him from serving on the Eastern Front and provided him with considerable scope for financial gain.

The danger of his being discovered by the Abwehr increases with every day which passes. He may be arrested by the Gestapo and compromise our agents under the stress of interrogation or to turn his own knowledge to his advantage. The sudden loss of a large number of our B1A agents would in itself be a serious blow, but it would be far more serious if this loss occurred after the agents have embarked on the implementation of the Overlord deception plan [i.e. Fortitude], since it would enable the Abwehr to read their traffic in the opposite sense. The sole function of a B1A agent at the present time is to play a part in the implementation of the deception plan. Any agent who is unable to fulfil this role is unworthy of reservation. Clearly the Tricycle organisation can play no part in the deception plan, since the fact that Tricycle is operating under control is liable at any time to come to the knowledge of the Germans. Under no circumstances should Artist be allowed to remain in the Peninsula.

'I agree with his arguments on all points,' wrote Tommy Harris, Garbo's case officer. 'I am quite convinced that each day longer he remains there, the risk to the whole of the Garbo case is increased. Unless steps are immediately taken to cease contact with Artist completely or evacuate him forthwith from Spain, then grave risks of blowing the Garbo case are inevitable.' If Jebsen was whisked to Britain, MI5 could 'interrogate him at leisure', argued Harris. 'We would be able to glean a considerable amount of reliable information from Artist and the danger of a number of our most valued agents becoming compromised would be averted.' But if Jebsen disappeared, the Germans would immediately suspect Popov: to protect the deception plan, Agent Artist must be extracted immediately, and Agent Tricycle must be shut down.

It fell to Ian Wilson, Popov's case officer, to make the opposing argument. A solicitor by training, dry and precise, Wilson had made a study of Johnny Jebsen, and he leapt to his defence with lawyerly ferocity.

I find myself in complete disagreement with Mr Harris and Mr Astor. I think I can claim to have a more detailed knowledge of Artist's outlook and position than anyone else in the office. The risk of Artist disclosing information has been greatly exaggerated. I cannot imagine circumstances in which it would cease to be to Artist's own interest, as well as his inclination, to continue to act in a manner advantageous to ourselves. I entirely disagree that he is unscrupulous and dishonest. He may be unscrupulous and dishonest towards the present German government, but he has been taking every care to protect the double agents of whom he has knowledge [Tricycle, Balloon and Gelatine]. Jebsen has been endeavouring to tell the truth to Tricycle, and has been doing so in the knowledge that Tricycle will pass the information to the British. There is no evidence that any statement he has made to us was not true. Of his own accord he ran the personal risk of endeavouring to maintain his own position. I do not, therefore, agree that he has always acted out of the sole desire to serve his own interests. Artist himself fears that he is in jeopardy, but we have no independent evidence to that effect. If Artist is grilled by the Abwehr or Gestapo, he will obviously endeavour to conceal that he has directly been giving information. It seems to me the height of folly deliberately to throw away a large part of our organisation at this stage.

Like most official bodies, when faced with competing factions and equally unpalatable alternatives, MI5 opted to do nothing but wait, watch and worry. The fate of the Double Cross system now hinged on the character of Johnny Jebsen, a brave and loyal spy in Wilson's estimation, but a dodgy, self-serving opportunist in the eyes of his MI5 colleagues.

There was 'less danger of Gestapo surveillance' in Lisbon, said Wilson, and Most Secret Sources would be scanned for any hint that the authorities were closing in on Jebsen: 'Should Artist find himself in danger of being kidnapped, he will be evacuated forthwith.'

Jebsen arrived in Lisbon on 16 October 1943, where he was taken 'under the wing' of a local MI6 officer, Charles de Salis. A thirty-three-year-old linguist and poet recruited to MI6 by Kim Philby (the head of MI6's Iberian desk later exposed as a Soviet spy), de Salis had spent much of his early life in Spain, where he became a friend of the poet Federico García Lorca. He was 'a modest aesthete', according to one account, 'an amusing raconteur and a mimic'. He and Jebsen hit it off at once. De Salis was under strict instructions: 'Artist is determined to carry on to the last possible moment, but should it become clear that the game is up, we feel that to prevent his being grilled we should send him to Gibraltar. You have full authority to get Artist out if, in your judgment, the game is up, leaving his associates in complete doubt as to his fate and destination.'

The Abwehr station in Madrid was large and well-organised, with more than 200 officers and some 300 secretaries. It spied around the clock, in obedience to the strenuous work ethic of Karl-Erich Kühlenthal who, though gullible, was considered by MI5 to be 'a very efficient, ambitious and dangerous man, with an enormous capacity for hard work'. By contrast, the Abwehr in Lisbon, under Ludovico von Karsthoff, ran at a leisurely pace. The Abwehr headquarters, a comfortable flat near the Embassy, consisted of about thirty personnel, half of whom were secretaries, as well as a number of dubious hangers-on with indeterminate roles. The Abwehr officers did little other than collect letters sent to the various Lisbon cover addresses. Indeed, there was very little work to do since the Germans believed that 'the characteristics of the Portuguese – their love of the melodramatics, their rumour-mongering and their general undependability – made them poorly fitted for the work of agents'. The only local informant of note was Paul Fidrmuc, Agent Ostro, who was, of course, a charlatan.

While Kühlenthal and his colleagues sweated away in Madrid, the officers of the Lisbon Abwehr station devoted themselves to pleasure, led by von Karsthoff, who 'set the example for their gay existence'. With money skimmed from Popov's payments, von Karsthoff had purchased a new Cadillac, a house in the country near Sintra, and another pet monkey. An Abwehr officer who arrived in Lisbon shortly before Jebsen was shocked by the behaviour of his new colleagues, who 'were leading a rather loose and immoral life in Lisbon, with little concern for their duties'. Some were sleeping with their secretaries. Others were cocaine abusers. 'All had enormous amounts of money, most had their own cars, made frequent pleasure trips throughout Portugal and spent their evenings gambling in the casinos.' Jebsen felt entirely at home. Since von Karsthoff was as dependent on Popov as he was, the Abwehr station chief was unlikely to make trouble – particularly after Jebsen promised him a 'post-war job as manager in a Vienna firm'. Jebsen began to relax, confident that his friends in Berlin would tip him off if his enemies were closing in, and the British would whisk him to safety.

There was even a possibility, if a crisis occurred, that Jebsen could be extracted without wrecking the Tricycle set-up. For Jebsen had contrived a bizarre fall-back plan, by convincing his bosses that he might be able to smuggle himself into England as a spy, with the help of one of the richest men in Britain. The tale Jebsen spun for the Abwehr went like this: his father had once saved the life of Lord Rothschild, of the banking family, who therefore had 'a debt of gratitude which he is anxious to repay by doing everything possible to assist him'; Rothschild had agreed to ask his 'influential friends' to arrange for Jebsen to enter the country as a refugee and avoid internment; once in Britain, posing as 'a discontented German out of favour with the regime', he would spy for Germany.

This story was completely fabricated, but to lend it credibility, Jebsen had 'for some months been conducting a completely fictitious correspondence with the Lord Rothschild whom he has invented'. British intelligence had followed this peculiar plot through wireless intercepts, and knew that 'there is a whole file deposited with the Abwehr containing carbon copies of Artist's letters and Rothschild's replies'. In reality, it would have been quite impossible for any private citizen, no matter how rich, to bend the rules so that a German citizen could enter Britain and 'remain at large'. The Abwehr did not know this, and in accordance with the Nazi convictions about the power of Jewish bankers, it was assumed that with 'the powerful backing of Lord Rothschild', any string could be pulled. When told about the Rothschild ruse, one senior Abwehr official observed: '*was diese Juden sich alles leisten*' (these Jews can get away with anything).

If Jebsen discovered that he was about to be arrested by the Gestapo, he would tell his Abwehr colleagues that the visa promised by his friend Rothschild had come through, and then vanish. The British would spirit him to London; the Germans would believe he was a loyal agent working in the UK, and B1A would deploy him as yet another double agent. To bolster the deception, MI5 faked a letter from the Home Office stating that 'Lord Rothschild has made a request that the case be given special treatment', which Jebsen could show to his colleagues as proof of his story. Robertson gave cautious approval to this convoluted charade, pointing out that the plan was 'ingenious, but not without dangers'.

Victor Rothschild, MI5's sabotage expert, was a real Lord Rothschild, and somewhat put out to discover that his name was being manipulated in this way. He had no connection whatever with Jebsen, and worried that if the story leaked out, people might leap to the wrong conclusions. 'It might appear unnecessarily finicky on my part but it might be as well to have it permanently on record that the whole Lord Rothschild–Artist saga is imaginary.'

On 10 November 1943, the DC3 to Lisbon took off from Whitchurch airport with no fewer than three Double Cross aficionados on board. Ian Wilson of MI5 and Major Frank Foley of MI6 travelled together as Mr Watson and Mr Fairclough. In another seat, studiously ignoring his case officers and travelling under his own name, was Dusko Popov. It had been decided that sending Tricycle back to Portugal would further strengthen his hand in the run-up to D-Day: 'After he returns to England, any deceptive material which we can pass over through him will have greater prospect of being implicitly believed.' Because of the uncertainty surrounding Jebsen, Popov did not yet pass over any positively misleading material, in case he was rumbled. Instead he carried a Yugoslavian diplomatic bag stuffed with the highest-grade chicken-feed for von Karsthoff: notes, photographs and documents, information that was accurate and apparently useful to the enemy, but essentially worthless. If all went according to plan, he would be back in Britain soon after Christmas, 'in time to participate in any major deception'.

Wilson and Foley intended to meet Jebsen in Lisbon, assess his character, debrief him, and boost his resolve: 'To make him feel that we regard him as being of great value to us; to prevent him from feeling he is betraying his own country; to treat him as a far-sighted and internationally minded man, who realises that the war is going to be won by the Allies, and that the Nazi party and military power in Germany will be eliminated.' They would tell him that 'any action that helps towards bringing the war to a speedy end will be to the advantage of Germany as well as the rest of the world in saving unnecessary loss of life by continued warfare'. Then they would quiz him on every aspect of German intelligence, from spies, to secret inks, to pigeons.

Charles de Salis of MI6 had arranged a rendezvous at a safe house in Lisbon. They had been waiting an hour when Jebsen shuffled in, an unkempt figure in a dark Homburg, dirty raincoat and unpolished shoes. He smiled broadly, and stuck out a hand. Wilson noted his nicotine-stained fingers, and ostentatious ruby wedding ring. Wilson was a deeply conservative English lawyer, a stolid upholder of all that was traditional and established; Johnny Jebsen was an international chancer, louche and unconventional. They had almost nothing in common. Yet from first sight, they established an affinity that would deepen with time. Johnny was a deal-maker, and before getting down to business, he wanted some guarantees: immunity from prosecution for anything he might have done in connection with the forgery swindle; help to obtain Danish or British citizenship after the war; and a promise that 'should anything happen to him, we will take care of his wife'. The final clause was a characteristic touch: Jebsen had started an affair with a secretary in the Lisbon Abwehr office; he had one mistress in Paris and another, of more recent acquisition, in Madrid. Yet he remained, despite his chronically adulterous habits, profoundly

loyal to his actress wife Lore. His final request was a humane
one: 'If through information obtained through Artist we are
successful in arresting German agents, such agents will not be
executed.'

Wilson's response was carefully couched: 'I made it clear that
any assurances which he might receive from us were conditional
on our being satisfied, when we had full information after the
war, that he had in fact assisted us to the best of his ability
and had not at any time endeavoured to mislead us.' This was
enough for Jebsen: for all his cynicism, he believed profoundly,
as a devotee of P. G. Wodehouse, that an Englishman's word
was his bond.

Reassured, Jebsen began spilling the beans. Over the next four
days, smoking an endless succession of cigarettes and drinking
champagne as if it was water, he painted a detailed picture of
the interior workings of the Third Reich intelligence apparatus,
and the battle for power within the Nazi High Command. 'The
Abwehr generally is demoralised and cynical and in fact the
OKW [Oberkommando der Wehrmacht] have known for at
least a year past that Germany has lost the war,' he said. German
intelligence was in disarray, riddled with corruption and beset
by internal feuding. Canaris was under intense pressure, with
Himmler actively plotting to take over the Abwehr with his own
SD, the Nazi party intelligence service. 'Himmler is the most
ambitious man in Germany but knows that the army would
not tolerate him in Hitler's place, so remains loyal. Contrary to
popular belief, Hitler does not believe in shooting his old friends
unless they have become a danger to himself. The leaders of the
SS will remain loyal to Hitler and the rank and file of the SS are
entirely under the influence of their leaders.' Jebsen's powers of
recall were extraordinary; this nervous little man was 'a living
dictionary on the whole of the Gestapo'.

Earlier that year, in Madrid, Jebsen had told Benton the
rumours about a 'rocket gun' being developed by Hitler's
scientists. Now he had more solid information, picked up not on

the grapevine, but in the bedroom. While in Spain, in between defecting to MI6 and visiting his favourite pornographic cinema, Jebsen had found time to start an affair with a married woman, one Baroness Gertzen. She was secretary to a German aircraft manufacturer named Henschel, whose factories supplied parts for the flying bomb project. 'The Baroness is very much in love with Artist [and] was easily induced to talk about the likelihood of severe bombardment of the UK.' Jebsen told her that he would soon be travelling to Britain, and slyly pretended to be fearful 'of going to a country which might be the object of an attack by Hitler's secret weapon'. Jebsen even 'spun a yarn to the effect that there had been a prophecy about him being struck by lightning in December!'

Baroness Gertzen was privy to all her boss's correspondence, and remarkably naive: 'She immediately promised to give him all details of the weapon [and] guarantees to send a cable to Artist wherever he is as soon as she gets information that the rocket will be used. If he is in England, this will give him time to escape to Scotland!' The rocket gun, Jebsen reported, was being built at an 'experimental station located at Peenemünde' on Germany's Baltic coast. The British already had an idea of what was happening in Peenemünde. Indeed, the RAF had attacked the site back in August. Jebsen's willingness to hand over such explosive information, gleaned from pillow talk, was a measure of his commitment, and his guile.

One by one, he listed the German spies operating on British soil, and how they were rated in Berlin: Popov, under suspicion during his American sojourn, was once again cherished by the Abwehr; Balloon was 'lazy'; Gelatine patchy, but occasionally useful. The much-feted Agent Ostro 'never disclosed to anyone who his agents are or where he gets his information'. He promised to find out more about the mysterious Ostro. Jebsen went on to recite chapter and verse on the Garbo network, with 'full details of most secret agents', including how and what they were paid.

This was exactly what British intelligence had hoped he would not do. Wilson was dismayed: 'He has given us certain information which ought to have assisted us to trace these agents if they really existed and we did not already control them, and he may have drawn correct inferences from our reactions.' Jebsen observed that he had long been suspicious of the ease with which Garbo (Agent Arabel, as he was to the Germans) transmitted reports from Britain, and speculated that Kühlenthal himself might be in the pay of MI6: 'He left us in no doubt that he was personally convinced that we control that organisation.' Wilson did his best to 'confuse Artist's state of mind about B1A agents' and put him off the scent. Rooting out spies in Britain was 'relatively unimportant work', he blustered. But Johnny Jebsen was no fool. 'Artist left me with the clear impression that he did not believe that any agents purporting to write letters or send messages from England were genuine', and suspected that these spies were all either 'controlled or non-existent (or partly one and partly the other)'. When MI5 failed to act on the information he had supplied, he would know for certain that the German espionage network was a sham.

Jebsen's own position, he said, had 'considerably improved' since his arrival in Lisbon. Both Canaris and Georg Hansen, the head of Abwehr foreign intelligence, were protecting him, and he was under specific orders not to return to Germany until the Gestapo business had been sorted out. He knew there was still a danger 'that the Gestapo will effect his return to Germany and he will be summarily disposed of', but a friend in the SD had told him that 'kidnapping in Portugal was now almost impossible'. Even so, Jebsen knew what would happen if he was uncovered as a British spy: the Ablege Kommandos hit squad would be sent to get him. 'They have a poison which can be dissolved in water or added to food which is quite tasteless,' said Jebsen grimly. 'Twenty minutes after death there is no trace in the body.' He was confident he would be alerted to any imminent threat in time to act, but as an extra precaution he had started an affair with Lily Grass, secretary to Aloys Schreiber, the newly appointed head of counter-intelligence in Lisbon. If the Gestapo made a move on Jebsen, they would tell Schreiber beforehand, in which case Lily Grass would hear of it, and tip him off.

'Jebsen has been giving Lily Grass considerable attention,' reported Wilson. 'She is in love with Artist and if the latter takes the trouble to hide the fact that he finds her tedious, he will able to count on her support.' Wilson was impressed by Jebsen's resolve and ingenuity: 'We have formed a favourable impression of his nerve and do not believe he will seek shelter unless it is necessary.'

Wilson ran through Jebsen's 'highly complex' motives: 'A genuine dislike of Nazism; a belief in the British political system; a conviction that Germany has lost the war; a fear of communism which can only be avoided by increased English influence in Western Europe; a contempt for the corruption and inefficiency of the Abwehr; the realisation that his own future as a big businessman depends on the restoration of normal trading activities; a desire to reinsure himself.' Jebsen seemed impelled by a combination of opportunism, idealism and above all personal loyalty to Popov. If he had a credo, it was P. G. Wodehouse's 'Code of the Woosters': 'Never let a pal down'. 'He at no time spoke of any financial reward and I am sure he does not expect any financial assistance.' He was even prepared to fake information for the Germans on Britain's behalf: 'Artist says that if we want foodstuff we should let him write it – he knows exactly what the Germans want and has been writing the stuff for years.'

Jebsen was an odd figure, Wilson reflected, raddled and raffish but oddly romantic. 'Looks ten years older than his thirty years; reddish, blond hair combed back; heavy moustache; very slender, body bent forward; grey blue eyes and very pronounced cheekbones; unhealthy pale complexion (lung disease?); smokes

about 100 cigarettes over a day; very bad teeth from frequent
smoking; eats little and drinks only champagne; unable to drive;
rides horseback; writes philosophical books.' Yet as Jebsen's trail
of seduction showed, there was something intensely attractive
about him, and a core of strength that belied his twitchy manner.
Wilson trusted him. 'No doubt Artist is acting mainly out of self-
interest but of a clear-sighted and long-term character. A man
of his undoubted intelligence is unlikely to try to deceive us
on any matter where he is liable to be found out after the war.'
Wilson was quite sure that Jebsen was prepared to risk his life for
the Allied cause. 'I am convinced that Artist sincerely desires to
continue to work wholeheartedly with us.' When they parted,
Wilson told him: 'I hope our collaboration will endure a very
long time.'

Wilson's report caused both delight and consternation in
London. This was intelligence of the highest quality, with the
promise of more to come. On the other hand, as Astor and Harris
had feared, Jebsen was in a position to expose the falsity of the
German networks in Britain, now supplying actively deceptive
material in the run-up to D-Day. 'The extent of Artist's possible
knowledge of Garbo is a matter of some concern,' wrote Tar,
who wondered whether Jebsen knew, or merely suspected that
the German agents in Britain were frauds. 'Obviously if Artist
were approached directly on this matter it would immediately
arouse his suspicion.' Wilson assured him: 'I do not think he
has any positive proof.' But then, Jebsen did not need any. The
continued flow of information from the D-Day spies would
be proof enough of the massive hoax being perpetrated on the
German High Command.

'Artist's zeal and ability,' Churchill was told, 'has verged upon
the embarrassing. He has begun to provide us with information
about the networks maintained by the Germans in this country.
Of these the principal one is the Garbo organisation of which
it is clearly undesirable that he should make us too fully aware.
We are engaged at the moment in the delicate operation of

diverting this valuable agent's attention elsewhere. There is good promise of success.'

While Jebsen was getting to know his new British spymasters, Dusko Popov settled back in with his German handlers. Von Karsthoff was genuinely glad to see him: Popov was not only his most valuable intelligence asset, but the guarantor of his profligate lifestyle. He examined Popov's haul of information, with something less than a critical eye, and pronounced it excellent. Canaris had recently questioned whether Popov was 'worth his pay', but the latest batch of intelligence, von Karsthoff predicted, would convince the Abwehr chief that he was 'really valuable'. He threw a dinner party in Popov's honour, and invited Jebsen, Aloys Schreiber, the new head of counter-intelligence, and their secretaries. It was a bizarre occasion. Two of the guests were German intelligence officers, and two others were secretly working for British intelligence; Jebsen was sleeping with Schreiber's secretary, who was spying on her boss; the married von Karsthoff was having an affair with his secretary Elizabeth Sahrbach, while ripping off the Abwehr. Popov was conducting at least six love affairs. Everyone was involved in the lying and cheating game . . . except Mabel Harbottle, who was not sleeping with, or deceiving, anyone, and probably never had. Von Karsthoff proposed a congratulatory toast, declaring that, in return for his latest intelligence haul, Popov could expect a payment of $15,000.

Aloys Schreiber agreed that Popov's report was 'good and had been sent by courier to Berlin'. His manner, however, was chilly.

After the dinner party, von Karsthoff flew to Baden Baden for an Abwehr conference and returned ecstatic: Popov was now considered 'the best man the Abwehr have'. The accolade was duly passed back to Wilson in London, who observed: 'This may well have been deliberate flattery, but there seems to be no doubt he is at the moment extremely highly regarded.' With greedy relish, von Karsthoff told Popov that 'if his work was really good he could get almost anything he asked for'. Plans were already being laid to send him back to Britain, with more money, a fresh batch of secret ink, and a new questionnaire demanding a range of information on just about everything, as Popov later put it, 'short of a detailed account of Churchill's digestive processes'. Popov was instructed to begin transmitting from outside London, as Hitler's flying bombs would soon be laying waste to the capital.

For Popov and Jebsen, these weeks in Lisbon offered the first opportunity, since war began, to speak to one another without dissembling, or inferring, what could not be spoken. They were now officially on the same side in the game, though utterly different in temperament. As P. G. Wodehouse once remarked of cricket: 'Some batsmen are nervous all through a long innings. With others the feeling disappears with the first boundary.' Popov was unflappable, where Jebsen was a jangle of jagged nerves, but they made an outstanding partnership. They spent many happy, dissolute hours together: a pair of British spies pretending to be German spies, spending Hitler's money on themselves. Jebsen took a house in Estoril, with four servants, while Popov lived at the Palacio Hotel. They celebrated Christmas together, and Popov sent a cheery seasonal message, in secret ink, to MI5: 'I shall spend my Christmas in Portugal buying National Lottery tickets and letting people shine my shoes,' he wrote. 'Wishing you and all our friends a happy Christmas.'

But as he boarded the plane for London a week later, Popov's spirit was troubled. He knew he was leaving his old friend in dire peril. If Jebsen had asked for asylum, he would have been safely alongside him on the plane to Britain. But he had not. The Tricycle files contain a handwritten letter Popov wrote to Jebsen soon after his return to London. It offers a glimpse into what he called the 'dilemma' of spying, balancing duty against friendship, risking the life of someone he loved to protect thousands he would never know.

Given the choice between 'helping a friend and ruining a much bigger cause, or making a friend take a chance and try to save the cause,' he wrote, 'I would opt for the second solution. What is more, I am sure you would do the same.' In his uncertain English, Popov tried to tell Jebsen how much their friendship meant to him, and to the cause they now shared: 'If this case would depend on anybody else but you, I would be desperate.'

Monty's Double

On the day Popov landed back in Britain, a brilliant British Army officer and part-time transvestite emerged from an army cinema south of Naples, after a screening of the Billy Wilder film *Five Graves to Cairo,* with one of the last (and oddest) elements of the deception swirling around in his mind. Lieutenant Colonel Dudley Clarke was the head of 'A Force', a highly successful deception unit based in Cairo, and one of the architects of Bodyguard. He was a film buff with a flair for the dramatic. Indeed, Clarke's taste for dressing up had landed him in hot water a year earlier, when he was arrested in Madrid wearing women's clothes. *Five Graves to Cairo* was set in the North African campaign and starred Erich von Stroheim as Rommel. But it was Miles Mander, the actor playing a remarkably plausible General Montgomery, that set Clarke's peculiar mind whirring.

Montgomery would be Allied ground troops commander for the D-Day invasion. If an actor playing Montgomery were to be spotted somewhere else in the world, immediately before the invasion, then the Germans might assume the cross-Channel attack was not imminent. It could buy precious time, and soften German defences at a vital moment.

Clarke's idea was adopted with enthusiasm by the deception planners at LCS, and Operation Copperhead was born. But casting the right actor for the part proved tricky. Mander was found to be several inches taller than the real general, 'a physical handicap it was impossible to disguise'. A substitute was found, who then 'fell victim to a road accident and broke his leg'. The search was about to be abandoned, when a Soho theatrical agency came up with Meyrick Clifton James, an Australian-born lieutenant in the Army Pay Corps and a former variety performer. James was not a good actor. He could neither sing nor dance, and he had lost a finger in the trenches. He had volunteered to entertain overseas troops, but instead wound up in Leicester, performing in the Pay Corps' Variety Troupe. But he had one act that never failed to get the audiences cheering: with his thin face and grey, drooping moustache, he could do a splendid Monty impersonation. The actor David Niven, then a colonel in the Army Film Unit, contacted James and asked him to come to London where he was assigned to Montgomery's staff, under cover as a journalist, to study the general's speech patterns and mannerisms.

In February 1944, it was publicly announced that the victor of El Alamein had arrived in Britain to take command of Allied land forces. 'From then onwards it was certain that German agents would do their best to watch his movements.' But where should the fake Monty be exhibited for German viewing? 'Supposing he were to be seen somewhere in the Mediterranean a day or two before the Normandy invasion, the Germans would take it as a certain indication that they had at least a week or more to wait before the landings.' Gibraltar was selected as the ideal stage for Monty's double. The airfield there was known to be kept under surveillance by the Germans. The Rock was also the stamping ground of a particularly efficient and unscrupulous spy, Major Ignacio Molina Pérez, who had been in MI5's sights for some time.

Molina was on the staff of the Algeciras military governor and liaison officer between the Spanish government and the British authorities in Gibraltar. Spanish officials were supposed to be neutral; in reality, MI5 knew that Molina was a fully paid-up German spy codenamed 'Cosmos' and 'bad from head to foot':

'Molina has been decorated by the German government on various occasions, and it has been proved, with a wealth of detail, that Molina is the prime mover in an extensive Nazi secret service organisation in Spain and Morocco. Molina himself is not aware we are out for his blood,' the Defence Security Officer in Gibraltar reported. 'One of the most irritating aspects of the case is that although we know him to be a German agent, he continues to enjoy every facility to enter and leave the fortress. We have not been able to catch him *in flagrante delicto*. Something more must be done since at any moment he may get hold of some really valuable information.' Molina was the ideal target for the hoax: if he spotted Montgomery in Gibraltar, he would immediately alert the Germans, and the British would have copper-bottomed proof of Molina's espionage. Operation Copperhead might have the satisfactory side-effect of stuffing Agent Cosmos.

The ground was prepared by spreading rumours that Montgomery was coming to North Africa, via Gibraltar, in order to discuss plans for the invasion of southern France before the launch of the main invasion in the north. James began rehearsing his part, which meant changing his habits: James was a heavy drinker and smoker, whereas Monty was teetotal and loathed smoking. A prosthetic finger was constructed to replace the missing one. The fake Monty trimmed his moustache, dyed his sideburns and was issued with khaki handkerchiefs monogrammed 'B.L.M.'. 'Monty is rather flattered by the whole plan which, of course, is based on the theory that the Second Front could not possibly start without him,' Guy Liddell reported. 'This is just the sort of plan that might conceivably come off, like [Operation] Mincemeat.' In obedience to bureaucratic niceties, James would be paid the equivalent of a general's pay for every day he impersonated Monty.

While a boozy actor was rehearsing the part of a fake general, a real general was preparing to take over a fake army. With the bogus First US Army Group (FUSAG) supposedly assembling in Kent, the deception team needed someone to take command. George Patton, the inspiring, swashbuckling and supremely unpleasant general who had led US troops into Sicily, was under a cloud for abusing and slapping soldiers traumatised by battle in the belief that they were malingering cowards. 'I ought to shoot you myself,' General Patton told one terrified man. 'There's no such thing as shell shock. It's an invention of the Jews.' Eisenhower forced him to apologise and, to Patton's fury, denied him overall command of ground forces for the coming invasion. Instead Patton was ordered to serve under Montgomery, as commander of the Third Army.

The Germans rated Patton highly – 'that's the best man they have', Hitler insisted – and so, at the suggestion of Christopher Harmer, he was appointed commander of the ghost army. By a judicious combination of leaks, newspaper reports and double agent messages, the belief that General Patton was in command of FUSAG took root in German thinking. Patton stomped around England acting the part. He called himself 'a goddam natural born ham', which he most certainly was, loudly hailing other officers with such remarks as 'see you in the Pas de Calais!' The scandal over the slapping incident even reinforced the deception, since the Germans assumed this was an invented story to disguise Patton's command of the most important D-Day army. The General's outspoken tactlessness enraged Eisenhower. 'I am thoroughly weary of your failure to control your tongue,' he told him. But the intelligence services were delighted. Whenever Patton said something like 'it is the evident destiny of the British and Americans to rule the world', this made headlines, and the headlines made their way to Germany, keeping Nazi eyes firmly focused on Patton, and his bogus army.

The components of the plan were slotting into place. To keep enemy forces pinned down in Norway, Allied intelligence imagined into being the British Fourth Army, poised to attack from Scotland, supported by American Rangers deployed from Iceland. Fortitude North was backed up by wireless traffic mimicking a real army preparing for an amphibious landing and mountain warfare – in reality wireless trucks driving around Scotland sending volleys of Morse code into the ether, some 350 people representing a force of 100,000 men.

The officer in command of this notional force was General Sir Andrew 'Bulgy' Thorne, a whiskery First World War veteran who had met Hitler when he was military attaché at the British Embassy in Berlin in the 1930s. Thorne and Hitler had fought on opposite sides of the trenches at Ypres, and discussed their shared experiences. Hitler, it was calculated, would be more likely to take seriously an army under the command of an old warhorse he knew personally. Thorne even inspected real American troops in Northern Ireland as if he were their commanding officer, in the hope that German spies in Ireland would feed the information back to Germany. As the northern deception gathered speed, the planners would add additional touches: declaring the Firth of Forth a 'protected area', as if a great and secret host was assembling there; Soviet forces would mass on the Norwegian border, suggesting a simultaneous assault from the East. At the same time, diplomatic approaches were made to neutral Sweden, requesting the use of its airfields and asking the Swedish air force commander to consider a peacekeeping role in Norway in the event of an Allied invasion. (The pro-Nazi Swedish police chief was bugging the room in which this conversation took place, and the lie flew back to Berlin.)

The officer responsible for implementing Fortitude North described the 'strange mental attitude' brought on by inventing, organising and then deploying a completely invisible army: 'As time went on we found it hard to separate the real from the imaginary. The feeling that the Fourth Army really existed and the fact that it was holding German troops immobilised made one almost believe in its reality.' This was precisely the mesmeric effect the planners hoped to induce in Hitler. The Führer had always considered Norway his 'zone of destiny'; the aim of

Fortitude North was to keep his attention – and hundreds of thousands of German troops – fixed there.

A similar and even more elaborate charade was under way along the Channel coast. German forces defending Normandy, the Seventh Army, were formidable enough, but if they were reinforced by General Hans von Salmuth's mighty Fifteenth Army, currently defending the Pas de Calais, then Normandy would be all but impregnable. The Calais troops must be kept where they were, not only before, but for as long as possible after the first attack on Normandy. The real Allied army massing in southwest England to attack Normandy should be as invisible as possible, while the fake army, supposedly gathering in the southeast, should be as loud and noticeable as Patton himself. Like stage managers on a massive scale, the planners began assembling props, scenery and backdrops all over the southeast coast to simulate the mighty FUSAG, a force of 150,000 men, forming up, training and preparing for battle: fake troop camps, bogus airfields, more than 250 dummy assault landing craft known as 'wetbobs', and dummy tank landing craft known as 'bigbobs' (a 'wetbob' being public school parlance for a rower, while a cricketer was a 'drybob'). The bigbobs, built from hollow steel tubes and canvas, were so light that in high winds they broke loose and flew through the air, like enormous misshapen kites. Stray cows tended to eat the fake aircraft made from wood and canvas.

From April, wireless operators drove around Kent simulating the wireless traffic of an entire corps preparing for battle. Plans were drawn up to establish a ten-mile exclusion zone around the coast. Robertson could never be fully certain he had intercepted every spy, so as a precaution misleading signs were erected in Kent, pointing to fake embarkation points. In Dover, all was commotion as engineers scurried to and fro pretending to build tunnels and wireless stations. Imitation docks and an oil storage complex were constructed by set builders from Shepperton Studios following plans drawn up by the architect Basil Spence. King George VI's tour of this impressive and entirely unusable installation was duly reported in the press for the Germans to read.

German intelligence, watching and listening, could not fail to realise that the *Schwerpunkt,* the focal point of the cross-Channel attack, must be the Pas de Calais. The only problem was the Germans were not able to see clearly, and were hardly listening at all. Indeed, it has since emerged that they barely bothered to pick up the vast scree of wireless traffic, and were unable to locate where it was coming from when they did. Allied air supremacy meant that German reconnaissance was strictly limited. Huge effort went into physical deception, camouflage and signals traffic, but the Germans were not really paying attention. And why would they? They had numerous spies, on the ground, providing copious evidence of exactly what was going on. Why go to the trouble of intercepting, deciphering and translating an avalanche of 13,358 coded wireless messages, when they had direct information from Garbo and Brutus?

On 21 January, Tar Robertson had announced to the 'W Board', which provided operational intelligence for Double Cross purposes, that the moment of truth had arrived. He was, he said, '98 per cent certain that the Germans trusted the majority of their agents', although 'there must always remain the additional 2 per cent of doubt'. The odds were good enough for the board, which authorised the Twenty Committee to deploy the Double Cross agents in the way that had always been envisaged: to blow the entire project in the most elaborate and dangerous deception yet. Only agents in whom the Germans had absolute faith, as reflected in Most Secret Sources, would be selected, and since the postal service would be cut off in the run-up to invasion, active deception would be restricted to agents with wireless transmitters: Garbo, Brutus and Agent Tate (Wulf Schmidt) all had well-established radio contact; Treasure, it was hoped, would soon get a radio set from Kliemann. Bronx would continue her letters as long as possible and then send a last-minute message by telegram using the agreed plain language code.

That left Popov. Lingering uncertainty over Jebsen's safety and reliability provoked another heated debate, with some arguing that the Tricycle channel should not be used, and possibly dismantled altogether. It fell once more to Ian Wilson, his case officer, to mount the defence:

It has been suggested that Tricycle and his group are barred from conveying deceptive material because of the risk that Artist will, willingly or under duress, disclose the fact that this group is controlled. The risk is extremely slight. It seems unthinkable that Artist would voluntarily blow this case in view of the care he has taken in the past to protect double agents and of the very considerable body of information he has given us, which has proved true whenever we have been able to check it. His motives for working for us are extremely complex [but] he is absolutely sincere in his actions. He cannot blow Tricycle without imminent danger of death to himself, his family, and Tricycle's family. Artist will be protected by the Abwehr from any attack on him by the Gestapo. Whatever danger existed has now diminished. Even if the Gestapo could get hold of Artist's person and extort a confession that Artist's agents were double-crossing, then the Abwehr would have to believe the confession. All the Abwehr officers, from the highest to the lowest, have a vested interest in supporting the *bona fides* of Tricycle. I very much doubt any of them would have the moral courage to admit that for years they have been fooled.

The Twenty Committee agreed to lift the veto on using Tricycle for deception. 'No ban', Wilson scrawled triumphantly across his memo. Popov was 'passed fit' to play in the final championship match.

The Double Cross team had presented their case with supreme confidence, but there was apprehension in St James's Street. Knowledge of the double-agent network, 'once confined to a small esoteric group of persons', was now widely distributed among civilians and military personnel, with an increased danger of leakage. Paul Fidrmuc, the rogue freelancer in Lisbon, was still spraying conjecture and fantasy at the Germans, but 'it was not impossible that Ostro might by fluke give the exact area of attack on the Continent, and thus destroy the deception plan'. And the Abwehr, the familiar enemy, was falling apart. If the organisation collapsed, or was subsumed by Himmler's SD, the intelligence agency of the SS and Nazi party, then the corrupt, lazy and gullible officers B1A had got to know so well might be replaced by men of a different, more effective stamp. Rats would begin to desert the leaking ship. Already a number of disaffected Abwehr officers were extending feelers, hinting at possible desertion. Here was the Artist problem writ large. If an officer with knowledge of the German spy network in Britain defected, his colleagues would naturally assume he had betrayed those networks; and if the networks continued regardless, they would realise the spies were under Allied control. 'In short, the German turncoat, in trying to assist us, would in fact destroy our entire system.' Even stone-souled John Masterman confessed to a 'gnawing anxiety' as the pace of deception accelerated. 'The whole existence of the double cross system hung in the balance just before D-Day,' he wrote. 'Failure was dangerously close.'

When the final, definitive deception plan was approved by Churchill in late February 1944, with just over three months to go, Christopher Harmer, the link between the double agents and the military planners, turned to Roger Fleetwood-Hesketh, his opposite number, and uttered the thought that all wondered, but few dared voice: 'I can't believe we will ever get away with it.'

The Double Dash

The participants in the deception, great and small, set to work. Flight Lieutenant Walker gathered his flock of second-rate pigeons; an Australian actor worked on his Montgomery impersonation; General Patton stamped around England, drawing attention to himself; and the American double agents, led by Max Rudloff, the libertine Argentinian, fed shreds of falsehood, indicating the attack would be delayed. But the central, swelling chorus of lies would come from the Double Cross spies, Hitler's most trusted source of information on the military build-up in Britain, and Churchill's trump cards.

The deception was built from myriad tiny fragments of misinformation, a mosaic for the enemy to piece together. Directly pointing to the Pas de Calais as the target area would be far too obvious, and exceedingly dangerous if the plot was rumbled. 'You cannot baldly announce to the enemy that such and such an operation is in preparation,' insisted Masterman. 'You cannot just volunteer information.' Instead, the great lie would be made up of snippets, gleanings and hints, buried in a mass of other information, some of it true.

Roman Czerniawski began implementing the bogus threat to Norway. Chopin, his wireless operator, sent a message to Oscar Reile reporting that the Polish spy was heading north for a Polish military conference. 'He had a good reason for visiting Scotland inasmuch as the majority of Polish troops were stationed there and he was recognised by the Germans as a highly trained military observer.' Agent Brutus began relaying the fake Allied Order of Battle, just as he once reported on the real strength of German troops in occupied France. He provided the Germans with the insignia and location of the Fourth Army headquarters in Edinburgh, described large bodies of troops in Stirling and Dundee, and offered evidence that American and Norwegian forces were also gathering. Brutus followed up by describing the arrival of Soviet staff officers in Edinburgh, to back up the notion of a pincer movement. The Norwegian agents Mutt and Jeff made similar observations, and Garbo's Scotland-based sub-agents pitched in, with troop-sightings in Dundee and major naval exercises on the Clyde. Freak, Popov's radio operator, invented a talkative American naval officer who revealed he would shortly be joining General Thorne's staff. The Germans were pleased. 'Your latest wires very satisfactory. Congratulations. Please state exact number of Divisions etc. belonging to Fourth Army under General Thorne.'

Like a spoilt lover, Czerniawski badgered his German handlers for expressions of affection and support, demanding money 'to increase the efficiency of his espionage activities' and new equipment: 'Urgently require two new wireless sets and two new codes. As result of my visit to Scotland I have report of many pages to send you urgently, and without the necessary assistance from you it will be impossible to transmit the information which I am collecting at sufficient speed.' The Germans responded soothingly: 'Many thanks for your hard and valuable work. What place can we best send you the money and the piano? Can you suggest a place which would be suitable for a plane to come low enough to drop what you want?' Czerniawski advised the Germans to parachute a package to him at a remote spot near Beccles in Suffolk. When there was no response, he sent a peevish message demanding to know 'whether the lack of reply was due to a lack of confidence in him'. Reile was unctuous: 'I have complete confidence in you but there are still difficulties.' German plans for re-equipping him came to nothing, but their willingness to try confirmed the esteem in which Czerniawski was held. 'He is a man who succeeds in creating the impression of Herculean ability, and from their knowledge of him the Germans will expect him to achieve the impossible or bust. Brutus is a professional spy and an artist at producing the most detailed and illustrated reports.'

The D-Day spies all swung into action for Fortitude South. By mid-February, Garbo's doughty team of fictional Welsh fascists were deployed all along the south coast, and Pujol was commended by Kühlenthal for the 'amplification of your network'; the Welsh spies, in particular, were 'giving the best results'. The Gibraltarian waiter was also well placed after supposedly getting a job in a canteen at a Hampshire military base. The sub-agents sent information to Pujol, which he gathered, graded, put into his own, inimitably dense prose, and then sent on by radio to Madrid, where Karl-Erich Kühlenthal consumed it with insatiable appetite. Garbo sent himself on a notional tour of the south coast: he reported seeing American soldiers but predicted the invasion 'would not happen for a long time', and certainly not 'until an assault force immeasurably greater in number than that which exists has been assembled'. The Germans could relax. 'I am surprised to hear of the nervousness which exists in official circles with regard to the Allied offensive ... I recommend once again calm and confidence in our work.' That work was already monumental, and would grow steadily in the following weeks: between the beginning of January and D-Day 500 wireless messages passed between Garbo and his controllers. Harris worried that no single person could, in reality, have marshalled such an enormous quantity of information. This thought never struck the Germans.

Dusko Popov gathered intelligence of a quality, complexity and duplicity greater than anything he had supplied before. He made his own tour of the Kent coast, and reported that preparations for a great armada were plainly under way, but incomplete. 'An extensive programme for preparing and improving cook houses, wash houses, tented camps and landing grounds has been drawn up, but nearly all of it still has to be done. In spite of intensive preparations there are no signs that invasion is imminent.' Dover harbour was being overhauled to accommodate a huge task force, he reported, but again, 'a lot of work still had to be done'. From Dover, he travelled on to Portsmouth, Southampton and Exeter, describing intense military commotion in the east, and inactivity in the west.

Tar debated whether to send Tricycle into the enemy camp once again. Alone among the double agents, only he could place the deception, physically, in enemy hands. 'His stock is very high in German eyes and it is desired to take advantage of this fact, and of the opportunity of his being able to take documents to the Germans.' Popov would go back to Lisbon one last time, carrying a 'mass of detailed information' to support the deception: eyewitness reports from the Channel ports, doctored documents, and conversations with Norwegian government officials in London who said they expected to be home before summer.

Johnny Jebsen reported that von Karsthoff was swallowing Popov's reports unchewed, and proclaiming that 'the landing in Western Europe will not take place until next spring'. Berlin's response was equally positive. Colonel Georg Hansen declared Popov the Abwehr's top spy and his radio connection 'the best in the whole Abwehr'. Jebsen shone a light directly into the minds of his colleagues. 'Their chief hope is to receive reports about the date of the landing in France,' he told MI6. 'It is quite possible to deceive with regard to the date as Tricycle's reliability is no longer in doubt, but all reports must contain a saving clause so that when an event which has been announced does not occur, the blame can be attributed to wrong information received. Reports submitted with a reservation are more easily believed than categorical statements.' These reports should be sent 'containing a wealth of small detail'. Jebsen was now actively coaching the Allied team.

While Brutus focused on the north, and Garbo and Tricycle worked on the southern deception, Bronx looked west. Most Secret Sources showed that Elvira's reports were now graded 'very important' and distributed to both the operational sections of the Abwehr and army intelligence HQ in Berlin. She still addressed her letters, in secret ink, to Bleil, unaware that the man who had recruited her in France was no longer handling her case. Her new controller was one Hauptmann Dr Berndt Schluetter, a former officer in the Paris Abwehr, now operating out of Cologne and an altogether more formidable figure than the feckless, drunken Bleil. Incoming letters to Bronx took on a more urgent tone: 'Important. Invasion details: Eisenhower's and Montgomery's HQs? Parts of coast evacuated? Concentration of ships and barges? Admiralty circles talk of invasion? Arrivals of American troops? Expenses and bonus for invasion news.' Bronx bolstered both Fortitudes South and North, but her singular hold on the Germans, it was decided, should be employed elsewhere in the deception.

The Germans had substantial forces deployed in the Bordeaux area of southwest France, most notably the feared 17th SS Panzergrenadier division. Once the invasion was under way, its tanks would certainly be deployed north to try to repel the Allies. Every hour the Panzers could be detained in the southwest would help. Just as the Fifteenth Army might be tied down in Calais by Operation Fortitude, so a new and equally fictitious threat would be aimed at the Bordeaux area: this was Operation Ironside. The imaginary assault would begin with an attack in the Bay of Biscay from the west coast ports of the UK, opening the way for an American force sailing directly from the US. Several double agents would contribute: Rudloff in the US reported that a force trained in fording rivers was assembling to tackle the watery terrain of southwest France; Tate said his girlfriend Mary, who worked in the Admiralty, had returned from Washington after working on a plan for a US expeditionary force.

Bronx had already agreed a code to be sent by telegram to warn of an invasion. 'She is independent and aloof from all our other agents, so that reasonable risks can be taken in running her without compromising any other agent.' Elvira would implement Operation Ironside almost single-handed, no small feat for an agent once dismissed as 'a good-time girl with no allegiance to anyone except herself'.

Timing was critical. 'In order to achieve our object of containing the German Panzer division in the region of Bordeaux, it will be necessary to time the telegram to arrive on D-2 [two days before D-Day].' Telegrams to Lisbon took five days. To reach the Germans in time, the message would have to be sent on or before 29 May. The telegram would 'indicate to the Germans that an attack will definitely be made against the Bay of Biscay', to be followed by a letter in secret ink, once the invasion was under way and the postal service was restored, 'providing a get-out for Bronx' by explaining how she had made a mistake. The only objection, as usual, came from MI6, sniping from the sidelines. Claude Dansey told Elvira it was 'ludicrous' to expect the Germans to swallow such an 'implausible' ruse. Astor reported: 'I told her I consider his opinion to be completely fallacious and that we were best qualified to decide on running her case.' The secret services tended to get far angrier with each other than they ever did with the enemy.

Mary Sherer spent three weeks coaching Lily Sergeyev on her cover story. In the evenings she took her to the theatre, or a movie. 'Sometimes Louisa [Gisela Ashley] comes as well,' Lily wrote. 'I'm very fond of Louisa, but somehow I just can't bring myself to trust her, or Mary, or Robertson. I suppose if I lived a long time in England, I would become like the English: cold, reserved, impersonal.' Even when Mary laughed in the cinema, it struck Lily as forced, 'a polite little laugh, prim and restrained, sort of a miser's laugh'. Since the death of her dog, she had begun to refer to the B1A team as 'Robertson and his gang'.

When Tar came to say farewell, Lily asked him: 'If Kliemann questions me about the invasion, do I say yes or no?'

'What do you think yourself?' he replied cryptically.

'I think it'll be soon.'

'Then tell him so.' There was a pause. 'You know how much we are counting on you.'

Agent Treasure shook Tar's hand without enthusiasm. 'His words don't make much impression on me.' She had bought a gift for Kliemann at Dunhill's on Piccadilly, a pigskin wallet engraved with the words: 'For Octave. A souvenir from London. 29th February, 1944. Solange.' She told Mary: 'I am absolutely sure of being able to cope with him.' In truth, she was looking forward to seeing Kliemann again.

Treasure landed in Lisbon on 1 March 1944. She had sent a letter ahead, telling Kliemann when she would be arriving. Inevitably, he wasn't there. She checked into the Palacio Hotel, telephoned the German legation, and left a message for Kliemann. A few hours later, 'a slim, fair youngster with slicked back hair and an ingratiating smile' knocked on her hotel room door and introduced himself as 'Hoppe'. Kliemann, he said, would be arriving soon. Treasure waited.

After the damp gloom of London, Lisbon in early spring was enchanting. She wandered the bazaars and fruit stalls, admiring the black and white marble pavements and the trees in bloom: these were Judas trees. The irony of the name was not lost on her. She made contact with MI6 and was told to be patient. Privately, the British wondered if Kliemann was a busted flush. A message had recently appeared in Most Secret Sources, indicating that 'Berlin were very pleased with the work she was doing, but were not pleased with Kliemann who was considered slack and inefficient' and might 'get the sack'. After twelve days of waiting, Treasure's patience was exhausted: she summoned Hoppe to her hotel, and blew a gasket. 'Kliemann is a saboteur,' she shrieked.

'He has no order, no method. He ought to be shot. You are all hopelessly incompetent. I am fed up with it.' Still, it took three more days before Hoppe reappeared, 'very excited', to tell her: 'Our friend is here!'

On the morning of 14 March, Hoppe drove her to the Place Pombal, at the top of Avenida Liberdade. A familiar, square-shouldered figure appeared, melodramatically, from behind the fountains. Kliemann embraced her warmly. He was smartly dressed, as always, in a blue suit and felt hat, but thinner, his hair greyer than before. She noted, for the first time, that his upper teeth were false. 'He looks much older,' she wrote. 'Something akin to pity stirs in me.'

Kliemann was delighted to see her, and as self-centred as ever. 'My stock has gone up recently because of your success,' he declared. 'You are the first person to have achieved this: to have got yourself into England, to have come out again, and to be able to return. I am very proud of you, Lily! Your success has helped my position a good deal. I nearly lost my job. If you give up now it'll be the end of me.'

In the back of Hoppe's car, Kliemann talked non-stop, mostly about himself. His leg had recently been poisoned, which is why he had lost weight, he said. He had spent Christmas with Yvonne at Thonon-les-Bains on the Swiss-French frontier. He wanted Yvonne to fire her maid who was 'lazy and impertinent and always answering him back'. Like all truly selfish people, Kliemann believed the minutiae of his life must be fascinating to all.

The car stopped outside an apartment block, and Kliemann led her upstairs to an empty flat. On the table lay a parcel, wrapped in paper and string. He was beaming with pride. She unwrapped it to find what looked like an ordinary transistor radio in a 'shabby' wooden case; inside was a transmitter, almost certainly a wireless taken from a captured British SOE agent. 'Here are the two holes to which you connect your tapper. It's the only outward sign that could arouse suspicions,' said

Kliemann. A wireless expert would show Lily how to make a Morse code tapper from household items. But first, Kliemann declared brightly, some sightseeing, and then lunch.

A few hours later Lily stood on the ramparts of the Castelo dos Mouros, the great Moorish fort looking out over Sintra. On the fifteen-mile drive from Lisbon, Kliemann had happily prattled away about how satisfied the bosses were with Lily and, more importantly, with him. 'Berlin was very pleased with her for getting to Bristol. Her descriptions of divisional signs were very well given and very precise. She was to send more like that.' In the future she must also send bomb damage reports. 'It is a very worrying business running agents,' he remarked. 'Because with most of them, I am always worrying about whether they are double-crossing or not. With you, in whom I have complete confidence, it makes me feel bad to be sending you to do such unpleasant things and to run such risks.' Still, he reflected, the war might soon be over: 'The situation is quite hopeless and it is only a matter of time before Germany will have to give in.' He did not seem unduly concerned.

They drove through delightful scenery, with blossoming fruit trees along the roadsides. Lily remembered thinking that she didn't feel like going back to England.

Lily had brought with her a small Zeiss camera. As they toured the castle, she said: 'What about a picture? It would be a souvenir.'

'What a good idea. You did well to bring your camera,' said Kliemann, never suspecting that the camera had been supplied by MI5 for the express purpose of obtaining his picture for their files. Lily snapped Kliemann as he clambered up through one of the castle turrets. Then she set the automatic shutter and took another photograph of the two of them together, beside a fountain. She is smiling a little coquettishly. He strikes his best spymaster pose. They are both visibly happy.

Kliemann ordered lunch at a small restaurant. While they were waiting for the food to arrive, she presented him with the wallet. His face lit up. Then he reached in his pocket and handed Lily a packet. Inside was a pretty bracelet, forty-five diamonds set in platinum, £300 in notes and 20,000 escudos. He was gathering more money, he said, which he would give her 'at midday tomorrow'. After the meal was cleared away, Kliemann grew serious.

'Do you think there is going to be an Allied invasion?'

Lily recalled what Tar had said. 'Yes.'

'I too. When do you think it will take place?'

'I think the landing is imminent.'

Kliemann frowned, and then launched into a prepared speech. 'Now listen to me carefully, Lily. The next big move in the war will be the Allied landing. Our only chance of winning, at the moment, is to throw them back into the sea. To do that we must know in advance where they are planning to land, so that we can prepare a hot reception. It could be in Holland or Belgium, but we don't think so. We are fairly sure that it will be in France, and there are two possibilities: either the Pas de Calais or Normandy. If they choose the Pas de Calais, the Allied troops will be concentrated on the Channel coast; but if it is to be Normandy, they will move them into the area around Bristol. Do you understand? What you must tell us is whether there is a build-up of troops and other activities, so we can work out where the enemy is making for.'

She should spend as much time as possible visiting her relatives in the West Country, paying particular attention to any military activity on Salisbury Plain, and reporting 'everything seen in or around Bristol'. Where was Eisenhower's headquarters? What exercises were taking place? Were invasion barges arriving in Bristol from America, and if so in what numbers? 'Information obtained by observation is of interest, but high-level gossip is not of much interest as it rarely proves accurate.' When her radio was working, she should transmit on Mondays, Wednesdays and Fridays, at 11 p.m. 'I want the transmissions to be as short as possible. The shorter the better.' Kliemann reached into his

wallet, and presented Lily with a single British stamp, explaining
that on the top left-hand corner was a microdot: 'These are the
instructions for the transmitting set in case you forget anything.'
She put the stamp in her note case.

Only now did Kliemann ask how she had managed to travel
to Lisbon. Lily launched into her cover story about her job at
the Ministry of Information and the propaganda films for which
she was gathering material. Kliemann nodded approvingly. She
had memorised numerous corroborative details, including how
Alfred Hitchcock was working for the ministry's Film Division
and exactly where the canteen was located. But he asked not a
single question.

After lunch they strolled along the waterfront, and watched
the fishing boats pull away from the coast. Kliemann turned to
her. 'What is our hold over you?'

'My parents are still in Paris, as you once reminded me . . .
but it would be better for you to realise that I am acting freely,
rather than under pressure. You'd feel much surer of me.'

The answer seemed to satisfy this most incurious of spies. It
was dark when they climbed into Hoppe's car for the drive back
to Lisbon. As they passed through Estoril, Kliemann remarked:
'I would like to have shown you the casino and take you to a
chic restaurant for dinner, but it wouldn't be wise. The place
is full of international gangsters, double agents and intelligence
agents. It is better that we shouldn't be seen together in public.'

The next morning, Hoppe showed her how to make a Morse
code tapper using a block of wood, a nail, a kitchen knife and
a book. He then handed over two new transmitting crystals
and a list of frequencies, and taught her a new code. Kliemann
arrived, carrying a large paper bag. Inside were 1,500 £1 notes.
He explained that he had 'planned to hide the money in a cigar
box but could not find one large enough'. He would try to find
banknotes of a larger denomination, he said, and a bigger box.

Lily now explained that, as part of her propaganda work, she
had made contact with the press attaché at the British Embassy

and he had agreed to send the radio to London in the diplomatic bag. This was a most implausible story. The diplomatic bag was used to transfer sensitive information; it was not a free luggage transportation service for civilians. But once again, Kliemann evinced no suspicion, and happily agreed that 'this was a wise move, to avoid any possible curiosity by security officials at the airport'.

There was one more important piece of business. Now that she had a wireless, Lily would need a 'control signal', a way to indicate that she was now transmitting under British control, should she be caught. 'We must take all possible precautions,' said Kliemann. 'Suppose the British unmask you. They won't arrest you. They'll watch you for a short time. They'll register all your transmissions to make sure they know your methods. Then they'll force you to work for them, under the threat of a revolver. I want to give you some means of warning us, some sign which they cannot detect, but for which we'll be watching very carefully.' Kliemann's plan was simple: 'If she was discovered by the British and told to go on transmitting, she was to call PSE QSL SK' – Morse shorthand for 'Please acknowledge reception'. Lily replied that this was 'silly' – which it was, since if she added something new to a message 'the British would know that this was some sort of sign'. She suggested a more subtle danger code.

'At the beginning of the message, between KA and the call-sign, there is a dash. Sometimes I do it, sometimes not. If I do it twice – once in the message and once in the repetition of the message – it'll mean I'm no longer a free agent. But only if the dash is there *both* times. If it's only in once, it doesn't mean anything. Because now and then I may send it just to make it less noticeable. If they comb through a series of my messages, they will see that it varies and won't pay any attention when I repeat it.'

Kliemann was impressed: 'That's excellent.' In his notebook he wrote: '*Strich zwischen Anfang und Nummer*', dash between the beginning and number.

They arranged to meet the next day at 11.00 a.m. in the Praça di Commercio, a few hours before Lily's flight. Kliemann, astonishingly, was waiting, with a very large box of cigars under one arm. Inside, he whispered, under a layer of cigars and a false bottom, was £500 in £5 notes. They walked around the square, arm in arm. Kliemann paused by a fountain, lit a cigarette, and looked solemn.

'Even if it meant the end of my career, if you said you did not want to go back to England, I would not force you.'

'I would rather go on until the end,' said Lily.

Kliemann was a ridiculous spy, a vain and fragile egotist, but he was also capable of gentleness, and he was offering his spy a way out. Lily's British spymasters had never shown her such care.

Kliemann kissed her hand, and walked away.

In her diary Lily wrote: 'Five months ago I was so full of enthusiasm, so ready to love the British, so eager to help them. I admired them; I trusted them; I had faith in British fair play. I worked readily for them; I took risks on their behalf. In return, I only asked for one thing: to keep my dog. It wasn't asking much, but it was too much for them! Tomorrow I'll be in London, I'll hand them over the money, the code, the radio, everything . . . except for a dash! A dash that will enable me to destroy all my work, all *their* work, the minute I want to. I shall not use my power. I know that. But I will know that I have them at my mercy!'

Agent Treasure landed at Bristol airport at 5.30 the next morning, in thick fog, and was driven to a hotel. There she was given a cup of tea and some toast, along with a tiny square of margarine and half-teaspoonful of marmalade. A few minutes later, Mary Sherer strode in, bustling and businesslike. Lily handed over the box of cigars with the cash inside, the radio crystals, the stamp with the microdot, the diamond bracelet, and the photographs of Kliemann, smiling in the sun.

'He must be daft,' said Mary. 'The Colonel will be absolutely delighted.'

Robertson came to Rugby Mansions the next day to congratulate Lily in person. 'So here you are again!' he said jovially. 'We didn't really expect you.' And added: 'They are very fine cigars.'

The radio, money and bracelet were examined by MI5's experts. The transmitter was pronounced to be 'indistinguishable from an ordinary radio to the untrained eye'. Exactly thirty-nine of the £5 notes were forgeries. The bracelet was valued at £175.

Lily described her conversations with Kliemann, his hunger for information about military manoeuvres in the southwest, and his almost endearing naivety. 'I have nothing against Kliemann personally,' she told Mary. 'He has always treated me very well and it makes me feel very badly to have to lie to him and cheat him.'

'What would he do if he thought you were controlled?' Mary asked. 'Presumably he would not tell Berlin because this would make him look such a fool.'

'I am absolutely sure that if he thought I was double-crossing, he would report it.'

Mary sent a glowing report to Tar: 'Treasure gave a very good account of herself, particularly given the flimsy nature of her story. She did very well in Lisbon and has provided us with a new, very valuable channel of communication.'

Yet there was one aspect of Lily's story that troubled her. Mary had studied the files in B1A. So far, every wireless agent sent by the Germans had a 'control signal', a way to tip off the Abwehr that they had been caught and were sending messages under British direction. Sometimes this was merely a misspelling, or an added comma. Kliemann had briefed her intensively on how to operate her wireless, but 'no suggestion for indications of operation under duress was made'. Lily never mentioned a control signal: 'She states she was never given any security check or other means of informing the Germans if she was controlled by the British. In fact, they never spoke of the possibility of this happening.' Having made a note of this anomaly, Mary Sherer promptly forgot about it.

On 13 April, Mary took Lily to Hampstead Heath, to a house with a royal blue front door. The little radio transmitter had been set up in a top-floor bedroom. At twelve minutes past midnight, Lily sent a message to Kliemann: 'Arrived Safely'. She did not insert a dash, either in the message or its repetition. Over the next two months, whenever she tapped out a message, she thought about the dash. 'Every time I know that I can destroy the work of three years. Just a dash, and the Germans will know that I work under the control of the Intelligence Service . . . and the British will suspect nothing. This is my revenge – they made me a promise and they didn't keep it. Now I shall have them in my power.'

Jebsen's New Friend

Johnny Jebsen was a one-man production line of secrets. His reports, funnelled back to Britain via MI6 in Lisbon, contained an extraordinary wealth of detail about flying bombs, economic conditions in Germany, intelligence reports, and 'even an account of opinions expressed by Hitler and Himmler and Kaltenbrunner', the chief of the Reich Main Security Office (RSHA). Artist's information was gleaned from no less than thirty-nine sub-sources and informants, ranging from Abwehr secretaries to Canaris himself, and the quality was so good that MI6, territorial as ever, wondered whether it should be shared with other branches of intelligence, since there was 'no authority from C to act as a circulating section'. Jebsen grew bolder. The V2 rocket, the world's first long-range ballistic missile, was being manufactured at the Rax-Werke factory in Wiener-Neustadt, using slave labour from Mauthausen concentration camp. Passing on this information, he 'seriously and earnestly put the proposition that when his trouble with the Gestapo is cleared up he should return to Germany and organise the sabotage of the factory at Wiener-Neustadt'. Jebsen was now offering to sabotage the most potent secret weapon in the German arsenal. 'This proposal sounds fantastic, but I repeat that Artist takes it very seriously.' Even more extraordinary was Jebsen's suggestion that MI6 should recruit as a spy the wife of one of Britain's most famous novelists.

P. G. Wodehouse was now living with his wife Ethel in Paris, where the couple had regular contact with a number of high-ranking Germans. Jebsen saw an opportunity. Charles de Salis of MI6 reported:

P. G. Wodehouse and his wife were great friends of Artist, who helped them financially from time to time. They are at the moment in Paris. Mrs Wodehouse is very pro-British and is inclined to be rude to anyone who dares address her in German. She has on occasion said loudly in public places: 'If you cannot address me in English don't speak at all. You had better learn it as you will have to speak it after the war anyway.' Artist thinks she might be a useful source, as both she and her husband are in close touch with [Paul-Otto] Schmidt, Hitler's interpreter, who often talks to her of the conversations he has had to interpret between Hitler and the various foreigners who visit him. Wodehouse himself is entirely childlike and pacifist.

It is not known whether MI6 acted on this suggestion and recruited Ethel Wodehouse, but Jebsen's suggestion casts a new light on their time in Paris. Critics accused the novelist and his wife of living in queasy accommodation with the Nazis, after Wodehouse foolishly agreed to make radio broadcasts at the Germans' behest. Jebsen's report proves that while Wodehouse himself may have been passively apolitical, his wife was so anti-Nazi that she was considered a potential spy.

Jebsen believed he was safe. Elements within the Abwehr saw him as 'anti-Nazi and latterly defeatist', but he had his defenders. A colleague in Berlin promised to warn him of any imminent danger: if he received a 'telegram saying "come back immediately" this was a pre-arranged signal which in fact meant "do not come, the Gestapo are after you".' He had also recruited a new bedroom mole within the Lisbon Abwehr station: Baroness Marie von Gronau, the twenty-three-year-old daughter of a pioneer aviator who was the Luftwaffe attaché in Tokyo. Marie was a secretary in the counter-intelligence section, and happily told Jebsen whatever was passing across her boss's desk. In jest, he asked Marie to marry him. She turned him down, but was 'fascinated by his intelligence and wide knowledge'. She may have been equally attracted to the 'seemingly inexhaustible funds at his disposal'. After the war, Marie von Gronau was asked if she had known Jebsen was a British agent. She replied that he had denied it so often she assumed he must be, and recalled how he dropped telltale remarks such as: 'I am His Majesty's Most Loyal Enemy' and 'Friendship goes across borders of nations, regardless of a state of war'.

Marie von Gronau was generous with her favours. When Jebsen arrived in Lisbon, she was already the mistress of the Italian air attaché, and being courted by an SD officer named Volbrecht. One evening Volbrecht told Marie that Jebsen was a '*macaco*', a Portuguese term of abuse meaning 'monkey', and the Baroness passed the insult on to Jebsen. 'Although he had not the slightest idea what a *macaco* was, he did not like the sound of the word and challenged Volbrecht to a duel with pistols.' Volbrecht refused, 'saying his department did not allow duels'. During this period, Jebsen's wife Lore came to Lisbon to see him, a visit that seems to have done nothing to slow down his extra-marital liaisons.

Jebsen's was spiralling into a most volatile frame of mind. Lily Grass, he declared, was still 'infatuated' with him, and passing on useful titbits from the correspondence of her boss, Aloys Schreiber, the head of counter-intelligence: 'Schreiber has written to Berlin that in his opinion Tricycle is absolutely reliable and should be given the biggest and most secret tasks for big money,' she told him. This was reassuring, yet 'Jebsen's nervousness and excitability' was a headache. In late January, Charles de Salis telephoned Jebsen's villa in Estoril to find that he had vanished. A discreet but intensive manhunt was launched. After three days British intelligence was starting to panic, when

Jebsen reappeared, none the worse for his disappearing act save for a hangover: he had been on an almighty binge with his new best friend, Hans Brandes.

Hans Joachim Brandes was one of numerous shady characters loosely attached to the Lisbon Abwehr station. He was twenty-four years old, fair-haired, half-Jewish, Swiss-educated, and so overweight that he had been declared unfit for military service. His father had owned a large machine tool factory in Berlin, and on the outbreak of war Brandes and his brother, principally through bribery, had successfully registered themselves as non-Jewish. Brandes spent money liberally wherever he went, and was 'known to give as much as 30,000 marks to reserve officers whose salary is only some 700 marks monthly, merely to make things easier for himself'. A shareholder in a Berlin armaments firm, he won a contract to supply arms to the Portuguese government.

Arriving in Lisbon in 1943, Brandes set himself up as a trader in platinum, diamonds and shoe leather, and occasional spy. 'He is personally befriended by Canaris who has sent him here to be out of harm's way as he is partly Jewish,' reported Jebsen. 'He is supposed to report through von Karsthoff but he does practically nothing' and seemed to have some sort of 'hold over' the Abwehr station chief, almost certainly financial: 'His bribes go a long way and he is certainly a specialist in that art.' Brandes claimed to be running his own espionage network, including an IRA spy in Ireland, agents in Switzerland and a Frenchman in North Africa named Barinki d'Arnoux. Brandes liked to boast: 'With a great deal of cunning and craftiness I have succeeded to settle down here in Lisbon for the duration of the war.' He shared Jebsen's tastes and, it seemed, his politics. 'He made no secret of the fact that he is not only very anti-Nazi but very pro-British and hoped England would win the war.' Together, they roistered around Lisbon, with secretaries in tow. 'Relations between Artist and Brandes seem to have grown very close,' MI6 reported. Early in January, Brandes told his new friend that he was going to Berlin and would 'try to persuade Canaris to cancel his order against Artist's return to Germany'. Jebsen did not tell Brandes about his work for the British, but he believed his new chum could easily be recruited as another double agent.

In fact, MI6 had been tracking the mysterious Brandes ever since his arrival in Lisbon, and had come to the conclusion that, like Ostro, he was a hoaxer. Kim Philby, the head of the MI6 counter-intelligence Iberian desk, followed the progress of Brandes through Most Secret Sources, and concluded 'the organisation he claims to run is fictitious'. Brandes was perpetrating a 'deliberate fraud on the Abwehr', which made him susceptible to blackmail. 'He is only twenty-four and half-Jewish,' wrote Philby. 'It is certain, therefore, that if he fails to maintain his position he would find himself fairly rapidly on the Eastern Front. He is strongly anti-Nazi and has never made any serious attempt to provide the Abwehr with genuine information. He would have a positive motive for accepting our proposition.'

Brandes knew Jebsen had secret agents in Britain, but he assumed that Jebsen's reports to Berlin, like his own, were what he called 'constructive fantasy'. He even offered to back up anything Jebsen might be sending to Berlin with his own inventions. Jebsen told de Salis he had 'enough confidence in Brandes to reveal to him that he was working for the British', but 'had not done so and would not do so without agreement'. Brandes was a 'slippery opportunist', said Jebsen, but he could be a useful ally: 'If he knew the truth he would probably want to join the game.'

MI6 decided to keep a close eye on Jebsen's new friend; if and when the time seemed ripe, he could be brought into the game. 'I think Brandes might develop into a useful straight agent if he has any guts and strong anti-Nazi convictions,' wrote Frank Foley of MI6. Jebsen was certain Brandes would persuade Admiral Canaris to 'lift the veto for my return which was made for my safety, as the Gestapo does not want anything from me any longer. I myself will be able to leave shortly.'

But before Canaris could do any such thing, he was toppled. Early in February, an Abwehr officer named Erich Vermehren slipped out of the Abwehr station in Istanbul, and defected. He and his wife were smuggled to Britain via Cairo and Gibraltar, and took up residence in a South Kensington flat belonging to Kim Philby's mother. Vermehren's defection was the excuse the enemies of Canaris were waiting for. Hitler was enraged. Canaris had long been suspected of being disloyal (which he was) and of working to undermine Hitler (which he probably was too). He was dismissed, given a meaningless job, and finally placed under house arrest. The Abwehr would soon be taken over by the SD and subsumed into the Reich Main Security Office under the control of Himmler and Kaltenbrunner, and then abolished entirely. Jebsen had been predicting 'the downfall of Canaris' for some time. His ousting brought with it an orgy of chaotic score-settling and internecine feuding: some Abwehr officers demanded to be sent to the front; others were dismissed; those remaining in place did so in an atmosphere of crippling paranoia and uncertainty. 'Further dismissals will probably take place,' Jebsen reported, 'together with a weeding out of unsatisfactory double agents.' The British would continue to refer to 'the Abwehr', although the old organisation was effectively obsolete.

The chaos within German intelligence, and the SD's seizure of power at the expense of the Abwehr, sent a shudder of anxiety through the Double Cross team. The Abwehr officers were the devils they knew. There was now a danger, as Masterman observed, that 'new brooms would sweep away much which we had tried to preserve'.

Jebsen had been at university in Freiburg with Erich Vermehren, and had helped him get a job in the Abwehr. The Vermehren family, from Lübeck, was ardently anti-Nazi. Erich's mother, Petra Vermehren, a distinguished German journalist, had come to Portugal early in the war in order to get out from under the Nazi regime. Jebsen knew her well, and on hearing of Vermehren's defection, he rushed to her home to find Petra packing. She explained that she had been recalled to Germany to explain her son's defection. 'Jebsen tried to persuade her not to go,' telling her 'he was on friendly terms with Lord Rothschild who has asked him to come to England' – a hint that he could help arrange her defection. Petra insisted she was not afraid and caught the next plane to Berlin, knowing that under the Nazi system of collective punishment she was probably doomed. She was arrested at the airport and sent to Sachsenhausen concentration camp. Her husband, son and two daughters were also interned in concentration camps.

Vermehren's defection made Jebsen's own position more vulnerable. His friendship with the family was well known, and he was sure to be tarred by association. Canaris, 'the old fox', was no longer on hand to protect him. The 'younger and more energetic' Georg Hansen was appointed head of counter-intelligence, and set about merging the remnants of the Abwehr into a new unified intelligence service. 'He is not a Nazi,' reported Jebsen, 'but he is determined to prevent Germany's defeat. There is no doubt that Hansen means to reform the Abwehr completely.' This new intelligence service would bear little relation to the dozy, dishonest and partly disloyal organisation Jebsen had joined back in 1939. Many of his supporters had been swept away with the fall of Canaris, replaced by men not at all to Jebsen's liking. 'The new officers have no experience of intelligence work, but they are keener and more active than their predecessors and will probably succeed in tightening up the organisation.' One of these new appointees, in particular, made Jebsen 'a little uneasy'.

Major Wilhelm Kuebart was one of the stiffest new brooms in German intelligence. A professional soldier from East Prussia, he had fought on the Eastern Front before transferring to the Abwehr in July 1943, as Hansen's deputy. Kuebart was twenty-eight, 'wide awake', ruthlessly proficient, and 'the most intelligent man in the Abwehr', Jebsen reported. The young Major swiftly concluded that German intelligence was composed of 'elderly men with little or no idea of military organisation'. The Lisbon office, in particular, was 'discharging its functions most unsatisfactorily'. Kuebart paid a visit to Portugal and was 'shocked at the general immorality'. Half the staff appeared to be sleeping with the other half. At least two of the secretaries were passing information to Jebsen. Von Karsthoff might insist that Jebsen was 'an extremely able man', but Kuebart smelled something 'rather fishy'. On returning to Berlin, he drew up a damning report, recommending that von Karsthoff be 'removed and replaced', and the 'sleeping secretaries' fired. 'This brothel must be shut,' Kuebart declared.

Ludovico von Karsthoff, Popov's indolent, charming, corrupt spymaster, was reprimanded for 'indiscretion and inefficiency' (which was putting it mildly), sacked from his post, and sent to the Eastern Front. Dr Aloys Schreiber was now, in effect, the head of German intelligence in Lisbon.

Schreiber was a puzzle. A forty-four-year-old Bavarian, with an oval face and greying hair, he was a First World War veteran with a doctorate in law from Erlangen University. He had been the personal courier to his close friend Canaris, before being sent to Lisbon to take over from Jebsen's arch-enemy Kammler as head of counter-intelligence, although he spoke not a word of Portuguese. 'His specific duties were obtaining intelligence information concerning enemy armies', gathering information about 'the possibility of Allied invasion, and in particular the time, location and strength of such a proposed landing'. Bookish and serious, Schreiber was openly disdainful of his dissolute colleagues, and had a reputation among the Abwehr roustabouts and layabouts for being 'pedantic and ambitious'. Jebsen was unsure what to make of this clever, sober, anti-social man: 'Schreiber is not a Nazi, but nor particularly anti-Nazi,' he reported.

In fact, Schreiber was not only anti-Nazi, but a conspirator in the spreading plot to topple Hitler. Like some others in the Abwehr, he nursed a quiet but profound hatred of Nazism.

In 1942, on the orders of Hans Oster, the deputy head of the Abwehr and a significant figure in the German resistance, he smuggled a Jewish couple named Weiss and their children to Switzerland, and was arrested 'on suspicion of aiding, abetting and camouflaging the illegal departure' of Jews. He was exonerated after his Abwehr bosses intervened. Before leaving for Portugal, Colonel Georg Hansen, another key conspirator, quizzed him closely about 'his general political attitude'. Schreiber was left in no doubt that the conspirators were sounding him out: 'Something was being planned and he was under the impression that they wished to ascertain exactly who belonged to them in sentiment, so they would know on whom they could count.' They could count on Schreiber. As defeat loomed, a determined band of officers, led by Claus von Stauffenberg, began planning Hitler's assassination in the attempted putsch codenamed 'Valkyrie'. These were not soft-hearted liberals, but ruthless military men determined to salvage German honour by destroying Nazism, making peace with the Americans and British, and then turning, with full ferocity, on the Bolshevik menace in the East. A postwar investigation concluded that Schreiber 'belonged to the group of militarists who sponsored the attempt of 20 July 1944' and 'he was sent to Portugal by the 20 July conspirators to ensure having a dependable man in a strategic position who could be called upon'. Schreiber would soon receive the call, with calamitous consequences for the Double Cross plot.

Marie von Gronau, Jebsen's latest 'sleeping secretary', reported that Berlin was demanding 'the names of Abwehr members who are believed to be in touch with the British'. Jebsen relayed this disquieting news to de Salis: 'We must reckon that they will in future pay special attention to us. Even greater care is necessary with regard to meetings.' The danger was reflected in Most Secret Sources. 'Berlin has ordered that a close watch be kept on Artist, presumably on account of the flight of the Vermehrens as he is known to be a friend of theirs,' wrote Tar. 'Artist's friends are not now in Berlin, and his enemies are going to make things unpleasant for him.'

Jebsen was confident: Brandes had been to Berlin, and reported that he had 'defended him strongly'; the secretaries were keeping him fully informed of the correspondence with Berlin; Schreiber did not seem particularly hostile, and the order to keep an eye on him was probably just a routine response to the defection of his friend, Erich Vermehren. 'The clouds are nearly over,' he told de Salis, who reported back to London: 'Artist in extremely good form, owing to fact that suspicions against him have died down due to prompt action by his allies, including Brandes.' Jebsen's confidence rose further with the news that he would soon be reunited with Popov.

Popov landed at the now-familiar Lisbon airport on 26 February, bearing with him another large slice of Operation Fortitude, including photographs of Admiralty documents, notes on aircraft types, information on rationing and a doctored parliamentary speech. Within Popov's cache, as Jebsen had advised, lay a wealth of smaller details which, when put together, would reveal a mighty army assembling in the southeast. Popov had been told to take Jebsen aside as soon as discreetly possible, and 'exert his influence over Artist to prevent the latter from getting nervous or excited and doing foolish things or taking any avoidable risks'. If Jebsen raised the idea of bringing Brandes into the plot, he should be urged to 'take no steps whatever to bring this about, although we would welcome suggestions as to how it might be possible to recruit Brandes'. Above all, Jebsen should be encouraged to find out whether the deception was working, by obtaining 'up-to-date details of the German knowledge of the British Order of Battle'.

Popov's reception was very different from the sort of welcome laid on by von Karsthoff. This time he would be debriefed by Aloys Schreiber, a man who, Jebsen warned, 'had a very great experience of interrogating prisoners'.

Schreiber asked Jebsen to sit in on the debriefing, which was as intense and penetrating as von Karsthoff's had been cheery and perfunctory. For two days and nights, pausing only for beer and sandwiches, Schreiber grilled Popov. Jebsen chipped in from time to time with his own sharp questions. Popov later reported that his friend had 'assisted him cleverly during his interrogation while deliberately appearing to be rather hostile, with the result that Schreiber is satisfied there is no collaboration between Artist and Tricycle'. Popov put on a dazzling performance. Indeed, as he later told Wilson, 'he was sure he was definitely on top and, as he modestly put it, being the younger man he stood the strain better than Schreiber'. The German station chief seemed utterly convinced by Popov's report, and immediately dictated a telegram to Berlin stating that he was 'an excellent agent and he had no suspicions'. Marie von Gronau passed the note on to Jebsen, who gave it to de Salis, who sent it on to London, where the news was passed to Churchill: 'His first interview with his spymasters passed off in a most satisfactory manner.' Popov's confidence was validated when Bletchley Park decoded a message to the German High Command, noting that Agent Ivan had furnished 'particularly valuable information about the British formations in Great Britain. The report confirmed our own overall operational picture.'

After the debriefing, Popov and Jebsen hit the town, hard. Jebsen was 'in funds, having managed to wangle authority to transfer some gold he has put by in Paris', and had bought himself a Rolls-Royce, which he could not drive. Jebsen did not seem unduly anxious for his own safety, and spoke of maintaining 'long-term contact with the British secret services' and wanting 'to be regarded by them as a reliable agent even after the war'. Popov was confident his own high standing in Berlin would protect his friend. They were joined in their carousing by Hans Brandes, Jebsen's new friend. Brandes seemed wary of Popov. Jebsen later suggested why:

'He is afraid that he [Popov] will report the date and place of the invasion and thus prolong the war.' It was an odd thing to say. Brandes often made overtly anti-Nazi remarks, as if fishing for a reaction. De Salis reported: 'Although convinced that Brandes is not trying to trap him, Artist always reacts to such suggestions as a good German should.'

Ian Wilson flew out to Lisbon and met Popov and Jebsen at the safe house. Jebsen was ambitious to do more for the cause. 'He is keen to go to Germany as he wanted to do something big for us,' Wilson reported. 'He could arrange to be sent to Germany for a visit under a false name if we really desired it.' Wilson thought it safer for Jebsen to remain in Lisbon, particularly after he casually referred to 'Kühlenthal's controlled agents in UK', and the need for these to back up whatever Popov reported. Here was proof positive that Jebsen knew the Garbo network, or 'the Spaniards', as he called them, were bogus. Brandes had 'brought word back from Berlin on how the British spies were seen in Berlin', which suggested that Popov was now even more valued than Pujol. 'Ivan [Popov] is now considered to be by far the best connection and the Spaniards, as regards quality, are following a long way behind,' Brandes reported. 'The confidence in him has grown very much.' Such comparisons were of limited value since, as Jebsen observed, it was 'common for members of the Abwehr to run down each others' agents'.

Still, Brandes was being remarkably helpful, and Jebsen again urged his recruitment: 'He is certain that Brandes would collaborate with us.'

Jebsen did not realise, and MI5 did not tell him, that Brandes was an even more slippery opportunist than he knew. Brandes had his own wireless transmitter. With this he was sending messages to Berlin, reporting on Jebsen – who he was meeting, where he was going, and what he was saying. These transmissions, decoded at Bletchley Park, revealed yet another layer of deception: the man Jebsen considered his close friend, to whom he was prepared to entrust his life by inducting him into his terrifying secret, was betraying him behind his back.

'Brandes is playing a game of his own,' reported Ian Wilson, a note of fear creeping for the first time into his words. 'Brandes is clearly telling tales.'

'Am I Not Always Careful?'

Brutus, Bronx, Treasure, Tricycle and Garbo would never meet. Yet individually, and together, as spring advanced and the Allied armies prepared for the biggest amphibious assault in history, they spun a tapestry of lies so thick and wide it would envelop the entire German intelligence system. In April 1944, anxiety was still high, and expectations low: Tommy Harris declared that the effort would be worthwhile if the deception caused just '*one* division to hesitate *48 hours* before proceeding to oppose our landing in the Cherbourg peninsula'. As the real army mustered in the southwest to attack Normandy, the double agents deployed their fake army in the southeast and the north. At first Pujol and Harris had merely sprinkled untruths among the chicken-feed, but now they began to 'increase the percentage of false in the mixture until the entire substance of our reports would be based on the false or notional', a creeping barrage of deception.

Popov's latest report to Lisbon had established the names and locations of units within the fictional invasion force; knowing that the Germans would now be paying attention, the double agents started to move these south and east. Most Secret Sources showed that Garbo's reports, five or six a day, were being relayed to Berlin, promptly and almost verbatim, along with his analysis of their meaning. The hoax was being injected straight into the central nervous system of the Third Reich.

The deceivers wondered if they were being too subtle. Would the Germans pick up the hints and reach the right conclusions? As a test, Tar Robertson called in a 'military expert who had no previous dealings with B1A', sat him down with forty boxes of paper – the entire double-agent traffic from March 1943 to April 1944 – and asked him to interpret the lot. The poor man ploughed through the files every day for two weeks, and then offered his conclusions as to what the Germans must be thinking:

1. Agents have been at pains to make no definite forecast.
2. Strong likelihood of attack in the Mediterranean at same time.
3. An attack in Norway, possibly of a diversionary nature, prior to the main attack.
4. The initial landings will be made against Belgium and the Pas de Calais.

The assessment fitted with the deception almost perfectly.

A German intelligence report of 4 April stated that the Fourth Army was assembling in Scotland, and cited a 'credible Abwehr source'. This source was Roman Czerniawski, whose reputation expanded with every message: 'He is very well regarded and up till now has produced much accurate information,' Oscar Reile noted. Hugh Astor hit on a way to bind Brutus even more firmly to the Germans, while reinforcing the lie that a fictional American-led army was assembling in Kent: 'If Brutus were posted notionally to FUSAG just before D-Day, he would be in an excellent position to report on the Order of Battle and operational intentions of FUSAG.' When the time was ripe, Czerniawski would announce that, 'on account of his intimate knowledge of France and French military procedure', he had been ordered to join a special unit 'set up under FUSAG with the object of recruiting Poles who worked in the German-occupied territory which was likely to be overrun in the near future'. Since many Poles worked in the coalfields east of Calais, this would in itself bolster the idea that the US Army Group was poised to attack the Calais area. Installed at the heart of the fictional army, the little Pole would be perfectly placed to report exactly what was happening or, more accurately, what was not happening.

While Brutus focused on military matters, Bronx fed her handlers 'the opinions of those whose names and pictures appeared in the column of fashionable newspapers', a peculiar admixture of the weighty and the irrelevant. Beneath the fluff, she pointed unmistakably to forces assembling to attack the Pas de Calais: Lord Kimberley told her an armoured division had moved from Yorkshire to Brighton; one Major Bulteel suggested 'Montgomery's HQ may be near Canterbury'; a friend in the Army petroleum department visited Dover and Folkestone and told her of 'large invasion stores'; another, George Mitchell, resident in Kent, informed her 'roads to beaches widened and concrete barriers removed', suggesting a mass military deployment towards the coast. She helped to focus attention on Scandinavia, relaying a conversation with Commander Sir Guy Domville, who 'believes Denmark place for invasion. S. Norway may be occupied.' Her reports were calculated to maintain German uncertainty about the date: 'Invasion seems imminent,' she reported on 25 April. 'Many US troops leaving west coast for S. E. Command.' A few days later, she corrected herself: 'Prime Minister's conference indicates invasion not imminent. Montgomery still training invasion force.'

As Emile Kliemann had instructed, Lily Sergeyev headed to Bristol to stay with her relatives, and toured the south coast by bicycle, while never leaving London. 'I make imaginary visits to places which I did not know existed, and from which I bring back rich harvests of information,' she wrote in her diary. 'In this world of fiction, I spend my time in trains, clubs, messes, canteens. I transmit a hodgepodge of descriptions of badges, vehicles, tanks, planes and airfields, garnished with conversations overheard, from which the Germans cannot fail to derive the correct conclusions.' Like many spies, caught up in the make-believe, she began to wonder who she really was. 'For three years I have been acting a part . . . If I survive the war, will I be able to readapt? Will I be able to become *normal* again?'

Mary was pleased with Lily's compliant attitude, and her apparent recovery from the death of Babs: 'She is working hard on her transmissions,' she told Tar. Inside, Lily was still seething, and her resentment was redoubled by some ill-advised penny-pinching on the part of MI5. She was told to make her own way to Hampstead by Tube: 'I don't think it would break the War Office to take me there by car,' she grumbled. She was moved out of Rugby Mansions and into a smaller flat at 39 Hill Street, where she had to pay rent, albeit reduced. A stern note from John Marriott instructed her: 'The furniture, fittings and books will be maintained in the condition that they are now in and expenses for cleaning etc. will be paid promptly. I shall expect you to carry out this undertaking.' It was the wrong tone to use to an agent who had just risked her life. As Lily pointed out, Kliemann was eating out of her hand – 'the German intelligence service seems entirely satisfied with the information I supply. From time to time there are congratulations in their messages.' The British, on the other hand, were charging her rent, and telling her to keep the carpet clean.

MI5 refused to reimburse Lily for her lost suitcase, while O'Shagar, the MI6 officer who had promised to look after Babs when she left Gibraltar, had also failed to send on the case's contents: Lily demanded their return, but her possessions were irretrievably lost in the fog of war. The suitcase had contained a jade necklace, a chamois leather pillow, two dozen handkerchiefs in a red leather case and, oddly, 'three shoes (not pairs) valued at £12'. Lily reckoned the total value was £128 2s 6d, but said she would settle for £50. MI5 declined to pay her a penny.

'I think we ought NOT to pay up,' declared Marriott, and listed the reasons why: 'She has no legal claim. She has behaved in an unreasonable fashion in the past and may therefore do so again. She is trying to bully us.' John Masterman agreed: 'We owe nothing.' Mary Sherer was appalled:

> Treasure is not a money grubber. In view of what she has accomplished and what we hope to get out of her case, I urge you very strongly to reconsider your decision. I have had a difficult time with Treasure on more than one occasion in the past and it will not make things any easier if she has a private grudge against the department and British authorities on the whole because of their apparently niggardly behaviour towards her for the sake of £50.

But the bosses were adamant. John Masterman did not like women in general, and Lily in particular, considering her 'exceptionally temperamental and troublesome'.

A few days later, as she and Mary were preparing a wireless message, Lily remarked darkly: 'It is very difficult not to take advantage of one's strength when one is the strongest.' Mary assumed she was referring to the parsimony of MI5 with its 'meticulous accounts'. Most likely, she was alluding to her own secret strength: the knowledge that a couple of undetected dashes in a mass of Morse could bring the entire Double Cross system crashing down.

Dusko Popov arrived back in Britain on 13 April, with a spring in his step, a fresh batch of questionnaires and a wad of cash. His last days in Lisbon had been spent wrangling over money, the sort of negotiation at which Popov excelled. He told Aloys Schreiber he wanted a staggering $150,000 as an advance payment on future information about Allied invasion plans, and declared that 'any further activities on his part would depend on the receipt of the stipulated sum'. When this was relayed to Berlin, the demand was flatly refused. Popov was offered just 1,500 Swiss francs a month. He threatened to resign. This gave

Wilhelm Kuebart, the officer who had ousted von Karsthoff, an 'uncomfortable feeling' about Popov, 'as it seemed to him highly improbable that an agent who was really independent and acting for himself could afford to threaten the Abwehr in this manner'. Even MI5 considered Popov's demands 'outrageous', and his threat to quit an unauthorised gamble. In the end, Popov was given $14,000, with the promise of more to come. Before leaving, he had been interviewed again by Schreiber, who told him to find out the date and target of the invasion, which attacks would be real, and which merely diversions. If the landings started, he should 'stay in London and give up-to-date news on what was happening'. Schreiber also asked him to report on bomb damage when the V1s started landing, but Popov refused, saying they could 'send some lower-grade agent round to look for holes in London'.

Popov and Jebsen spent a last night together at the casino in Estoril. At dawn, they shook hands and parted, but as Popov was walking away, Jebsen called him back: 'I just wanted to have a good look at you,' he said. 'It's going to be a while. I feel we are going in different directions.' Then he walked away.

Back in London, Popov was ebullient, convinced the Germans had 'complete faith in him'. Schreiber had no idea he was playing a double game. The Germans were paying good money. Johnny was safe. 'Tricycle is now considered to be the Abwehr's best agent in the UK,' MI6 reported.

The B1A case officers pored over Popov's latest offerings from the other side, which included a long questionnaire largely composed of wishful thinking: 'What are Churchill's prospects of remaining at the helm? How is his health? Does he by any chance already think of retiring, and if so, when?' To which the answers were: 'good', 'good', 'no' and 'never'. Popov's briefcase contained no fewer than five typed reports from Jebsen, on aircraft production, industrial output, military reserves and the restructuring of German intelligence: he noted the rise of SS officer Walter Schellenberg, 'personally agreeable and quite ruthless', who would eventually take over as intelligence supremo.

Popov was 'not unduly worried' for Jebsen's safety, since the Gestapo had apparently rescinded an order to have him arrested if he returned to Germany. Even so, Tar insisted 'it was much safer that he should remain in Lisbon rather than return to Germany, where he might find himself in an awkward position, under which his nerves would give way'. Before leaving Lisbon, Popov learned from Marie von Gronau that the SD was 'sending a representative to interrogate Artist at the end of April or beginning of May in Lisbon, in order to clear up certain financial matters', but this was no cause for concern. 'These allegations have nothing to do with activities on behalf of the British, but relate to questionable financial transactions. He is satisfied that he can easily clear himself. The intended interrogation is likely to be a formality, so that the file against Jebsen can be closed.' Popov was convinced his friend was finally 'free from danger'.

MI5 knew otherwise.

On 11 February, Hans Brandes, using the codename 'Ballhorn', sent a message to Berlin, reporting that Jebsen was asking suspicious questions, and 'trying to find out about Ostro'. The message was intercepted and decoded at Bletchley Park. Under British instructions, Jebsen was investigating the fake agent Paul Fidrmuc, whom MI5 had considered eliminating a few months earlier. Another intercepted message referred to 'oral reports made by Ballhorn', indicating that Brandes had been snitching during his trip to Berlin. The next day brought further evidence of his duplicity, when Brandes reported that through the secretaries, Jebsen 'learns everything' that happened in the German intelligence station. Schreiber fired off his own message to Berlin: 'As cannot continue to work in such circumstances, it is urgently requested that Grass and Von Gronau be immediately recalled, giving routine reduction of staff as justification in order not to give Johnny prior warning.'

What was Brandes up to? Why was he dripping poison into his superiors' ears about a man supposed to be his friend? Brandes 'might be playing some deep game for his own interests', thought Wilson, 'possibly with the ultimate intention of blackmailing Artist, or ourselves. He is far from stupid and quite unscrupulous, as are so many spoilt children of rich German industrialists.' Brandes had recently been ordered to send his agents 'to France for instruction'. But Brandes had no agents. He had made them all up, and he was now trying to find a way of 'worming, or bribing, his way out of this dilemma'. Ratting on Jebsen would divert attention. 'It may well be that in order to prevent his being discovered he is trying to build himself up with the Abwehr by unmasking Artist.' Ambitious and avaricious, Brandes knew how much money was being passed to Popov, and what Jebsen and von Karsthoff had made on the side. A postwar investigation revealed that Brandes was 'very jealous of the fact that Artist was in touch with Tricycle, the best German secret intelligence man in England. Brandes wanted to get rid of him so that he might get the credit for Tricycle's work.'

The evidence of Brandes's treachery presented MI5 with an appalling dilemma. If Jebsen was warned that his friend was betraying him, he would immediately wonder how MI5 had come by that information, and perhaps conclude that the British must be intercepting German wireless messages. At all costs, Most Secret Sources must be protected. After an intense debate, it was agreed that MI6 would pass on a general warning to Jebsen, hinting that Brandes should not be trusted because some of what he had told Jebsen had turned out to be inaccurate. A telegram was sent to Charles de Salis in Lisbon: 'Strong impression that Brandes is playing a game of his own and may be trying to provoke Artist into confidences which he might use for his own interests. Instruct Artist not to expose himself in any way to Brandes, even if this restricts his acquisition of information on our behalf.' De Salis was not told that MI5's 'impressions'

came from Most Secret Sources. Wilson meanwhile sounded out
Popov on how well Jebsen might hold up under interrogation,
should he be arrested. Popov replied that he had 'absolutely no
doubts whatsoever that Artist would never betray Tricycle or
confess his own work for the British under any normal form
of interrogation [but he] doubts his powers to withstand any
physical violence'.

Jebsen had been 'hasty in assuming that the clouds have quite
rolled away'. A storm was gathering with terrifying speed. On
16 April, Schreiber informed Jebsen that they had both been
ordered to travel to Biarritz, in the South of France, to meet
the paymaster of the reformed German intelligence service and
discuss Popov's demands for money. Sensing a trap, Jebsen
refused to go, claiming that this would blow 'his cover' as an
independent businessman, since travelling to France required
official German approval. Schreiber insisted the telegram from
Berlin 'should be looked upon as an order', and refusal to
obey 'would be considered desertion'. Jebsen dug in his heels.
Schreiber reported this back to Berlin, and headed off to Biarritz
alone. Jebsen, deeply alarmed, told Brandes what had happened;
Brandes immediately sent a telegram to Berlin:

> On the 17th Johnny told me he had been ordered to a
> conference in Biarritz on the subject of Ivan. Johnny said
> he saw a clear trap in this and was certain that his immediate
> arrest was intended in Biarritz. Johnny added that if in the
> next few days any further signs of mistrust existing towards
> him on the part of Berlin are to be observed he intends to
> draw his own conclusions and will inform Ivan in good
> time.

Further signs of mistrust were not long in coming. The next
day the office secretaries, Lily Grass and Marie von Gronau,
were ordered to return to Berlin within twenty-four hours. This
was 'a routine reduction of staff', Schreiber claimed, since 'all

secretaries who have been here more than two years are to leave
on the principle that they have had a long period of work in
a pleasant place and should therefore be moved to somewhere
less pleasant'. But Jebsen knew his moles within the system were
being weeded out. The women were instructed not to speak
to him before they left; both ignored the order. Jebsen even
escorted Marie to the airport. As they parted, he said something
that made her even more convinced that he must be a British
agent. 'Three days after the end of hostilities, a British pilot
will report to a restaurant in Flensburg, Schleswig-Holstein, the
Grossadel Bylond, and if you are present he will pick you up
and bring you to England.' Marie promised to be there.

Jebsen met Charles de Salis at the safe house. He was deeply
agitated, smoking furiously with trembling fingers. The MI6 man
passed on the veiled warning about Brandes, but Jebsen seemed
preoccupied with the forced departure of the secretaries. 'Artist
does not consider this a very good sign,' de Salis reported. 'He feels
very bitter. He rails against the pig-headed administration which
has ordered this.' The order to go to Biarritz with Schreiber had
been a 'test' of his loyalty and obedience: 'Further traps of this
nature will be laid,' he predicted. Despite the precariousness of
his own position, Jebsen had some important new intelligence
to report: the latest strategic assessment by the German General
Staff, as presented to a conference of generals in France. This
predicted a 'large-scale invasion attempt' across the Channel
and in southern France, revealed doubts as to 'whether Norway
could be defended successfully', and concluded that a precise
assessment of American troops in the UK would be 'decisive'.
The Germans appeared to be concentrating on exactly the right
areas. Before she was ordered home, Lily Grass had passed on
some good news. 'Tricycle's reports have made a tremendous
impression in Berlin and the General Staff are considering
modifying their plans in consequence. The last report had already
been classified as being "as good as sure", which is an almost
unparalleled evaluation.' By the end of the meeting, Jebsen had

regained some of his composure. 'Artist is confident that Brandes will keep him warned of future traps, and hopes that in this way the "tests" may be negotiated successfully. If this can be done, Tricycle's position as the Ace Abwehr agent in the UK will be assured and all thenceforward should be comparatively easy.'

Before they parted, de Salis told Jebsen to be careful.

'Am I not always careful?' said Jebsen, with a pale smile.

The warning about Brandes had not registered. Or perhaps Jebsen chose to ignore it. He was a firm believer in friendship. Later the same day, he showed a document to Brandes, who was on the radio to Berlin within hours. 'A telegram which has just arrived from England was shown to me by Johnny at his house. It was signed by his friend Baronet Anthony Rothschild. The contents read as follows "Don't worry, our business shall be finished very soon".'

This was, of course, part of Jebsen's elaborate tale about a rich member of the Rothschild family (now downgraded from peer to baronet) who was helping him get a refugee visa to Britain. He probably showed it to Brandes, knowing he might soon have to disappear. There was no such person as Sir Anthony Rothschild. But Brandes did not know this, and to his mind the 'telegram conveyed a hidden meaning, that the time was nearly due for Artist to come over to the British with such information as he had been able to gather'. Brandes told Berlin that Jebsen was again showing 'noticeable curiosity about Ostro'.

Robertson brought together Masterman, Marriott and Wilson for a crisis meeting. The intercepts revealed that 'while Artist considered Brandes to be entirely his friend, Brandes was reporting unfavourably on Artist'. On the other hand, Most Secret Sources indicated that the Gestapo was no longer on his trail, and although the authorities wanted to interview him, they were concerned 'solely with financial matters'. If Jebsen was asked why he was so interested in Ostro, he could 'take a bold line' and insist that it was his 'desire to expose Ostro if he could find proof that Ostro was a fraud'. (Which, as MI5 well knew, he was.)

Wilson summed up the situation, while admitting this was 'too complicated to enable one to make any very confident appreciation of the position':

Brandes is clearly telling tales about Artist but there is no indication, at least so far, that Brandes is trying to suggest Artist is working for the British. I am personally satisfied that the telegram [summoning Artist to Biarritz] was not a trap, but Artist is apt to get into a state of nerves where he quite genuinely imagines traps which do not exist. He may not have seen as clearly as we have that the Gestapo seems now to be convinced that he is best left in Lisbon, and he may quite honestly fear that the Gestapo are behind the attempt to get him into occupied territory where they will arrest him. No immediate action can be taken by us. There is a risk that, despite our warning, Artist may continue to place some confidence in Brandes, but we cannot strengthen our warning without danger to our sources.

They agreed to do nothing. The protection of Most Secret Sources was paramount. 'I see no reason to be unduly nervous,' said Wilson, with a confidence he certainly did not feel.

Jebsen, meanwhile, decided to brazen it out with his bosses, and conduct his own 'test'. He told Schreiber he had received a message from Popov, stating he would 'brook no further delay over money'. To Jebsen's surprise, Schreiber was most accommodating. He agreed to cable Berlin immediately, and came back with the answer that he had 'received immediate instructions to hand over all available funds to Artist'. He then presented Jebsen with $75,000 in cash. This, he said, was only a down payment. Jebsen was ecstatic.

'Artist considers this proof all is well and that general staff will repeat will act on strength of Tricycle's reports,' Charles de Salis reported back to London. 'He now believes the investigation is over and Abwehr are satisfied both he and Tricycle are sound.

Tricycle's position as an ace agent is assured.' The crisis was over. Schreiber could not have been more friendly, and told him that Berlin had cabled 'at the last minute' to say that Jebsen was not needed at the Biarritz meeting after all. There was even talk of bringing back his lover Marie von Gronau. Jebsen wrote a triumphant letter to Popov:

> You will know by reports coming from Cobb [de Salis's cover name] about the tests the Abwehr tried to carry out. I am quite happy that it is over now and I congratulate you on being my beloved Führer's best agent without any doubt, because, after having hesitated for some time, the Abwehr have decided the money should be transferred to you as arranged. I got 75,000 dollars, of which I will send 50,000 today. We might settle accounts later, but my share I am keeping here because I might be in need of some money to bribe heaven knows whom. Please give my best greetings to Ian, Frank and the Bentons. Be a good boy, and try to behave . . . Yours always, Johnny.

Relief flooded through B1A. The Tricycle network was safe, and with it, the rest of the Double Cross deception. This called for a celebratory dinner with Popov as guest of honour, to be held at the Hyde Park Hotel on 26 April. A report was sent to Churchill:

> The agent Tricycle has now returned from visiting his masters in Lisbon. He has once more succeeded in persuading them of his complete reliability and has extracted from them a large sum of dollars as an advance against his future services. He has received an interesting questionnaire. They appear to have the highest respect for him.

The day before the dinner, Jebsen met de Salis again and 'confirmed that everything was fine'. Schreiber had congratulated him on his handling of Popov, and told him he was to receive a medal, a War Merit Cross (*Kriegsverdienstkreuz*, or KVK) 1st Class without swords, a civilian medal usually awarded for bravery behind the lines. Now that he was no longer under suspicion, Jebsen said he planned to go to Berlin, where he would gather more information for British intelligence. 'From Artist's point of view the outcome is a complete triumph,' de Salis reported. 'To crown it all, Artist has been awarded the KVK 1st Class, an honour shared by no one in Lisbon. Schreiber in particular is envious.'

Jebsen dictated a letter to Mabel Harbottle (now fully in his confidence) telling Popov the good news:

A proof of the fact that Schreiber did not tell me stories [i.e. lie] is that I got another decoration, and this time the KVK First Class. First Class probably was given because you double-crossed them first class! I feel a little bit ashamed of getting the decoration for the work you and Ian did. I made up my mind to give it to Ian. Unfortunately I cannot get the Germans to put his name on the certificate, but I shall give him the decoration itself. If, as I hope, he collects curiosities, he might find a place for it in his collection. After all, he is an exceptional man and has the exceptional honour of getting a decoration with a swastika on it.

Schreiber had promised more money:

Knowing your mentality, I am sure you are much more interested in this than in the really funny story of my decoration.

Brandes is no longer your friend because he is terribly afraid you might betray the circumstances and date of the invasion and not only prolong the war but endanger his position as only 50% Aryan which must be more and more difficult. It might come out in the end that he is going to hang instead of the Nazi leaders if the war goes on for a very long time. Last time I forgot to send my best greetings to Frano [de Bona, Agent Freak]. This was because at the time I didn't remember that he should know that I know what after all we all know. I sometimes forget to whom I have to cover what, and what I have to cover to whom. I think this letter is too long already. Besides, I have to think of the poor lady who has to type it and probably has something better to do than to amuse you. [Mabel Harbottle wrote in the margin with what, for her, was very nearly coquetry: *'The lady herself is of course delighted at the thought of helping to keep you amused.'*]

He ended with a flourish:

I hope you will give my love to all you can give it to without spoiling your, my, or anybody else's cover. To you I can give my love anyhow, yours, as always, Johnny.

The letter was typical Jebsen: funny, insouciant, mercenary, and more worried about the fate of Hans Brandes than his own. De Salis reported that Jebsen had been 'in a very good mood and the difference between this and the last meeting, when he was obviously worried, was very noticeable.' Jebsen agreed to return to the safe house on 5 May, one month and one day before D-Day.

Amid all the excitement and relief, no one spotted a message, sent the day before Popov's dinner, from Aloys Schreiber to Georg Hansen, the new head of German counter-intelligence: 'The carrying out of the threatened plan is imminent. Request your permission to prevent this plan even if it should become necessary to use extreme measures.' Hansen gave his permission.

The dinner at the Hyde Park Hotel was most convivial. The key players in the Tricycle case were all there, in evening attire: Guy Liddell, Tar Robertson, John Masterman, John Marriott and Ian Wilson, who had just steered the network through such rocky waters. MI6 was represented by Frank Foley. MI5's Director General, Sir David Petrie, raised a toast to Agent Tricycle. Popov was 'full of praise for Wilson for whom he clearly has the greatest respect', Liddell noted in his diary. 'I think he realises that if Wilson had not been at his side coaching him, he could never have achieved the position which he has now reached. He told me also that Wilson had made a very good impression on Artist.' In a rare departure from intelligence protocol, as a mark of trust in Popov, 'all those present used their own names'.

They did however, keep one secret from Popov: 'It was unknown to Tricycle that the cigars smoked at dinner were kindly provided by Dr Emile Kliemann of the Paris Abwehr station.'

Operation Dora

On the afternoon of 29 April, Aloys Schreiber telephoned Johnny Jebsen and asked him to come to the offices on Rua Buenos Aires, as he wanted to discuss the award of his War Merit Cross. Jebsen had a friend staying with him in Estoril, Heinz Paul Moldenhauer, a young Abwehr officer from the Cologne branch. Schreiber suggested that Jebsen bring Moldenhauer along, as he would like to discuss some intelligence matters with him.

Jebsen and Moldenhauer arrived at the office at dusk. The place was deserted. In Schreiber's outer office sat two men Jebsen knew only vaguely, a signals officer named Bliel and Karl Meier, a burly civilian car mechanic. Schreiber welcomed Jebsen and Moldenhauer warmly, and after chatting for a few minutes, invited Jebsen to step into the inner office alone. Once Jebsen was seated and the door closed, Schreiber calmly explained that he had orders to take him 'to Berlin by force, since he would not go of his own free will'. Jebsen made a bolt for the door, but Schreiber was faster, and fitter. He punched Jebsen once, and knocked him cold. When Jebsen came to, he found himself tied to a chair, along with Moldenhauer, who had been overpowered by Meier in the adjoining room.

Schreiber told his captives what would happen next: 'They would be knocked out and while unconscious placed in two large trunks, in which they would be shipped by car the same evening over the Portuguese-Spanish and Spanish-French borders to Biarritz. To guard against all possible surprises at the borders, he had decided to drug them by injections.' Schreiber asked them to surrender without a struggle. Jebsen seemed to realise that the time to fight would come later. 'Both of them submitted to the injections.'

At around 2 a.m., a Studebaker sedan with diplomatic plates and two large trunks in the boot arrived at Badajoz, the border crossing into Spain. In the rear seat sat Schreiber. Meier knew 'border conditions and officials personally', and the car was waved through. They drove north, stopping only for 'a few rests in the open'. From Madrid, Schreiber sent a telegram to Hansen: 'Mission has been carried out as far as Madrid'. At midnight the following evening, the party crossed into France. In Biarritz, Jebsen and Moldenhauer, still heavily drugged, were removed from the trunks and handed over to an intelligence officer named Fuchs. Schreiber sent another cable: 'Luggage handed over Biarritz to be sent on to Berlin. Undertaking was successful and everything all right.'

The following day Hans Brandes in Lisbon received a message of congratulations from Georg Hansen: 'Many thanks for reports and special recommendation'.

Plans for the kidnapping of Johnny Jebsen had been laid two weeks earlier. The message from Brandes, warning that Jebsen might be about to defect, had 'provoked considerable excitement' in Berlin. 'Jebsen's desertion had to be prevented at all costs,' Hansen told Kuebart, who was instructed 'to see personally that Jebsen reached German-occupied territory or at any rate to thwart any attempt on his part to reach Allied territory'. Kuebart briefed Schreiber, telling him that 'Berlin had proof that Jebsen had been working for both sides for some time and was now prepared to go over to the Allies' while also 'seeking to take financial advantage of the Abwehr'. Stopping this defection was 'of extreme importance to the war effort'.

Schreiber had tried to object, pointing out that this was surely 'a police matter', but Kuebart was insistent. The operation should be conducted in strict secrecy: neither the counter-espionage section in Lisbon, nor the Gestapo, nor the Portuguese police 'were to know anything about the affair'. The Abwehr and the SD, the Nazi party intelligence service, were not yet fully merged, and this was strictly a matter for the Abwehr: 'Once Jebsen was in Berlin, he would have to answer only to the military authorities and under no circumstance to the SD.' Still dubious, Schreiber cabled Berlin asking Hansen to 'accept full responsibility, in case the abduction caused difficulties with the Portuguese'. Hansen replied 'specifically charging Schreiber with the task' and telling him to hurry up: how Jebsen was bagged and delivered to Berlin was 'left entirely up to Schreiber'.

The Nazis had a taste for attaching female codenames to the most secret operations. Their espionage campaign against Britain was 'Lena'; the plan to seize the Canary Islands was 'Isabella'. The kidnapping of Jebsen was codenamed 'Operation Dora'.

Jebsen was suspected of being a double agent and probably a crook, but the real reason for the urgency and secrecy of Operation Dora had little to do with either his spying or his dodgy dealings. Hansen, Kuebart and many other intelligence officers were now actively plotting to kill Hitler. Jebsen, if he absconded, would derail those plans.

Hansen was deeply implicated in the anti-Nazi conspiracy that would culminate in the 20 July plot to assassinate the Führer. His home at Rangsdorf was used as a meeting place for the conspirators. Like many of the plotters, Hansen's loathing for Hitler was coupled with a deeply conservative patriotism, the urgent desire to save Germany before Hitler destroyed the Fatherland utterly. He wanted to remove Hitler and then launch a concerted assault on the Soviets, even if that meant Germany ended up with the 'status of a British dominion'. Kuebart shared his views, believing Hansen was 'the man to put things right'. The previous March, Hansen had begun to 'instruct Kuebart in the details of his machinations against the German regime'. By May, a plot was in place: Hansen told Kuebart he had 'arranged for someone to place some British-manufactured explosives in an aircraft in which Hitler was to fly'. Once Hitler was dead, the anti-Nazi resistance would rise up and overthrow the regime. But Jebsen was in the way.

Himmler's SD was itching for an opportunity to purge the remaining Canaris loyalists and anti-Nazi elements within German intelligence – men like Hansen, Kuebart and Schreiber. If Jebsen defected, Hansen feared, then the blame would be pinned on what remained of the Abwehr, as yet more proof of treachery: Hitler's henchmen would 'pounce on the Abwehr as they had done after the Vermehren incident', Hansen told Kuebart, which would 'put an end to schemes he was already concocting for the liquidation of Hitler and Himmler and the ultimate overthrow of the Nazi party'. A postwar investigation into the power struggle within German intelligence concluded that Operation Dora was a pre-emptive strike aimed at shielding the conspirators from their Nazi enemies. 'The Vermehren case had been used by Himmler and Schellenberg as a lever for gaining control of the Abwehr. Hansen and Kuebart were particularly concerned to prevent another desertion.'

Jebsen was kidnapped to preserve the plot to kill Hitler, a plot in which Jebsen would have been delighted to participate.

Schreiber had lulled Jebsen into thinking he was safe: the cash, the medal, the soothing words were all aimed at ensuring Jebsen did not flee before Schreiber was ready. The unexpected appearance of Heinz Moldenhauer at Jebsen's house complicated matters. Moldenhauer was the half-Jewish son of a former German minister and 'one of a number of anti-Nazis who have avoided active participation in the war by undertaking service with the Abwehr which they make no effort to carry out conscientiously'. He was regarded with suspicion in Berlin. Schreiber assumed that he must also be planning to defect, and decided to abduct him too. 'If innocent, Moldenhauer would have no trouble clearing himself with the military authorities in Berlin.' But Moldenhauer was not planning to defect: he was simply in the worst place at the worst possible time.

On 27 April, the day after the party for Popov, Hansen authorised the payment of 25,000 escudos to Schreiber 'in order to ensure the execution of Operation Dora'. Schreiber bought a sleeping drug from a Lisbon chemist, a syringe, rope and two trunks 'large enough for a grown person, fitted with adequately large openings for ventilation'. Four days later, Jebsen, dazed, battered and terrified, was lying on the floor of a cell in the Gestapo prison in Berlin.

Jebsen's disappearance sent a bolt of pure horror through the Double Cross team. The dreadful news arrived in a single line from Lisbon: 'Artist has disappeared since the afternoon of 29.4 and investigations have been instituted.' Most Secret Sources offered no clues to explain the mystery. 'This has clearly been done in great secrecy,' wrote Wilson. The first the SD in Lisbon knew of it was a message stating that Jebsen had been 'taken to France by the Abwehr as he was acknowledged as being unreliable'.

But what did 'unreliable' mean? The stakes went far beyond the fate of one man. If Jebsen's captors considered him untrustworthy, they might well suspect Popov, his best friend and agent, and if Popov was identified as a double agent that would inevitably cast suspicion on the other controlled agents in the UK. But worse than that, Jebsen knew the entire Garbo network was fiction, feeding false information in huge quantity back to Berlin. He had told Wilson he believed all the German spies in Britain were frauds. If Jebsen revealed this to his captors, the Germans would re-examine all the information received from their agents and look for the patterns of disinformation; they would quickly work out that the spies were directing them to defend the Pas de Calais and Norway. Operation Fortitude would be blown, with incalculable consequences. The invasion

was just one month away, and the immense machinery of
Operation Overlord was already in motion. Popov had told Ian
Wilson he was 'afraid that Jebsen would break down if physical
pressure were applied'. His abduction could spell disaster.

Wilson frantically combed Most Secret Sources for evidence
of what might have happened to Jebsen: 'A number of messages
on MSS have become available,' he reported, 'but none of them
seem very conclusive.' Two days after Jebsen's disappearance,
Popov's brother in Yugoslavia was still at large; if Dusko was
under suspicion, they would surely have pulled in Ivo. Wilson
tried to sound a positive note:

> Artist's present troubles arise primarily from the reports
> against him made by Brandes. The general tenor of the
> intercepts seems to be that the Abwehr are afraid that Artist
> was intending to go over to the British or to cause the
> Tricycle messages to be intercepted rather than that Artist is
> already a traitor to Germany or that Tricycle is a controlled
> agent. If they do not yet suspect the latter there is a good
> chance that Artist will not be subjected to pressure which
> will break him.

There was no sign that the Germans suspected Popov.
Indeed, the capture of Jebsen may have been ordered in part
because it was feared that if he defected to the Allies, this would
compromise a spy that Hansen considered 'the one agent of
real value in the UK'. Here was yet more black irony. Jebsen,
it seems, had been abducted not because the Germans suspected
Popov was a double agent, but because they didn't.

If Jebsen remained out of the hands of the Gestapo and the SD,
there was just a chance that the self-interest of those involved
might protect him. 'All the parties involved have their weak
spots. Brandes will fear a counter-investigation. Schreiber will
not willingly admit that Tricycle has been fooling them. Hansen
will not willingly reach a conclusion that will undermine the

whole Abwehr.' But these were fragile hopes, and Wilson knew it: 'The next few days will provide evidence to show clearly whether he is merely to be interrogated on relatively minor charges and kept in preventive custody, or forced to disclose the true position of Tricycle and possibly other controlled agents.' If Jebsen was made to talk, then instead of pulling off a great deception coup, the Double Cross team would have set the scene for a bloodbath on the beaches of Normandy.

At a crisis meeting on 9 May, John Masterman laid out the grim situation:

The cover plan has been to a considerable extent built up on the reports of XX agents. The fact that Artist, who is fully cognizant of the Tricycle network and has some knowledge of the other cases, has fallen under suspicion and been removed to Berlin therefore threatens the whole cover plan. We cannot tell exactly why Artist has fallen under suspicion – we only know that he is regarded as 'unreliable'. His 'unreliability' may be connected with his financial operations, his intrigues, or his unwise inquisitiveness about the undertakings of Brandes and Ostro, and not with his dealings with Tricycle at all. There is no proof that treason on the part of Artist is part of the charge. But obviously under interrogation at Berlin, he may reveal what he knows. We must act on the assumption that the Tricycle case may be blown. In these circumstances, what should be done?

We should leave the door open to continue our present policy in the hope that the Berlin investigation may be confined to Artist's personal delinquencies and leave Tricycle untouched. With good fortune we should get information through secret sources telling us how the inquiry proceeds. It may be that Tricycle will be confirmed in his position of trust and that we can operate him as before. The case of the other agents is more difficult. Clearly they must not change their style in any way, but should they, or should they not, continue to implement Fortitude? The danger of their doing so is that if all or most of them are blown as a result of Artist's revelations, their traffic will be 'read in reverse' and interpreted accordingly.

Masterman laid out the options:

1. They should for the time being continue to operate without change, though specific indication of the false objective should be avoided.
2. Attempt by diversity of messages to create confusion in the enemy's mind even though we have to abandon the hope of getting a complete cover plan over to the enemy.
3. If we come to the conclusion that practically all the agents are in fact blown we could take the extreme step of abandoning all efforts at deception and deny all information to the enemy by closing down all agents.

Shutting down the Double Cross system would nullify more than four years of hard work and extreme risk, but it would leave the enemy 'deprived of all information from agents at a time when he needs it most and would have to prepare himself in the dark to meet any eventuality'. Masterman's recommendation was to continue the deception but 'if, and only if, the blowing of Tricycle and Garbo is certain, we close down *all* agents shortly before D–Day'.

Within B1A, Jebsen's capture sparked a blazing row, the worst so far. Tommy Harris was particularly enraged. He had warned that Jebsen was a liability, and now the delicate structure of deception he had created with Juan Pujol was liable to be smashed to pieces. 'The confidence which has been deposited in Artist during the last few months has left him in little doubt that Kühlenthal's network in this country is controlled by us. Developments in the Artist case have, to say the least, very seriously compromised the Garbo channel for passing operational deception.' Harris did not believe that Most Secret Sources would give sufficient warning of disaster. The intercepts, after all, had failed to alert MI5 before Jebsen was snatched – 'the same night that our confidence in him was at its height'. Garbo could be blown 'without our getting any warning on MSS that he has been denounced by Artist'. The Tricycle network should be shut down, said Harris, immediately and permanently. It took Guy Liddell to point out that this would amount to Jebsen's death sentence, for it would prove to his captors that both he and Popov had been in league with the British: 'Packing up Tricycle will finish Artist,' he observed.

If the double agents were exposed, would the Germans be able 'to deduce the cover plan and the real plan from the previous traffic'? Could the Germans extract, in less than a month, the essence of Operation Fortitude from the reams of misinformation they had received? Masterman thought it would require a 'lengthy and exhaustive study [to] sift the truth from the falsehood', but Harris disagreed: 'I maintain that the enemy could, within twenty-four hours, analyse the entire B1A traffic for the [last] two months and they would be able to draw the conclusions that the cover plan threat is against the Pas de Calais, and we wish the enemy to believe that the assault will be two-pronged. Such a discovery by the enemy would be catastrophic.'

In the hands of the Gestapo inquisitors, Jebsen might reveal the true state of affairs and so compromise the entire network of controlled agents in this country. From now onwards the Germans might, at any moment, tumble to the fact that all their spies in England were under Allied control. They would then conclude that the messages they were receiving were the opposite of the truth. There could only be two reasonable objectives for the cross-Channel assault, namely the Pas de Calais and Normandy. If the Germans perceived we were trying to induce them to believe that we were

coming to the Pas de Calais, the true objective would thus
be automatically disclosed.

As the dispute raged, Tar Robertson found himself under
attack from MI6. Charles de Salis had lost not only a valued
agent, but a friend. The MI6 officer had been instructed only to
warn Jebsen that Brandes was an unreliable informant; he was
not told that Brandes was informing on Jebsen, and had warned
Berlin that he was about to flee. When de Salis discovered that
he had been given a doctored version of events, he hit the roof,
and accused MI5 of throwing Jebsen to the wolves.

'Why lead *me* up the garden path? The obvious way of putting
this over to Artist was to attribute the information to one of
23700's sources [a reference to MI6 informants].' Jebsen's
'respect for 23700 penetration of the German services was
profound', de Salis argued, and if told that the warnings came
from a British spy, he 'would have been really on his guard, and
would no doubt have been suspicious enough not to fall into the
German trap'. de Salis accused MI5 of giving him misleading
information, of which the acute danger to Jebsen was 'the most
flagrant and tragic example'. If he had been allowed to warn
Jebsen properly, de Salis railed, then the kidnapping could have
been thwarted. 'If I cannot be trusted to act a little comedy as
simple as this, I should not be here at all.'

Tar struggled to defend himself.

No one can have greater concern than I do over the
affairs of Artist, but a direct warning could not be given to
Artist. We had no indication that there was any imminent
danger of an attempt to kidnap Artist. The most careful
consideration was given to whether we should inform
Artist that Brandes was reporting on him, and it was
accepted by all the numerous officers here that we could
not run the risk to the source [Most Secret Sources] that
would be involved in warning Artist. All we could do was

warn Artist against putting confidence in Brandes. At my suggestion the warning was based on the suspicion we had of the accuracy of Brandes' reports. Operation Dora was not known to us until after the event had taken place. There was a message the day before, not mentioning Artist by name which, had we at the time had sufficient knowledge to link it with Artist, would have indicated that he was in danger of some sort. But because of the source, we could not have taken the risk of giving him any additional warning. I have naturally given a great deal of thought to this matter and I am satisfied that we went as far as we possibly could in protecting Artist.

Tar was blustering. His excuses were thin, as he was well aware. He knew there was a world of difference between the suggestion that Brandes was unreliable, and a tip-off that he was actively betraying Jebsen. He knew that a warning, carefully couched, would not necessarily have alerted Jebsen to Most Secret Sources. He knew that he and his team, paranoid about protecting the Allies' most valuable secret, had failed to appreciate the mortal danger to Jebsen, and as a consequence he was in prison, probably undergoing torture, and possibly already dead. Tar was a good and honourable man, and in his heart he must have known that Jebsen had trusted the British completely, and they had let him down. This was the worst moment of his war; perhaps, the worst moment of his life.

Dread throbbed through the building at 58 St James's Street. 'Anthony Blunt told me Tommy Harris was extremely worried about the Artist situation,' Liddell wrote. 'The whole situation is rather worrying. Tricycle has been told that all is not well with Artist who has disappeared. This news obviously caused Tricycle considerable worry as it obviously showed it was possible that Artist had been kidnapped.' MI5 could not reveal Most Secret Sources evidence of his abduction, but Popov soon reached the independent realisation that his friend had, 'by trick or by force, been taken back to Germany'. Another Abwehr defector, Hans Ruser, who knew Jebsen well, was asked whether his former colleague would be able to withstand interrogation. 'Jebsen was a mine of information and had always talked too much,' he said. 'Under third degree pressure, he would tell the Germans everything.'

As the crisis erupted, Winston Churchill was kept, if not exactly in the dark, then certainly in the shade. Blunt's report was a masterpiece of deliberate understatement:

> There has been an unfortunate development in the case of Tricycle, the true purport and consequences of which have not yet been determined. It was learnt from Most Secret Sources that Artist, his spymaster, was lured with great secrecy into France and there dispatched to Berlin. The reasons for this action are for the moment obscure, but it is certain that the Tricycle case is passing through a most critical phase and must be handled with the greatest care in view of Overlord.

'Unfortunate', 'rather worrying', 'most critical': these were delicate British euphemisms for what one officer described as 'near-panic'. MI5 had once worried Churchill might go 'off the deep end' if he knew too much about espionage matters. It can only be imagined how far off the deep end he would have plunged had he learned not only that the Double Cross system was in danger of unravelling, but that the invasion itself was in jeopardy.

Popov had already sent the Germans copious deceptive material relating to Fortitude. But could he continue to do so, given that Jebsen might expose him at any moment? If he suddenly ceased to send good information, or altered the thrust of the deception, the Germans would smell a rat. One option was to shut him down, but as Liddell pointed out this 'would undoubtedly put Artist completely in the cart and seriously jeopardise Tricycle's

brother'. By sheer good fortune an opportunity presented itself
to suspend the Tricycle network without further endangering
Jebsen. Earlier in May, a message was intercepted revealing that
German intelligence knew Frano de Bona, Agent Freak, was
suspected by some of his fellow Yugoslavs of spying for Germany.
If de Bona was under suspicion, he would naturally be brought
in for questioning. 'This gives us an opportunity of closing down
Tricycle's transmitter, at any rate temporarily,' wrote Liddell. 'If
we see from the traffic that Artist is once more on a good wicket
we can go on the air again.' On 18 May, de Bona sent a message
to Lisbon saying he was going off the air, which was followed
by a letter from Popov, in secret ink, reporting that 'certain
inquiries were in progress against Freak and for that reason they
had temporarily hidden the wireless set'.

The other double agents would continue building Operation
Fortitude to its climax. Henceforth, Brutus, Garbo, Bronx and
Treasure would only hint that the Pas de Calais was the target,
but not state this as bald fact in case Jebsen revealed the deception.
Once the troops had landed, the spies would point specifically
to Calais as the target of a second, even bigger assault, by the
fictional FUSAG: 'After D-Day we can go absolutely all out.'
At the same time, Most Secret Sources would be dissected daily
for any indication that Jebsen had confessed, either willingly or
under duress. If it became clear he had told all, B1A would shut
down Double Cross, and hope the Germans would not have
time to work out Operation Fortitude. The race was on: to put
as much of the deception in place as possible before D-Day, and
pray that Jebsen did not crack too soon.

The deception – and perhaps the success or failure of the
invasion itself – now depended on the fortitude of Johnny
Jebsen, a strange and dishonest spy with unhealthy habits, who
might, even now, be languishing in a Nazi torture cell.

Masterman was pessimistic: 'Under interrogation it was to
be presumed that much, if not all, of the history of his activities
would come to light, and in that case many of our best cases

were doomed. The whole deception through Double Cross was in danger.' Every hour mattered. The longer Jebsen held out, the less time the Germans would have to unravel the deception.

All the Double Cross team knew was that Jebsen had been bound for Berlin. 'We do not know how quickly the interrogation of Artist will be started,' Wilson remarked miserably. 'I hope the RAF have made the train journey from Biarritz to Berlin a lengthy matter.'

Guest of the Gestapo

The double-crossers needed to get inside Hitler's head, and for their purposes the most direct access to the mind of the Führer was via Lieutenant Colonel Alexis von Roenne, the head of Fremde Heere West, or FHW, the intelligence branch of the High Command of the German army. The FHW gathered information from all branches of German intelligence – aerial reconnaissance, wireless intercepts, POW interrogations, captured documents and spy reports – and tried to make sense of it. Every letter from Bronx, every transmission by Treasure and Brutus, every report from Tricycle, ended up, eventually, with this 'erudite, imaginative, level-headed' intelligence expert, whose monumental task it was to explain what, in military terms, it all amounted to.

Every day von Roenne's intelligence branch, a secret hive inside a concrete bunker at Zossen, south of Berlin, produced a three-page situation report with an update on enemy military activity. The intelligence unit also compiled a more detailed picture of the Order of Battle every fortnight, and an occasional long-range forecast of Allied intentions. These were distributed to the relevant intelligence agencies, the High Command, and commanders in the field: in the case of France, Field Marshal Gerd von Rundstedt, Supreme Commander of the German armies in the West. Von Roenne, an aristocrat with refined manners, pious beliefs and a sinuously clever mind, was aided by the head of the English section, Major Roger Michael, who could not have been more different from his boss. Half-English and half-German, Michael was a bald, back-slapping, heavy-drinking hearty who had played rugby for Germany. He had a 'jolly, easy, happy disposition', but 'a quick understanding of essentials'. He was also credited with insight into the British mentality, having spent much of his youth in Britain. He was Gisela Ashley's opposite number.

Hitler had complete faith in von Roenne. As Anton Staubwasser, Rommel's intelligence chief, put it, 'the opinions held by Hitler and OKW about the invasion were based principally on the information supplied by FHW and did not deviate from that department's ideas in essentials'. If von Roenne and his analysts could be fooled into thinking that another army, far larger than the real D–Day force, was assembling on Britain's coast, then Hitler himself would probably fall for the deception. What Hitler did not know, and never knew, was that Alexis von Roenne and Roger Michael were running their own deception operation.

From 1943 onwards, von Roenne overestimated the strength of Allied forces in Britain consistently, massively and quite deliberately. Once an enemy army unit had been identified and logged by the analysts, it was never removed from what von Roenne called the *Feinbild*, his picture of the enemy. More than that, by the spring of 1944 he was intentionally embellishing the picture. In January 1944, Michael told von Roenne that the troop estimates they sent to the High Command were being deliberately reduced by the SD (which took every opportunity to undermine the experts in military intelligence) before being passed to Hitler. Michael reckoned the numbers were being halved. So he made a suggestion that was logical, daring and extremely dangerous. Why not double the figures? Then something close to the right number would be achieved. That, at least, was how he rationalised the plan to von Roenne, who went along with it, knowing that inflating these vital numbers might cost him his life. Every single sighting of an Allied unit was chalked up as genuine, no matter how feeble the evidence; if only part of a troop was spotted, it was assumed the entire force was present, even when other parts of the unit were spotted elsewhere. Every anomaly was quietly wished away. Gradually at first, and then faster and faster, the numerical gap between the forces that were really poised to invade France and the statistics being relayed to Hitler grew ever wider. At the beginning of 1944, FHW estimated there were fifty-five divisions in Britain, when there were really only thirty-seven. By mid-May, von Roenne calculated that seventy-seven enemy divisions were in place. And by D-Day he had magnified the forty-four divisions in Britain to a remarkable eighty-nine, more than enough men under arms to launch diversionary attacks on Normandy and Norway, and a main assault on the Pas de Calais.

Quite why von Roenne exaggerated the Allied Order of Battle so extravagantly remains a matter of debate and conjecture. He may simply have been covering his back, knowing that if he underestimated enemy strength he would be in serious trouble. Perhaps, like many purveyors of official statistics, he moulded his numbers to fit what his audience wanted to hear. Perhaps his act of rebellion was just another skirmish in the bitter internecine battle within German military intelligence.

What is certain is that von Roenne was bitterly opposed to the Nazi regime, and actively plotting to oust Hitler, whom he detested. He had already played an important part in Operation Mincemeat in 1943 by giving the firm stamp of approval to documents he had every reason to distrust. Some historians believe von Roenne was deliberately sabotaging the German war effort from within. His precise motives may never be known, because Hitler, when he discovered von Roenne's disloyalty, had him murdered. Roger Michael's purpose was possibly more straightforward. After the war, unlike most officers of the German General Staff, Michael was quickly released. He was said to have been seen in Heidelberg, wearing an American army uniform and claiming to be part of the US Counter Intelligence Corps. He then vanished, having apparently defected to the Soviet Union. He was never seen again. The cheery, rugby-playing, half-English Major Michael may have been a spy, for Britain, America or the Soviets, and conceivably all three.

Piece by piece, the double agents dropped the jigsaw into the hands of FHW, where they were slotted together in the ever-expanding projections of von Roenne. Czerniawski reported the 4th US Armoured Division in Bury St Edmunds; one of Garbo's Welsh Aryans saw the 6th Armoured Division in Ipswich, while another spotted the 28th Infantry Division in Kent. Pujol himself reported troops of the 83rd Infantry Division gathering in a Dover car park. Lily sent a wireless message confirming that the First US Army was serving under Montgomery, to reinforce the idea that US troops could serve under British command, and vice versa. Bronx was vaguer, but the very insouciance with which she relayed her information lent it greater force: 'To Newmarket for the races. Expected invasion has produced political unity. Many US troops in East Anglia.' On 18 May, as planned, Czerniawski told his handlers that he had joined FUSAG itself. Henceforth he would be able to relay the fake Order of Battle from within the fake army. The loss of the Tricycle network, wrote Masterman, meant that 'a heavier burden had to be carried by Brutus'. He lifted it with ease.

Pujol told Kühlenthal he had obtained a job in the Ministry of Information, and now had access to propaganda documents intended to 'hide the facts in order to trick us' that would offer new insight into the Allies' real intentions. Wulf Schmidt, Agent Tate, was the longest serving double agent of all, but B1A had doubts about using him, largely because his handlers communicated with Berlin by telephone and there was therefore no way to check his status through Most Secret Sources. Even so, it was decided to move him, in German minds, from a farm in Hertfordshire to another in Kent, where he could observe

Clifton James,
Australian actor,
playing the part of
General Bernard
Montgomery.

Winston Churchill and the real Monty, preparing for battle.

Dummy tanks ready for Operation Fortitude: hundreds of fakes would be deployed across southeast England, to give the impression of a vast army preparing to attack Calais.

The dummy tanks were easy to move, but tended to take off in high winds.

A dummy Hurricane fighter aircraft. It was hoped that no enemy spy would get close enough to spot the fake.

Dummy landing craft at anchor in the River Orwell, part of the fake flotilla ready to transport a bogus army in an invasion that would never take place.

Dusko Popov: a
dashing spy at war.

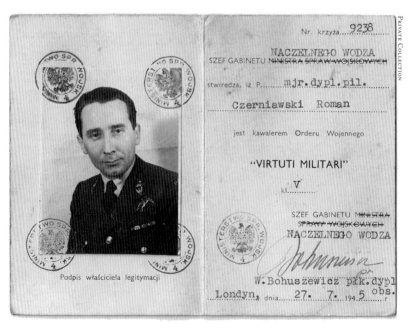

Nr. krzyża.....9238

NACZELNEGO WODZA
SZEF GABINETU ~~MINISTRA SPRAW WOJSKOWYCH~~

stwiredza, iż P.......mjr.dypl.pil.

Czerniawski Roman

jest kawalerem Orderu Wojennego

"VIRTUTI MILITARI"

V
kl...........

SZEF GABINETU ~~MINISTRA~~
~~SPRAW WOJSKOWYCH~~
NACZELNEGO WODZA

W.Bohuszewicz płk.dypl
obs.
Londyn, dnia.....27. 7. 194.5.........r

Podpis właściciela legitymacji

Roman Czerniawski's certificate for the award of the Virtuti Militari, Poland's
highest military decoration.

Emile Kliemann and Lily Sergeyev in the Castelo dos Mouros, Sintra, Portugal, March 1944. The photograph was taken with a Zeiss camera provided by MI5.

Claus von Stauffenberg,
ringleader of the July 1944
plot to assassinate Hitler.

Georg Hansen, anti-Nazi
plotter and head of German
counter-intelligence.

Baron Hiroshi
Oshima, Japanese
Ambassador to
Berlin, presents
his credentials
to Hitler, while
Foreign Minister
Von Ribbentrop
looks on.

Tar Robertson: 'immensely personable and monstrously good looking'.

Ian Wilson, the introverted but dedicated case officer for Dusko Popov and Johnny Jebsen.

Charles de Salis, MI6 officer in Lisbon and Jebsen's point of contact with British intelligence.

General Dwight
Eisenhower
and Winston
Churchill prepare
for the 'Great
Crusade'.

General George
Patton: 'a goddam
natural born ham'.

Erwin Rommel inspects German Channel defences, confident that the Atlantic Wall could not be breached.

German officers on the coast of France, 1944, awaiting the invasion.

Hans Brandes, arms dealer, spy and Jebsen's 'friend'.

Major Wilhelm Kuebart: 'the most intelligent man in the Abwehr'.

Marie von Gronau, secretary at the Lisbon Abwehr station and Jebsen's lover.

Heinz Paul Moldenhauer, the Abwehr officer kidnapped with Jebsen.

Lieutenant Commander Mike Cumberlege, the piratical Royal Navy officer captured while attempting to blow up the Corinth canal.

Johnny Jebsen on the waterfront in Estoril, Lisbon, 1944.

One of the thirty-nine solitary cells in the basement of the Gestapo prison.

8 Prince Albrecht Strasse, Berlin: the Gestapo prison where Jebsen was held.

Invasion troops disembarking on D-Day. 'Just keep the Fifteenth Army out of my hair for two days,' said Eisenhower.

Troops reinforced the beachhead after the Normandy landings.

The vast artificial ports known as 'Mulberry Harbours', built in Britain and then floated across the Channel.

GROUP II/1A
MADRID 1 TO BERLIN
RGS 128, 130/9/6/44
TRC on 12996 kcs.   1050 GMT   9/6/44
AUI on 9288 kcs.   1107 GMT   8/6/44
256

267. To HAROLD. Please inform LUDWIG MARTIN at
your end. Other Stellen not informed. V ALARIC
ARABAL reports on 9th June from GOLFPLATZ via
FELIPE: after personal discussion on 8th June in
LONDON with my agents DONNY DICK and DORICK, whose
reports were passed over today, I am of the opinion,
by reason of the large troop assemblage in Southeast and East ENGLAND which are not taking part in
the present operations, that these operations are
diversionary manoeuvres aiming to draw on themselves
enemy reserves in order subsequently to make a
decisive blow at another place. Having regard to
the air-raids carried out there and the situation,
strategically favourable for this purpose, of the
above mentioned assembly area, this [blow] might well
be made in the PAS DE CALAIS area, especially as, if
there were such an attack, the nearer air-bases would
facilitate a continuous and very strong support by
the air force for such an undertaking. According to

Abwehr message intercepted three days after D-Day, in which Garbo warns the Germans to expect a second 'decisive' invasion in the Pas de Calais.

Fortitude North: In
Norway, German troops
waited for an invasion
that never came.

Fortitude South: a German tank of the Fifteenth Army defending the beaches of Calais.

The heavily fortified coast of the Pas de Calais, where the Germans expected a second, even larger Allied invasion.

Calais: 'It is here that the enemy must and will attack,' said Hitler.

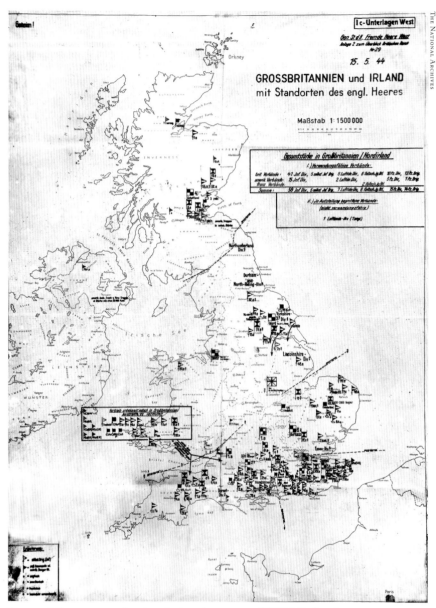

Captured German map showing the invasion troops of FUSAG, the phantom army, clustered in southeast England: 'It was almost identical with Plan Fortitude'.

the deployment of the fictional FUSAG at first hand. 'Have found first-class lodgings with elderly couple in Wye,' he told his handler. 'So far as I can see, ideal for radio purposes.'

Von Roenne was too busy adding weight to his already bloated Order of Battle to wonder why three key agents had suddenly, and almost simultaneously, moved into positions where they had access to the highest-grade information. Perhaps, through his monocle, he turned a blind eye. At the expeditionary force headquarters, Fleetwood-Hesketh and Harmer moved their fake units to where they wanted them to be in German minds; the double agents passed them on, bit by bit, to the Germans; and von Roenne and Michael reassembled the map, and passed it up the military chain to Hitler.

The pins on the board at the intelligence office in Zossen were massing in the right places, but MI5 remained fretfully aware that if Jebsen cracked and Double Cross was revealed, von Roenne's projections, built up from the spies' reports, would show exactly where the Allied armies were *not* assembling. Guy Liddell was certain that once the Gestapo went to work on Jebsen, he would eventually crack 'under duress'.

Ian Wilson scanned the intercepts with dread. If Jebsen's friends and associates were rounded up, if his Abwehr colleagues were interrogated, if Popov's brother was arrested, then that would prove the game was up. The moment Jebsen revealed that the double agents were all part of a grand sham, the evidence would crackle like lightning across Most Secret Sources. Incompetence was a crime under Hitler's rule, and guilt came by association: Kühlenthal, Kliemann, Reile, Bleil and von Karsthoff would all find themselves hauled in to explain how they had been hoodwinked for so long. Everyone Jebsen knew would be considered suspect, and probably arrested: wife, lovers, friends, even Mabel Harbottle. The bloody retribution would start immediately, and be reflected in the intercepts. Here was cold consolation: if Double Cross was rumbled, at least they would know it.

At first, Most Secret Sources were mute, save for some baffled enquiries from German officials in Lisbon who were not privy to Operation Dora, wondering where Jebsen had gone. But within a week of the kidnapping, it became clear that an interrogation must be under way, as a flurry of messages were intercepted relating to Jebsen's financial activities. Berlin asked Madrid to 'report whether 2.7 million Moroccan francs which Johnny is alleged to have remitted to Tangier have been received'. This was followed by an even more cryptic message from Schreiber to Berlin: 'French money Dora can be received to the full amount through Dora friends here. Furthermore we may also count on receiving shortly through Dora friends here the original material about Dora which was asked for by his fat friend.' Dora was a reference to the kidnapping, and 'his fat friend' was probably Hans Brandes; but the only thing to be deduced with any certainty was that Jebsen's finances were being probed, and large sums of money were involved. Berlin was also trying to trace the cash handed to Jebsen for Popov.

After two weeks, Ian Wilson reported that there was still 'no evidence to prove conclusively what effect the return of Artist to Germany has had'. Encouragingly, there was not yet a general round-up of Jebsen's contacts. Freak's control station in Germany was still sending messages on the agreed frequency; if the Germans were trying to get in touch with Popov then they must still trust him, which might indicate that Jebsen had not betrayed the network. Unless, of course, that was just what the Germans wanted the British to think. Wilson allowed himself a glimmer of hope. The references in Most Secret Sources, he wrote, 'are consistent with the theory that Artist was taken to Germany so that his financial dealings could be probed and for fear that at some future date he might come over to the Allies. If he has confessed, one would have expected that some of the Abwehr officials closely connected to Artist and Tricycle would have ceased to carry out their normal functions' – like breathing. Wilson began to wonder if, by some miracle, Jebsen could yet be rescued. Hans Brandes had betrayed him; perhaps he might now be bribed, beguiled, bullied or blackmailed into saving him, or at least providing information on what had become of him. Might now be the moment to revive Kim Philby's idea of recruiting this horrible man to British intelligence?

If Brandes could be persuaded to play with us, he could as well as informing us of the position of Artist, give us a lot of information about what is going on in the inner circles of the Abwehr, and particularly the political struggle which seems to have resulted in the Abwehr coming under the control of Himmler. I do not regard Brandes as being in the least bit reliable. There is plenty of evidence that Brandes is unprincipled [but] if the proposition was put to him that he should re-insure himself with the British he might accept it. If he reported the approach to the Germans we would know that fact from MSS.

John Masterman stamped hard on this idea. Brandes was a snake, and if he told Berlin that British intelligence was sniffing around, this would reinforce suspicion that Jebsen was a British spy and plunge him into even hotter water. 'I do not agree with the proposal to approach Brandes,' he wrote on Wilson's memo, underlining the word 'not' three times. But Wilson was not going to give up on Jebsen. 'I feel a strong personal sense of responsibility in this matter,' he wrote. Wilson liked and trusted Jebsen; he had encouraged him to stick to his mission, and he had lost him. He would make it his own mission to find him.

Popov waited anxiously for news. Frano de Bona, no longer transmitting to Germany, was also at a loose end. They distracted themselves in the usual way. When MI5 found out that women of the Auxiliary Territorial Service were 'being introduced to the Clock House for immoral purposes and that there might be security interest involved', Wilson told them sharply to 'stop drawing attention to themselves in this manner'. Unable to play an active part in the deception, Popov fired off letters to Churchill, offering to intercede in Yugoslavia between the forces of Mihailović and Tito's communists. He was told that while Churchill 'had a paternal interest in his wellbeing', he did not want him meddling in politics. He should stay calm, stay put and stand ready in case there should be news of Jebsen: 'This was not the time for hasty or violent action . . . The only course for the time being was to take no action and await results.'

On 19 May, Bletchley Park deciphered a personal message from Georg Hansen to Aloys Schreiber in Lisbon: 'I wish to convey special appreciation and thanks for carrying out Operation Dora.' Schreiber replied that 'a written report on Dora matters was following by air'.

Then, just two weeks before D-Day, the references to 'Johnny', 'Dora' and all the missing money abruptly ceased. Ian Wilson wondered if the sudden silence was ominous: 'It seems to me not unlikely that Artist may have been shot, or may have committed suicide shortly after his arrest.' Yet he tried to look on the bright side: 'There is still no indication that Artist has made any confession.'

Wilson's flicker of hope would have been swiftly extinguished had he known where Jebsen was at that moment.

Jebsen and Moldenhauer had arrived in Berlin by train, under guard, on 1 May. From there they were driven to the military prison at Wünsdorf, near Zossen, and lodged in separate cells, while Georg Hansen made 'arrangements for their interrogation by legal experts'. The SD, however, had already got wind of Jebsen's abduction, and demanded that Hansen put 'the captive at the disposal of Kaltenbrunner as soon as possible'. A full investigation into another potential defector was exactly what Hansen hoped to avoid. He refused to surrender the prisoners, and instructed Kuebart to tell the SD that 'as Jebsen was a soldier he regarded it as a matter within the exclusive jurisdiction of the Abwehr'.

For several days, Kuebart 'did his best to place difficulties in the way of Jebsen being handed over'. The dispute even reached the desk of Field Marshal Wilhelm Keitel, head of the OKW. Finally a 'brusque ultimatum' arrived from SS Obergruppenführer Heinrich Müller, demanding that Jebsen be handed over to the Gestapo at once. Among the murderous sycophants surrounding Hitler, Müller stood out for his brutality: the head of the secret state police, he was a principal architect of 'the final solution', directed the SS murder squads that followed the German army into the Soviet Union, and personally presented Himmler with evidence of Canaris's links to the anti-Nazi resistance. He loathed anyone with an education – 'One really ought to drive all the intellectuals into a coal mine and then blow it up,' he declared – and he was not a man who took anything but yes for an answer. The demand to surrender Jebsen had already 'produced a great deal of ill-feeling in the Abwehr', according to Kuebart, but there was no point in arguing with 'Gestapo' Müller. Jebsen was taken into police custody by one Sturmbannführer Schmitz, an aide to Schellenberg, who accused Jebsen of 'having betrayed the work of the SS to the Abwehr', and consigned him to a cell in the notorious Gestapo prison on Prinz Albrecht Strasse to await interrogation.

Jebsen had often hinted to his British handlers that he was involved in shady business deals with high officials. Indeed, he had told Marie von Gronau he had 'so much information on the SD they would not dare investigate him'. But his financial chicanery, it seems, went far beyond the forgery scam that had first put him on the wrong side of the Gestapo. Jebsen had been using diplomatic bags to smuggle money from one occupied country to another, and 'engaging in large-scale manipulations of currency and gold' with the connivance of high-ranking officers, who got a cut of the profits but had since 'got into difficulties because it became apparent they had more money to spend than could be justified by their apparent incomes'. In addition, some senior SS and

Gestapo figures had used Jebsen as an unofficial banker: 'Certain sizeable sums of money [have] been given to Jebsen, who deposited the sums in such a way as to render the sums inaccessible.' He was also back in the forgery business: 'Some SS officials had been printing foreign currency and he had exchanged it for gold value. He was now suspected of having made too much profit for himself and the SS wanted to remove him for knowing too much.' To cap it all, he was accused of 'improperly converting SD monies for his own use'. Jebsen was nothing if not bold in his financial corruptions: he had contrived to diddle senior officers in each of the three most brutal elements of the Third Reich – the Gestapo, the SS and the SD – and they were out for his blood.

MI5 was right to believe that Jebsen was being investigated for his financial dealings, but wrong to assume that this was the only, or even the main reason he had been kidnapped. Müller was in no doubt that Jebsen was a British spy. Schellenberg confirmed in a postwar interview that Jebsen had been 'accused of working for Britain'. According to Eduard Waetjen, an Abwehr officer with links to American intelligence, Jebsen had been tipping off members of the anti-Nazi resistance when they were about to be arrested. 'Because of good connections he helped many people who had difficulties with the Nazi organisation,' Waetjen testified. 'By his warning, many people were saved.' Kuebart's postwar testimony also confirms that Jebsen was suspected of conspiring with the British and planning to defect. The extent of that guilt was, as yet, undetermined, but Müller and his thugs intended to find out.

The two officers in charge of Jebsen's case were SS Standartenführer Eugen Steimle, and Obergeheimrat Quitting. They went to work on Jebsen at once.

The Gestapo prison at 8 Prinz Albrecht Strasse, a neo-classical former Museum of Decorative Arts, consisted of thirty-nine basement solitary cells, and one communal cell. Torture was conducted in specially equipped rooms in the upper floors.

The term *Verschärfte Vernehmung*, or 'sharpened interrogation', was coined by Müller himself in 1937 to describe the torture techniques used on 'Communists, Marxists ... saboteurs, terrorists, members of the resistance movement, asocial persons, Polish or Soviet persons who refuse to work'. By 1944, the extraction of confessions had been refined to a vicious art. Müller's Gestapo torturers were masters of the electrode and rubber nightstick, the genital vice, the soldering iron and the ice-cold bath, in which prisoners were thrust to the point of drowning. Captured members of the French resistance were told to try to resist torture for at least twenty-four hours; the Gestapo boasted that in forty-eight hours they could squeeze any man or woman dry.

Gestapo interrogation records were destroyed before the end of the war. The only evidence of what happened to Jebsen comes from a handful of witnesses, postwar interviews and the testimony of other prisoners. Karl Weigand, an Abwehr officer in Madrid, was summoned to Berlin to discuss the interrogation of Jebsen and returned, according to colleagues, 'in a highly nervous condition and mentioned something about the unpleasantness of having one's fingernails torn off'. Hjalmar Schacht, once Hitler's trusted economist who was arrested on suspicion of resistance activities, briefly occupied the cell next to Jebsen. According to Popov, Schacht 'caught a glimpse of Johnny once as he was being brought back from an interrogation. His shirt was drenched with blood. As the guards were about to lock him in his cell, Johnny turned to them, haughty as ever, saying "I trust I shall be provided with a clean shirt".' A former Abwehr colleague who visited Jebsen in prison (itself a brave act) described Jebsen as looking like a 'typical concentration camp victim'. Jebsen was never a physically robust man, with his varicose veins and rattling smoker's cough, but after the attentions of the Gestapo he was barely recognisable: 'His flesh and muscle had melted away, and his head looked enormous, sitting on top of his wasted neck and shoulders.'

Torture usually extracts a confession in the end. But it does not always work quickly, and it doesn't work on everyone, and sometimes it extorts information that is wrong. 'Violence is taboo,' wrote Robin 'Tin-eye' Stephens, who ran Britain's wartime interrogation centre in London. 'Not only does it produce answers to please, but it lowers the standard of information.' A person in terror and pain will often tell their torturers what they imagine they want to hear, just to stop the agony, just for a while.

Johnny Jebsen knew much that Steimle and Quitting wanted to hear – for a start, the details of his various business operations. Merely offering up the names of officers implicated in his financial dealings would have provided Müller with useful ammunition and bought, perhaps, some respite. He could have confessed to everything he had told MI6 about Hitler's secret weapon, the workings of German intelligence and even his suggestion that the wife of P. G. Wodehouse would make a good spy. The Gestapo, the SS and the SD would have been more than interested. He could have revealed that Popov was a double agent, and that every German spy in Britain was either turned or invented, by admitting that he had identified them all to the British, and they were still functioning. He could have told them enough to scupper the looming invasion, and change the course of the war. But by 20 May, with less than three weeks to go until D-Day, he had told them nothing at all.

Bronx Gets Toothache

As D-Day approached, MI5 told Winston Churchill that Jebsen seemed to be holding out – 'there is still no indication that Artist has made any confession, or that the Abwehr have come to realise the true position', wrote Guy Liddell. In further evidence that the deception remained on track, the Germans continued to shower the double agents with praise, encouragement and even medals. When Agent Tate 'transmitted his 1,000th message', the Prime Minister was informed, 'he took the opportunity of referring to this fact and expressing his loyal devotion to the Führer. A cordial reply has been received, and it is hoped that this will be followed up by the further advancement of Tate in the order of the Iron Cross, of which he already holds the first and second class.'

The case officers were now competing for German decorations. Eddie Chapman, Agent Zigzag, had been awarded the Iron Cross; Agent Tate might get as many as three; Jebsen had promised Wilson his War Merit Cross. Hugh Astor believed Brutus deserved a decoration, and began actively lobbying for a Nazi gong. He suggested that Chopin, Brutus's fictional wireless operator, send a message to Oscar Reile recommending that 'Agent Hubert' be awarded a medal, since this would 'remind the Germans Brutus is running great risks and working under great difficulties solely for ideological motives'. Astor drafted a message, in what he hoped was the style of a 'not very intelligent old man':

Colonel, please forgive me for troubling you with a personal matter . . . Hubert would never forgive me if he got to learn about it. He has made great personal and financial sacrifices in the interests of our work. He frequently works until the early hours of the morning preparing lengthy reports. He has mentioned casually to me the daring exploits which he has carried out in order to obtain the information and I am sure that his honour would be more than satisfied if you could recommend him for some decoration.

Wireless intercepts showed that the Germans thought Lily Sergeyev's wireless was 'functioning flawlessly'; her messages were being conveyed, word for word, to the intelligence analysts at Zossen. By comparing her original message with its coded repetition on the German intelligence network, the cryptanalysts at Bletchley Park could break that day's code almost immediately: 'The messages of Treasure and Brutus are being so consistently relayed verbatim on the German w/t [wireless] network that, with the assistance of this "crib", there has been a very considerable saving of time and manpower in deciphering Most Secret Sources.' For the first time, a note of excited pride crept into the report to Churchill. The Double Cross agents, he was told, 'have, at a critical moment, acquired a value which it is scarcely possible to overestimate'.

But just as this upbeat assessment was handed to Churchill, fresh disaster loomed in the shape of a small, dead dog.

On 17 May, Mary Sherer took Lily Sergeyev to see *Gone with the Wind* in the West End. Lily's kidneys ached, and she was running a temperature. She had convinced herself, once again, that she was dying. Mary decided she needed a treat. Both women wept copiously during the film, and emerged red-eyed and in high spirits. 'I always cry in the cinema,' said Mary. They linked arms as they walked home. In her diary, Lily wrote: 'Mary crying at the cinema! Is she human, after all, this Mary with whom I've been working for seven months, trying to discover some signs that she is a living being and not an automaton.'

Perhaps it was this newfound amity, or perhaps her premonition of impending death prompted the revelation, or perhaps, frankly, she didn't give a damn. But the next morning, as they were preparing another wireless message, Lily leaned over with a conspiratorial air and observed that if she should die, Mary should not try to work the transmitter without her.

Mary, suddenly alert, asked her what, exactly, she meant by that remark. Lily, realising she had revealed too much, was defensive, and dug herself in deeper.

'I didn't mean to warn you; I'm not concerned about what happens to your people. I don't owe them anything. I trusted them. You know the result! But I have told you now. You are warned.'

With a flush of horror, Mary understood that this was not a warning but a thinly veiled threat. Lily must have been given a control signal after all – otherwise why should they not run the transmitter without her? Indeed, she might already have alerted Kliemann that she was being run as a double agent. Mary was appalled, and suddenly very worried.

'The landing is very near, and thousands of lives depend on our ability to deceive the Germans . . .'

'Why do you suppose I have told you all this?' asked Lily.

Mary knew the answer. 'You were very fond of Babs.'

She demanded that Lily describe her control signal, and reveal whether she had used it. Lily refused, on both counts. 'You can go through all my transmissions with a mathematical genius, but you won't find it.'

'You realise I must warn Colonel Robertson,' Mary said. She immediately sent a message to the head of B1A that was short, precise, and deeply alarming.

Sergeyev made a statement to the effect that when she visited Lisbon she fixed up a control signal with Kliemann which she had not told us about on her return. She had meant, on her return, to get the W/T working well and then blow the case. She confessed that her motive was revenge for the death of her dog for which she considered we were responsible. On return from Lisbon she had changed her mind about blowing the case. She refused to divulge what the signal was.

Tar Robertson was not merely displeased, he was scorchingly furious. Lily was holding Operation Fortitude to ransom over a dog. She might have alerted the enemy already, but as she refused to divulge the signal there was no way of checking. Kliemann's messages of congratulation might be bluff. And if the Germans had realised Lily was passing over deceptive material, they would compare the thrust of her messages with information from the other agents, spot the similarities, and find out the truth. Robertson faced a dreadful choice: if he shut down Treasure's wireless and she had not warned Kliemann she was controlled, it would immediately arouse German suspicions while depriving Bletchley Park of its useful 'crib' at a time when breaking the codes quickly was vital. But keeping the channel open would be a dangerous gamble, since he had only Lily's word (whatever that was now worth) that she had genuinely changed her mind about wrecking the deception. But however fickle she might be, Treasure was too enmeshed in the deception to be extracted now. Mary wrote: 'In spite of Sergeyev's confession, she should carry on operating her W/T herself. However the nature of her traffic would have to be altered and anything of a deceptive nature would now be out of the question.'

An emergency plan was drawn up. 'We see no particular object in having a showdown with her at this moment,' wrote Liddell; the showdown would come later. Lily would be kept under surveillance. Her past and future transmissions would be closely monitored for any evidence of the control signal. Her telephone would be tapped. A radio technician would stand by, ready to take over and mimic her radio 'fist' at the first sign she had alerted Kliemann. And then, as soon as D-Day was over, Lily would be admonished, fired and quite possibly arrested. She had deceived her case officers, conspired with the enemy, and perhaps tipped off Kliemann, putting countless lives in jeopardy for reasons of personal pique and in retaliation for a dog-killing that may, or may not, have taken place.

The Double Cross team, so confident in its report to Churchill, was plunged back into a state of roiling insecurity. On top of the continuing uncertainty over Jebsen's fate, now came the gnawing fear that Lily was lying, and Kliemann – tardy, inept Kliemann – might be stringing them along. Since Lily was working her own radio, she might yet be able to scupper the operation. 'Treasure is in a position to blow her case to the Germans at any time she wished to do so,' wrote Liddell. 'She is a very temperamental person. Although her statement may not be true, it shows she is unreliable.' The Tricycle network had already been shut down as a means of deception, and now Treasure had been taken out of the equation too. That left Garbo, Brutus and Bronx.

On 27 May 1944, Antonio Manuel de Almeida, director and general manager of the Banco Espirito Santo in Lisbon, received a telegram, in French, from one of the bank's London clients. It read: '*Envoyez vite cinquante livres. J'ai besoin pour mon dentiste*': 'Send £50 quickly, I need it for my dentist'.

Señor Almeida knew that this particular client was always short of money; he knew, too, that any message relating to her doctor or dentist was intended for the Germans: he immediately passed the telegram to the German intelligence station on Rua Buenos Aires. From Lisbon the messáge passed to Hauptmann Schluetter in Cologne, then to Berlin, and from Berlin to Zossen, where Elvira de la Fuente Chaudoir's telegram would be interpreted not as a dental emergency, but as a warning: 'I have definite news that a landing is to be made in the Bay of Biscay in one week.'

On the day she sent the telegram to Lisbon, Elvira wrote a letter in secret ink which would arrive in Lisbon after D-Day, *ex post facto* evidence that her tip-off had been genuine. It was one of Bronx's finest confections.

> After a cocktail party I stayed on at the Four Hundred Club with Captain David Ormsby-Gore. After having a good deal to drink, he told me that I should hear some startling news on the wireless the next day, as there was to be an airborne attack on the U-boat base at Bordeaux, preliminary to the invasion. Yesterday he came to see me, very much upset, and asked me to swear not to repeat anything as he had been drunk and now the attack had been postponed by a month, and if I repeated the conversation I would endanger thousands of lives. I am convinced that he spoke the truth and have, therefore, decided to send you a telegram to warn you of the raid.

David Ormsby-Gore was a figure of profound respectability. Son of a baron, grandson of a marquis, and great-grandson of a prime minister, he was an officer in the Royal Artillery serving in a secret reconnaissance unit with airborne troops and special forces. After the war, he became an MP, Ambassador to the US and a peer. He was a pallbearer at Robert Kennedy's funeral. He supplied John F. Kennedy with Cuban cigars, brought in by diplomatic bag. Elvira had never clapped eyes on him. He was not a heavy drinker, and would never have been so imprudent as to discuss an imminent invasion with someone like Elvira. He was press-ganged into the fiction; he had no choice in the matter. David Ormsby-Gore died in 1985, a pillar of the British establishment, wholly unaware that he had taken part, unwittingly, in tipping off the Germans to an invasion that never was.

★

On the day Elvira sent her telegram to Lisbon, Major Ignacio Molina Pérez, Spanish liaison officer and spy for the Germans, was looking out of a window of Government House, Gibraltar, into the courtyard below, when he saw a large car draw up, out of which hopped an instantly recognisable figure, 'wearing battledress and famous beret'. He was greeted by the Governor, Lieutenant General Sir Ralph 'Rusty' Eastwood. With the window open, Molina could hear every word.

'Hello, Monty, glad to see you,' said Sir Ralph.

'Hello, Rusty, how are you?' said Lieutenant Clifton James, until recently a star turn on the Leicester variety stage.

Molina had been invited to Government House to discuss routine business with the Colonial Secretary, who had stepped into the next room, the better to allow Molina a free view of the courtyard. 'His interest in happening on this significant scene was too great to hide,' reported the Colonial Secretary who, when quizzed by Molina about what Montgomery was doing in Gibraltar 'with well-feigned embarrassment, was forced to confess that the commander-in-chief was on his way to Algiers'.

James was suffering an attack of stage fright, but he 'played his difficult part with expert skill', MI5 recorded. He had breakfast with the Governor, who congratulated him on his performance, and told him: 'You *are* Monty. I've known him for years.' Then, with perfect stage management, 'His Excellency was handing "General Montgomery" into his car', at the very moment Molina emerged from the building.

The spy sped away in his own car, and was observed making 'an urgent trunk call' in the Spanish town of La Linea. 'The material reached Berlin in twenty minutes,' MI5 estimated. Molina even embellished his own role, telling one of his confidants (who happened to be a spy working for the British) that he had shaken hands with Montgomery himself. 'The Governor introduced me to him. He seems *muy simpatico*.' This informant (who rejoiced in the codename 'Pants') reported that Molina was 'very satisfied with himself'. The next day, Bletchley

Park intercepted a message from Madrid to Berlin which read: 'General Montgomery arrived Gibraltar. Discussions held with Governor and French General.' The British had a double agent working in Algiers airport codenamed 'Gaol', a former wireless operator for the Free French. Gaol informed Berlin of Monty's arrival in Algiers, and his reception by General Maitland 'Jumbo' Wilson, the Supreme Allied Commander in the Mediterranean. German reviews of the performance, as revealed in Most Secret Sources, were uniformly positive, and a subsequent report by von Roenne concluded that the presence of Monty in North Africa 'might point towards additional operations in South of France in addition to the main invasion'. Liddell wondered if the masquerade had been performed 'a little too early', but German intelligence seemed satisfied that Monty was still in North Africa on 28 May. And if he was there, then he could hardly be organising a massive assault across the Channel. The plot 'had gone through from start to finish without a hitch, and we knew that the main feature of its story had reached the Germans', MI5 reported.

Clifton James found playing the part of Monty extremely stressful. He was taken to a safe house in Cairo where he remained, with a copious supply of whisky, until the Normandy landings were under way. Like all method actors, he struggled to get out of character: 'He was under terrible pressure and strain,' said the wife of an intelligence officer detailed to look after him as he decompressed following the performance of his life. 'Coming out of that part was very difficult for him.'

On the sunny afternoon of 27 May, Adolf Hitler had tea with one of his favourite guests in the Berghof, his chalet in the Bavarian Alps above Berchtesgaden. General Baron Hiroshi Oshima, Japan's Ambassador to the German Reich, was a regular visitor to Hitler's private retreat, and the Führer's closest foreign confidant. A deep-dyed fascist and fawning Hitler devotee, Oshima had first met Hitler in 1935, when he was Japanese military attaché in Berlin. No one worked harder than the Japanese Ambassador to cement the alliance between Germany and Japan. The American journalist William L. Shirer called him 'more Nazi than the Nazis'. He spoke German fluently, and shared Hitler's views on Jews, the iniquity of the Soviet Union and the need to kill the survivors of U-boat attacks. If Hitler had been able to make friends with a racially inferior being, then he might have counted Oshima as a friend. A professional soldier with formidable powers of recall, after each cosy and informal chat with the Führer, Oshima compiled a detailed update on Hitler's military thinking and planning, which was encrypted and sent by wireless, with German approval, to the Japanese Foreign Office. These reports were read with avid interest in Tokyo; and Washington, and London.

American cryptanalysts had broken the Japanese wireless code in 1940. Using a duplicate of the cipher machine used by Japanese Foreign Office officials, the Allies were able to read the enemy's sensitive diplomatic cables as soon as they were sent. Indeed, the messages were sometimes read by the Allies *before* they were read in Tokyo, since wireless traffic from Germany to Japan was often held up in transmission. This was the Japanese equivalent of Most Secret Sources, codenamed 'Magic', an almost miraculous insight into Japan's secrets. Oshima supplied the most interesting reading of all: some seventy-five of the Ambassador's reports were picked up in 1941, a hundred in 1942, 400 in 1943, and no less than 600 in 1944. His commentaries were like having a bug in Hitler's headquarters, only more efficient, since the Japanese Ambassador was a military expert with a crisp prose style, who boiled down his conversations with Hitler to the essentials – so Allied intelligence analysts did not have to.

Oshima furnished copious information on U-boats, mobile forces, military production, technological developments, the effects of Allied bombing and the state of the German economy. In November 1943, he was taken on a four-day tour of German fortifications on the Channel coast of France. His resulting twenty-page report described the location, strength and weaponry of every German division, the dimensions of anti-tank ditches and the layout of machine-gun emplacements. If the invaders landed there, he predicted, 'lateral shell fire from the neighbouring posts and the appearance of mobile forces would annihilate them'. Allied intelligence could not have produced a better picture of the enemy's defences had they been invited on the tour themselves. As early as December 1943, Oshima reported that his friend, Joachim von Ribbentrop, Hitler's Foreign Minister, expected an invasion in Belgium or across the Dover Straits. In January 1944, he informed Tokyo that Hitler was speculating that the Allies might attack Bordeaux – giving hope to Operation Ironside. General George Marshall, the US Army Chief of Staff, paid tribute to Oshima's contribution to the Allied war effort: 'Our main basis of information regarding Hitler's intentions in Europe was obtained from Baron Oshima's messages from Berlin.' If Baron von Roenne was the best way of planting an idea in Hitler's head, then Baron Oshima was the most reliable way of finding out if it had lodged there.

Hitler was ludicrously proud of his hideously kitsch, self-furnished chalet at Berghof, purchased with the profits from *Mein Kampf*. 'This place is mine,' he told *Homes and Gardens* magazine in 1938. 'I built it with money that I earned.' The Führer welcomed the Japanese Ambassador into an entrance hall 'filled with a curious display of cactus plants in majolica pots'. Together, they strolled down a path to the Tea House in the woods. On the way, Hitler remarked that the Japanese government ought to publicly hang every US pilot captured during air raids on Japan. 'Our attitude cannot be ruled by any humane feelings,' he believed, a view with which Oshima heartily concurred. This was the kind of brutal small-talk they enjoyed. Tea was served by members of the SS acting as waiters. The two allies sat on the wooden terrace, under a large colourful parasol, overlooking the Berchtesgaden valley.

'What is your feeling about the Second Front?' Oshima asked.

'I believe that sooner or later an invasion of Europe will be attempted,' mused the Führer. 'I understand that the enemy has already assembled about eighty divisions in the British Isles. Of that force, a mere eight divisions are composed of first-class fighting men with experience in actual warfare.'

'Does Your Excellency believe that those Anglo-American forces are fully prepared to invade?'

'Yes.'

'I wonder what ideas you have as to how the Second Front will be carried out.'

'Well, judging from relatively clear portents, I think that diversionary actions will take place in a number of places – against Norway, Denmark, the southern part of Western France, and the French Mediterranean. After that – when they have established bridgeheads in Normandy and Brittany, and have sized up their prospects – they will then come forward with an all-out Second Front across the Straits of Dover. We ourselves would like nothing better than to strike one great blow as soon as possible. But that will not be feasible if the enemy does what I anticipate; their men will be dispersed. In that event we intend to finish off the enemy's troops at several bridgeheads. The number of German troops in the west still amounts to about sixty divisions.' Oshima scurried back to Berlin to write up his notebook.

When Oshima's report of his teatime conversation with Hitler duly arrived in Britain on 1 June, relief flooded through Allied intelligence. In almost every respect, Hitler's assessment mirrored what the framers of Operation Fortitude had hoped for. 'It gave the first definite assurance that the Germans greatly overestimated our strength,' wrote Roger Fleetwood-Hesketh. Hitler believed the major assault would come in the Pas de Calais, with precursor attacks in Norway and southwestern France; he believed von Roenne's wildly inflated estimates of Allied troop strength; he had faith in the 'clear portents' being fed to Germany by the double agents; he expected a number of attacks at different points, whereas the Allies were even now preparing, in Hitler's own words, 'one great blow', at Normandy. Some were uneasy that Hitler had, correctly, predicted an attack on Normandy, but he had made clear that he believed this would be nothing more than a diversionary assault, a prelude to the main invasion across the Straits of Dover.

Hitler told Oshima he thought an attack would come 'sooner or later'. With five days until D-Day, the attack would come far sooner than he imagined.

Garbo's Warning

The Allied armies streamed down the country lanes of southern England, like water running through numberless rivulets and channels towards the coast, gathering and spreading into a wide estuary of men, weapons, tanks and ships. 'The south coast was just unimaginable,' recalled Private Fred Perkins of the Royal Berkshire Regiment. 'It was just one vast marshalling yard of men and materiel all the way along.' Sergeant Joe Stephens of the Royal Artillery was waiting on the parade ground at Hawick camp when Montgomery arrived for a last, sinew-stiffening visit. Monty climbed onto the bonnet of his jeep. 'Gather round me, men,' he said. 'We're going to Europe; the Germans know we're going to Europe, but they don't know when and where, and this will be the deciding factor. I wish you good luck.' Then he drove away.

Major Peter Martin led his men past ripening fields towards the coast, wondering at the 'unreal feeling' of marching to war through this gentle bucolic landscape. 'Everything was totally normal and the countryside was gorgeous, and in a few days' time one would be going into an absolute charnel house.'

Within a week, 7,000 warships and landing craft, 11,000 planes and nearly 160,000 men would be hurled at the Atlantic Wall, the largest amphibious invasion ever attempted, and the first and naval phase of Operation Overlord, codenamed Neptune. German defences would be pummelled by air and naval bombardment; one British airborne division would try to secure the eastern flank, while American forces would land to the west by parachute and glider; shortly after dawn, six Allied infantry divisions – three American, two British and one Canadian – would storm onto five selected Normandy beaches.

Eisenhower called it the 'great crusade', but in his pocket he carried a scribbled note, the basis of what he would say if D-Day did not succeed, and his forces 'failed to gain a satisfactory foothold'. In the General's mind, victory was anything but certain. 'The troops, the air and the navy did all that bravery and devotion to duty could do,' he wrote, in dread anticipation. 'If any blame is found attached to the attempt it is mine alone.' Before turning in for the night on 5 June, Churchill, haunted by memories of slaughter on the beaches of Gallipoli in the First World War, told his wife Clementine: 'Do you realise that when you wake up in the morning, 20,000 men may have been killed?'

As a real army along the southern edge of England prepared for battle, another deployment, even larger, but wholly bogus, was under way in two quite unremarkable, pebble-dashed semi-detached houses in the London suburbs. With Treasure and Tricycle *hors de combat*, it fell to Brutus and Garbo to ram home the Fortitude deception in the hours before D-Day. Mr and Mrs Roman Czerniawski had recently moved into 61 Richmond Park Road, Barnes: from here, Agent Brutus 'drew all the loose threads together'. Through his invented wireless operator Chopin, Brutus laid out the Order of Battle for the fake army FUSAG, with its HQ in Wentworth, under the command of George Patton. In three long reports, packed with details supposedly gathered from within the army's operations room at Staines, and tours of Kent and East Anglia, he was able to present the Germans with, as Fleetwood-Hesketh put it, 'the entire chain of command of the shadow army group in southeast England'. Patton's army, he warned, gave 'the impression of being ready to take part in active operations in the near future'.

While Brutus sketched out the contours of the fake army, on the other side of London, at 35 Crespigny Road, Garbo added the shading and colours. From Scotland came reports of major naval exercises in Loch Fyne, soldiers seen wearing Arctic uniforms, and troops assembling in east coast ports, preparing for an assault on Norway. Garbo reported that his sub-agent in Exeter, one of the Welsh Aryans, had been arrested for lacking the correct documentation in a prohibited zone, a convenient explanation for the lack of intelligence from the southwest. Backing up Bronx's warning of an assault on Bordeaux, Garbo's agent in Liverpool spotted American forces 'destined for an attack on the South Atlantic French coast in cooperation with another army which will come direct from America'. Pujol himself described troops assembling in East Sussex. The Germans were so convinced of Garbo's accuracy that on at least one occasion his report was simply tacked, unedited, onto the German situation analysis. But in case the enemy was unable to reconstruct this 'imaginary Order of Battle' without help, Garbo, the 'self-trained military reporter', offered his own conclusions, leading the enemy by the hand to the wrong place: 'I conclude that the Harwich-Ipswich area has become an important operational base for future operations,' he advised, while news from the north 'indicates the possibility of an imminent attack against Norway'. No one asked him for his opinion, he merely proffered it, and the Germans grabbed it.

As the reports poured in from Britain, von Roenne faithfully drew and redrew his map: 'The main enemy concentration is showing itself ever more clearly to be in the south and southeast of the island,' the German analysts noted on 15 May. Then, two weeks later: 'Further transfer of formations to the south and southeast of the British Isles again emphasises that the main point of enemy concentrations is in this area.' By 2 June, the two-army scheme laid out by Brutus was as good as gospel: 'According to a reliable Abwehr message of 2nd June, the forces at present in the south of England are organised into two army groups (twenty-one English and First American).' The German spymasters asked for details about the 21st Army Group under Montgomery, the real army, but entirely failed to sense danger in the way their agents seemed so much keener to report what was happening farther east.

There is often one much-praised player on a team who fails to perform on the big day. Wulf Schmidt, Agent Tate, the veteran slogger who had clocked up more than 1,000 messages, was not playing at anything like the expected level. He fed the enemy a 'sustained diet of high-grade deceptive intelligence', but none of it was being swallowed. The bogus units and their locations identified by Brutus and Garbo reappeared dependably in the German military summaries, but for some reason Tate scored a duck. 'By the date of the invasion, not one of the messages which we had sent through him had found a place in the OKW intelligence summary,' wrote Fleetwood-Hesketh.

Even more worrying than the reluctance to accept Tate's deceptions was the danger that they might believe the fabrications of another informant, which just happened to be correct. Paul Fidrmuc, Agent Ostro, had been inventing reports for the Abwehr since 1940, based on gossip and guesswork. MI5 had long feared that Ostro might hit the truth with his scattergun inventions and, since he was evidently trusted by Berlin, draw the enemy towards the landing site by accident. Sure enough, in early June, Bletchley decoded a message in which Ostro reported that one of his non-existent informants, a colonel on Montgomery's staff, had identified Normandy as the *Schwerpunkt*. 'Ostro, in a long message, though entirely inaccurate, has hit on the target area,' Liddell wrote in his diary for 5 June. With just twenty-four hours to go, there was nothing to do but hope that one lucky, accurate falsehood would not be enough to outweigh the great mass of misleading untruths that had already been dumped on the enemy.

★

Shortly before midnight on the eve of D-Day, in deep blackout, a peculiar little procession entered the house at 35 Crespigny Road in Hendon. Leading the way was Juan Pujol, followed by Tar Robertson, Tommy Harris and Roger Fleetwood-Hesketh. Bringing up the rear was Sergeant Charles Haines, the former bank clerk who operated Garbo's wireless. All wore civilian clothes. Earlier in the evening, they had enjoyed dinner at Harris's home in Mayfair, lubricated with a magnum of Château Ausone 1934 from his excellent cellar. Refreshed, eager and extremely tense, this oddly assorted group was about to commit what was, on the surface, an act of astounding treachery, by tipping off the Germans to the time and place of the D-Day landings.

Harris had argued strenuously that in order to maintain Garbo's standing with the Germans, Pujol must be allowed to send advance warning of the invasion – not so soon as to make any military difference, but sufficiently early that when the Allies duly landed in Normandy, Pujol would be able to say he had told them so. This was not vanity. The follow-up phase of Fortitude – maintaining the threat to the Pas de Calais to prevent the Germans redeploying forces to Normandy – was as important as the first, and sustaining German belief in Garbo's infallibility was crucial. After some hesitation, Eisenhower had agreed that the Double Cross team could alert the Germans no more than three and a half hours before the first troops landed at 6.30 a.m. The delay in transmission from Madrid to Berlin was about three hours, so by the time the German High Command got the message, the invasion should be under way. Pujol had told Kühlenthal he was expecting important news from Scotland, and asked him to ensure that the wireless operator in Spain was waiting to receive a message at 3.00 a.m.

Number 35 Crespigny Road was and is a perfectly nondescript house on a quiet street in an unremarkable corner of London. It looked like every other house in the road and a million other houses across Britain which was, of course, why MI5 chose it.

If any building could claim to be a master of disguise, it was this one. But if the house seemed innocuous, unlikely to play any part whatever in winning the war, then so did Juan Pujol. He was now all but bald, and wore large glasses, which made him seem less like the fighting bantam he had resembled on first arriving in England, and more like a tiny, intensely focused owl. He appeared to be exactly what his neighbours in Crespigny Road thought he was: a shy, polite foreign gentleman who did something dull at the BBC.

Just before 3.00 a.m., with Allied paratroopers already in action in France, the five men gathered around the wireless in the upstairs bedroom, and Haines prepared to send the message. The story, as befitted the occasion, was a dramatic one, although buried, as usual, in Pujol's nomadic circumlocutions. Fred, the Gibraltarian waiter, had linked up with two American deserters from Hiltingbury Camp, and gone AWOL in order to bring Garbo the news that the invasion had started.

> He has told me that three days ago cold rations and vomit bags had been distributed to troops of the 3rd Canadian Division and that the division had now left the camp, its place now taken by Americans. There were rumours that the 3rd Canadian Division had now embarked. The situation of this agent is very compromising because his absence must have been noted due to the many hours which have elapsed since he left the camp. In order to protect the service [i.e. the network] I have taken a decision to put him into hiding.

If the Canadian troops had not returned, that could only mean they had set sail for France; and since Hiltingbury is just eight miles from Southampton, and Southampton is opposite Cherbourg, then the logical target must be Normandy. The Germans would read the clues instantly.

At 2.59 a.m., Tar told Haines: 'All right Sergeant, let them have it!' Haines keyed in the call sign. The only response was a crackle of static. 'I don't get it,' said Haines. 'Normally Fritzy answers right away.' He repeated the call after fifteen minutes. Again there was no reply. The radio operator had either left his post, or fallen asleep. Haines kept calling. Harris observed: 'The trouble is, life in Madrid really only begins at midnight. Kühlenthal's operator is probably at Chiquotes having a *copita* with his friends.' Robertson and Fleetwood-Hesketh eventually made their excuses and went home to bed, like guests peeling off from a dud party. The message was strengthened, adding information that would have breached security a few hours earlier, to make the warning more stark and enhance Garbo's standing further. Finally, at 8 a.m., the Madrid wireless operator either woke up or came into work, and the message was picked up and acknowledged. By which time the Canadian Third Division was no longer gathering up its vomit bags and preparing to embark, but under heavy fire from the German 716th Division on Normandy's Juno beach.

So far from being an anticlimax, Garbo's carefully timed non-warning had achieved its purpose. He had passed over what must be seen, in German eyes, as the most important intelligence tip-off of the war, and they had missed it. Like the Madrid radio operator, the Germans had been caught napping.

On the afternoon of 4 June, Lieutenant Commander George Honour gingerly manoeuvred his midget submarine into its reconnaissance position, a quarter of a mile off the beach codenamed Sword; the most easterly of the landing beaches where, in just thirty-six hours, the British 3rd Infantry Division was due to attack. He raised the periscope and peered towards the shore. 'We saw a lorry-load of Germans arrive. They started playing beach ball and swimming and at the back of my mind I thought, "I hope there are no Olympic swimmers and they don't swim out and find us." There were the Germans having a Sunday afternoon recreation and little did they know what was sitting and waiting for them.'

The invasion of Normandy came as a stunning surprise to the

senior German commanders who were not only unprepared, but positively relaxed. Rommel, in charge of improving the Channel defences, was 500 miles away at home in Ulm, celebrating his wife's birthday. Hans von Salmuth of the Fifteenth Army, defending the Calais area, was on a hunting expedition. The intelligence chief Colonel Georg Hansen was taking the waters at Baden Baden. Divisional commanders in Seventh Army's area had left for a war-gaming exercise in Rennes, designed to simulate an Allied landing. The German navy, having reported that an invasion was 'improbable' owing to the poor weather, cancelled patrols in the Channel, and the troops in their dugouts and bunkers were told to get some rest. Von Roenne's situation report for 6 June did not even mention Britain, and focused almost exclusively on the Mediterranean.

The day before D-Day, Rundstedt, with 1.5 million men of the Wehrmacht under his command, sent out a reassuring situation report: 'That the invasion is actually imminent does not seem to be indicated as yet.' Even his convoluted grammar suggests a man who thought he had time on his hands. The defenders manning the great Atlantic Wall were assured of its impregnability – convinced that the enemy would be repulsed – and thoroughly disinclined to get agitated. When a private in the German Seventh Army Intelligence Corps informed the duty officer that the front line was reporting an attack, he was told 'Don't make a big production of it. Remember Dieppe' – a reference to the failed Allied raid of 1942.

Colonel Oscar Reile, Brutus's wily case officer in Paris, had become an expert in interpreting hidden messages to the French resistance contained in apparently meaningless phrases broadcast in French by the BBC. On 5 June, German intelligence picked up fourteen such messages and concluded that the invasion was imminent. The Seventh Army, in Normandy, ignored the warning; the Fifteenth Army, at Calais, raised its state of alert, but von Salmuth remained catatonically calm: 'I'm too old a bunny to get excited about this,' he said.

Hitler had stayed up late on 5 June, discussing films with Eva Braun and Goebbels. Since the Normandy attack was assumed to be a diversion, it was not thought necessary to wake Hitler and tell him it had started. On D-Day he slept in until 10 o'clock. When finally told the invasion had begun, he was cheerful, convinced the attack would be repelled with ease.

The Double Cross team could not (and did not) claim sole credit for wrong-footing the Germans on 6 June. The bombing campaign in northeast France had steadily increased, until every bomb that landed on Normandy was matched by two dropped on the Pas de Calais; twice as many radar stations were attacked outside the invasion zone as in it. Far behind the lines, paratroopers set off flares and fireworks, and blasted out recordings of small-arms fire to draw German troops away from the landing beaches, while an airborne army of dummy parachutists compounded the confusion. As the real army ploughed through the waves towards Normandy, two more fake convoys were scientifically simulated heading for the Seine and Boulogne, by dropping a blizzard of tin foil from planes, codenamed 'Window', which would show up on German radar as two huge flotillas approaching the French coast.

The Germans might have been taken by surprise, but they were far from defenceless. The coastline bristled with field and coastal batteries, mortars, machine guns and snipers; barbed wire, wooden stakes, mines, anti-tank 'hedgehogs' made from welded steel girders; concrete pyramid-shaped 'dragon's teeth' to slow down and channel tanks into 'killing zones', and more than a million upright stakes in the fields beyond, known as 'Rommel's Asparagus', to impede airborne landings. From bunkers, machine-gun nests, trenches and gun emplacements, the German defenders poured fire onto the attackers. At Omaha beach, the first men to land faced an 'inhuman wall of fire'. More than 2,400 were killed or wounded. At Juno, the Canadians suffered 50 per cent casualties in the first hour. Beyond Sword beach, where German forces had played Sunday beach ball a few hours earlier, the Gestapo began reprisals: at the city prison in Caen, more than seventy members of the French Resistance were marched into the courtyard and shot.

News of the landings was brought back to Britain by Gustav, an RAF homing pigeon released by the Reuters war correspondent Montague Taylor. 'His name might sound suspiciously foreign,' said the bird's trainer, Frederick Jackson of Cosham in Hampshire, 'but he was as English as they come.' Montague reported: 'The invasion army has thought of everything, including carrier pigeons to carry the big news home if all else fails. A wing commander arrived here only a few hours before I embarked on my landing ship and presented me with a basket of four pigeons, complete with food and message-carrying equipment.' At 8.30 a.m., Montague released Gustav. Flying through 30 mph headwinds, dense cloud and sporadic enemy fire, the pigeon completed the journey to his home loft in Thorney Island, near Portsmouth, in just five hours, sixteen minutes – a D-Day record. Sergeant Harry Halsey removed the message strapped to his leg, and relayed it to London: 'We are just 20 miles or so off the beaches. First assault troops landed 0750. Steaming steadily in formation. Lightnings, Typhoons, Fortresses crossing since 0545. No enemy aircraft seen.'

D-Day was the reason for the Double Cross system, the grand finale to which every preceding deception was a foretaste. The men who fought that day have become lasting symbols of courage and skill. But while they battled their way up the bloody dunes, an unseen force fought alongside them, from many miles away, not with guns, bullets and bombs, but with subterfuge and stealth, to whittle away German strength and confidence, to confuse, surprise and mislead, and shield the invaders with lies. By the end of the first day of the invasion, the Allies had suffered at least 10,000 casualties, and 2,500 dead. But 156,000 men had landed in France from the sea and 23,000 from the air, thrusting a spearpoint into occupied France.

What those numbers might have been without the Fortitude deception, and what measure of that deception was attributable to the double agents is, of course, impossible to judge.

But this is certain: if the Double Cross deception had backfired, if Johnny Jebsen had cracked, if Lily Sergeyev had inserted her control signal, if the great defensive net of lies had unravelled and the Germans had been ready and waiting in Normandy, reinforced and alert, then the invasion would have failed, and D-Day would have ended in a massacre.

25

Second Innings

The 6th of June was the longest day. It had been assumed that for the double agents, it might also be the last, once the Germans realised they had fallen victim to an elaborate hoax. They did not, and the Double Cross team now had a second innings to play: to foster the illusion that another, even larger invasion, would soon strike the Pas de Calais – and maintain that sham as long as possible. The spies would surely soon be exposed, but every hour that the fiction held, every hour that the Fifteenth Army awaited the fake invasion, could make a critical difference in blood spilled and territory won. The planners hoped the twin threats to Norway and Calais might be maintained for as much as ten days. Eisenhower would have settled for less. He knew that if even a part of the mighty German army in the north moved its guns to the fragile Normandy bridgehead, the invasion could still fail: 'Just keep the Fifteenth Army out of my hair for the first two days,' he told the deception planners. 'That's all I ask.'

The Double Cross agents plunged back into the shadow battle, following up the D-Day invasion with a volley of apologies from the spies who had failed to give prior warning, and a blast of recrimination from the only one who had.

Brutus's excuse was that he had been busy finding out about the other army poised to cross the Straits of Dover: 'Unfortunately, by remaining without contact with 21 Army Group and through awaiting a state of alert at FUSAG, I was not able to give you details of the first landings.' Tate was also contrite, pointing out that more troops seemed to be arriving in Kent. As soon as the Normandy invasion was publicly announced, Bronx sent a letter in secret ink, knowing it would not arrive for many weeks, insisting that her prediction of an attack on Bordeaux had been sent in good faith. 'Distraught by the news of invasion and convinced of the genuineness of the information given by Captain Ormsby-Gore. Dined with him last night but he did not respond to my teasing on the subject of his indiscretion, merely reminding me that I had promised never to speak of it again. Can only suppose there has been a change of plan or else that this attack, also, will take place.'

Garbo, by contrast, took a verbal flame-thrower to his German handler for failing to pick up the warning message sent before the invasion began:

This makes me question your seriousness and your sense of responsibility. I therefore demand a clarification immediately as to what has occurred. I am very disgusted in this struggle for life or death. I cannot accept excuses or negligence. Were it not for my ideals and my faith I would abandon this work. I write these messages to send this very night though my tiredness and exhaustion, due to the excessive work I have had, has completely broken me.

Kühlenthal squirmed. He blamed the weather. He blamed Garbo's wireless operator, and his own. He blamed anyone but himself, and offered a flood of grovelling flattery.

I wish to stress in the clearest terms that your work over the last few weeks has made it possible for our command to be completely forewarned and prepared. Thus I reiterate to you, as responsible chief of the service, and to all your collaborators, our total recognition of your perfect and cherished work and I beg of you to continue with us in the

supreme and decisive hours of the struggle for the future of
Europe.

Churchill made what he doubtless thought was a helpful
contribution, by lying to the House of Commons and
announcing that the assault on Normandy was 'the first of a
series of landings'. The only problem was that Garbo had already
reported to Madrid, from his notional perch within the Ministry
of Information, that officials had been specifically ordered *not*
to allude to further attacks in order to preserve the element of
surprise, and here was the Prime Minister doing just that, in the
most public way. Pujol scrambled to explain that Churchill's
failure to follow the directive had caused consternation, and an
investigation was under way. In the end, the Prime Minister's
gaffe probably did more good than harm.

So far the double agents had dropped hints of an impending
invasion of the Pas de Calais; now they could 'go all out', and baldly
state that FUSAG was preparing to 'attack across the Channel at
any moment'. If the deception before D-Day was composed of
subtle hints and nudges, the second phase was spoon-fed to the
Germans, with a spade. 'Fortitude requires a threat to the Pas
de Calais to be continued indefinitely,' wrote Astor, 'to contain
the maximum number of troops during the next few critical
days.' Brutus immediately sent a message to Reile depicting the
Normandy invasion as merely a starter before the main course.
'It is clear that the landing was made only by units of the 21st
Army Group,' he radioed on the evening of D-Day. 'FUSAG,
as I reported, was ready for an attack which is capable of being
released at any moment, but it is now evident that it will be
an independent action.' The agents reported American troops
pouring into southeast England, radio traffic was increased, and
sabotage in the Calais area was intensified, all pointing to a second
army in an 'advanced state of preparedness for offensive action'.

Garbo was also categorical. 'I never like to give my opinion
unless I have strong reasons to justify my assurances,' he told

Kühlenthal. (This was hardly true, since he gave his opinions all the time, on everything.) In the longest message to date, sent from Crespigny Road in the early hours of 9 June, he and Harris laid out exactly what the German High Command ought to think.

> After personal consultation on 8th June with my agents . . . I am of the opinion, in view of the strong troop concentrations in S.E. and E England which are not taking part in the present operations, that these operations [in Normandy] are a diversionary manoeuvre designed to draw off enemy reserves in order then to make a decisive attack in another place. It may probably take place in the Pas de Calais area, particularly since in such an attack the proximity of the air bases will facilitate the operation by providing continued strong air support . . . The constant aerial bombardment which the area of the Pas de Calais has suffered and the strategic disposition of these forces give reason to suspect an attack in that region of France which at the same time offers the shortest route for the final objective of their illusions, which is to say Berlin.

Garbo listed every unit, genuine and invented, in the south of England, and calculated the Allies must be 'left with some fifty divisions with which to attempt a second blow'. He concluded with what sounded like an order.

> I trust you will submit urgently all these reports and studies to our High Command since moments may be decisive in these times and before taking a false step, through lack of knowledge of the necessary facts, they should have in their possession all the present information which I transmit with my opinion which is based on the belief that the whole of the present attack is set as a trap for the enemy to make us move all our reserves in a hurried strategical disposition which we would later regret.

If the receivers of this vast scree had paused to reflect, they might have registered how unlikely it was that a wireless would have been able to operate for more than two hours without detection. But they did not. Garbo's report, boiled down to readable form, hurtled up the chain of command, gaining traction as it went: from Madrid it passed to Berlin, and then on to Berchtesgaden. There it was read by Freidrich-Adolf Krummacher, the head of the High Command intelligence branch, who underlined the sentence describing the Normandy landing as 'diversionary', and passed it on to General Alfred Jodl, head of the OKW operations staff, who underlined 'S.E. and E England'. Then it was handed to Hitler.

The Führer's response may be deduced from the resulting intelligence assessment, which embraced Garbo's conclusions with the sort of blind enthusiasm ideologues usually display on being told what they already believe.

The report is credible. The reports received in the last week from the Arabel undertaking have been confirmed almost without exception and are to be described as exceptionally valuable. The main line of investigation in future is to be the enemy group of forces in south-eastern and eastern England.

Elvira lent a hand with a letter in secret ink reporting: 'Only part of Allied force in Normandy operation, bulk remains here at present.' The very artlessness and apparent naivety of her letters made them, in a different way, as powerful as Czerniawski's military reportage and Pujol's detailed analysis. Two weeks after D-Day, she was still hinting at a looming second invasion, worrying about her overdraft, and wondering what to spread on her toast. 'Lord Stanley of Alderney says bad weather hinders ships leaving south coast ports,' she wrote. 'Fruit spoiled by frosts, jam to be sent from America. Still no money.'

As planned, as soon as Overlord was under way, Treasure, once the darling of the Double Cross team, was unceremoniously fired. Lily Sergeyev had taken extraordinary risks on behalf of British intelligence, and played a crucial part, not just in the deception, but in winning Kliemann's trust to the extent that her wireless traffic, relayed verbatim, had 'absolutely saved the bacon of GC and CS [the Government Code and Cipher School at Bletchley] during June'. But she had allowed her feelings to intrude into a business that had little time for such things; she had loved her dog too much, and in withholding information and seeking revenge for its death, she had broken the most fundamental rules of intelligence. And she was still refusing to reveal her control signal.

Three days after D-Day, Tar came to the Hill Street flat to sack her in person, accompanied by Mary Sherer. He was wearing his Glengarry cap and the trousers of the Seaforth Highlanders. He sat in the armchair. Mary took up a position by the window.

'I have some hard things to say. I'll come straight to the point.'

'Go ahead,' she said, with mock insouciance.

Tar did not easily rise to anger, but when he did, he flushed scarlet. Gripping the arms of the chair, Robertson leaned forward: 'Mary has told me that when you were in Lisbon you arranged a security check. We have accordingly decided that you are no longer trustworthy. It is quite impossible for me to place any confidence in someone who behaves in this manner. You will not transmit any more. We'll do that ourselves. We have already started to work without you.'

Lily smiled. Tar turned a deeper shade of red.

'The situation is as follows: you cease to work for us; we shall continue to pay you £5 a week for your maintenance; as soon as possible I shall organise your return to Paris. You must leave this flat. You have a fortnight to clear out.'

Lily still said nothing. Tar was beginning to boil.

'If I have any cause to think that you are in any way acting contrary to the interests of the Allied cause, I will at once take severe action and either put you in prison or hand you over to the French authorities, who would no doubt deal with you pretty severely.'

Lily noticed a darning hole in the left knee of his tartan trousers. Tar was unshaven, and looked tired and a little shabby, she thought.

Tar waited for a response: 'What do you have to say?'

'Your first allegation is correct,' said Lily. 'And you can keep your money.'

'You will take the money whether you like it or not. You can do what you like with it after that. I suppose that you don't want to give us the security check?'

Lily shrugged. 'You said a while ago I couldn't be trusted,' she muttered. 'If I gave you the sign, how would you know it is not exactly the opposite of what you wanted?'

Tar had had enough of the game. 'I didn't say we would believe you.'

Without another word, he left, followed by Mary Sherer. As soon as she heard the front door close, Lily burst into tears, of self-pity, perhaps, but also of regret. This had been, as she later put it, the 'big scene from Act Three'. She had planned to end the drama in her own way, either as a heroine for the Allies or by blowing the whole operation in retaliation for the death of Babs. Instead, she was being sent away with a meagre pay-off, and a dressing down from a man with a red face and a hole in his trousers.

In a last attempt to get Lily to divulge the control signal, Tar sent Gisela Ashley to see her. They had always got on well, and Gisela was a dab hand at extracting information.

'Why did you do it?' she asked.

'I refuse to be beaten by them, by your damned intelligence service.'

Gisela Ashley put her arm around Lily. 'Ducky, that's just pride.'

In a rare moment of self-knowledge, Lily wrote in her diary: 'I have destroyed my own work, or at any rate rendered it useless.'

★

Double Cross was built on sideways thinking. But as Operation Fortitude stretched beyond D-Day, the thinking went from lateral to outlandish. Intoxicated by their success, Hugh Astor and Roman Czerniawski came up with an idea that was ingenious, daring, and quite mad: what if they could entice the Germans into sending an assassination squad to kill General Eisenhower and his senior officers at the fake headquarters of the fake army?

The plan was simple: Brutus would send an urgent radio message to Reile 'inviting the Germans to make an airborne raid on the notional FUSAG Headquarters at Wentworth'. The message would read: 'General Eisenhower and a few other eminent persons are holding a conference, at the end of which Eisenhower is to address all officers. This represents an ideal and unprecedented opportunity for capturing or destroying some of the most eminent personages on which the success of the invasion depends.' Wentworth, Brutus would point out, is 'surrounded by golf courses suitable for airborne landings'. Czerniawski himself would 'flash a torch to indicate the exact landing point, and direct the raiders to the mess where the exalted persons will be holding their post prandial celebrations'. Immediately on landing, the German paratroopers would be ambushed and taken prisoner. 'Arrangements will have to be made to give the raiders a suitable reception and to ensure none of them escape.' Czerniawski would need an excuse for why the assassination plot had failed. 'On the following day Brutus will himself transmit a furious message explaining that although he was vigorously flashing his lantern, the airborne troops landed several fields away, where they were naturally rounded up by the Home Guard.' The plot, Astor argued, would reinforce German belief in the invented army in the southeast: 'If the Germans refuse to play, no harm will have been done, as the threat to the Pas de Calais will have been continued and Brutus will again have shown himself to be a man of courage and resource.' The Germans surely could not resist this 'appetising dish'.

Tar Robertson rejected the idea out of hand, pointing out that there were easier ways to catch German attention than inciting heavily armed Nazi assassins to run around the golf courses of the Home Counties in the middle of the night, looking for American generals to kill.

Some elements of the grand deception were more effective than others. Flight Lieutenant Richard Walker had spent months preparing his pigeon double-cross scheme. He recruited hundreds of second-rate homing pigeons, equipped them with faked German leg rings, and dropped them over occupied Europe, in the expectation that they would destroy the German pigeon service from within.

Walker's grand deception was a damp squab: there is no evidence that it had any effect whatever. The Germans never detected the double-agent pigeons in their midst. Indeed, when the Wehrmacht officer in command of the pigeon service was interrogated after the war, and asked whether his lofts might have been infiltrated by Allied pigeons, he responded that such a thing was impossible since the impostors would have been spotted immediately: no one, he said, could attach a fake leg ring to a pigeon without soldering it. This, of course, was precisely what Walker had managed to do. The plot failed because of its excessive ingenuity. The double-agent pigeons, too feeble to fly home, simply blended in with the local pigeon populations, and like so many ex-combatants, made new lives for themselves, their wartime heroics unsuspected and, until now, unsung.

The charade of Monty's double may also have had only a limited effect on German thinking. The *mise-en-scène* in Gibraltar was certainly reported back to Berlin, but as MI5 candidly admitted, 'what they deduced from it, and how far it had any effect upon their plans, unfortunately we have never been able to find out'. The ruse may have concentrated German attention on a possible landing in the South of France, but the meeting between the fake General Montgomery and the real General Wilson at Algiers does not appear to have been reported to von

Rundstedt, or to have affected German defence of the Channel. The most that can be said of Operation Copperhead is that it compounded German confusion, and provided considerable entertainment for its organisers. It also put paid to Molina Pérez, whose career as a Nazi spy came to an abrupt end. Armed with hard evidence of his espionage activities, the British declared the Spanish officer *persona non grata*, and permanently excluded him from Gibraltar, much to his baffled annoyance.

Elvira's telegram warning of the imminent attack on the Bay of Biscay undoubtedly reached German intelligence, although the invasion was graded, at most, a 'small calibre' operation. Even so, it was considered real enough that when German reconnaissance spotted Allied convoys near Brest it was assumed these must be heading for the Biscay area for a 'diversionary attack'. Allied military planners had anticipated that within a week of D-Day, two Panzer divisions would be sent from southwest France to Normandy. In fact, only one, the 17th SS Panzergrenadier Division, headed north to join the counter-attack, and even that did not move immediately: it finally reached Normandy and engaged in combat on 11 June. The 11th Panzer Division remained in position, defending southwest France from an attack that never came. John Masterman was sure that this was attributable to Elvira: 'When the invasion took place, the Panzer division *was* kept in the Bordeaux area and not pushed north at once towards Cherbourg.' Astor agreed: 'Their movement of a Panzer division to the Bordeaux area may to some extent be attributed to Bronx's telegram', ensuring those troops remained 'impotent near Bordeaux while the battle raged in Normandy'.

Elvira's follow-up letter, suggesting that the Biscay invasion might yet happen, further muddied the waters. As late as July, General Jodl told Admiral Abe, the Japanese naval attaché in Berlin, that a second series of invasions was expected: 'We are prepared for landings in the vicinity of Bordeaux.' Agent Bronx and Operation Ironside may not have fully convinced the Germans that an attack on southwest France was imminent, or even likely, but it undoubtedly added to German confusion. And the credit for that uncertainty goes, in large part, to a frivolous party girl who lied about meeting a drunken officer in a club, and told her spymasters of a conversation that never took place.

The stated, limited aim of Fortitude North had been to 'contain some first quality divisions' in Scandinavia by a threatened assault on Norway. In this, it succeeded, though perhaps less dramatically than hoped. The Germans certainly believed in the fictional Fourth Army under General Thorne, but they seem to have assumed that it was not big enough, or sufficiently backed by air cover, to do more than mount a diversionary attack. In early May, the Germans had described an attack on Norway as a 'strong possibility', and action against Denmark as a 'certainty'. The seventeen German divisions across Scandinavia were put on full alert. The Germans certainly feared an attack, albeit not on a large scale. The deception may not have persuaded Hitler to do anything he was not already disposed to do; but it undoubtedly encouraged him to continue doing something he was already doing, and the Allies needed him to continue doing. At no point did Hitler redeploy the 250,000 troops in Norway to the real zone of destiny, in northern France.

If some subsidiary elements of Operation Fortitude were of debatable effectiveness, the main thrust of the deception was an undisputed, unalloyed, world-changing triumph. As the Battle of Normandy raged, the Germans held fast to the illusion, so carefully planted and now so meticulously sustained, that a great American army under Patton was preparing to pounce and the German forces in the Pas de Calais must remain in place to repel it.

On D-Day itself, von Roenne insisted that 'another landing would come in the Fifteenth Army area and no troops would be withdrawn from there'. Rommel agreed, arguing that the forces in the north should not be weakened. Nonetheless, the Fifteenth Army reserves were mobilised and on 9 June, the mighty 1st

Panzer division, 25,000-strong, was ordered to head south from the Pas de Calais to join the counter-attack against the Allied bridgehead. But then came Garbo's explicit warning that the Normandy invasion was a ruse, specifically designed to draw off troops from Calais before the main assault. The order to the 1st Panzers was countermanded. The division would remain in place for another, crucial week. Several factors were at work in that decision, but Field Marshal Keitel later stated he was '99 per cent certain' that the warning from Garbo 'provided the reason for the change of plan'.

A week after D-Day, only one German division had moved from the Pas de Calais to Normandy. German belief in the phantom army was unshakeable. On 23 June, Oshima reported to Tokyo that 'twenty-three divisions commanded by General Patton are being held in readiness to make new landings. This is one reason why Germany has avoided pouring a great number of men into the Normandy area.' Physical proof of success came when the British forces in Italy captured a map, drawn up by German intelligence on 15 June, which showed exactly where the enemy believed the second Allied army was waiting in southeast England to cross the Channel. 'It was almost identical with Plan Fortitude,' wrote Liddell.

A month after D-Day, no fewer than twenty-two German divisions were still held back in the Fifteenth Army sector. 'Patton's army group,' Jodl reported, 'is being made ready in London and in southern England for the next landing.' The ever-helpful Oshima confirmed that the Germans still expected that 'Patton's forces will land in the neighbourhood of Dieppe'. Hitler had 'reposed an almost mystic confidence in Garbo', MI5 later concluded, and even in late July he 'still could not rid his mind of the belief that a second landing was intended'. But von Roenne was now starting to have doubts, or pretending to. After warning for weeks that another, even larger attack was coming, he began to hedge his bets, suggesting that FUSAG 'has not been given the decisive role' after all. Perhaps, like all experts, he was just adopting new certainties as events unfolded. But perhaps von Roenne had never been fooled by the chimera of Patton's army, which he had done so much to reinforce. By 27 July he was singing a new tune: 'A second major landing on the Channel Coast no longer seems to be so probable in view of the situation in Normandy.' Seven weeks after the first landings, four divisions were finally released from the Fifteenth Army to head south, far too late. As Eisenhower put it, 'every additional soldier who then came into the Normandy area was then caught up in the catastrophe of defeat'. The bridgehead, so vulnerable in the first days and weeks, was firmly established. The war was not won, but the end was in sight.

Looking back, the most clear-sighted German officer knew that the failure to counter-attack in Normandy had cost them the battle, and perhaps the war. Shortly before he was forced to kill himself, Rommel conceded that it had been a 'decisive mistake to leave the German troops in the Pas de Calais'. But so far from realising they had been fooled, the Germans assumed that Allied plans had changed. On 30 August, Garbo reported that the planned attack on the Pas de Calais had been cancelled, and the Germans believed him, as they had believed him from the start. Only later did the truth dawn. 'All this Patton business wasn't a trick, was it?' Professor Percy Schramm, the keeper of the OKW War Diary, asked his interrogators. 'Were all those divisions sent to southeast England simply to hold our forces in the Pas de Calais?' But others clung to the deception long after the war was over. Jodl was interrogated in 1946, still congratulating himself on being fooled:

We knew that you had one Army Group in the south of England and one in the southeast. We know now that the South-Eastern Army Group was not in fact launched against the Channel coast, but its continued presence in the southeast of England constituted a threat which it was not possible for us to ignore. We therefore did not feel justified in authorising any large-scale release of Fifteenth

Army formations for use in Normandy until a considerable time after the invasion had started. Had our picture of your dispositions in the UK been less complete and had we not been aware of the presence of the First US Army Group in the southeast of England we might have dispatched more of the Fifteenth Army to Normandy earlier, which might have had very serious results for yourselves.

On the Allied side, there was no doubt that the Germans had been induced into making what Major General Kenneth Strong, Eisenhower's intelligence chief, called an 'unparalleled blunder'. If the huge German army in the north had been deployed to Normandy at once, instead of waiting for a second invasion, then the Allies would have faced an even bloodier fight, with every possibility of defeat. Those additional forces 'might well have tipped the scales against us', wrote Eisenhower: 'I cannot overemphasise the importance of maintaining as long as humanly possible the Allied threat to the Pas de Calais area, which has already paid enormous dividends and, with care, will continue to do so.' Montgomery concurred: 'The deception measures,' he wrote, 'played a vital part in our successes in Normandy.' The Double Cross report for Churchill was a fully justified hymn of self-congratulation.

It seems from all indications that the Germans have accepted the stories which we have told them about an impending attack on the Pas de Calais. It seems pretty clear that the congratulatory messages, especially to Garbo, to some extent reflect the general military appreciation of the German High Command. It is known for a fact that the Germans intended at one time to move certain Divisions from the Pas de Calais area to Normandy but, in view of the possibility of a threat to the Pas de Calais area these troops were either stopped on their way to Normandy and recalled, or it was decided that they should not be moved at all.

John Masterman knew, as Churchill did not, just how close the deception had come to disaster: 'We were not very far from failure just before the period of our greatest success,' he later wrote. But the team had put on a superb all-round performance in what his colleague in American intelligence, Norman Holmes Pearson, called 'the greatest Test Match of the century'. After the war, British intelligence combed through captured records and established exactly which elements in German military thinking could be traced directly to agents' reports: only eleven of Tate's messages registered with the German analysts; Garbo's network clocked up an impressive eighty-six, but it was Brutus who made the highest score, with no fewer than ninety-one messages reflected in the German intelligence summaries, just nine short of his century.

The post-match analysis was, and remains, universally admiring. Thaddeus Holt, author of the most comprehensive account of wartime deception, has called Operation Fortitude 'the most successful strategic deception of all time'. Even Kim Philby, that master of deceit, called it 'one of the most creative intelligence operations of all time'.

But the most important tribute to the deception's success came from the Germans themselves. On 29 July, nearly two months after D-Day, Kühlenthal sent a wireless message to Garbo:

> With great happiness and satisfaction I am able to advise you today that the Führer has awarded the Iron Cross to you for your extraordinary merits, a decoration which, without exception, is granted only to front-line combatants. For that reason we all send you our most sincere and cordial congratulations.

In reply, Garbo professed to be so overcome with pride and emotion that he was lost for words. Then the words came tumbling out in a great, frothing torrent.

I cannot at this moment, when emotion overcomes me, express in words my gratitude for the decoration conceded by our Führer, to whom humbly and with every respect I express my gratitude for the high distinction which he has bestowed on me, for which I feel myself unworthy as I have never done more than what I have considered to be the fulfilment of my duty. Furthermore, I must state that this prize has been won not only by me but also by the other comrades, who, through their advice and directives, have made possible my work here, and so the congratulations are mutual. My desire is to fight with great ardour to be worthy of this medal which has only been conceded to those heroes, my companions in honour, who fight on the battlefront.

You can almost hear Pujol and Harris sniggering with glee in the background. But Garbo was right to see the award as a collective honour. He had not mounted the deception alone. His 'comrades' included the agents he had invented, the other agents and their own inventions, and behind them the men and women who built the system, the case officers, spymasters and inspired dissemblers who imagined the Double Cross project, and the far-sighted planners who, amazingly, let them get on with it. Those who fought on the battlefront of D–Day never knew that a Polish patriot, a Peruvian gambling-girl, a French dog-lover, a Serbian playboy and a Spanish chicken farmer, together and in deepest secrecy, had lied them to victory.

Agent Garbo accepted the Iron Cross on behalf of them all.

Aftermath

In German eyes, Agent Brutus had proved himself 'the noblest Roman'. In the wake of D-Day, having failed to predict the real invasion and pumped his handlers full of lies about the false one, he could do no wrong. Most Secret Sources showed that his reports were being 'studied not only by the operational sections, but by the most prominent persons in Berlin, including Hitler and Goering'. German intelligence regarded him as an oracle, a sage: 'We shall presently reach a stage where high-level questions on military matters are addressed personally to Brutus,' Astor crowed. In July 1944, a flying bomb landed in Barnes in southwest London, blowing out the windows of 61 Richmond Park Road, and leaving Monique Czerniawski with serious facial injuries. MI5's bean-counters agreed to pay the £50 needed for plastic surgery, noting that Czerniawski had 'worked valiantly for us over a long period of time without receiving any remuneration'.

In his assumed role as a secret international statesman, Czerniawski bombarded the Germans with unsolicited and unhelpful advice. 'Nobody here believes any more in a German victory,' he told them. 'As a Pole, can I suggest that neither is it in our interest nor in yours [that] the Russians be allowed to occupy Central Europe . . . I believe this is a good psychological moment for attempting to reach an agreement with the Anglo-Saxons, and I am inclined to think they may

accept your military propositions.' The reply came back from
Reile: 'Once again I thank you with all my heart for your
excellent work. I have passed on all your political propositions,
especially concerning your country, recommending them to
accept them.' Still hungry for an Iron Cross, Astor longed to
deploy Czerniawski on one final deception, and suggested
parachuting him into France ahead of the retreating German
forces. Once there, he would contact German intelligence
and explain that he had been sent by the British 'to recruit
and organise an intelligence service behind the lines' – and
offer to work for Germany, again. He would then be 'in a
position to receive the Germans' deception plans which
might reveal their real intentions'. No other spy had made so
many journeys back and forth between loyalty and betrayal:
first as an agent in occupied Paris; then a double agent for
the Germans; then a triple agent, working for the Allies once
more; he now offered to go back to France, as a quadruple
agent, while in reality a quintuple agent, still working for
Britain.

By the terms of the deal
with the Germans, Czerni-
awski's family and former
colleagues in the Interallié network would not be
harmed if he played his
part. When Paris was liberated, so were the hostages.
Before leaving, the Germans
left a final token of their
faith. Beside the road
out of Paris, Reile dug a
hole, in which he buried a
new radio transmitter and
50,000 French francs, in
the expectation that if the

Roman Czerniawski (*right*) and Hugo
Bleicher, the German intelligence
officer who captured him, reunited in
Paris in 1972.

indefatigable Agent Hubert arrived with the advancing Allied troops, he would wish to keep in touch – an act which hardly squares with Reile's later claim that he knew Czerniawski was a double agent. 'On Nationale 3 between Paris and Meaux there is a milestone which, according to the inscription upon it, is 2.3 km from Claye and 12.4 km from Meaux. The equipment is concealed 5 metres from this stone in a ditch under a mark on the grass, buried 10 cm deep.' The German retreat was too swift to put the Quintuple Cross plan into operation, and Czerniawski's parting gift from his German spymaster was forgotten. In the 1960s, Route Nationale 3 was widened, covering over the hiding place. Every day, thousands of motorists on the road from Paris to the German border pass over this buried memento to Agent Brutus.

After the war, Roman Czerniawski settled in Britain. Though he thought a 'Polish government set up by Moscow is a degree better than having no Polish government at all', he could never return to his homeland with a communist regime in power. He was secretly appointed OBE for his wartime role. He became a printer, settled in West London, amicably divorced Monique, remarried, divorced, married again. He adored cats, and in old age he liked to sit in his front room, watching James Bond films, with his cats. The cat population in the Czerniawski household eventually reached thirty-two. He never lost his heavy Polish accent, or his whole-souled Polish patriotism, and he intrigued to the end, spending his final years secretly working for the Solidarity movement. He died in 1985, aged seventy-five.

Mathilde Carré, once Czerniawski's partner in the Interallié network, was extradited to France in January 1949 after six years in British prisons, and charged with treason. The trial of 'The Cat' was a sensation. She sat wordless throughout, with a 'withdrawn air of detachment', as thirty-three witnesses came forward to denounce her for sleeping with the enemy. The prosecution summed up with an entry from her own diary from the night she first made love to Hugo Bleicher: 'What I

wanted most was a good meal, a man, and, once more, Mozart's
Requiem'. Mathilde was sentenced to death, later commuted
to hard labour for life. In Rennes prison she suffered cat-filled
'nightmares which turned into hallucinations'.

She was finally released in 1954. A few months later she was
approached by Bleicher, who had served time in prison and
was now running a tobacconist in Württemberg. He asked her
to write a book with him, a 'harmless literary collaboration',
he called it. She had done enough collaborating with Bleicher,
and wrote her own book, *I Was The Cat*, insisting that her
crimes had been 'committed to achieve a noble, patriotic
ideal'. Few believed her. She died in 1970, a recluse. Mathilde
Carré was either treacherous, or just desperately unlucky. Like
Czerniawski, she claimed she had only worked for the Germans
in order to betray them. As her lawyer argued, 'at certain
moments in the life of a spy, the double-cross is all part of the
game'. Czerniawski felt a residual sympathy for his fellow spy,
forced by war to make impossible choices in circumstances
not of her making. Years later, he was still troubled by her fate.
'I don't know how I would have behaved,' he wrote. 'Do
you?'

A month after D-Day, Lily Sergeyev divulged her last secret.
Mary Sherer had turned up with a cake, and invited Lily to
come for a walk. She was still fishing for the control sign, and
as they walked down Piccadilly she asked Lily, for the last time,
to reveal the arrangement she had made with Kliemann. She
asked her not as an MI5 case officer, but as a friend. It was
the nearest these two diametrically different women – one
melodramatically French and the other so stolidly English –
had come to intimacy.

Lily suddenly turned to her former case officer: 'OK, you
win.'

On a piece of paper, she sketched out the system of dashes
agreed with Kliemann to indicate when she was operating her
wireless under British control.

'Is that all?'

Lily nodded.

Mary raced back to the office, pulled out the file for Agent Treasure, and extracted the wireless traffic, every message sent by Lily since her return from Lisbon. Sometimes Lily had put a dash in the original, sometimes in the repeated message, and sometimes in neither. But never in both. There was no double-dash. Lily had never gone through with her threat. MI5 had been sent into a completely needless tailspin by the fear that their D-Day plan had been scuppered by a hysterical woman in mourning for her dog. But by putting her British handlers through the mill, Lily felt she had evened up the score. 'I will be able to close my notebooks and forget,' she wrote in her diary. 'One forgets quickly. Maybe it's for the best.' Babs was avenged.

When peace came, Lily was soon reunited with her parents in Paris. 'My joy has no end,' she wrote. She then took a job with the US occupation forces in Germany, helping to administer vaccinations under the command of Major Bart Collings, a bluff former parachutist from the Midwest, who was most attentive to her. 'I've lost my solitary state,' she wrote. 'I'm no longer alone.' Her health improved and, for the first time in her life, she was completely happy. But Lily had not quite finished tormenting MI5.

In March 1946, Billy Luke warned Tar Robertson that Lily was planning to write a book about her wartime experiences: 'You may find your name appearing in a first-class spy thriller.'

Tar was aghast. 'I don't honestly think there is anything we can do with this wretched woman,' he told Gisela Ashley. 'She will always be a source of trouble to us, no matter what restrictions we put on her, short of imprisonment for life. I don't know if there is anything you can say which might appeal to her better nature, if she has one.'

He need not have worried. The book would not appear for another twenty years. Lily was simply doing what she had done before: driving the strait-laced British into a lather with a threat she would not carry out.

In 1947, Bart Collings and Lily Sergeyev married, and moved to Michigan. Theirs was a happy marriage, though childless, and tragically brief. Lily's illness returned, this time with a vengeance. She died of kidney failure in 1950. Determined, petulant and spirited, she had played a double-edged role in the Double Cross story; a mainstay of the deception, she had also planned to destroy it. The good folk of St Mary's Avenue, Detroit, had no inkling that Mrs Collings, the excitable Frenchwoman with many dogs who lived at number 17542, was really Agent Treasure, a spy of the highest value, whose life, in her own words, had been one of 'unbelievable reality'.

Juan Pujol maintained the façade, and the Germans loved him to the end: 'We have in your personality, your character, your valour, all those virtues that become a gentleman.' As the Third Reich disintegrated in a welter of blood and fury, Garbo exhorted his handlers to keep the Nazi faith. 'The noble struggle will be revived,' he told Kühlenthal. 'I only regret not being at your side.' The last act of the drama was the dismantling of a network that had never existed. Even the Welsh fascists were becoming disillusioned, Pujol reported: 'They cannot hope for anything from us.' Garbo's final wireless message was a wordy eulogy to the martyred Hitler: 'His deeds and the story of his sacrifice to save the world from the danger of anarchy which threatens us will last forever in the hearts of all men of goodwill,' he waffled. 'I am certain that the day will arrive in the not too distant future when the noble struggle will be revived.' On 8 May 1945, the Catalan watched the crowds celebrating in central London, and allowed himself a flush of private pride.

After the war, MI5 wondered whether to continue his espionage career, by 'selling' him to the Soviets; if recruited by Moscow, he might be able to deceive the KGB as he had once foxed the Abwehr. But Garbo knew when to leave the stage. He had extracted an estimated $350,000 from the Germans, and

Juan Pujol, MBE, outside Buckingham Palace, 1985

an Iron Cross. The British gave him £15,000, and an MBE. He divorced Aracelli, and settled in Venezuela. A lifelong lover of language and literature, he became a Spanish teacher for Shell Oil and opened a bookshop. At his urging, Tommy Harris spread a rumour that Pujol had died of malaria in Angola. Garbo slipped quietly and completely out of the limelight, settling in Zulia, on the shores of Lake Maracaibo. 'No one knew about my past. Nobody knew what I had done.' In 1984, he briefly emerged from the shadows, when the writer Nigel West found him and persuaded him to return to London for a formal recognition of his wartime achievements at Buckingham Palace. He then disappeared back to Venezuela. He died in 1988, and is buried in Choroní, by the sea. 'My main pride and satisfaction,' he wrote, 'has been the knowledge that I contributed to the reduction of casualties among the tens of thousands of servicemen fighting to hold the Normandy beachheads. Many, many more would have perished had our plan failed.' Pujol was a warrior who fought to save lives, not to take them, using words as his only weapons.

Elvira de la Fuente Chaudoir, the sexually venturesome, boredom-prone gambler with the elegant fingernails, had proved her worth: as the Third Reich collapsed, she was deployed to find out which elements in the German hierarchy might sue for peace. 'Bronx is the most suitable of all B1A cases for a political role,' wrote Astor. 'They will take the initiative in putting out definite peace feelers through Bronx.' Elvira wrote a letter on 15 August 1944, offering her continued services to Germany, at a price.

> It is quite evident that you have lost the war [and] I am extremely worried that the advancing Allied armies may come into possession of my dossier which would provide evidence of my espionage activities. Will you please give me an assurance that all incriminating evidence will be destroyed? I am prepared to go on working, even after the war if you wish, provided that you continue to pay me . . .

The response was as keen as ever: 'Good work. Write quickly and often.'

Elvira was instructed to go to Madrid, make contact with German intelligence, and 'learn as much as possible about German ideas on peace terms but not in any way attempt to act as intermediary between the two powers'. The idea that Elvira could conceivably have acted as an international go-between would once have been regarded as ludicrous: the good-time girl had come a long way.

Elvira flew to Madrid on 19 December 1944. 'I believe that she will make a good job of it,' Astor wrote. 'She is likely to be closely questioned about her telegram threatening Bordeaux. Bronx has never met Ormsby-Gore but I have attempted to give her a description of him and believe that she is now able to give a colourful account of the incident.' Before leaving she told Astor that 'if any mishap should befall her I should notify her friend Miss Monica Sheriffe'. With that, she set off, 'in cheerful heart'. But by now the German intelligence organisation in Madrid, once a byword for ruthless efficiency, had all but disintegrated. Elvira could not find a single German spy.

Back in London, she dispatched a furious letter of complaint to the Germans: 'Absolutely livid about the uselessness of the journey which was expensive and disagreeable. You let me down. I only made the journey because I was expecting a handsome bonus.' She received an abject apology, and a request to send word if she learned of another Allied invasion in Scandinavia or northern Germany. The suggested code was almost identical to the one she had used before D-Day. This time, the demand for £50 for her dentist would indicate Denmark, whereas a request for £100 would mean 'parachuting to the west of Berlin and landing in the German Bay'.

Here was fresh evidence that the earlier ruse had worked. 'It is difficult to believe that the Germans would have used this same code again,' Masterman observed, 'if they had been dissatisfied with its use by Bronx in May 1944.'

The Germans 'eagerly await her news and will probably believe any information she puts over', said Astor, and as the end drew near, she passed on news intended 'to lower the German will

Elvira Chaudoir, 1995

to resist', and encourage capitulation. 'Guerrillas will be treated without mercy,' she reported, citing her friends in the government. Agent Bronx was helping to shape post-war Germany. The debt-driven spy recruited as a gamble and picked up in a French casino had paid huge dividends. MI5 was delighted: 'Her long-term possibilities should not be overlooked.'

There would be no long-term career. The declaration of peace brought a simultaneous declaration from Elvira that she was retiring from espionage. She received a parting gift of £197. 'Words of gratitude and appreciation were freely expressed on both sides.' She moved to a small village in the South of France, having inherited the remains of her father's guano fortune. For the next half a century, she ran a gift shop in Beaulieu-sur-Mer on the Côte d'Azur. She avoided casinos, but ran short of money nonetheless. In 1995, Hugh Astor informed Stella Rimington, then Director General of MI5, that the former Agent Bronx was broke. In December 1995, Elvira received a cheque for £5,000, as 'a way of making the point that her wartime service is still remembered and appreciated'. Elvira died the following month at the age of eighty-five. To some, her later life may have seemed dull, but Elvira was never bored again. Of her role in the war, she remarked: 'I recall the adventure as the most wonderful and intense period of my life.'

With the coming of peace, Dusko Popov, the playboy spy, got married, became British, and was awarded a medal, marks of respectability that did nothing whatever to change his habits. 'I am getting fed up with my married friends criticising my immoral life,' he told Billy Luke, his first case officer, adding that his fiancée was a 'young and pretty French girl (just your type)'. He married Janine on 6 March 1946, in Megèves, France. Popov's bride was just eighteen, but 'apparently entering into this matrimonial adventure with her eyes open', MI5 noted sardonically. His application for citizenship was swiftly approved: 'I will try to do my best to be worthy of my new country,' he told Tar Robertson. 'I am still at your disposal whenever you think I might be useful.' A year later, they met at the bar of the Ritz, where Tar handed Popov a leather box containing an OBE, in recognition of his role 'in deceiving the enemy prior to the Normandy invasion'. Tar apologised for the unorthodox presentation ceremony, but the setting could hardly have been more appropriate: an espionage relationship that had started at the Savoy was brought to a close at the Ritz.

The British secret services were still trying to disentangle Popov's finances long after the war ended. 'We are making arrangements as regards the receipts for his furniture,' wrote Kim Philby in 1948, with infinite weariness. Popov's businesses prospered, though never conventionally: one week Tarlair Ltd was trading cholera serum to the Egyptian government, the next Popov was importing Peugeot cars, selling rubber hosepipes to the French and setting up a German textile industry. 'His activities have freewheeled far outside any MI5 commitment,' observed Ian Wilson, who started acting as Popov's solicitor as soon as he ceased to be his case officer. Popov purchased a castle overlooking

PRIVATE COLLECTION

Dusko Popov, 1974

Nice. His marriage did not last. In 1961, he met a blonde eighteen-year-old Swedish student named Jill Jonsson, and married her the following year. They moved into the former summer palace of the Bishop of Grasse. His finances remained opaque, his tastes extravagant, and his mysterious glamour undimmed.

Only in 1974, when the truth about Britain's wartime deceptions began to emerge, did Popov reveal that he had been Agent Tricycle. His book *Spy/Counterspy* was vigorously written, entertaining, and partly invented. James Bond was all the rage, and the book contained scenes straight from the 007 playbook – gorgeous women appearing naked in his hotel bedroom, punch-ups with evil Nazis, the staking of thousands of dollars on the turn of a card. Popov was a conscientious spy who told his British case officers everything; none of these episodes appears in the MI5 files. Popov's true story reads like fiction, but like most spies, he could not resist making it up. In the 1970s Popov and his brother Ivo, the former Agent Dreadnought, opened a rejuvenation clinic in the Bahamas, an appropriate last venture for a man who continued to live life like a twenty-five-year-old. He died in 1981, at the age of sixty-nine.

Most of the B1A team drifted back into civilian life. In 1948, Tar Robertson retired to Worcestershire to look after sheep, farming his flock as gently and diligently as he had tended the Double Cross agents. John Masterman, soon 'Sir John, OBE', became Provost of Worcester College, Oxford, then Vice-Chancellor of that university. He played cricket, wrote detective novels, sat on various worthy boards, and scandalised some of his former colleagues in 1971 by publishing his account of the Double Cross system in defiance of the Official Secrets Act. Hugh Astor became Middle East Correspondent of *The Times*, and covered the birth of an independent Israel, before joining the newspaper's board in 1956. Billy Luke resumed his business career, and in 1958 became Master of the Worshipful Company of Makers of Playing Cards of the City of London. Christopher Harmer returned to practising law. In memory of his favourite double agent, the Harmers would occasionally go to the Hyde Park Hotel bar and drink a cocktail made from rum, orange juice and vermouth, called a Bronx. Mary Sherer met Phyllis McKenzie, who had worked for British intelligence in New York during the war, and the two women became inseparable. They lived together for the rest of their lives, 'perfect foils for each other'. Within MI5 they were assumed to be lesbians or, rather, Lesbians. Together they moved to Rome, and opened the Lion Bookshop on Via del Babuino near the Spanish Steps. 'Mary was a very fast runner and would think nothing of pursuing the rather numerous petty thieves that abounded in Rome during and after the war. She loved a challenge.' This formidable pair of English ladies, known as 'the Lionesses', spent their days surrounded by books and a large posse of dogs: Pekinese, French bulldogs and pugs, 'all of which Mary doted on'.

Flight Lieutenant Walker spent the rest of his days happily breeding pigeons. Gustav, the pigeon who brought back the first news of D–Day, was awarded the Dickin Medal, the animal equivalent of the Victoria Cross, to 'signalise its performance on D–Day', but died soon after the war when his breeder trod on him while mucking out his loft.

Tommy Harris settled in Spain after the war, where he painted, and gave memorable parties at which he told outrageous spy stories which few believed. He was killed in 1964 at the age of fifty-four after his car spun off a road in Majorca and crashed into a tree. Some saw the accident as sinister.

Guy Liddell remained in MI5, a continued fount of good humour and good sense. 'There is no doubt that the Russians are far better in the matter of espionage than any other country in the world,' he wrote prophetically in 1945. 'They will be a great source of trouble to us when the war is over.' When the Cambridge spies were finally exposed, Liddell would be caught up in the scandal, and even, unfairly, suspected of being a double agent himself.

Anthony Blunt left MI5 as soon as the war ended, and resumed his career as an academic. He was knighted, courted, feted and went on to become Professor of the History of Art at the University of London, Director of the Courtauld Institute of Art, and Surveyor of the Queen's Pictures. When he was finally outed as a spy in 1979 and publicly disgraced, he became a semi-recluse, taking refuge in 'whisky and concentrated work'. In a posthumously published memoir, Blunt wrote that spying for the Soviets had been 'the biggest mistake of my life'. Yet soon after his exposure as a double agent, he bumped into Tar Robertson, and told the former boss of B1A: 'It has given me great pleasure to have been able to pass the names of every MI5 officer to the Russians.'

Other players in the Double Cross team faded into obscurity. Wulf Schmidt, Agent Tate, became Harry Williamson, a British citizen, a photographer on the *Watford Observer*, a breeder of tropical fish and a 'respected judge at cage bird exhibitions around the country'. Paul Fidrmuc, Agent Ostro, invented spy reports for the Germans until the end of the war, and then vanished. He achieved immortality eleven years later when Graham Greene, who had seen reports on both Garbo and Ostro as a young MI6 officer, combined them as the inspiration for Wormold in *Our Man in Havana*, the spymaster with the imaginary network. Clifton James published a book in 1954 entitled *I Was Monty's Double*: he acted the part of himself in the film adaptation, and of Monty.

Emile Kliemann, Lily's case officer, was arrested by American troops in Louveciennes on 20 August 1944. He might easily have escaped with the rest of the German intelligence officers, but he was running late. The preceding weeks had been most unsettling for Kliemann: suspected of involvement in the July Plot (wrongly, he was far too idle for conspiracy), his flat had been searched by the Gestapo and he had then come under machine-gun fire from the Free French forces as he tried to flee the city. He surrendered with alacrity, and was imprisoned in Fresnes, where Czerniawski had once been held. Yvonne Delidaise and her brother Richard were arrested the same day.

Kliemann's American interrogators found him 'somewhat shifty; responds well to flattery; talking as much to save his own skin and that of his fiancée as anything else'. Quizzed about his intelligence work, Kliemann grew crafty, explaining that he had run a top-level woman agent in Britain codenamed 'Tramp', and was 'very proud and gratified at the results achieved'. Kliemann then played what he thought was his trump card, and suggested that Treasure should be run, with his help, as a double agent, entirely unaware that she had been one from the start. 'He has no idea,' wrote Liddell, 'that he himself is the sucker.'

Kliemann was released in May 1945. He returned to Austria, and his wife, taking with him memories of Yvonne, and a pigskin wallet from Dunhill's of London, inscribed to 'Octave . . . a souvenir from London'. In the 1960s, an over-excited newspaper article on German spies described Kliemann as having a 'sharp and ruthless brain'. The clipping was inserted into his MI5 file, with an eloquent, one-word comment alongside that description: 'Kliemann?!'

More than 5,000 people were arrested in the orgy of violence and score-settling that followed the July plot of 1944. A few days before the attempt to assassinate Hitler, Georg Hansen told his deputy, Wilhelm Kuebart, to stand by to 'arrest various Nazis on the day of the attempt'. The day after the bomb planted by Claus von Stauffenberg failed to kill the Führer, they were both arrested. Heinrich Müller, the Gestapo chief, orchestrated the bloody reprisals against anyone considered defeatist, disloyal or ideologically suspect. Hansen and Kuebart were soon joined in Lehrterstrasse prison by Alexis von Roenne, the anti-Nazi intelligence expert. Kuebart was interrogated as to why he had 'made difficulties' over surrendering Johnny Jebsen. His answers were dismissed as a 'tissue of lies'. Brought before the Volksgerichtshof, the People's Court, the prisoners were accused of conspiring with a 'small clique of cowardly officers to murder the Führer, to overthrow the National Socialist regime and conclude an unworthy peace pact with the enemy'.

Hansen was executed by hanging on 8 September 1944 at Plötzensee jail, Berlin. Von Roenne was executed next, without ever explaining whether his falsification of the Allied Order of Battle had been a deliberate act of sabotage. Canaris, the former Abwehr chief, was kept alive by Himmler as a possible pawn for use in negotiating with the British; but finally he, too, was killed in Flossenbürg concentration camp in April 1945, along with his deputy Hans Oster, two weeks before the camp was liberated. Kuebart, surprisingly, survived. He had already written farewell letters, after his lawyer said 'he considered the case already lost from the intrinsic gravity of the charge', when he learned he had been acquitted for lack of evidence. He was dishonourably discharged from the German army, and spent the remainder of the war working on a farm.

'Gestapo' Müller was last seen in the Führerbunker the day before Hitler's suicide. 'Defend Berlin to the last man, the last bullet,' he ordered, and then disobeyed himself by vanishing. His fate remains a mystery. Documents discovered in 2001 appeared to indicate that he was still in American custody at the end of 1945. Over the years, Müller was variously 'sighted' in East Germany, Czechoslovakia, Switzerland, Brazil, Argentina, Paraguay, Cairo, Damascus, Moscow, Washington DC and New Hampshire.

Aloys Schreiber, Jebsen's kidnapper, went back to teaching the law. Ludovico von Karsthoff (or Kremer von Auenrode, to restore his real name), the pleasure-loving Lisbon Abwehr chief, fell into the hands of the Soviets, and is believed to have been executed. Oscar Reile returned to Germany and wrote no fewer than three academic works on the theory and practice of intelligence, in one of which he claimed, not quite credibly, that he had always suspected that Roman Czerniawski was a double agent. The spy-catcher Hugo Bleicher wrote a substantially misleading autobiography, *Colonel Henri's Story*, and died in 1982. Karl-Erich Kühlenthal became a wealthy and respected clothing retailer in Koblenz. He died in 1975, unaware of how thoroughly he had been duped.

Hans Brandes, the betrayer of Johnny Jebsen, was arrested

in Portugal, and held in a civilian internment camp in the American–occupied zone in Germany. He convinced his captors that he was 'a poor, half-Jewish businessman and as a result was cleared, used as a trustee and eventually released'. MI5 was enraged to find Brandes had slipped through the net, describing his interrogation as 'pure whitewash' and his release as a 'grave miscarriage of justice'. Tar Robertson launched a manhunt: 'Brandes was mixed up with the kidnapping of Johnny. It would be a good idea to lay hands on him.' But as time passed, the memory of his perfidy faded. By 1954, he was back in the family firm, as managing director of Fritz Werner Machine Tools. On 15 April 1971, Hans Brandes was found in his car on a dirt road in Schäftlarn, near Munich, dead from poisoning.

Johnny Jebsen was dragged into the Oranienberg sector of Sachsenhausen concentration camp in July 1944, a month after D-Day. Skeletally thin, he could hardly walk and 'his hair had fallen out in patches'. The camp, thirty miles north of Berlin, was a place of unimaginable horror. More than 30,000 political prisoners, homosexuals, gypsies and Jews died there during the course of the war from exhaustion, disease, malnutrition, execution, or under brutal medical experimentation.

Petra Vermehren, the journalist arrested after her son defected in Istanbul, was interned at Sachsenhausen and learned of Jebsen's arrival through the camp barber. She found out which cell he was in, and threw stones at the window 'until she attracted his attention'. Jebsen was overjoyed to see his old friend. In a whisper, 'he told her that the Gestapo had abducted him because he had divulged information to the British'. He had been arrested on a charge of high treason, he said, but because he had refused to talk, he was now under investigation for *Devisen Verbrechen*, the foreign currency crime of exchanging forged British £5 notes. Jebsen did not know it, but in Sachsenhausen, Himmler had employed a team of 140 imprisoned Jewish photographers, lithographers and photoengravers to churn out forged British and American currency. His 'crime' had been started in this prison camp, by the very people accusing him.

For the next two months, Jebsen lay on his bunk, his ribs too badly broken to stand. Completely cut off from the outside world, he was unaware that in Frankfurt, his wife Lore was expecting his child. Slowly, despite the starvation rations and freezing cold, his strength started to return, and with it, hope. Jebsen began to imagine ways to escape. A number of British prisoners were held at Sachsenhausen, including Lieutenant Commander Mike Cumberlege, a piratical Royal Navy officer with a gold earring, and Lieutenant Colonel John Churchill, widely known as 'Mad Jack', a commando who fought armed with a claymore, longbow and bagpipes. Cumberlege had been captured in 1943 while attempting to blow up the Corinth canal. Churchill had led an ill-fated commando attack on the German-held island of Brač in Yugoslavia in 1944: surrounded with six of his men, he played *Will Ye No Come Back Again* on the bagpipes until a mortar shell landed, killing everyone but him, and he was captured. These were men, as the writer Saki put it, 'who wolves have sniffed at'. Jebsen, a man who would have run a mile from a wolf, struck up an unlikely friendship with them both.

In September 1944, Jack Churchill crawled through an abandoned drain under the camp wire, and set off on foot for the Baltic coast. He was recaptured, transferred to a camp in the Tyrol under SS guard, and then set free by a German army captain after the SS moved out. He walked ninety-three miles into Italy, and linked up with an American armoured unit. When Churchill finally got back to Britain, he produced a letter written by Mike Cumberlege to his wife. The letter contained a message, in code, which read: 'JOHNNY JEBSEN HUN HELD HIGH TREASON CAN D REPEAT D POPOFF HELP URGENT FO KNOW OF JJ ALL CHARGES AGAINST

US ARE BASELESS.' The Foreign Office had never heard of
Johnny Jebsen, and to make matters worse, as the message was
passed around, his name was garbled. 'I can make little of this.
We appear to have no record of any Johnny Jebsen or Debsen,'
wrote one official.

In February 1945, a Gestapo escort arrived from Berlin
with orders to collect Jebsen and Heinz Moldenhauer. Petra
Vermehren saw the two men leave under guard. On 12
April, Moldenhauer was returned to the camp alone. He
told Vermehren that he was surprised not to find Jebsen
back in Sachsenhausen already. The Red Army was now
closing in. A week later, the SS ordered 33,000 inmates to
begin the forced march northeast. Moldenhauer was among
the thousands killed on the way. Mike Cumberlege had
already been transferred to Flossenbürg camp, where he was
executed, five days before it was liberated. Petra Vermehren
was one of 1,400 women still in Sachsenhausen when the
camp was liberated on 30 April. She returned to Hamburg,
and resumed her writing career.

Johnny Jebsen had vanished. Ian Wilson, Artist's one-time
case officer, set out to find him. Wilson was a man of deep, if
well-hidden, feelings and granite loyalty. It was, he said, 'my
personal wish to help those who helped us', and none had been
more helpful than Jebsen. 'I do feel that it is up to this office to
use all possible diligence in finding out exactly what happened.'

Wilson owed Jebsen a debt and, with the single-mindedness
that was his trademark, he meant to discharge it. Recalling that
Jebsen had spoken about meeting Marie von Gronau in a café
in Flensburg three days after the end of the war, in May 1945 he
wrote to the British intelligence officer in that part of Germany,
and asked him to be ready in case Jebsen turned up.

My old friend Johnny Jebsen stated long ago that when
the Allies defeated Germany he would hope to have
made his way to Flensburg in Schleswig Holstein. It is

just possible that he may have been able to get himself to SH, in which case I have little doubt that he will get in touch with British intelligence. Should he come to your notice it might be as well to have him sent to this country, purely for his own cover and protection. He knows my own name which will serve as a password. I hope he has got the KVK [War Merit Cross] First Class which he said he was going to give me.

Jebsen did not appear. Recalling the 'assurance we gave Johnny that if anything happened to him we would look after the welfare of his wife', Wilson went looking for Lore Jebsen, who had by now given birth to their son. With the help of Popov, he found her in the Russian sector of Berlin, arranged for her to move to the British zone, helped her get a job back on the stage, lobbied MI5 to request the German government for a state pension, and found a lawyer to untangle Jebsen's financial affairs. 'She will be able to live in comfort,' he wrote. John Marriott could not understand why his colleague was going to such lengths: 'We have no financial and very little moral responsibility for Mrs Jebsen,' he wrote. 'Wilson is, as you know, obstinate, pertinacious and kind-hearted and he feels a great sense of responsibility.' He shared that responsibility with Popov, who, heartsick at the disappearance of his friend, had launched his own hunt for Jebsen and those who had abducted him. He travelled to Switzerland and Germany, interviewing anyone who might know of his fate.

Wilson and Popov tracked down Jebsen's business associates, his lovers and his secretary Mabel Harbottle. 'None of these people had any definite information about what had happened to Artist.' One of Jebsen's business partners, a Yugoslavian named Glusevic, said the Gestapo had quizzed him about Jebsen, and formed the impression they 'had not extracted full information about anything from Artist'. Wilson went hunting for the German officers, notably chief investigator Obergeheimrat Quitting, 'who would be most likely to know of Artist's ultimate fate'. Popov was keen for vengeance: 'If you have luck and find the man, keep him alive until I come.' Quitting never resurfaced.

The NKVD, it seemed, was also on the trail of Jebsen. Soviet intelligence officers had interrogated Popov's family in Yugoslavia before the war's end, and seemed to 'know everything about Jebsen, including his visits to Lisbon'. Wilson wondered 'how the NKVD could be aware of Jebsen's movements?' – the answer of course was Anthony Blunt.

Wilson refused to lose hope. 'We do not know whether or not Artist is still alive, but if he is, he may yet prove to be a valuable agent.' He went back to work at McKenna & Co. Solicitors, but continued the search. Others came to the conclusion that Jebsen must be dead. Tar Robertson had shared Wilson's determination to find out 'what actually happened to him in the end, as Johnny did some extremely good work on our behalf', but reluctantly decided he must have been transferred to Mauthausen concentration camp, 'which was the normal place for internees to be sent who were to be killed'. Popov eventually came to believe that his friend had been 'shot while trying to escape'. On 17 February 1950, a court in Berlin formally pronounced Johnny Jebsen dead.

Wilson was not convinced, and nor was Lore. 'She refuses to believe he is dead,' wrote Wilson. Petra Vermehren, 'the last person to see him alive', was also 'emphatic that he did not die' in Sachsenhausen. A rumour persisted that Jebsen 'was liberated by the Russians only to be rearrested and consigned to some camp in Russia'. That might explain the interest of the Soviet NKVD. A strange report from MI6, citing an American source in Lisbon, reported that 'Johnny Jebson [sic] has left for England.' In a postwar interrogation, Walter Schellenberg, the Nazi intelligence chief, stated categorically: 'Jebsen has not been killed.'

The mystery lingered, but Wilson's investigations had proved one thing beyond doubt: Jebsen had 'kept the faith'; he had never revealed anything to his captors about the Double Cross plot, either before D-Day, or after it. 'There is nothing to indicate that whatever may have happened to him he was forced to disclose facts which we wanted kept secret.' Jebsen had taken his secret with him to the grave, or wherever else he had vanished to.

Perhaps Jebsen was caught up in the last murderous spasms of the Nazi regime, as Tar believed, killed and tossed into some unmarked mass grave, like so many others. Or perhaps he made good his escape. In the chaos and confusion of those final days, it was easy to disappear. Heinrich Müller vanished, as did Quitting and other Nazis. So did Juan Pujol and Paul Fidrmuc, Agents Garbo and Ostro. Roger Michael, von Roenne's assistant who may have spied for all sides, or none, reached the end of the war, and then evaporated. Johnny Jebsen had the ingenuity, the means and the motive to disappear. His funds had seemed, to his colleagues, 'inexhaustible', and he was an acknowledged expert in bribery. He had many debts to call in, many an underworld contact to shield him, and any number of places he could hide. He had bank accounts in Paris, London, Berlin, San Francisco, Dubrovnik and Shanghai. He had every reason not to stay in Germany to discuss his questionable business activities with the authorities, and every motive to want to start afresh, somewhere else, as someone else. Ian Wilson died in 1978, still wondering what had happened to his lost spy.

The Double Cross double agents spied for adventure and gain, out of patriotism, greed and personal conviction. They made an eccentric, infuriating, courageous and astonishingly successful team. And the most important of them has disappeared from history, just as he vanished from the world, at the age of twenty-seven: Johnny Jebsen, former international playboy turned 'businessman'; a man of cynicism, humour, deep intellect and frailty; the chain-smoking Anglophile who took up spying in order not to fight. He was unable to resist worldly temptations, but he resisted his Gestapo torturers to the end. Like many ordinary, flawed people, he did not know his own courage, until war revealed it. Jebsen might easily have turned history in a disastrous direction to save his own skin, and he chose not to. Agent Artist was not a conventional D-Day hero, but he was a hero nonetheless.

Johnny Jebsen

Notes

Citations
Citations marked KV refer to the Security Service files, CAB to Cabinet Office files and FO to Foreign Office files at the National Archives (TNA), Kew.

Epigraphs
vii 'Tangle within tangle': Winston Churchill, *Thoughts and Adventures* (London, 1991), p. 55.
vii 'The enemy must not': Sun Tzu, *The Art of War*, Chapter VII.

Preface
2 'It may well be the': Field Marshal Lord Alanbrooke, *War Diaries* 1939–1945, (London 2001), p. 554.
3 'In wartime, the truth': 4th Eureka meeting, 30 November 1943, quoted in Thaddeus Holt, *The Deceivers: Allied Military Deception in the Second World War* (London, 2004), p. 505.
3 'This is what we call': ibid.
3 'utterly impossible to disguise': J. C. Masterman, *The Double Cross System in the War 1939–1945* (London, 1972), p. 150.
3 It is here that the': Fuhrer Directive No. 51, 3 November 1943, cited in Joshua Levine, *Operation Fortitude: The Story of the Spy Operation that Saved D-Day* (London, 2011), p. 199.

Chapter 1: Raw Recruits
7 'We both had some intellectual': Dusko Popov, *Spy/Counterspy* (New York, 1974), p. 5.
7 'He smiles freely, showing': KV 2/846.
7 'A well-flattened': ibid.
8 'loose, sensual mouth': ibid.
8 'His coldness, aloofness': Popov, *Spy/Counterspy*, p. 6.
8 'He had much warmth too': ibid.
8 'deliberately stir up situations': ibid.
8 'not thinking my looks would be': ibid., p. 7.
9 'Some of my love of my country': ibid.
9 'like a young Anthony Eden': ibid.
9 'pro-Nazi student intelligentsia': ibid.
9 'Under that mask of a snob': ibid.
9 'Need to meet you urgently': ibid., p. 2.
10 'two girls from the chorus': ibid., p. 16.
10 'sharp intelligence, cynicism': ibid., p. 14.
10 'ordered his whiskies double, neat': ibid.
10 'because it saved him from': KV 2/845.
10 'a wangle by Canaris': KV 2/856.
10 'time travelling throughout Europe': KV 2/859.
10 'Hitler is the undisputed master': Popov, *Spy/Counterspy*, p. 23.

11 'Would you dine with a friend': ibid.

11 'No country can resist': ibid., p. 24.

11 'We have many agents': ibid.

11 'General. Political': ibid.

11 'a little idea of my own': ibid.

11 'our sole source of information': KV 2/72.

12 'His loyalty is entirely to his own': ibid.

12 'a man who lives and thinks': ibid.

12 'based on the highest ideals': Roman Garby-Czerniawski, *The Big Network* (London, 1961), p. 14.

13 'Every signpost': ibid., p. 21.

13 'vision': ibid., p. 22.

13 'small cells of resistance': ibid.

13 'She was small': ibid., p. 43.

13 'Thin and muscular': Lily Mathilde Carré, *I Was the Cat* (London, 1959), p. 69.

14 'in an appalling French': ibid., p. 68.

14 'under the eyes of an enormous': ibid., p. 66.

14 'Instead of throwing myself': ibid., p. 67.

14 'Every time he spoke': ibid., p. 70.

14 'A great bond of friendship': ibid., p. 69.

14 'he could count on her': Garby-Czerniawski, *The Big Network*, p. 47.

15 'you walk so quietly': ibid., p. 49.

15 'And I can scratch': ibid.

15 'It will be inter-Allied': ibid., p. 56.

15 'who had received a': Carré, *I Was the Cat*, p. 86.

15 'In her black fur coat': Garby-Czerniawski, *The Big Network*, p. 79.

15 'To defeat the enemy': ibid., p. 124.

16 'a tall, thin Pole': Carré, *I Was the Cat*, p. 81.

16 '*Remplacez le couvercle*': Garby-Czerniawski, *The Big Network*, p. 77.

16 'Big Network composed': ibid., p. 83.

17 'packed in such a way': ibid., p. 125.

17 'RE: GOERING TRAIN': ibid., p. 144.

17 'a typical little provincial': Carré, *I Was the Cat*, p. 98.

17 'no question of any jealousy': Garby-Czerniawski, *The Big Network*, p. 120.

17 'strange woman, idealistic': ibid., p. 58.

17 '*C'est la vie*': ibid., p. 180.

17 'You've kept us all busy': ibid., p. 188.

17 'the head of some business': ibid., p. 187.

17 'We are perfect partners': ibid., p. 194.

17 'I was petrified by the': ibid., p. 205.

18 'Subconsciously I felt': ibid.

18 'exceedingly dull': KV 2/2098.

18 'she had nothing in common': ibid.

19 'an utter shit, corrupt': Cited in Anthony Read & David Fisher, *Colonel Z: The Secret Life of a Master of Spies* (London, 1985), p. 361.

20 'I realised he must have': Nigel West, 'High Society Spy', *Mail on Sunday*, 7 May 1995.

20 'Attractive in appearance': KV 2/2098.

20 'tastes appear to be in the direction': ibid.

20 'hilarious parties': ibid.

20 'rowdy behaviour, singing': ibid.

20 'favours the companionship': ibid.

21 'apparently innocuous letters': West, 'High Society Spy'.
21 'Between the lines': ibid.
21 'She is very intelligent': KV 2/2098.
21 'she was being taught': ibid.
21 'she must abstain from': ibid.
22 'I must do something': Nigel West and Juan Pujol García, *Operation Garbo* (London, 2011), p. 48.
22 'a psychopath': ibid.
22 'I wanted to work for them': ibid., p. 49.
22 'My plans were fairly': ibid., p. 49.
22 'extremely busy': ibid.
22 'I was fascinated by the origin': ibid., p. 29.
22 'The pen is mightier': ibid.
22 'rant away as befitted': ibid., p. 50.
23 'He should be careful': Mark Seaman, Introduction to Tomás Harris, *Garbo: The Spy Who Saved D-Day* (London, 2004), p. 50.
24 'There are men here': ibid., p. 58.
25 'did not particularly like Germans': Lily Sergueiev, *Secret Service Rendered: An Agent in the Espionage Duel Preceding the Invasion of France* (London, 1968), p. 10.
26 'promised to obtain for her': José António Barreiros, *Nathalie Sergueiew: Uma Agente Dupla em Lisboa* (Lisbon, 2006), p. 34.
26 'let the French down badly': KV 2/464.
27 'It might be quite easy': Barreiros, *Nathalie Sergueiew*, p. 56.
27 'I am interested': Sergueiev, *Secret Service Rendered*, p. 32.
27 '*Why* do you want to work': ibid., p. 33.
27 'Major, you are an intelligent': ibid.
27 'I will make contact': ibid.
27 'Babs lifts up his shaggy': ibid., p. 15.
27 'I take Babs on my knees': ibid., p. 56.

Chapter 2: A Bit of an Enigma

28 'to get an easy living': KV 2/853.
28 'an awful crook': KV 2/859.
28 'Be a good thing for you': Dusko Popov, *Spy/Counterspy* (New York, 1974), p. 21.
28 'Continue your conversation': ibid., p. 29.
29 'insignificant letter in': KV 2/845.
29 'a young girl, about twenty-two': ibid.
29 'Your spymaster will be Major': Popov, *Spy/Counterspy*, p. 45.
29 'Who were Churchill's enemies': ibid., p. 31.
29 'We are now both': KV 2/845.
30 'strongly pro-British': ibid.
30 'British at heart': ibid.
30 'a bit of an enigma': ibid.
30 'What is Canaris like': ibid., p. 18.
30 'A sensitive man': ibid.
31 'There was a curious ambiguity': ibid., p. 45.
31 'blackish hair on his hands': KV 2/847.
31 'I have been instructed to': Popov, *Spy/Counterspy*, p. 47.
31 'He was tall and dark': KV 2/847.
32 'Popov, hello': Popov, *Spy/Counterspy*, p. 53.
32 'Let's get acquainted': ibid.

32 'many agents in England': Popov, *Spy/Counterspy*, p. 24.

32 'excellent': ibid.

33 Fifth Column Neurosis': KV 4/186, Diaries of Guy Liddell, 15 March 1940.

33 'the gentlemen who are': FO, TNA INF 1/264-8.

34 'junk': Liddell Diaries, 30 March 1941.

34 'a high proportion': KV 4/8, Robin 'Tin-eye' Stephens, Report on the Operations of Camp 020.

35 'You have forfeited your life': Cited in Emily Wilson, 'The War in the Dark: The Security Service and the Abwehr 1940–1944', PhD Thesis (Cambridge, 2003), p. 63.

36 'an almost suicidal appetite': Alistair Robertson, correspondence with the author.

36 'a perfect officer type': Thaddeus Holt, *The Deceivers: Allied Military Deception in the Second World War* (London, 2004), p. 131.

36 'friendly eyes and an assertive': Miranda Carter, *Anthony Blunt: His Lives* (London, 2001), p. 284.

36 'less than promising': Alastair Robertson, correspondence with the author.

36 'immensely personable': Christopher Harmer, address at Memorial Service for Tar Robertson, 17 October 1994.

36 'with a charm that could melt': ibid.

36 'unmistakable twinkle': Peter Stormonth Darling, address at Memorial Service for Tar Robertson.

36 'delightful chuckle': ibid.

36 'by and large pretty stupid': Christopher Andrew, *Secret Service: The Making of the British Intelligence Community* (London, 1985), p. 645.

36 'real genius': Hugh Trevor-Roper, cited in Wilson, 'The War in the Dark', p. 67.

37 'shifty look': KV 2/448.

37 'stupid little man': Joshua Levine, *Operation Fortitude: The Story of the Spy Operation that Saved D-Day* (London, 2011), p. 45.

37 'work on logical lines': ibid.

37 'saved us from absolute': Christopher Andrew, *The Defence of the Realm: The Authorised History of MI5* (London, 2009), p. 249.

38 'fanatical Nazi': Robin 'Tin-eye' Stephens, *Camp 020: MI5 and the Nazi Spies*, introduction by Oliver Hoare (London, 2000), p. 138.

39 'he had helped the man': KV 2/60.

39 'The double agent is a tricky': J. C. Masterman, *The Double Cross System in the War 1939–1945* (London, 1972), p. 52.

39 'blow our whole show': Andrew, *Defence of the Realm*, p. 258.

39 'they will be liquidated': ibid.

40 'I have a strong feeling': KV 2/845.

40 'absolutely obsessed with': ibid.

40 'It will be necessary': ibid.

40 'Skoot left an exceedingly': ibid.

41 'was obviously pleased': ibid.

41 'He enjoyed himself thoroughly': ibid.

41 'both viewing things': ibid.

41 'I much enjoyed': ibid.

42 'definitely members of the party': ibid.

42 'I found him a most charming': ibid.

42 'Giraffe's case died chiefly': Masterman, *The Double Cross System*, p. 55.

43 'The Club': Wilson, 'The War in the Dark', p. 138.

43 'Running a team of double': Masterman, *The Double Cross System*, p. 91.

43 'a thoroughly well-trained': ibid.
43 'required a good deal': ibid.
43 'initiated into the mysteries': See Oliver Locker-Lampson, 'Adolf Hitler As I Know Him', *Daily Mirror*, 30 September 1930.
43 'withdrawal of the use': ibid.
43 'bigger and harder ball': ibid.
43 'ready to take the field': Masterman, *The Double Cross System*, p. 91.
44 'The prime difficulty': ibid.
44 'We have in him a new agent': KV 2/845.

Chapter 3: Roman and the Cat

45 'I wonder if anybody': Roman Garby-Czerniawski, *The Big Network* (London, 1961), p. 218.
45 'a complete picture': ibid., p. 10.
45 'Many Happy Returns': ibid., p. 233.
45 'AGAINST THE GERMANS': ibid.
46 'overworked and was obviously': ibid.
46 'Why did you ask': ibid., p. 238.
46 'I must be tired': ibid., p. 237.
46 'The light was switched': ibid., p. 240.
46 'intelligent face': ibid., p. 142.
46 'If only someone': ibid., p. 245.
46 'It was a great gamble': Lily Mathilde Carré, *I Was the Cat* (London, 1960), p. 104.
46 'an ordinary denunciation': KV 2/72.
47 'wide boy': Carré, *I Was the Cat*, p. 90.
47 'I was like an animal': ibid., p. 107.
47 'You have committed enough': ibid.
47 'If you double-cross': ibid.
47 'Great Britain makes': ibid.
47 'inhumanely': ibid. p. 116.
47 'not only with handcuffs': ibid.
47 'the greatest act of cowardice': ibid., p. 115.
47 'purely animal': ibid.
47 'winning Bleicher's confidence': ibid., p. 126.
47 'You must behave': ibid., p. 112.
48 'You see how easy it is': ibid.
48 a strangely haunted': ibid., p. 110.
48 'one by one': ibid., p. 117.
48 'A few men proved': KV 2/72.
48 'We have decided': Carré, *I Was the Cat*, p. 119.
48 'I had felt the icy': ibid., p. 115.
49 'started to laugh contentedly': Garby-Czerniawski, *The Big Network*, p. 243.
49 'treated severely': KV 2/72.
49 'the completeness': ibid.
49 'intelligent and quick-witted': ibid.
49 'always boasting': ibid.
49 'Also a man of great': ibid.
49 'terrified eyes': Garby-Czerniawski, *The Big Network*, p. 242.
49 'given everything away': KV 2/72.
49 'the Germans felt': ibid.
49 'might exploit this': ibid.
50 'It is possible she': ibid.

50 'When working in this': ibid.
50 'by force': ibid.
50 'a firing squad did': ibid.
50 'If the German nation': ibid.
50 'thick grey hair': ibid.
51 'manicured': ibid.
51 'We do not deny': ibid.
51 'You have tied': ibid.
51 'By joining us': ibid.
51 'Whatever collaboration Poland': ibid.
51 'excellent knowledge': ibid.
51 'raise the Polish nation': ibid.
51 'war of nerves': ibid.
51 'as though I had really': ibid.
51 'In my opinion': ibid.
52 'The Germans were': ibid.
52 'be working for the': ibid.
52 'he would never under': ibid.
52 'The future of Poland': ibid.
52 'I am prepared': ibid.
52 'preparations for': ibid.
52 'do for Germany': ibid.
52 'I will group around': ibid.
52 'the moment that': ibid.
52 'That the agents': ibid.
52 'an extremely odd': Oscar Reile, *Geheime West Front* (Munich, 1962), p. 214.
52 'in unusually polite': KV 2/72.
53 'highly appreciative': ibid.
53 'I told them': ibid.
53 'Your companions': ibid.
53 'You know yourself': ibid.
53 'If I work for you': ibid.
53 'Should I fail': ibid.
53 'I knew that the fate': ibid.
53 'like an intelligent boxer': ibid.
54 'enable him to go': ibid.
54 'The prison would': ibid.
54 'The English knew': Reile, *Geheime West Front*, p. 214.
54 'If the enemy attempted': ibid.
54 'fantastic': ibid.

Chapter 4: Coat Trailing

55 'cosmopolitan cover': Nigel West, 'High Society Spy', *Mail on Sunday*, 7 May 1995.
55 'small class of': KV 2/2098.
55 'People who get all': ibid.
55 'altogether more agreeable': West, 'High Society Spy'.
55 'I felt I was doing': ibid.
56 'obviously rolling': KV 2/2098.
56 'very tall' : ibid.
56 'The German seemed': ibid.
56 'He was young': ibid.

56 'I'll introduce you': ibid.
56 'He is a secret agent': ibid.
56 'been recruited personally': ibid.
56 'one of the most expensive': ibid.
56 'graceful walk': ibid.
56 'obviously a gentleman': ibid.
56 'inferiority complex': ibid.
56 'spotted as a German': ibid.
56 'seemed to want': ibid.
56 'he laughed': ibid.
57 'pleasant fellow': ibid.
57 'enjoyed everything': ibid.
57 'The war was very silly': ibid.
57 'Why are you going' to 'How?': ibid.
57 'After the war': ibid.
57 'rather vague': ibid.
57 'You will have': ibid.
58 'to start with': ibid.
58 'marvellous trick': ibid.
58 'We just want facts': ibid.
58 'This is infinitely': ibid.
58 'He looked around': ibid.
58 'The Germans are': ibid.
58 'I always act on': ibid.
58 'I felt rather sorry': ibid.
59 'You must never': ibid.
59 'I have no desire': ibid.
59 'a nice girl but without': KV 2/464.
59 'pretty but rather fat': ibid.
59 'looked a little like': Lily Sergueiev, *Secret Service Rendered: An Agent in the Espionage Duel Preceding the Invasion of France* (London, 1968), p. 24.
60 'ordinary writing paper': KV 2/464.
60 'This has been dragging': Sergueiev, *Secret Service Rendered*, p. 53.
60 'I am sick of it': ibid.
60 'You shall not continue': ibid.
60 'It is the first time': ibid.
61 'serve the Allied': ibid., p. 53.
61 'He could recognise you': ibid.
61 'I have confidence': ibid., p. 53.
61 'I wave a handkerchief': ibid., p. 73.

Chapter 5: The Club

62 'scrofulous Nazi': Joshua Levine, *Operation Fortitude: The Story of the Spy Operation that Saved D-Day* (London, 2011), p. 125.
62 'manifestly unemployable': Robin 'Tin-eye' Stephens, *Camp 020: MI5 and the Nazi Spies*, introduction by Oliver Hoare (London, 2000), p. 156.
62 'He died at': ibid.
63 'newfound loyalty': Levine, *Operation Fortitude*, p. 88.
63 'a pearl among agents': J. C. Masterman, *The Double Cross System in the War 1939–1945* (London, 1972), p. 53.
64 'I cannot help regarding': KV 2/845.
64 'not very impressed': ibid.
64 'blind confidence': ibid.

64 'You'll soon want': Dusko Popov, *Spy/Counterspy* (New York, 1974), p. 95.

64 'expected much from': KV 2/845.

64 'London is rather': ibid.

65 'hinted that a little': ibid.

65 'suggestions as to possible': ibid.

65 'a woman purely': ibid.

65 'I won't be able': ibid.

66 'Complexion depends': ibid.

66 'typical Scottish scenery': ibid.

66 'filled with jovial': ibid.

66 'There was a law': Popov, *Spy/Counterspy*, p. 66.

66 'he made no effort': KV 2/845.

66 'He did not think it would': ibid.

66 'especially if he could': ibid.

66 'It may be desirable': ibid.

66 'He is quite definitely': ibid.

67 'Clever, versatile and firm': ibid.

67 'He is fond of the society': ibid.

67 'Skoot is an ingenious': ibid.

67 'he hates them all': ibid.

68 'link with people': ibid.

68 'in a position': ibid.

68 'They propose to buy': KV 2/860.

68 'the answers we had': KV 2/845.

68 'slight moral scruples': ibid.

68 'The strictest moral': ibid.

68 'that the work': ibid.

68 'It would be difficult': ibid.

68 'somewhat tired': ibid.

68 'an expensive evening': ibid.

68 'a small automatic': ibid.

68 'We could do nothing': ibid.

68 'a slightly rolling': ibid.

69 'A case officer should': Masterman, *The Double Cross System*, p. 70.

69 'command the best talent': Emily Wilson, 'The War in the Dark: The Security Service and the Abwehr 1940–1944', PhD Thesis (Cambridge, 2003), p. 96.

70 'The running and control': Masterman, *The Double Cross System*, p. 15.

70 'the whole-time service': ibid.

70 'the collector of facts': Peggy Harmer, cited in Emily Wilson, 'The War in the Dark', p. 127.

71 'overgrown schoolboys': Christopher Harmer to Hugh Astor, 28 October 1992, Collection of Robert Astor.

71 'casual agent': Christopher Andrew, *The Defence of the Realm: The Authorised History of MI5* (London, 2009), p. 242.

71 'real understanding': KV 2/1067.

72 'Thank God for Tar': Christopher Harmer to Hugh Astor, 28 October 1992, Collection of Robert Astor.

72 'born leader': J. C. Masterman, *On the Chariot Wheel: An Autobiography* (Oxford, 1975), p. 219.

72 'gifted with independent': ibid.

72 'In this game one never': KV 4/70.

72 'in an obviously': Masterman, *The Double Cross System,* p. 101.
73 'since he always does': Miranda Carter, *Anthony Blunt: His Lives* (London, 2001), p. 273.
73 'that's what Tiggers': ibid.
73 'He was a very nice': Andrew, *Defence of the Realm,* p. 270.
74 'I couldn't stick the man': Carter, *Blunt,* p. 284.
74 'Tony is a thorough': Andrew, *Defence of the Realm,* p. 272.
74 'He tries to fulfil': ibid.

Chapter 6: Garbo Takes the Stage
76 'Who was this Arabel': Nigel West with Juan Pujol García, *Operation Garbo,* (London, 2011), p. 88.
77 'drunken orgies': Christopher Andrew, *The Defence of the Realm: The Authorised History of MI5* (London, 2009), p. 254.
77 '87 shillings and 10 pence': Tomás Harris, *Garbo: The Spy Who Saved D-Day* (London, 2004), p. 59.
77 'very wild messages': Joshua Levine, *Operation Fortitude: The Story of the Spy Operation that Saved D-Day* (London, 2011), p.160.
78 'I do not see why': Guy Liddell, *The Guy Liddell Diaries, 1939–1945,* ed. Nigel West (London, 2005), 26 March 1942.
78 'The whole thing': ibid.
78 'a miracle that he': Harris, *Garbo: The Spy Who Saved D-Day,* p. 77.
78 'inexhaustibly fertile': ibid., p. 34.
79 'With fierce black': Sefton Delmer, *The Counterfeit Spy* (London, 1973), p. 73.
79 'He played his game': J. C. Masterman, *The Double Cross System in the War 1939–1945* (London, 1972), p. 118.
80 'mysterious business deals': KV 2/845.
80 'We are going': ibid.
80 'In time of war': KV 2/848.
80 'The Germans may': KV 2/847.
80 'His latest girlfriend': ibid.
80 'Missing you terribly': KV 2/846.
81 'degenerating in prison': KV 2/848.
81 'which makes for much': KV 2/847.
81 'I wonder whether': ibid.
81 'submitting to her': KV 2/1067.
81 'We are the Double': ibid.
81 'After all, any decent spy': ibid.
81 'He is by temperament': KV 2/848.
82 'some sort of decoration': KV 2/847.
82 'I do not like': ibid.
82 'I am still satisfied': KV 2/845.
82 'extremely pleased': KV 2/847.
82 'like whores on': Dusko Popov, *Spy/Counterspy* (New York, 1974), p. 109.
83 'in this business': KV 2/847.
83 'I am not cruel enough': ibid.
84 'If there is anyone': ibid.
84 'I would be willing': ibid.
84 'They are like cat': ibid.
84 'Whenever I go to': ibid.
84 'advised it was': KV 2/856.
85 'If this is Upper Silesia': Robert McCrum, *Wodehouse: A Life* (London 2004), p. 198.

86 'to take revenge': KV 2/856.
86 'I know too much': KV 2/847.
86 'If you are caught': KV 2/859.
86 'He is very pro-British': KV 2/847.
86 'placed in honourable': ibid.
87 'I am not at all sure': ibid.
87 'not as confident as': KV 2/848.
87 'virile telegraphese': Masterman, *The Double Cross System*, p. 17.
87 'I am beginning': Levine, *Operation Fortitude*, p. 126.
87 'I shit on Germany': ibid.
89 'He was in a complete': KV 2/848.
89 'I said enough to': ibid.
89 'Heartiest congratulations': Levine, *Operation Fortitude*, p. 138.
89 'On no account': ibid.
89 'The actual cash': Masterman, *The Double Cross System,* p. 16.

Chapter 7: Popov Goes Shopping
90 'Popov is a clever': KV 2/846.
90 'For the moment' Dusko Popov, *Spy/Counterspy* (New York, 1974), p. 112.
90 'we shall probably': ibid.
91 'greatest spy round-up': Russell Miller, *Codename Tricycle* (London, 2005), p. 94.
91 'His first innings': KV 2/849.
91 'It is a great pity': ibid.
91 'Hoover obviously only': Ewen Montagu, *Beyond Top Secret Ultra* (London, 1977), p. 89.
92 'The mistake we made': Joshua Levine, *Operation Fortitude: The Story of the Spy Operation that Saved D-Day* (London, 2011), p. 146.
92 'No one ever dreamed': ibid.
92 'The questionnaire indicated': J. C. Masterman, *The Double Cross System in the War 1939–1945* (London, 1972), p. 82.
93 'embarrass the bureau': ibid.
93 'gold-digger': Miller, *Codename Tricycle*, p. 98.
94 'His financial behaviour': KV 2/850.
94 'I cannot distinguish': ibid.
94 'Tricycle should have': KV 2/849.
94 'so that he should': ibid.
94 'found him depressed': Montagu, *Beyond Top Secret Ultra*, p. 92.
94 'Hoover's management of': ibid.
94 'that there were people': ibid.
94 'Berlin suspected Tricycle': KV 2/860.
94 'a larger sum in dollars': KV 2/850.
95 'I cannot continue': ibid.
95 'Tricycle suspects the evil': ibid.
95 'to maintain him': KV 2/849.
95 'Popov has been totally': Miller, *Codename Tricycle*, p. 132.
95 'I need not repeat': KV 2/850.
95 'He could end his': ibid.
96 'entertaining, social life': ibid.
96 'razor-keen mind': author's interview with Wilson's daughter, Fiona Agassiz, 18 May 2011.
96 'Quiet and introverted': ibid.
96 'failed to produce any': ibid.

96 'how he had': ibid.
96 'a very pro–British': ibid.
96 'extremely objectionable': ibid.
96 'The FBI have lost': ibid.
97 'to prevent any further': ibid.
97 'It is a very outspoken': ibid.
97 'Tricycle himself showed': ibid.
97 'His chances were nothing': Montagu, *Beyond Top Secret Ultra*, p. 92.
97 'an enormous number': KV 2/850.
97 'the greatest instance': Montagu, *Beyond Top Secret Ultra*, p. 92.
97 'Will telephone office': KV 2/849.
98 'stiff in manner': KV 2/850.
98 'as if he learned': ibid.
98 'some suspicion': ibid.
98 'very good . . . excellent . . . terribly bad': ibid.
98 'Now you know what': ibid.
98 'You send me there': Popov, *Spy/Counterspy*, p. 184.
98 'We did all we could': KV 2/851.
99 'embezzled': KV 2/850.
99 'Berlin are stupid': KV 2/851.
99 'might make a scene': KV 2/850.
99 'Kammler begged': ibid.
99 'severe': ibid.
99 'double work': ibid.
99 'Lisbon seem to have': ibid.
100 'Berlin wants information': ibid.
100 'we are not so': ibid.
100 'What about invasion': ibid.
100 'so that I can satisfy': ibid.
100 'voluble and rather confused': ibid.
100 'a great deal of vague': ibid.
100 'He is entirely friendly': ibid.
101 'extraordinary casualness': ibid.
101 'It is quite probable': ibid.
101 'both by making': ibid.
101 'I was cheated by Johnny': ibid.
101 'very anti-Nazi': ibid.
101 'Johnny would give': ibid.
101 'Any suspicion against': ibid.
101 'ability to impose': ibid.
101 'not in any way': ibid.
101 'Von Karsthoff has defended': ibid.
101 'We may be able': ibid.

Chapter 8: The Great Game

102 'in enormous quantities': KV 2/72.
103 'realised that any': ibid.
103 'a mere formality': ibid.
103 'starting to work': ibid.
103 'Long Live Hitler': ibid.
103 'super-spy': ibid.
103 'great daring and initiative': ibid.
103 'He is a natural leader': ibid.

103 'amazing': ibid.
103 'everyone was prepared': ibid.
103 'there was something': ibid.
104 'tiny, vivacious': Roman Garby-Czerniawski, *The Big Network* (London, 1961), p. 126.
104 'The plan was that': Lily Mathilde Carré, *I Was the Cat* (London, 1960), pp. 137–8.
104 'a couple of pairs': ibid., p. 143.
104 'Anglo-Saxon hypocrisy': ibid., p. 157.
105 'Her guilt is the greater': KV 2/72.
105 'but there is no excuse': ibid.
105 'the bombshell': ibid.
105 'The Germans are entering': ibid.
105 'the wireless crystals': ibid.
105 'carrying out a carefully': ibid.
105 'During the whole': ibid.
106 'I shall discuss personally': ibid.
106 'The story of my escape': ibid.
106 'I am convinced': ibid.
106 'demanded a revolver': ibid.
106 'certain of the degree': ibid.
106 'sinister individual': ibid.
107 'There are considerable': ibid.
107 'His loyalty is entirely': ibid.
107 'a loyal and fervent': ibid.
108 'As his condition': ibid.
108 'He finds that so': ibid.
108 'I do not think': ibid.
108 'There is no evidence': ibid.
108 'rendered very great': ibid.
109 'The Germans would': ibid.
109 'we are never going': ibid.
109 'the Germans have really': ibid.
109 'knowing pretty well': ibid.
109 'We are not yet': ibid.
109 'hell-bent on chopping': Christopher Harmer to Hugh Astor, 28 October 1992, Collection of Robert Astor.
109 'intrigued behind my back': ibid.
109 'one of the rudest': ibid.
109 'I loved the old boy': ibid.
109 'throw the case away': KV 2/72.
109 'under close supervision': ibid.
110 'non-job': ibid.
110 'The Germans lost': ibid.
110 'Roman Czerniawski had': Joshua Levine, *Operation Fortitude: The Story of the Spy Operation that Saved D-Day* (London, 2011), p. 175.

Chapter 9: The Flock

111 'one of the most': Nigel West, 'High Society Spy', *Mail on Sunday*, 7 May 1995.
111 'beautifully varnished nails': ibid.
111 'She was really': ibid.
111 'carried out to the': KV 2/2098.
111 'Mr Palmer': ibid.

111 'made a good impression': ibid.
111 'It is by no means': ibid.
112 'Lesbian tendencies': ibid.
112 'she would appear': ibid.
112 'disclosed no possible': ibid.
112 'We have not': ibid.
112 'We ought *not*': ibid.
112 'She is a rather': ibid.
112 'I think this woman': ibid.
112 'typical member of the': ibid.
113 'She replied that she had': ibid.
113 'impressed on her': ibid.
113 'I chose the name': West, 'High Society Spy', 7 May 1995.
113 'It was one': ibid.
113 'It was a very': ibid.
114 'remarkable talent': Tomás Harris, *Garbo: The Spy Who Saved D-Day* (London, 2004), p. 77.
114 'entire existence remained': ibid.
114 'absolute loyalty': ibid., p. 78.
114 'thoroughly undesirable': ibid., p. 318.
115 'to swamp the': ibid., p. 69.
115 'I do not wish to end': ibid., p. 95.
115 'in as much confusing': ibid., p. 69.
115 'The greater the work': ibid., p. 71.
115 'the fanatical loyalty': ibid., p. 78.
115 'temperamental genius': ibid., p. 70.
115 'expressions of high satisfaction': ibid.
115 'Why have I been made': ibid., p. 90.
115 'I want you to know': ibid.
116 'who seldom or never': Michael Howard, *Strategic Deception in the Second World War* (London, 1995), p. 12.
116 'the possible uses': T. A. Robertson to Major H. Petaval, 24 June 1943, CAB 154/35 (TNA).
117 'Years of breeding': KV 4/10.
117 'magical': ibid.
117 'Out of a hundred': ibid.
117 'Himmler, who has': ibid.
117 'any lofts where': ibid.
117 'to accustom as many': ibid.
118 'It was positively': Emily Wilson, 'The War in the Dark: The Security Service and the Abwehr 1940–1944', PhD Thesis (Cambridge, 2003), p. 169.
118 'accent': KV 4/10.
118 'they are easier to work': ibid.
118 'Both birds are now': ibid.
119 'The falconry unit proved': ibid.
119 'If all the fanciers': ibid.
119 'covered an area': ibid.
119 'Had they done': ibid.

Chapter 10: True Agent, False Agent, Double Agent
120 'the idea there might': J. C. Masterman, *The Double Cross System in the War 1939–1945* (London, 1972), p. 59.

120 'reasonably certain': Michael Howard, *Strategic Deception in the Second World War* (London, 1995), p. 20.

121 'powerful weapon': KV 4/70.

121 'The only network': ibid.

121 'fill the German files': Ewen Montagu, *Beyond Top Secret Ultra* (London, 1977), p. 102.

122 'It was always': Masterman, *The Double Cross System*, p. 72.

122 'The enemy is': Emily Wilson, 'The War in the Dark: The Security Service and the Abwehr 1940–1944', PhD Thesis (Cambridge, 2003), p. 174.

122 'if one pearl': ibid.

122 'It is always impossible': KV 3/7.

122 'the Nazis are very': KV 2/1067.

122 'carefully and cleverly': ibid.

122 'The very few really': Masterman, *The Double Cross System*, p. 152.

122 'glittering possibility': ibid.

123 'the most highly polished': Thaddeus Holt, *The Deceivers: Allied Military Deception in the Second World War* (London, 2004), p. 185.

123 'prepare deception': ibid., p. 189.

123 'any matter calculated to': ibid.

123 'We had an instrument': Masterman, *The Double Cross System*, p. 108.

124 'lingering malady': ibid., p. 119.

124 'I fulfil my duty': Tomás Harris, *Garbo: The Spy Who Saved D-Day* (London, 2004), p. 103.

124 'Your last reports': ibid., p. 104.

125 'The success was not': Masterman, *The Double Cross System*, p. 111.

125 'the team was distinctly': ibid., p. 126.

125 'If the agents': ibid., p. 72.

125 'an older, wiser': Christopher Harmer to Hugh Astor, 28 October 1992, Collection of Robert Astor.

125 'guaranteed to argue': ibid.

125 'come down with': ibid.

126 'without any training': ibid.

126 'What may appeal to': KV 2/1067.

126 'The case officer': Masterman, *The Double Cross System*, p. 22.

126 'He had to see': ibid.

127 'most careful psychological': ibid., p. 23.

127 'We were playing': ibid., p. 14.

127 'Gonorrhoea expert': KV 2/850.

127 'This might be a heavily': ibid.

127 'only a well-kept record': Masterman, *The Double Cross System*, p. 28.

127 'a truly formidable size': ibid., p. 68.

128 'the messages of any one': ibid.

128 'Tangle within tangle': Winston Churchill, *Thoughts and Adventures* (London, 1991), p. 55.

128 'could not claim': KV 4/70.

129 'on seeing some': Guy Liddell, *The Guy Liddell Diaries, 1939–1945*, ed. Nigel West (London, 2005), 10 March 1943.

129 'In all, 126 spies': KV 4/83.

129 'Deeply interesting': ibid.

129 'seen more detailed': Christopher Andrew, *The Defence of the Realm: The Authorised History of MI5* (London, 2009), p. 292.

129 'Why don't you': KV 4/83.

130 'very competent': Masterman, *The Double Cross System*, p. 123.

130   'no evidence of any': KV 2/2098.
130   'She plays bridge': ibid.
130   'She is not engaged': ibid.
130   'completely meaningless': ibid.
130   'This text is so': ibid.
130   'Last week I saw': ibid.
130   'Her friends are to': ibid.
131   'We took great care': Nigel West, 'High Society Spy', *Mail on Sunday*, 7 May 1995.
131   'I hope you won't': KV 2/2098.
131   'As she is woman': ibid.
131   'satisfactory regularity': ibid.
131   'minus several hundred': ibid.
131   'somebody on their': ibid.
131   'It was hoped that': ibid.
131   'ignored this suggestion': ibid.
132   'Tank production retarded': KV 2/3639.
132   'Money must be sent': KV 2/2098.
132   'a glowing account': Masterman, *The Double Cross System*, p. 9.
132   'the British had': Nigel West, 'High Society Spy'.
132   'we can in some': Masterman, *The Double Cross System*, p. 9.
132   'He has apparently': KV 2/2098.
132   'We have no knowledge': ibid.
132   'a member of the international': ibid.
133   'Bronx is believed': ibid.
133   'The evidence suggests': ibid.
133   'They had studied': Masterman, *The Double Cross System*, p. 145.
133   'sparingly': KV 2/72.
133   'allowed to lead': ibid.
134   'exceedingly good': ibid.
134   'lengthy report on the': ibid.
134   'telegraph French': ibid.
134   'Brutus is very easy': ibid.
134   'Several of my old': ibid.
134   'if I have your': ibid.
134   'Every now and then': Joshua Levine, *Operation Fortitude: The Story of the Spy Operation that Saved D-Day* (London, 2011), p. 31.
135   'Almost certainly Brutus': KV 2/72.
135   'a little anxious about': ibid.
135   'might warn the': ibid.
135   'evidence that he is': ibid.
135   'no qualification to suggest': ibid.
135   'very valuable wireless agent': ibid.
135   'As confidence grew': Masterman, *The Double Cross System*, p. 146.
135   'threw his weight about': KV 2/72.
135   'at loggerheads with': ibid.
135   'he is a vain and conceited': ibid.
135   'infernal nuisance': ibid.
135   'He spends his whole': ibid.
136   'embroiled in Polish': ibid.
136   'extreme anti-Bolshevism': ibid.
136   'sensed that he was hurt': ibid.
136   'In Defence of our': ibid.

136 'The Soviets committed': ibid.
136 'The Polish Air Force': ibid.
137 'the gravest military': ibid.
137 'little tin-pot hero': ibid.
137 'threatened the extinction': Masterman, *The Double Cross System*, p. 146.
137 'any patriotic Pole': KV 2/72.
137 'meddling in affairs': ibid.
137 'it was the duty': ibid.
137 'which demonstrate a desire': ibid.
137 'I foresee my arrest': ibid.
137 '20th June arrested': ibid.
137 'whether the Germans': ibid.
138 'indiscipline and offensiveness': ibid.
138 'for the harm he': ibid.

Chapter 11: Cockade

139 'perhaps the highest-grade': Guy Liddell, *The Guy Liddell Diaries, 1939–1945*, ed. Nigel West (London, 2005),, 5 June 1943.
139 'The one-man band': J. C. Masterman, *The Double Cross System in the War 1939–1945* (London, 1972), p. 146.
139 'Garbo himself works on': KV 4/83.
140 'hysterical, spoilt and selfish': Tomás Harris, *Garbo: The Spy Who Saved D-Day*, (London, 2004), pp. 327–34.
140 'for a week': ibid.
140 'unbalanced': ibid.
140 'I am telling you': ibid.
140 'a woman of Mrs G's': ibid.
141 'read her the Riot Act': Liddell, *Diaries*, 22 June 1943.
141 'outburst of jealousy': Harris, *Garbo: The Spy Who Saved D-Day*, pp. 327–34.
141 'ruin the whole undertaking': ibid.
141 'give the whole': ibid.
141 'hysterical outburst': ibid.
141 'her husband had': ibid.
141 'ninety per cent': ibid.
141 'She pleaded that': ibid.
141 'considerable comfort': Russell Miller, *Codename Tricycle: The True Story of the Second World War's Most Extraordinary Double Agent* (London, 2005), p. 163.
141 'Please try': KV 2/853.
142 'undoubtedly be an easier': KV 2/854.
142 'Your writing is wonderful': KV 2/853.
142 'He gets particularly obscure': ibid.
142 'humour and spirit': Dusko Popov, *Spy/Counterspy* (New York, 1974), p. 193.
142 'Everyone, the Germans included': ibid., p. 223.
142 'realised that Germany': KV 2/851.
142 'Johnny has never': ibid.
142 'full details of the': ibid.
142 'Johnny is always': ibid.
142 'amoral, opportunist': ibid.
143 'to arrange for Johnny': ibid.
143 'The Germans regard': KV 2/853.
143 'We must seek to take': KV 2/854.

143 'the shabbiest and coldest': KV 2/851.
143 'My heart is in very': ibid.
143 'The chocolates': ibid.
143 'We have done our best': ibid.
144 'Tricycle has the Balkan': ibid.
144 'The one thing that': KV 2/853.
144 'his desire to do': KV 2/851.
144 'certainly no intention': ibid.
144 'he was ready to': KV 2/853.
144 'white silk shirts': KV 2/846.
144 'Tricycle is continuing': KV 2/853.
144 'Every Double Cross': Masterman, *The Double Cross System*, p. 24.
145 'invasion questions are no': KV 2/854.
145 'he ought to be': ibid.
146 'in his best mood': KV 2/853.
146 'He should be back': ibid.
146 'taken his girlfriends to': KV 2/854.
146 'active as a supply': ibid.
146 'hospital arrangements': KV 2/3639.
146 'France to be attacked': ibid.
147 'in the hope that': ibid.
147 'I gather some': CAB 154/35.
147 'But some fall into': ibid.
147 'It occurs to me': ibid.
147 'the questionnaire carried': ibid.
147 'The mere fact of': ibid.
148 'It was an inspiring': Thaddeus Holt, *The Deceivers: Allied Military Deception in the Second World War* (London, 2004), p. 488.
148 'a German coast-artillery': ibid.
148 'disappointing in the': ibid.
148 'It appears the operation': ibid., p. 489.
148 'Your activity and': Harris, *Garbo: The Spy Who Saved D-Day,* p. 147.
148 'These reports': ibid.
149 'There can be no doubt': KV2/42.
149 'looked forward to the day': Masterman, *The Double Cross System*, p. 130.
149 'the actual uses that Pigeons': CAB 154/35.

Chapter 12: Discovered Treasure
150 'sly fox': Kenneth Benton, 'The ISOS Years: Madrid 1941–3', *Journal of Contemporary History*, vol. 30, no. 3 (July 1995), pp. 359–410.
151 'rather attractive' to 'first and foremost': ibid.
151 'doubtful': ibid.
151 'I should be very': KV 2/464.
151 'She has respectable': ibid.
151 'pro-German': ibid.
151 'a White Russian': ibid.
151 'perfectly sure that': ibid.
151 'something of an adventuress': ibid.
152 'often at other people's': Memoir of Mary Sherer, unpublished, by Prue Evill, 18 July 2011.
152 'Mary was someone': ibid.
152 'She appears to be': KV 2/464.
152 'had a great deal of character': Kenneth Benton, 'The ISOS Years'.

152 'full of menace': Lily Sergueiev, *Secret Service Rendered: An Agent in the Espionage Duel Preceding the Invasion of France* (London, 1968), p. 80.
152 'I have got very': ibid., p. 91.
153 'The heat in Madrid': KV 2/466.
153 'We know a certain': Kenneth Benton, 'The ISOS Years'.
153 'Babs licks his face': Lily Sergueiev, *Secret Service Rendered*, p. 92.
153 'I look at them': ibid.
153 'It will be quite something': ibid., p. 98.
154 'thoughtfully at the space' to 'Major Kliemann, I don't care': ibid., pp. 100–105.
155 'appears to be extremely': KV 2/464.
155 'pathologically jealous': ibid.
155 'the object of Kliemann's': Kenneth Benton, 'The ISOS Years'.
155 'Whatever the truth may': Sergueiev, *Secret Service Rendered*, p. 107.
155 'purely fictitious but reassuring': KV 2/464.
155 'who was under great': ibid.
155 'What view is taken': ibid.
156 'the personification': Sergueiev, *Secret Service Rendered*, p. 10.
156 'if any harm came': KV 2/464.
156 'Naturally, should she': ibid.
156 'help and sympathy': ibid.
156 'a cheery wave': Sergueiev, *Secret Service Rendered*, p. 109.
156 'He has gone': ibid.
157 'I was getting to know': Benton, 'The ISOS Years'.
157 'Mr Benton': Sergueiev, *Secret Service Rendered*, p. 87.
157 'That's exactly it': ibid.
157 'I'll see what I can do': ibid.
157 'If my work is important' to 'You shall not': ibid., p. 88.
158 'it was going to be': Benton, 'The ISOS Years'.
158 'Get her to Gibraltar': ibid.
158 'My Gibraltar colleagues': ibid.
158 'suspicious looks': ibid.
158 'I picked up Babs': Sergueiev, *Secret Service Rendered*, p. 110.
159 'From now on': ibid.
159 'Mr Benton's promise': ibid.
159 'see to that too': ibid.
159 'Why don't you' to 'You have my word': ibid.
159 'a rich dowry': Sergueiev, *Secret Service Rendered*, p. 10.
159 'feeling of guilt': Benton, 'The ISOS Years'.
160 'After all': ibid.

Chapter 13: The Walk-in
161 'First of all a very': KV 2/859.
161 'make it clear that': ibid.
161 'absolutely sure': ibid.
161 'The way he talks': ibid.
161 'that idiot Hitler': ibid.
161 'funny smile in': ibid.
162 'some new invention': KV 2/854.
162 'with the same effect': ibid.
162 'for the first time': KV 2/859.
162 'Tricycle has just returned': KV 4/83.
163 'I consider this plan': Russell Miller, *Codename Tricycle: The True Story of the Second World War's Most Extraordinary Double Agent* (London, 2005), p. 182.

164 'His main mission': KV 4/83.
165 'used as a bedroom' to 'No, I shook them off': Kenneth Benton, 'The ISOS Years: Madrid 1941–3', *Journal of Contemporary History*, vol. 30, no. 3 (July 1995), pp. 359–410.
166 'their special fields': ibid.
166 'There is hardly': KV 2/855.
166 'During an air raid': ibid.
166 'which would spread' : Benton, 'The ISOS Years'.
166 'I'm giving you': ibid.
166 'I shall take poison': KV 2/859.
167 'piece of extreme': ibid.
167 'He was an interesting': Benton, 'The ISOS Years'.
167 'He had a great': ibid.
167 'visible shudder': ibid.
167 'trained hijack team': ibid.
167 'It is in your interest' to 'He's a prolific agent': ibid.
168 'Artist is telling you': ibid.
168 'I was very sorry': ibid.
168 'You won't have to': Lily Sergueiev, *Secret Service Rendered: An Agent in the Espionage Duel Preceding the Invasion of France* (London, 1968), p. 112.
168 'should be dealt': KV 2/465.
168 'particularly anxious': ibid.
168 'fat, with big ears': ibid.
168 'rather ill-advised': ibid.
169 'on the edge of a chair': Sergueiev, *Secret Service Rendered*, p. 119.
169 'through slightly slanted': ibid.
169 'You can be extremely': ibid., p. 123.
169 'So you are here': ibid., p. 124.
170 'We look on you': ibid., p. 125.
170 'I want you': ibid.
170 'That only leaves': ibid.
171 'I am not': ibid.
171 'rather a far cry': KV 2/464.
171 'A French citizen': KV 4/83.
171 'to be informed when': KV 2/464.
171 'very strong conviction': Benton, 'The ISOS Years'.
171 'Poor girl': Geoffrey Elliott, *Gentleman Spymaster* (London, 2011), p. 246.
171 'clean and impersonal': Sergueiev, *Secret Service Rendered*, p. 124.
171 'bleak and gloomy': ibid.
171 'plain-fronted house': ibid.
172 'What strikes me': ibid., p. 126.
172 'I still cannot quite': ibid., p. 129.

Chapter 14: A Time for Fortitude

173 'haggard with sleeplessness': Thaddeus Holt, *The Deceivers: Allied Military Deception in the Second World War* (London, 2004), p. 505.
175 'one of the best claret': ibid., p. 478.
175 'charming and witty': ibid.
175 'most tidy and meticulous': Christopher Harmer to Hugh Astor, 28 October 1992, Collection of Robert Astor.
175 'essentially a scorer': ibid.
175 'impossible and insufferable': ibid.
175 'rewrote the thing entirely': Holt, *The Deceivers*, p. 536.

176 'We had always': J. C. Masterman, *The Double Cross System in the War 1939–1945* (London, 1972), p. 149.

176 'the German General': Joshua Levine, *Operation Fortitude: The Story of the Spy Operation that Saved D-Day* (London, 2011), p. 196.

176 'An agent who turned': Masterman, *The Double Cross System,* p. 151.

177 'I have managed':   Miranda Carter, *Anthony Blunt: His Lives* (London, 2001), p. 286.

177 'Our task is to understand': ibid.

178 'all the data': ibid.

178 'far more powerful': Masterman, *The Double Cross System,* p. 148.

179 'These bats should': John Crossland, 'MI5 planned to threaten Hitler with A-bomb', *Sunday Times,* 1 December 2002.

179 'It sounds like a': ibid.

179 'our pigeon expert': CAB 154/35.

179 'began to wonder': ibid.

179 'double-cross pigeon racket': KV 4/10.

180 'Pigeon Contamination Plan': ibid.

180 'A stray or lost pigeon': ibid.

180 'throw them off': ibid.

180 'perfectly invisible joint': ibid.

181 'when aircraft were': ibid.

182 'a tall, pleasant-looking': Holt, *The Deceivers,* p. 442.

182 'audition at the': ibid.

183 'an extremely selfish': ibid., p. 456.

183 'Although he might': ibid.

184 'regarded in Berlin': KV 2/856.

184 'If liquidation means': KV 2/197.

184 'We should try': ibid.

185 'try to discredit Ostro': KV 4/66.

Chapter 15: Enriching the Chicken-feed

186 'less than beautiful': Nigel West with Juan Pujol García, *Operation Garbo* (London, 2011), p. 122.

186 'delightfully indiscreet': ibid.

186 'I would never': Tomás Harris, *The Spy Who Saved D-Day* (London, 2004), p. 290.

186 'jocular and fairly talkative': West and Pujol, *Operation Garbo,* p. 124.

187 'There is no concentration': ibid., p. 130.

188 'more military in character': KV 2/2098.

188 'radio controlled rockets': ibid.

188 'big magnetic': ibid.

188 'showed German faith': ibid.

188 'Great invasion problem': KV 2/3639.

188 'hundreds of American': ibid.

188 'Good work. Good reward': ibid.

188 'The principal': ibid.

188 'Of the cases I have': KV 2/2098.

189 'a lot of perhaps interesting': ibid.

189 'Bronx assures me': ibid.

189 'She was a British': ibid.

189 'It is absolutely': ibid.

189 'to twist our tails': ibid.

189 'She has no right': ibid.

190 'absolutely certain of': ibid.
190 'the general manager': ibid.
190 'in view of the': ibid.
190 'If it is desired to send': ibid.
191 'would appear too professional': ibid.
191 'Anxious to hush': KV 2/72.
191 'declined to give': ibid.
191 'most unorthodox proposal': ibid.
191 'Ah, but you must': ibid.
192 'her personal loyalty': ibid.
192 'peculiar circumstances': ibid.
192 'We can never guarantee': ibid.
192 'Of all the agents': ibid.
192 'dynamic and industrious': ibid.
192 'an excellent agent': ibid.
192 'become sufficiently': ibid.
193 'an enemy radio-operator': Oscar Reile, *Geheime West Front* (Munich, 1962), p. 214.
193 'a probability bordering': ibid.
193 'Not the least of my': ibid.
193 'suggested, half-jokingly': KV 2/72.
193 'send a personal message': ibid.
193 'an excellent idea': ibid.
193 'I like the suggestion': ibid.
193 'Colonel! I conceive': ibid.
194 'The Germans appear': ibid.
194 'the Germans expressed': ibid.
194 'The Brutus case could': ibid.
194 'a complete waste': ibid.
194 'We have caught your man': ibid.
195 'the opportunities': ibid.
195 'Brutus is getting questions': ibid.
195 'even better wireless': ibid.
195 'The objectives': ibid.
195 'The risks involved': ibid.
195 'The information doesn't': Lily Sergueiev, *Secret Service Rendered: An Agent in the Espionage Duel Preceding the Invasion of France* (London, 1968), p. 134.
196 'lonely countryside': ibid.
196 'For the last few months': ibid., p. 125.
196 'I don't try to': ibid., p. 135.
196 'I want to love': ibid., p. 147.
196 'There is something': ibid.
197 'very unreasonable': KV 2/465.
197 'Treasure is very': ibid.
197 'I do not quite know': ibid.
197 'her *internal* troubles': ibid.
197 'seized with a fit': Sergueiev, *Secret Service Rendered*, p. 131.
197 'You cannot be ill': ibid.
197 'Mary, it's obvious' to 'My brain is empty': ibid., pp. 135–6.
198 'Treasure is behaving': KV 2/465.
198 'It seems I won't live' to 'I don't want to die': Sergueiev, *Secret Service Rendered*, pp. 140–41.
199 'Information very interesting': KV 2/465.

199 'Why should he have': Sergueiev, *Secret Service Rendered*, p. 143.
200 'Treasure could be': KV 2/465.
200 'There is something': Sergueiev, *Secret Service Rendered*, p. 143.
200 'If we let him': KV 2/465.
200 'I believe': ibid.
200 'first-hand information': ibid.
200 'You've made Kliemann': Sergueiev, *Secret Service Rendered*, p. 151.
200 'My poor Darling': ibid., p. 146.
201 'Everything is indifferent': ibid.
201 'Report from Mary Sherer': KV 2/465.
201 'in good spirits': ibid.
202 'I can change my': Sergueiev, *Secret Service Rendered*, p. 97.

Chapter 16: Artist Paints a Picture
203 'both in quantity': KV 2/855.
203 'violently against machinations': ibid.
203 'intention of throwing': ibid.
203 'malicious': ibid.
203 'the cover under': ibid.
204 'if, as he says': KV 2/859.
204 'He was convinced': ibid.
204 'unconditionally': ibid.
204 'The fact that Johann': Guy Liddell, *The Guy Liddell Diaries, 1939–1945*, ed. Nigel West (London, 2005), 2 September 1943.
204 'A difficult situation': KV 4/83.
205 'If Artist is energetic': KV 2/855.
206 'I agree with his': ibid.
206 'interrogate him at leisure': ibid.
207 'I find myself in complete': ibid.
207 'less danger of Gestapo': Kenneth Benton, 'The ISOS Years', *Journal of Contemporary History*, vol. 30, no. 3 (July 1995), pp. 359–410.
207 'under the wing': ibid.
207 'a modest aesthete': obituary of Charles de Salis, *The Times*, 26 March 2007.
207 'an amusing raconteur': ibid.
207 'Artist is determined': KV 2/855.
208 'a very efficient': Tomás Harris, *Garbo: The Spy Who Saved D-Day* (London, 2004), p. 69.
208 'the characteristics of': KV 2/3568.
208 'set the example': ibid.
208 'were leading a rather': ibid.
208 'All had enormous': ibid.
209 'post-war job': KV 2/855.
209 'a debt of gratitude': ibid.
209 'influential friends': ibid.
209 'a discontented German': ibid.
209 'for some months': ibid.
209 'there is a whole file': ibid.
209 'the powerful backing': ibid.
209 '*was diese Juden*': ibid.
210 'Lord Rothschild has made': ibid.
210 'ingenious, but not': ibid.
210 'It might appear': ibid.

210 'After he returns': KV 2/854.
211 'in time to participate': ibid.
211 'To make him feel': KV 2/855.
211 'any action that': ibid.
211 'should anything happen': ibid.
212 'If through information': ibid.
212 'I made it clear': ibid.
212 'The Abwehr generally': KV 2/856.
212 'Himmler is the most': ibid.
212 'a living dictionary': ibid.
213 'The Baroness is very': KV 2/855.
213 'of going to a country': ibid.
213 'spun a yarn to': ibid.
213 'She immediately promised': ibid.
213 'experimental station': ibid.
213 'lazy': ibid.
213 'never disclosed to anyone': KV 2/856.
213 'full details of most': KV 2/855.
214 'He has given us': KV 2/856.
214 'He left us in no doubt': ibid.
214 'confuse Artist's state': ibid.
214 'relatively unimportant work': ibid.
214 'Artist left me with': ibid.
214 'controlled or non-existent': ibid.
214 'considerably improved': ibid.
214 'that the Gestapo': KV 2/855.
214 'kidnapping in Portugal': ibid.
214 'They have a poison': ibid.
215 'Jebsen has been': ibid.
215 'We have formed': ibid.
215 'highly complex': KV 2/856.
215 'Never let a pal down': P. G. Wodehouse, *The Code of the Woosters* (London, 1938), p. 24.
215 'He at no time spoke': KV 2/856.
215 'Artist says that': KV 2/855.
215 'Looks ten years': KV 2/861.
216 'No doubt Artist': KV 2/859.
216 'I am convinced': ibid.
216 'I hope our collaboration': ibid.
216 'The extent of Artist's': KV 2/856.
216 'Obviously if Artist': KV 2/855.
216 'I do not think': KV 2/856.
216 'Artist's zeal and ability': KV 4/83.
217 'worth his pay': KV 2/856.
217 'really valuable': ibid.
217 'good and had been': ibid.
217 'the best man': ibid.
217 'This may well have': ibid.
218 'if his work was': ibid.
218 'short of a detailed': Dusko Popov, *Spy/Counterspy* (New York, 1974), p. 185.
218 'Some batsmen are nervous': P. G. Wodehouse, 'Now, Talking About Cricket', Essay in *Tales of St Austin's: A Selection of the Early Works of P. G. Wodehouse* (London, 2008) p. 143.

218   'I shall spend': KV 2/856.
218   'dilemma': KV 2/855.
219   'helping a friend': ibid.

Chapter 17: Monty's Double

220   'a physical handicap': KV 2/3123.
221   'fell victim to a road': ibid.
221   'From then onwards': ibid.
221   'Supposing he were': ibid.
221   'bad from head': ibid.
222   'Molina has been': ibid.
222   'One of the most': ibid.
222   'Monty is rather flattered': Guy Liddell, *The Guy Liddell Diaries, 1939–1945*, ed. Nigel West (London, 2005), 6 May 1944.
223   'I ought to shoot': Olivier Wieviorka, *Normandy: The landings to the liberation of Paris*, (London, 2008), p. 79.
223   'There's no such': Stanley Hirshon, *General Patton: A Soldier's Life* (New York, 2002), p. 203.
223   'that's the best': Thaddeus Holt, *The Deceivers: Allied Military Deception in the Second World War* (London, 2004), p. 541.
223   'a goddam natural': Joshua Levine, *Operation Fortitude: The Story of the Spy Operation that Saved D-Day* (London, 2011), p. 229.
223   'see you in the': ibid.
223   'I am thoroughly': ibid., p. 231.
223   'it is the evident destiny': ibid.
224   'strange mental attitude': ibid., p. 221.
224   'As time went on': ibid.
224   'zone of destiny': Henrik O. Lunde, *Hitler's Pre-Emptive War: The Battle for Norway, 1940* (London, 2010), p. 550.
226   '98 per cent': KV 4/70.
227   'It has been suggested': KV 2/856.
227   'No ban': ibid.
227   'passed fit': J. C. Masterman, *The Double Cross System in the War 1939–1945* (London, 1972), p. 153.
228   'once confined to': ibid., p. 154.
228   'it was not impossible': ibid., p. 155.
228   'In short, the German turncoat': ibid., p. 157.
228   'gnawing anxiety': ibid., p. 132.
228   'The whole existence': ibid., p. 153.
228   'I can't believe': Holt, *The Deceivers*, p. 538.

Chapter 18: The Double Dash

229   'You cannot baldly': J. C. Masterman, *The Double Cross System in the War 1939–1945* (London, 1972), p. 114.
229   'He had a good reason': Roger Hesketh, *Fortitude: The D-Day Deception Campaign* (London, 1999), p. 126.
230   'Your latest wires': ibid.
230   'to increase the efficiency': KV 2/72.
230   'Urgently require': ibid.
230   'Many thanks for your hard': ibid.
230   'whether the lack': ibid.
230   'I have complete': ibid.
231   'He is a man who': ibid.

231 'amplification of your network': Nigel West with Juan Pujol García, *Operation Garbo* (London, 2011), p. 137.

231 'giving the best results': ibid., p. 138.

231 'would not happen' : ibid.

231 'until an assault force': ibid.

231 'I am surprised to hear': ibid.

232 'An extensive programme': KV 2/863.

232 'a lot of work': ibid.

232 'His stock is very high': KV 2/856.

232 'mass of detailed': ibid.

232 'the landing in Western Europe': ibid.

232 'the best in the whole': ibid.

232 'Their chief hope': ibid.

232 'It is quite possible': ibid.

232 'containing a wealth': KV 2/857.

233 'very important': KV 2/2098.

233 'Important. Invasion details': KV 2/3639.

234 'She is independent': KV 2/2098.

234 'a good-time girl': ibid.

234 'In order to achieve': ibid.

234 'indicate to the Germans': ibid.

234 'providing a get-out': ibid.

234 'ludicrous': ibid.

234 'I told her I consider': ibid.

234 'Sometimes Louisa': Lily Sergueiev, *Secret Service Rendered: An Agent in the Espionage Duel Preceding the Invasion of France* (London, 1968), p. 196.

234 'a polite little laugh': ibid., p. 207.

235 'Robertson and his gang': ibid., p. 159.

235 'If Kliemann questions' to 'I am absolutely': ibid., p. 180.

235 'a slim, fair youngster': ibid., p. 157.

235 'Berlin were very pleased': KV 2/464.

235 'get the sack': ibid.

235 'Kliemann is a saboteur': Sergueiev, *Secret Service Rendered*, p. 164.

236 'very excited': ibid., p. 170.

236 'Our friend is here!': ibid.

236 'He looks much': ibid., p. 175

236 'My stock has gone': ibid., p. 173

236 'lazy and impertinent': ibid.

236 'shabby': KV 2/464.

236 'Here are the two': Sergueiev, *Secret Service Rendered*, p. 175.

237 'Berlin was very': KV 2/465.

237 'It is a very worrying': ibid.

237 'The situation is quite': Sergueiev, *Secret Service Rendered*, p. 180.

237 'What about a': ibid., p. 178.

237 'What a good idea': ibid.

238 'at midday tomorrow' to 'Now listen to me': ibid., pp. 179–182.

238 'everything seen in': ibid.

238 'Information obtained': ibid.

238 'I want the transmissions': ibid.

239 'These are the instructions': ibid.

239 'What is our hold': ibid., p. 183.

239 'My parents are still': ibid.

239 'I would like to': ibid., p. 182.

239　'planned to hide': ibid.
240　'this was a wise': ibid.
240　'We must take': ibid., p. 187.
240　'If she was discovered': ibid.
240　'silly': ibid.
240　'the British would': ibid.
240　'At the beginning': ibid.
240　'That's excellent': ibid., p. 188.
240　'*Strich zwischen*': ibid.
241　'Even if it meant': ibid., p. 173.
241　'I would rather go': ibid.
241　'Five months ago': ibid., p. 188.
241　'He must be daft': ibid., p. 192.
242　'So here you are' : ibid., p. 193.
242　'indistinguishable from' KV 2/465.
242　'I have nothing': ibid.
242　'What would he do': Sergueiev, *Secret Service Rendered*, p. 190.
242　'I am absolutely sure': ibid.
242　'Treasure gave a': KV 2/465.
242　'no suggestion for': KV 2/464.
242　'She states she': ibid.
243　'Arrived Safely': Sergueiev, *Secret Service Rendered*, p. 197.
243　'Every time I know': ibid., p. 200.

Chapter 19: Jebsen's New Friend
244　'even an account': KV 2/856.
244　'no authority from C': ibid.
244　'seriously and earnestly': KV 2/855.
244　'This proposal sounds': ibid.
245　'P. G. Wodehouse and his': KV 2/856.
245　'anti-Nazi and': ibid.
245　'telegram saying': ibid.
246　'fascinated by his intelligence': KV 2/861.
246　'seemingly inexhaustible': ibid.
246　'I am His Majesty's': ibid.
246　'Friendship goes': ibid.
246　'*macaco*': KV 2/856.
246　'Although he had': ibid.
246　'saying his department': ibid.
246　'infatuated': ibid.
246　'Schreiber has written': KV 2/855.
246　'Jebsen's nervousness': KV 2/856.
247　'known to give as': KV 2/3295.
247　'He is personally': ibid.
247　'He is supposed to': ibid.
247　'hold over': KV 2/856.
247　'His bribes go a long': KV 2/858.
247　'With a great deal': KV 2/856.
247　'He made no secret': ibid.
247　'Relations between Artist': ibid.
248　'try to persuade Canaris': ibid.
248　'the organisation he': KV 2/3295.
248　'deliberate fraud': ibid.

248 'He is only twenty-four': ibid.
248 'constructive fantasy': ibid.
248 'enough confidence in': KV 2/856.
248 'had not done': ibid.
248 'slippery opportunist': KV 2/857.
248 'If he knew the': KV 2/856.
248 'I think Brandes': KV 2/3295.
248 'lift the veto': KV 2/856.
249 'the downfall of': ibid.
249 'Further dismissals': KV 2/855.
249 'new brooms would': J. C. Masterman, *The Double Cross System in the War 1939–1945* (London, 1972), p. 156.
250 'Jebsen tried to': KV 2/861.
250 'he was on friendly': ibid.
250 'the old fox': KV 2/857.
250 'younger and more': KV 2/855.
250 'He is not a Nazi': ibid.
250 'The new officers': ibid.
250 'a little uneasy': ibid.
250 'wide awake': ibid.
250 'the most intelligent': ibid.
251 'elderly men with': KV 2/410.
251 'discharging its functions': ibid.
251 'shocked at the': ibid.
251 'an extremely able': ibid.
251 'rather fishy': KV 2/855.
251 'removed and': KV 2/410.
251 'sleeping secretaries': KV 2/857.
251 'This brothel must': ibid.
251 'indiscretion and inefficiency': ibid.
251 'His specific duties': KV 2/3568.
251 'the possibility of Allied': ibid.
251 'pedantic and ambitious': ibid.
251 'Schreiber is not a': KV 2/856.
252 'on suspicion of aiding': KV 2/3568.
252 'his general political': ibid.
252 'Something was being': ibid.
252 'belonged to the group': ibid.
252 'he was sent to Portugal': ibid.
252 'the names of Abwehr': KV 2/856.
252 'We must reckon': ibid.
252 'Berlin has ordered': ibid.
252 'Artist's friends': ibid.
253 'defended him strongly': KV 2/857.
253 'The clouds are': ibid.
253 'Artist in extremely': ibid.
253 'exert his influence': ibid.
253 'take no steps': ibid.
253 'up-to-date details': ibid.
253 'had a very great': ibid.
254 'assisted him cleverly': ibid.
254 'he was sure': ibid.
254 'an excellent agent': KV 2/72.

254 'His first interview': KV 4/83.
254 'particularly valuable': Roger Hesketh, *Fortitude: The D-Day Deception Campaign* (London, 1999), p. 112.
254 'in funds': KV 2/857.
254 'long-term contact': KV 2/856.
254 'to be regarded': ibid.
255 'He is afraid that': KV 2/858.
255 'Although convinced that': ibid.
255 'He is keen to': KV 2/857.
255 'Kühlenthal's controlled': ibid.
255 'the Spaniards': ibid.
255 'brought word back': ibid.
255 'Ivan [Popov] is now': ibid.
255 'The confidence in': ibid.
255 'common for members': ibid.
255 'He is certain that': ibid.
256 'Brandes is playing': ibid.
256 'Brandes is clearly': ibid.

Chapter 20: 'Am I Not Always Careful?'

257 '*one* division to hesitate': Tomás Harris, *Garbo: The Spy Who Saved D-Day* (London, 2004), p. 183.
257 'increase the percentage': ibid., p. 176.
258 'military expert': KV 2/858.
258 'credible Abwehr source': Roger Hesketh, *Fortitude: The D-Day Deception Campaign* (London, 1999), p. 95.
258 'He is very well regarded': KV 2/72.
258 'If Brutus were posted': ibid.
258 'on account of his': KV 2/72.
258 'set up under FUSAG': Hesketh, *Fortitude*, p. 126.
259 'the opinions of': KV 2/3639.
259 'Montgomery's HQ may': ibid.
259 'large invasion stores': ibid.
259 'roads to beaches': ibid.
259 'believes Denmark place': ibid.
259 'Invasion seems imminent': ibid.
259 'Many US troops': ibid.
259 'Prime Minister's': ibid.
259 'I make imaginary visits': Lily Sergueiev, *Secret Service Rendered: An Agent in the Espionage Duel Preceding the Invasion of France* (London, 1968), p. 204.
259 'In this world of': ibid.
260 'For three years I': ibid., p. 153.
260 'She is working hard': KV 2/465.
260 'I don't think it would': Sergueiev, *Secret Service Rendered*, p. 201.
260 'The furniture, fittings': KV 2/465.
260 'the German intelligence': Sergueiev, *Secret Service Rendered*, p. 206.
260 'three shoes (not pairs)': KV 2/465.
260 'I think we ought': ibid.
261 'We owe nothing': ibid.
261 'Treasure is not a money': ibid.
261 'exceptionally temperamental': J. C. Masterman, *The Double Cross System in the War 1939–1945* (London, 1972), p. 174.
261 'It is very difficult not': Sergueiev, *Secret Service Rendered*, p. 201.

261 'meticulous accounts': ibid., p. 196.
261 'any further activities': KV 2/861.
262 'uncomfortable feeling': KV 2/860.
262 'as it seemed': ibid.
262 'outrageous': KV 2/857.
262 'stay in London': ibid.
262 'send some lower-grade': ibid.
262 'I just wanted': Dusko Popov, *Spy/Counterspy* (New York, 1974), p. 245.
262 'Tricycle is now': KV 2/857.
262 'What are Churchill's': ibid.
262 'personally agreeable': KV 2/856.
263 'not unduly worried': KV 2/857.
263 'it was much': ibid.
263 'sending a representative': ibid.
263 'These allegations have nothing': ibid.
263 'free from danger': ibid.
263 'trying to find out about': KV 2/860.
263 'learns everything': ibid.
263 'As cannot continue': ibid.
264 'might be playing': KV 2/857.
264 'possibly with the': ibid.
264 'to France for': KV 2/858.
264 'worming, or bribing': ibid.
264 'It may well be that': ibid.
264 'very jealous of the': KV 2/860.
264 'Strong impression that': KV 2/857.
265 'absolutely no doubts': ibid.
265 'hasty in assuming': KV 2/858.
265 'his cover': ibid.
265 'should be looked': KV 2/857.
265 'would be considered': ibid.
265 'On the 17th Johnny': ibid.
265 'a routine reduction': ibid.
265 'all secretaries': KV 2/858.
266 'Three days after': KV 2/861.
266 'Artist does not': KV 2/857.
266 'He feels very': ibid.
266 'Further traps of this': ibid.
266 'large-scale invasion': ibid.
266 'whether Norway': ibid.
266 'decisive': ibid.
266 'Tricycle's reports have': ibid.
267 'Artist is confident': ibid.
267 'Am I not always': obituary of Charles de Salis, *The Times*, 26 March 2007.
267 'A telegram which has': KV 2/858.
267 'telegram conveyed': ibid.
267 'while Artist considered': ibid.
267 'solely with financial': KV 2/859.
267 'take a bold line': KV 2/857.
267 'desire to expose': ibid.
268 'too complicated': ibid.
268 'Brandes is clearly': ibid.
268 'I see no reason': ibid.

268 'brook no further': KV 2/858.
268 'received immediate': ibid.
268 'Artist considers this': ibid.
268 'He now believes': ibid.
269 'You will know': KV 2/857.
269 'The agent Tricycle': KV 4/83.
269 'confirmed that everything': KV 2/858.
270 'From Artist's point': ibid.
270 'To crown it all': ibid.
270 'A proof of the fact': ibid.
270 'Knowing your mentality': ibid.
271 'I hope you will': ibid.
271 'in a very good': ibid.
271 'The carrying out of': KV 2/3568.
272 'full of praise': Guy Liddell, *The Guy Liddell Diaries, 1939–1945*, ed. Nigel West (London, 2005), 26 April 1944.
272 'I think he realises': ibid.
272 'all those present': ibid.
272 'It was unknown': ibid.

Chapter 21: Operation Dora
273 'to Berlin by force': KV 2/3568.
273 'They would be knocked': ibid.
274 'Both of them': ibid.
274 'border conditions': ibid.
274 'a few rests': ibid.
274 'Mission has been': ibid.
274 'Luggage handed': ibid.
274 'Many thanks for': KV 2/858.
274 'provoked considerable': KV 2/410.
274 'Jebsen's desertion': ibid.
274 'to see personally': KV 2/3568.
274 'Berlin had proof': KV 2/861.
274 'seeking to take': ibid.
275 'a police matter': KV 2/3568.
275 'were to know anything': ibid.
275 'Once Jebsen was': ibid.
275 'accept full responsibility': ibid.
275 'specifically charging': KV 2/861.
275 'left entirely up to': KV 2/3568.
275 'status of a British dominion': KV 2/410.
275 'the man to put': ibid.
275 'instruct Kuebart in': ibid.
276 'arranged for someone': ibid.
276 'pounce on the Abwehr': ibid.
276 'put an end to': ibid.
276 'The Vermehren case': KV 2/860.
276 'one of a number': KV 2/859.
276 'If innocent': KV 2/861.
277 'in order to ensure': KV 2/3568.
277 'large enough for a': ibid.
277 'Artist has disappeared': KV 2/860.
277 'This has clearly been': KV 2/858.

277 'taken to France': ibid.
278 'afraid that Jebsen': KV 2/857.
278 'A number of messages': KV 2/858.
278 'Artist's present troubles': ibid.
278 'the one agent of real': KV 2/857.
278 'All the parties involved': KV 2/858.
279 'The next few days': ibid.
279 'The cover plan has': ibid.
280 'deprived of all': ibid.
280 'if, and only if': ibid.
280 'The confidence which': ibid.
281 'the same night': ibid.
281 'without our getting': ibid.
281 'Packing up Tricycle': Guy Liddell, The Guy Liddell Diaries, 1939–1945, ed. Nigel West (London, 2005), 10 May 1944.
281 'to deduce the cover plan': KV 2/858.
281 'lengthy and exhaustive': ibid.
281 'I maintain that the': ibid.
281 'In the hands': Roger Hesketh, Fortitude: The D-Day Deception Campaign (London, 1999), p. 111.
282 'Why lead me up': KV 2/859.
282 'respect for 23700': ibid.
282 'would have been': ibid.
282 'the most flagrant': ibid.
282 'If I cannot': ibid.
282 'No one can have': ibid.
283 'Anthony Blunt told me': Guy Liddell, Diaries, 10 May 1944.
283 'by trick or by': KV 2/858.
284 'Jebsen was a mine': KV 2/859.
284 'There has been': KV4/83.
284 'near-panic': Sefton Delmer, The Counterfeit Spy (London, 1973), p. 160.
284 'would undoubtedly put': Guy Liddell, Diaries, 10 May 1944.
285 'This gives us': ibid., 18 May 1944.
285 'certain inquiries': ibid.
285 'After D-Day we': Thaddeus Holt, The Deceivers: Allied Military Deception in the Second World War (London, 2004), p. 565.
285 'Under interrogation': J. C. Masterman, The Double Cross System in the War 1939–1945 (London, 1972), p. 159.
286 'We do not know': KV 2/858.

Chapter 22: Guest of the Gestapo

287 'erudite, imaginative': David Kahn, Hitler's Spies: German Military Intelligence in World War II (New York, 1978), p. 424.
288 'jolly, easy, happy': ibid. See also Anthony Cave Brown, Bodyguard of Lies, vol. 1 (London, 1976), p. 497.
288 'the opinions held': ibid., p. 496.
290 'To Newmarket for': KV 2/3639.
290 'a heavier burden' J. C. Masterman, The Double Cross System in the War 1939–1945 (London, 1972), p. 159.
290 'hide the facts': Nigel West with Juan Pujol García, Operation Garbo (London, 2011), p. 151.
291 'Have found first-class': Roger Hesketh, Fortitude: The D-Day Deception Campaign (London, 1999), p. 121.

291 'under duress': Guy Liddell, *The Guy Liddell Diaries, 1939–1945*, ed. Nigel West (London, 2005), 15 May 1944.
292 'report whether': KV 2/859.
292 'French money Dora': ibid.
292 'no evidence to prove': ibid.
292 'are consistent with': ibid.
293 'If Brandes could': ibid.
293 'I do not agree': ibid.
293 'I feel a strong': KV 2/860.
293 'being introduced to': KV 2/858.
293 'stop drawing attention': ibid.
294 'had a paternal interest': KV 2/859.
294 'This was not the': ibid.
294 'I wish to convey': KV 2/860.
294 'a written report': KV 2/859.
294 'It seems to me': ibid.
294 'There is still': ibid.
294 'arrangements for their': KV 2/860.
294 'the captive at the': KV 2/858.
294 'as Jebsen was a soldier': KV 2/860.
295 'did his best to': ibid.
295 'brusque ultimatum': KV 2/861.
295 'One really ought': Christopher Hudson, 'Architects of Genocide', *Daily Mail*, 19 January 2002.
295 'produced a great': KV 2/860.
295 'having betrayed': KV 2/861.
295 'engaging in large-scale': KV 2/859.
295 'got into difficulties': ibid.
296 'Certain sizeable': ibid.
296 'Some SS officials': ibid.
296 'improperly converting SD': ibid.
296 'accused of working for Britain': KV 2/860.
296 'Because of good': ibid.
297 'Communists, Marxists': Rebecca Wittmann, *Beyond Justice: The Auschwitz Trial* (Harvard, 2005), p. 120.
297 'in a highly nervous': KV 2/860.
297 'caught a glimpse of': Dusko Popov, *Spy/Counterspy* (New York, 1974), p. 261.
297 'typical concentration': ibid.
297 'His flesh and muscle': ibid.
298 'Violence is taboo': https://www.mi5.gov.uk/output/bad-nenndorf.html

Chapter 23: Bronx Gets Toothache

299 'there is still no': KV 4/83.
299 'transmitted his 1,000th': ibid.
299 'remind the Germans': KV 2/72.
299 'not very intelligent': ibid.
300 'Colonel, please forgive': ibid.
300 'functioning flawlessly': KV 2/464.
300 'The messages of Treasure': KV 4/83.
300 'have, at a critical moment': ibid.
300 'I always cry in': Lily Sergueiev, *Secret Service Rendered: An Agent in the Espionage Duel Preceding the Invasion of France* (London, 1968), p. 207.

300 'Mary crying at the': ibid.
301 'I didn't mean to': ibid., p. 205.
301 'The landing is very' to 'You realise I': ibid.
301 'Sergeyev made a': KV 2/466.
302 'In spite of Sergeyev's': ibid.
302 'We see no particular': Guy Liddell, *The Guy Liddell Diaries, 1939–1945*, ed. Nigel West (London, 2005), 28 May 1944.
303 'Treasure is in a position': KV 2/466.
303 '*Envoyez vite*': KV 2/2098.
304 'After a cocktail party': ibid.
305 'wearing battledress': ibid.
305 'Hello, Monty': KV 2/3123.
305 'Hello, Rusty': ibid.
305 'His interest in happening': ibid.
305 'with well-feigned': ibid.
305 'played his difficult': ibid.
305 'You *are* Monty': ibid.
305 'His Excellency was': ibid.
305 'The material reached': ibid.
305 'The Governor introduced': ibid.
305 'very satisfied with': ibid.
306 'General Montgomery': ibid.
306 'might point towards': ibid.
306 'a little too early': Liddell, *Diaries*, 28 May 1944.
306 'had gone through': KV 2/3123.
306 'He was under': Thaddeus Holt, *The Deceivers: Allied Military Deception in the Second World War* (London, 2004), p. 562.
306 'Coming out of that': ibid.
307 'more Nazi than': Reinhard R. Doerries, Gerhard L. Weinberg, *Hitler's Intelligence Chief: Walter Schellenberg* (New York, 2009), p. 99.
308 'lateral shell fire': Charles Fenyvesi, 'Japan's Unwitting D-Day Spy', *Washington Post*, 26 May 1998.
308 'Our main basis': ibid.
308 'This place is mine': Ignatius Phayre, 'Hitler's Mountain Home', *Homes & Gardens*, November 1938.
308 'filled with a curious': ibid.
308 'Our attitude cannot': *Trial of German Major War Criminals*, vol. 3, p. 387.
309 'What is your feeling' to 'Well, judging': Holt, *The Deceivers*, p. 566.
309 'It gave the first': Roger Hesketh, *Fortitude: The D-Day Deception Campaign* (London, 1999), p. 194.

Chapter 24: Garbo's Warning
311 'The south coast': Roderick Bailey, *Forgotten Voices of D-Day* (London, 2010), p. 38.
311 'Gather round me': ibid., p. 48.
311 'unreal feeling': ibid., p. 66.
311 'Everything was totally': ibid.
312 'great crusade': http://www.eisenhowermemorial.org/legacyreport/military-legacy.htm
312 'failed to gain a': ibid.
312 'The troops': ibid.
312 'Do you realise': Tony Hall, Bernard C. Nalty, *D-Day: The Strategy, The Men, The Equipment* (London, 2002), p. 8.

312 'drew all the loose': Roger Hesketh, *Fortitude: The D-Day Deception Campaign* (London, 1999), p. 176.
312 'the entire chain': ibid.
312 'the impression of being': Thaddeus Holt, *The Deceivers: Allied Military Deception in the Second World War* (London, 2004), p. 550.
313 'destined for an attack': Hesketh, *Fortitude*, p. 190.
313 'imaginary Order of Battle': ibid.
313 'self-trained military reporter': Tomás Harris, *Garbo: The Spy Who Saved D-Day* (London, 2004), p. 189.
313 'I conclude that the': ibid., p. 188.
313 'indicates the possibility': ibid.
313 'The main enemy': ibid.
313 'Further transfer': ibid.
313 'According to a': Harris, *Garbo: The Spy Who Saved D-Day*, p. 188.
314 'sustained diet of high-grade': Hesketh, *Fortitude*, p. 187.
314 'By the date of the': ibid.
314 'Ostro, in a long message': Guy Liddell, *The Guy Liddell Diaries, 1939–1945*, ed. Nigel West (London, 2005), 5 June 1944.
316 'He has told me': Juan Pujol and Nigel West, *Operation Garbo* (London, 2011), p. 154.
316 'All right Sergeant': Sefton Delmer, *The Counterfeit Spy* (London, 1973), p. 176.
316 'I don't get it': ibid., p. 177.
317 'The trouble is': ibid.
317 'We saw a lorry-load': Bailey, *Forgotten Voices of D-Day*, p. 192.
318 'improbable': David Kahn, *Hitler's Spies: German Military Intelligence in World War II* (New York, 1978), p. 512.
318 'That the invasion': Holt, *The Deceivers*, p. 579.
318 'Don't make a big': ibid.
318 'I'm too old a bunny': Kahn, *Hitler's Spies*, p. 513.
319 'inhuman wall of fire': Bailey, *Forgotten Voices of D-Day*, p. 269.
320 'His name might': KV 4/10.
320 'The invasion army': Montague Taylor, 'Carrier Pigeons Ready', *Belfast Telegraph,* 6 June 1944.
320 'We are just 20': ibid.

Chapter 25: Second Innings
322 'Just keep the Fifteenth': Thaddeus Holt, *The Deceivers: Allied Military Deception in the Second World War* (London, 2004), p. 579.
322 'Unfortunately, by remaining': Roger Hesketh, *Fortitude: The D-Day Deception Campaign* (London, 1999), p. 148.
323 'Distraught by the': KV 2/3639.
323 'This makes me question': Nigel West with Juan Pujol García, *Operation Garbo* (London, 2011), p. 161.
323 'I wish to stress in': ibid., p. 162.
324 'the first of a series': Christopher Andrew, *The Defence of the Realm: The Authorised History of MI5* (London, 2009), p. 305.
324 'attack across the Channel': Hesketh, *Fortitude,* p. 199.
324 'Fortitude requires a threat': KV 2/72.
324 'It is clear that': Hesketh, *Fortitude*, p. 199.
324 'advanced state of': ibid.
324 'I never like': Tomás Harris, *Garbo: The Spy Who Saved D-Day* (London, 2004), p. 188.
325 'After personal consultation': West with Pujol, *Operation Garbo*, p. 166.

325 'left with some': ibid.
325 'I trust you will': ibid.
326 'The report is credible': ibid., p. 167.
326 'Only part of Allied': KV 2/3639.
326 'Lord Stanley of Alderney': ibid.
326 'Fruit spoiled by frosts': ibid.
327 'absolutely saved the': KV 2/72.
327 'I have some hard' to 'I didn't say we': Lily Sergueiev, *Secret Service Rendered: An Agent in the Espionage Duel Preceding the Invasion of France* (London, 1968), pp. 209–11.
328 'big scene from': ibid., p. 209.
328 'Why did you': ibid., p. 212.
328 'I refuse to be': ibid.
328 'Ducky, that's': ibid., p. 213.
328 'I have destroyed': ibid., p. 212.
329 'inviting the Germans' to 'appetising dish': KV 2/72.
330 'what they deduced': KV 2/3123.
331 'small calibre': Holt, *The Deceivers*, p. 561.
331 'diversionary attack': ibid.
331 'When the invasion': J. C. Masterman, *The Double Cross System in the War 1939–1945* (London, 1972), p. 167.
331 'Their movement of': KV 2/72.
331 'impotent near Bordeaux': personal account of Elvira Chaudoir, collection of Robert Astor.
331 'We are prepared': KV 4/247.
332 'contain some': Joshua Levine, *Operation Fortitude: The Story of the Spy Operation that Saved D-Day* (London, 2011), p. 224.
332 'another landing': Holt, *The Deceivers*, p. 582.
333 '99 per cent': Levine, *Operation Fortitude*, p. 285.
333 'provided the reason': ibid.
333 'twenty-three divisions': Thaddeus Holt, *The Deceivers*, p. 581.
333 'It was almost': Guy Liddell, *The Guy Liddell Diaries, 1939–1945*, ed. Nigel West (London, 2005), 30 June 1944.
333 'Patton's army group': Holt, *The Deceivers*, p. 582.
333 'Patton's forces will': ibid.
333 'reposed an almost': KV 4/247.
333 'still could not': ibid.
333 'has not been given': Holt, *The Deceivers*, p. 589.
334 'A second major landing': ibid.
334 'every additional': Terry Crowdy, *Deceiving Hitler: Double Cross and Deception in World War II* (London, 2008), p. 272.
334 'decisive mistake': Holt, *The Deceivers*, p. 589.
334 'All this Patton': Levine, *Operation Fortitude*, p. 295.
334 'Were all those divisions': ibid.
334 'We knew that you': KV 4/247.
335 'unparalleled blunder': Crowdy, *Deceiving Hitler*, p. 272.
335 'might well have': Andrew, *Defence of the Realm*, p. 309.
335 'I cannot overemphasise': ibid.
335 'The deception measures': ibid.
335 'It seems from': KV4/83.
336 'We were not very': Masterman, *The Double Cross System,* p. 148.
336 'the greatest Test': Norman Holmes Pearson, introduction to Masterman, *The Double Cross System.*

336 'the most successful': Holt, *The Deceivers*, p. 590.
336 'one of the most': Kim Philby, *My Silent War* (London, 1968), p. 17.
336 'With great happiness': West with Pujol, *Operation Garbo*, p. 183.
337 'I cannot at this moment': ibid., p. 184.

Aftermath
338 'studied not only by': KV 2/72.
338 'We shall presently': ibid.
338 'worked valiantly for': ibid.
338 'Nobody here believes': ibid.
339 'Once again I thank': ibid.
339 'to recruit and organise': ibid.
340 'On Nationale 3': ibid.
340 'Polish government set up': ibid.
340 'withdrawn air of': Lily Mathilde Carré, *I Was the Cat* (London, 1960), p. 10.
341 'What I wanted most': ibid., p. 132.
341 'nightmares with': ibid., p. 202.
341 'harmless literary': ibid., p. 219.
341 'committed to achieve': ibid., p. 175.
341 'I don't know how': Roman Garby-Czerniawski, *The Big Network* (London, 1961), p. 246.
341 'OK, you win': Lily Sergueiev, *Secret Service Rendered: An Agent in the Espionage Duel Preceding the Invasion of France* (London, 1968), p. 214.
342 'Is that all': ibid.
342 'I will be able': ibid., p. 223.
342 'My joy has no': KV 2/465.
342 'I've lost my solitary': ibid.
342 'You may find': ibid.
342 'I don't honestly': ibid.
342 'She will always': ibid.
343 'unbelievable reality': Sergueiev, *Secret Service Rendered*, p. 7.
343 'We have in your personality': Nigel West with Juan Pujol García, *Operation Garbo* (London, 2011), p. 200.
343 'The noble struggle': ibid., p. 207.
343 'They cannot hope': ibid., p. 204.
343 'His deeds and': ibid., p. 206.
343 'I am certain': ibid.
343 'selling': Emily Wilson, 'The War in the Dark: The Security Service and the Abwehr 1940–1944', PhD Thesis (Cambridge, 2003), p. 227.
344 'No one knew': West with Pujol, *Operation Garbo*, p. 216.
345 'My main pride': ibid., p. 217.
345 'Bronx is the': KV 2/2098.
345 'They will take': ibid.
345 'It is quite evident': ibid.
345 'Good work': ibid.
345 'learn as much': ibid.
345 'I believe that': ibid.
346 'if any mishap': ibid.
346 'in cheerful heart': ibid.
346 'Absolutely livid': ibid.
346 'parachuting to the': ibid.
346 'It is difficult to': J. C. Masterman, *The Double Cross System in the War 1939–1945* (London, 1972), p. 167.

346 'eagerly await': KV 2/2098.
346 'to lower the German' : ibid.
347 'Guerrillas will': ibid.
347 'Her long-term': ibid.
347 'Words of gratitude': ibid.
347 'a way of making': Stella Rimington to Hugh Astor, 6 November 1995, Collection of Robert Astor.
347 'I recall the adventure': Nigel West, 'High Society Spy', *Mail on Sunday*, 7 May 1995.
347 'I am getting fed up': KV 2/861.
347 'young and pretty': ibid.
347 'apparently entering': ibid.
347 'I will try to do': ibid.
348 'in deceiving the': ibid.
348 'We are making': ibid.
348 'His activities have': ibid.
350 'perfect foils for': Memoir of Mary Sherer by Prue Evill, 18 July 2011.
350 'Mary was a very': ibid.
350 'the Lionesses': ibid.
350 'all of which': ibid.
350 'signalise its performance': KV 4/10.
350 'There is no doubt': Emily Wilson, 'The War in the Dark', p. 228.
350 'They will be a great': ibid.
351 'whisky and concentrated': 'Anthony Blunt: Confessions of a spy who passed secrets to Russia during the war', *Daily Telegraph*, 28 May 2010.
351 'the biggest mistake': ibid.
351 'It has given me': Chapman Pincher, *Too Secret Too Long* (London, 1984), p. 351.
351 'respected judge': obituary of Wulf Schmidt, *Daily Mail*, 28 October 1992.
351 'somewhat shifty': KV 2/278.
352 'very proud and': ibid.
352 'He has no idea': Guy Liddell, *The Guy Liddell Diaries, 1939–1945*, ed. Nigel West (London, 2005), 22 October 1944.
352 'sharp and ruthless': KV 2/278.
352 'arrest various Nazis': KV 2/410.
352 'made difficulties': ibid.
352 'tissue of lies': ibid.
352 'small clique of': ibid.
353 'he considered the': ibid.
353 'Defend Berlin to': 'US may have used Gestapo chief as cold war warrior', *Sunday Times*, 8 April 2001.
354 'a poor, half-Jewish': KV 2/3295.
354 'pure whitewash': ibid.
354 'grave miscarriage': ibid.
354 'Brandes was mixed': ibid.
354 'his hair had': Dusko Popov, *Spy/Counterspy* (New York, 1974), p. 261.
354 'until she attracted': KV 2/861.
354 'he told her that': ibid.
355 'who wolves have': Saki, *The Unbearable Bassington* (first published 1912; London, 2008), p. 108.
355 'JOHNNY JEBSEN HUN': Communications from Lt Cdr Cumberlege, Code 92 File 10046 FO 371/48935.
356 'I can make': ibid.

356 'my personal wish': KV 2/860.
356 'I do feel that': KV 2/861.
356 'My old friend Johnny': KV 2/860.
357 'assurance we gave': ibid.
357 'She will be able': KV 2/861.
357 'We have no financial': KV 2/862.
357 'None of these people': KV 2/859.
357 'had not extracted': ibid.
357 'who would be': KV 2/860.
357 'If you have luck': ibid.
358 'know everything about': ibid.
358 'how the NKVD could': ibid.
358 'We do not know whether': ibid.
358 'what actually happened': KV 2/861.
358 'which was the normal': ibid.
358 'shot while trying': Popov, *Spy/Counterspy*, p. 263.
358 'She refuses to': KV 2/861.
358 'the last person': ibid.
358 'emphatic that he did': ibid.
358 'was liberated by': Sefton Delmer, *The Counterfeit Spy* (London, 1973), p. 162.
358 'Johnny Jebson': KV 2/860.
358 'Jebsen has not': ibid.
358 'kept the faith': Delmer, *The Counterfeit Spy*, p. 164.

Select Bibliography

Archives

British Library Newspaper Archive, Colindale
Bundesarchiv-Militärarchiv, Freiburg
Churchill Archives Centre, Churchill College, Cambridge
IWM Archives, Imperial War Museum, London
National Archives, Kew
National Archives, Washington DC

Published Sources

Andrew, Christopher, *Secret Service: The Making of the British Intelligence Community* (London, 1985)
———————— *The Defence of the Realm: The Authorised History of MI5* (London, 2009)
Bailey, Roderick, *Forgotten Voices of D-Day* (London, 2010)
Barbier, Mary Kathryn, *D-Day Deception: Operation Fortitude and the Normandy Invasion* (Mechanicsburg, PA, 2009)
Barreiros, José António, *Nathalie Sergueiew: Uma Agente Dupla em Lisboa* (Lisbon, 2006)
Beesley, Patrick, *Very Special Admiral: The Life of Admiral J. H. Godfrey* (London, 1980)
Beevor, Antony, *D-Day* (London, 2009)
Bennett, Gill, *Churchill's Man of Mystery: Desmond Morton and the World of Intelligence* (London, 2007)
Bennett, Ralph, *Behind the Battle: Intelligence in the War with Germany 1939–45* (London, 1999)

——————*Ultra and Mediterranean Strategy 1941–1945* (London, 1989)

Benton, Kenneth, 'The ISOS Years: Madrid 1941–3', *Journal of Contemporary History*, vol. 30, no. 3 (July 1995)

Bower, Tom, *The Perfect English Spy: Sir Dick White and the Secret War, 1935–1990* (London, 1995)

Bristow, Desmond, with Bill Bristow, *A Game of Moles: The Deceptions of an MI6 Officer* (London, 1993)

Carré, Lily Mathilde, *I Was the Cat* (London, 1960)

Carter, Miranda, *Anthony Blunt: His Lives* (London, 2001)

Cave Brown, Anthony, *Bodyguard of Lies*, vol. 1 (London, 1975)

Crowdy, Terry, *Deceiving Hitler: Double Cross and Deception in World War II* (London, 2008)

Curry, J., *The Security Service 1908–1945: The Official History* (London, 1999)

Delmer, Sefton, *The Counterfeit Spy* (London, 1973)

Elliott, Geoffrey, *Gentleman Spymaster* (London, 2011)

Farago, Ladislas, *The Game of the Foxes: The Untold Story of German Espionage in the US and Great Britain During World War Two* (New York and London, 1972)

Fest, Joachim, *Plotting Hitler's Death: The German Resistance to Hitler 1933–1945* (London, 1996)

Foot, M. R. D., *SOE: The Special Operations Executive 1940–1946* (London, 1999)

Garby-Czerniawski, Roman, *The Big Network* (London, 1961)

Gilbert, Martin, *Winston S. Churchill, Vol. 6: Finest Hour, 1939–1941* (London, 1983)

Harris, Tomás, *Garbo: The Spy Who Saved D-Day*, introduction by Mark Seaman (London, 2004)

Hastings, Max, *Finest Years: Churchill as Warlord 1940–45* (London, 2009)

——————*Overlord: D-Day and the Battle for Normandy, 1944* (London, 1984)

Hennessy, Thomas, and Claire Thomas, *Spooks: The Unofficial History of MI5* (Stroud, 2010)

Hesketh, Roger, *Fortitude: The D-Day Deception Campaign* (London, 1999)

Hinsley, F. H., *British Intelligence in the Second World War: Its Influence on Strategy and Operations*, vol. 1 (London, 1979)

Hinsley, F. H., and C. A. G. Simkins, *British Intelligence in the Second World War: Security and Counter-Intelligence,* vol. 4 (London, 1990)

Holmes, Richard, *Churchill's Bunker: The Secret Headquarters at the Heart of Britain's Victory* (London, 2009)

Holt, Thaddeus, *The Deceivers: Allied Military Deception in the Second World War* (London, 2004)

Howard, Michael, *British Intelligence in the Second World War, vol. 5: Strategic Deception* (London 1990)

——————— *Grand Strategy* (London, 1972)

Jeffery, Keith, *MI6: The History of the Secret Intelligence Service 1909–1949* (London, 2010)

Johnson, David Alan, *Betrayal: The True Story of J. Edgar Hoover and the Nazi Saboteurs Captured During WWII* (New York, 2007)

——————*Righteous Deception: German Officers against Hitler* (Westport, Connecticut, 2001)

Kahn, David, *Hitler's Spies: German Military Intelligence in World War II* (New York, 1978)

Knightley, Philip, *The Second Oldest Profession* (London, 1986)

Levine, Joshua, *Operation Fortitude: The Story of the Spy Operation that Saved D-Day* (London, 2011)

Liddell, Guy, *The Guy Liddell Diaries, 1939–1945,* vols 1 & 2, ed. Nigel West (London, 2005)

McLachlan, Donald, *Room 39: Naval Intelligence in Action 1939–45* (London, 1968)

Masterman, J. C., *On the Chariot Wheel: An Autobiography* (Oxford, 1975)

——————*The Double Cross System in the War 1939–1945* (London, 1972)

Miller, Russell, *Codename Tricycle: The True Story of the Second World War's Most Extraordinary Double Agent* (London, 2005)

Moen, Jan, *John Moe: Double Agent* (London, 1986)

Montagu, Ewen, *Beyond Top Secret Ultra* (London, 1977)

Mure, David, *Practise to Deceive* (London, 1997)

Paine, Lauran, *The Abwehr: German Military Intelligence in World War II* (London, 1984)

Philby, Kim, *My Silent War: The Autobiography of a Spy* (London, 1968)

Popov, Dusko, *Spy/Counterspy* (New York, 1974)

Rankin, Nicholas, *Churchill's Wizards: The British Genius for Deception 1914–1945* (London 2008)

Reile, Oscar, *Geheime West Front* (Munich, 1962)

Rose, Kenneth, *Elusive Rothschild: The Life of Victor, Third Baron* (London, 2003)

Sebag-Montefiore, Hugh, *Enigma: The Battle for the Code* (London, 2000)

Sergueiev, Lily, *Secret Service Rendered: An Agent in the Espionage Duel Preceding the Invasion of France* (London, 1968)

Smith, Michael, *Foley: The Spy Who Saved 10,000 Jews* (London, 1999)

Stafford, David, *Churchill and the Secret Service* (London, 1997)

——————*Roosevelt and Churchill: Men of Secrets* (London, 1999)

——————*Ten Days to D-Day* (London, 2004)

Stephens, Robin 'Tin-eye', *Camp 020: MI5 and the Nazi Spies*, introduction by Oliver Hoare (London, 2000)

Waller, John H., *The Unseen War in Europe: Espionage and Conspiracy in the Second World War* (New York and London, 1996)

West, Nigel, *At Her Majesty's Secret Service: The Chiefs of Britain's Intelligence Agency, MI6* (London, 2006)

——————*Mask: MI5's Penetration of the Communist Party of Great Britain* (London, 2005)

——————*MI5: British Security Service Operations 1909–45* (London, 1981)

——————*Venona: The Greatest Secret of the Cold War* (London, 1999)

West, Nigel, and Oleg Tsarev, eds, *Triplex: Secrets from the Cambridge Five* (Yale, 2009)

West, Nigel, with Juan Pujol García, *Operation Garbo* (London, 2011)

Wilson, Emily Jane, 'The War in the Dark: The Security Service and the Abwehr 1940–1944', PhD Thesis (Cambridge, 2003)

Winterbotham, F. W., *The Ultra Secret* (London, 1974)

Acknowledgements

Once again, I am deeply indebted to scores of people who have helped me to write this book by generously providing guidance, hospitality, gentle mockery, food and fellowship, as well as access to documents, photographs, recorded interviews and memories. I am particularly grateful to the families of the agents and their case officers, German as well as British, who provided me with so much valuable material: Fiona Agassiz, Robert Astor, Marcus Cumberlege, Gerry Czerniawski, Prue Evill, Jeremy Harmer, the late Peggy Harmer, Anita Harris, Caroline Holbrook, Alfred Lange, Karl Ludwig Lange, David McEvoy, Belinda McEvoy, Marco Popov, Misha Popov and Alastair Robertson. I have benefited greatly from the expertise of a number of brilliant historians and writers, including Christopher Andrew, Michael Foot, Peter Martland, Russell Miller, Nigel West and Paul Winter. My thanks to Jo Carlill for her superb picture research, Ben Blackmore for long hours of research at Kew, Mary Teviot for her genealogical sleuthing, Manuel Aicher for research work in Germany, José António Barreiros in Lisbon, and Begoña Pérez for her help with translations from the Portuguese. I am also grateful for the advice, help and encouragement of Hugh Alexander, David A. Barrett, Paul Bellsham, Roger Boyes, Martin Davidson, Sally George, Phil Reed, Stephen Walker, Matthew Whiteman, and all my friends and colleagues at *The Times*. I owe a particular debt to Terry Charman, Robert Hands and Mark Seaman for reading the manuscript and saving me from some excruciating howlers. The remaining errors are all my own work. To those who prefer not to be named, I am deeply grateful for all your help.

It is a pleasure and a privilege to be published by Bloomsbury; my thanks go to Anna Simpson and Katie Johnson for their unfailing efficiency and patience, and to Michael Fishwick, loyal editor and dear friend. My agent, Ed Victor, has been a rock of support throughout my writing career. My children have kept me sane through another book with their support and good humour; and to Kate, as ever, all my love.

Index

Page numbers in **bold** refer to illustrations.

A NOTE ON THE AUTHOR

Ben Macintyre is a columnist and Associate Editor on
The Times. He has worked as the newspaper's correspondent
in New York, Paris and Washington. He is the author of eight
previous books including *Agent Zigzag*, shortlisted for the
Costa Biography Award and the Galaxy British Book Award
for Biography of the Year 2008, and the no. 1 bestseller
Operation Mincemeat. He lives in London with his wife
and three children.